Seven Minutes

Seven Minutes

The Life and Death of the American Animated Cartoon

NORMAN M. KLEIN

VERSO

London · New York

First published by Verso 1993
© Verso 1993
All rights reserved

Verso
UK: 6 Meard Street, London W1V 3HR
USA: 29 West 35th Street, New York, NY 10001-2291

Verso is the imprint of New Left Books

ISBN 0-86091-396-1

British Library cataloguing in publication data
A catalogue record for this book is available from the British Library

Library of Congress cataloging-in-publication data
A catalogue record for this book is available from the Library of Congress

Designed by Claire Brodmann
Typeset by MHL Typesetting Ltd, Coventry
Printed in Great Britain by The Bath Press, Avon

Contents

CONTENTS

Acknowledgments

Ralph Bakshi, Mel Blanc, Bob Clampett, Robert Clampett, Jr, Sody Clampett, Donald Crafton, Marc Davis, Al Dempster, Harvey Deneroff, Jules Engel, June Foray, Friz Freleng, Milt Gray, Ollie Johnston, Chuck Jones, Hugh Kenner, Ward Kimball, Walter Lantz, Leonard Maltin, Bill Melendez, Phil Monroe, William Moritz, Grim Natwick, Maurice Noble, Virgil Ross, Milt Shaffer, Dave Smith, Charles Solomon, Dave Tendler, Frank Thomas.

The author and publisher acknowledge permission granted by the Walt Disney Company to reproduce illustrated material from *The Band Concert*, *Plane Crazy*, *Shanghaied* and *Musicland* (all material © The Walt Disney Company). Illustrations from *Felix Woos Whoopee* are reproduced courtesy of the copyright holders (© King Features Syndicate and Felix the Cat Productions). Illustrated material from *Betty Boop's Snow White*, *Betty Boop for President* and *Beware of Barnacle Bill* is reproduced courtesy of Fleischer Studios, Inc. The cartoon and comic strip characters Felix the Cat, Popeye and Betty Boop are copyright King Features Syndicate. The drawing 'What Makes Betty Boop?' originally appeared on the cover of *L.A. Reader* (1980). The Disney strip autographed by Sergei Eisenstein was originally reproduced in Jay Leyda (ed.), *Eisenstein on Disney* (London: Methuen, 1988). Illustrations by Chuck Jones are reproduced courtesy of the artist (© 1993, Warner Bros, Inc., LJE, Inc.). The caricature by T. Hee of the Schlesinger Studio staff is reproduced courtesy of Betty Brenon. The drawings of Bosko, Honey and Bruno in chapter 9, story sketches from *Coal Black and de Sebben Dwarfs* and illustrated material in chapters 16 and 17 (all characters owned by Warner Bros, Inc.) are reproduced courtesy of the Bob Clampett Collection (© Bob Clampett Productions, Inc.). (All rights reserved including the right to reproduce in any form.) The self-portrait by Tex Avery is reproduced courtesy of the artist. Illustrations from *Bad Luck Blackie* (MGM) and *Rabbit Seasoning* (Warner Bros, Inc.) are reproduced courtesy of the Turner Entertainment Company. The drawings for *Gerald McBoing-Boing* are reproduced courtesy of Jules Engel and UPA; the illustration from *Madeleine* is reproduced courtesy of Jules Engel. Other illustrated material in this volume originally featured in Nat Falk, *How to Make*

ACKNOWLEDGEMENTS

Animated Cartoons (New York: Foundation Books, 1941) and *The Sho Card Cartoonist* (Minneapolis: Bart Publications, 1929). The author and publisher have made every effort to trace relevant copyright holders for all illustrated material reproduced in this volume.

The American Theatrical Cartoon, 1928–63

The average cartoon runs approximately seven minutes, with subtleties that can easily be hidden from the viewer. Cartoons are a record of consumer rituals over the past seventy years: of transitions away from print media toward cinema, and then video; of the streets and stores where audiences shopped; and of the interior of the consumers' homes. They are, above all, a narrative built around the expressive possibilities of the anarchic. They are another deterritorializing object, a tribute to the power of the naked line as transgressor.

Cartoons are also a tribute to the ruthlessness of the film industry. For thirty years, from the marketing of newspaper chains in the twenties to the marketing of television in the fifties, cartoons were continuously given the short end. They bear witness to the best and worst of American mass culture, condensed, as indeed all of our civilization has become, into small, brilliantly manipulated blasts of imagery.

I will examine the fabric of these seven minutes piece by piece, starting with the coming of sound in 1928, and continue to 1960, reviewing the graphics, scripts, and marketing of each era, to locate an aesthetics for the theatrical cartoon — the antic parody ever shifting, continually vulnerable.

Why start in 1928? So much was put in place before that year. The systems for running an animation studio had been established — an artisan shop which mildly resembled the factory models of the time. The cartoon was already an industrial art. Each stage of production required a different hand, from early thumbnails, to poses, layout, transfer to cels (i.e. celluloids), and inking. The first major cartoon star had already appeared by 1928: Felix the Cat, who was followed by a barrage of merchandising.

The essential links to graphic storytelling had been made, as well as the first links with film language. However, what came after 1928 was far more convulsive, and made on a far grander scale. Steadily, through the thirties, this small industry, centered in New York, was absorbed directly into the film business out west. The distribution and financing for cartoons were transformed, as were the graphics, rhythm, and story. Block-booking through movie studios liberated the cartoon, but also indemnified it.

This is a social history of what emerged on the screen as the movie industry took charge, as its control advanced, from 1928 to 1934, then 1934 to 1937, and 1937 into the Second World War, and then into decline after 1947. I have based much of the material in this book on interviews with veteran animators, mixed with the history of illustration, cinema, mass culture, architecture, and materials located in animation archives. But the essential research revolves around the ten thousand American theatrical cartoons produced between the twenties and the sixties; the information contained in the layout, the design of characters, the rhythm, music, dialogue; and in the reception by the audience. In even broader terms, this is a history of perception, of the imagery used to identify how audiences remembered their daily life. All in seven minutes, a digest turned upside down and set to spin.

CHAPTER ONE

Graphic Narrative: 1928

Any essay about the history of the American cartoon must begin officially somehow with the first sound shorts from Disney. That does not privilege Disney's work above Fleischer, or other studios. It simply divides epochs. Much has been written about the eras "before Mickey," but in 1928 Disney still remains the measure. How do we explain the enormous impact that these Mickeys and Silly Symphonies had? In part, it was clearly the novelty of sound. Once music and squeaks were added to Mickey's airplane ride in *Plane Crazy*, the cartoon became vivid in a way that was impossible for any live-action film made in America in 1928.

When Chaplin was an old man, he was once asked what had disturbed him most about working in sound. He answered: the tangle of machinery. The technical details had appalled him, the hours of preparation added before shooting. The spontaneity of the gags had been lost, he felt.[1] The stiffness of many early sound films reflects this confusion: Where should the microphones be placed? How to control the new sound stages? What style of acting helped the voice? and so on. Was film moving backward as an aesthetic form and losing its independence? Was it being forced into an unholy marriage with theater?

By contrast, the sound cartoon was liberated. There were casualties, of course, Sullivan Studios and Messmer's Felix the Cat being the most famous. But essentially the cartoon achieved a synthesis with sound which defined the medium for fifty years.

This synthesis is typically associated with Disney and the incunabula on mimeograph that was distributed to Disney employees during the thirties: the handbooks on character and "personality," on drawing volume, on the rules of storytelling for cartoons. This became the state of the art, and the illusionist style of animation the measure of progress. However, the earliest Mickey shorts — and early sound animation in general — differ greatly from the canon of later Disney. These cartoons, from 1928 to 1934, are anti-realist, drawn specifically for the flat screen. In short, they continued a tradition of graphic narrative which dates back to the eighteenth century, but particularly stems from nineteenth-century illustration.

3

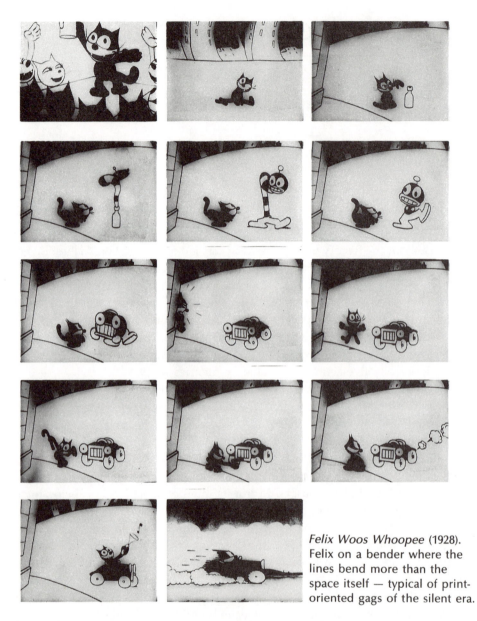

Felix Woos Whoopee (1928). Felix on a bender where the lines bend more than the space itself — typical of print-oriented gags of the silent era.

They were animated comic strips with a frantic life of their own. They borrowed very little from live action, except from silent comedy, and much from Chaplin, but not the point of view of an imaginary camera (as in Disney later on), nor the cartoon zooms, pans and cinematic simulacra. They did not pay homage to Griffith's montage, but rather to a cartoon montage of their own.

Let us try to recreate the style of narrative of the hand-drawn animated short before sound in 1928. What was the central tradition? From that center, the rest of character animation follows, and there is indeed a miraculous syntax within the seven-minute cartoon, the great American genre — first with line, then sound, color, and, above all, with continuing characters. As in a Cubist painting, there is an algebra of paint within the thumping, panting, and groaning, the colossal pratfalls and impossible escapes. The visual language can be so complex at times that one expects a modernist theory from Eisenstein or Viktor Shklovsky, rather than the Fleischer Studio in New York.

CARTOON GRAPHICS BEFORE SOUND

Were this a modernist document on cartoons, say an addendum to Eisenstein's *Film Form* or Brecht's *Short Organum*, it would begin — even before any reference to Mickey Mouse — with a statement of first principles. Ironically enough, in animation (at least for cartoons made before 1934) a single generic summary can be made quite easily. Put simply, character animation is a *graphic* art medium, not a photographic one. I do not mean graphic in the sense of a Rembrandt etching or a poster; more in the sense of Hogarth or the Sunday funnies. It is *graphic narrative*. But while it makes allusion to story, its primary responsibility is to surface, rhythm, and line.

When Felix the Cat uses the horizon as a laundry cord and walks on it, going forward and backward simultaneously into a non-existent distance, the audience is reminded of the flat screen. To paraphrase Resnais, if we ask how far back the castle is in *Felix in Fairyland*, the answer might be: about five feet from the bottom, along the surface of the screen.

The silent cartoon, like all animation, was supposed to defy perspective or plausibility. It managed this in a unique way. Felix uses his ears as scissors. He attaches his tail to his heart and plays it as a banjo. He climbs question marks up to the giant's castle. Resembling Keaton more than Chaplin (though he is indeed a cartoon Tramp), Felix is inventive purely within the restraints (or freedom) of the flat screen. Every object he transforms is flat ink.

Felix is a typographical creature, reminding us of Russian typography of the twenties. Of course, Otto Messmer, Felix's creator, knew absolutely nothing of Modernist design, particularly Russian Futurism or Productivism. Rather, the source for Felix came directly from nineteenth-century popular culture. After 1850, regionally printed imagery was transformed into mass-produced, international graphic forms, like the Sunday funnies in the Hearst newspapers or film animation — and finally the animated cartoon with continuing characters. That is more the source of Felix's modernity. The cartoon was an expansion of the illustrated or printed page — the typographical cartoon.

By typographical I mean the cartoons in newspapers so familiar to readers in the twenties. Borrowing from Russian theory of the twenties, they resembled *ideograms*, like comparing Felix the Cat to Russian posters and books, and how these influenced the way films were made there (for example, Eisenstein on "hieroglyph," and its links to "intellectual" montage).[2]

An *ideogram* is similar to a logo; it makes words and images interchangeable on a flat surface. Posters or title pages are transformed into independent language systems. Very often, these were compared to Chinese characters, which is revealing. Over millennia, a picture of the sun or a horse will simplify, but, on careful observation, will still suggest, in the way the brush draws the word, something of its origins. Calligraphy has enormous significance in Chinese art, even in the literature. It identifies an abstract surface that continually intrudes into the story. Any form of *graphic* storytelling will intrude in that way if it has enough memory behind it, a memory shared by artist and audience. In the case of American cartoons by 1928, the memory came primarily from the printed page — not exclusively, of course, but at its core, and, to some extent, ever since.

Consider the balloon dialogue in Krazy Kat, or the interjected signs in Clampett cartoons, or Chuck Jones' Roadrunner cartoons, but particularly the silent uses of type and language. A word could be as much a "character" in the story as an image.

And images can be simplified until they resemble letters. This remains true of all character animation; all bodies are stripped down for motion and easy readability. One can see this in the initial sketches: circles and oblongs, a mobile shape, with a face attached. It is also evident in the objects and space — instant readability: Felix at the garbage pail, confronting the Oily Boid, then taking his famous pensive strut; Bugs Bunny's rabbit hole, with carrot disposal nearby; or Pluto snarling to protect his food bowl. Relationships and simple drives are reduced to a visual phrase, an engine rather than a plot. It takes little to start up the engine, nothing more than a contrasting set of circles and oblongs, like a thirsty kitten sidling up to Pluto's bowl. These are then broken down into brief "cycles" of action, which might be repeated in the same cartoon, to save money.

Even the costume becomes standardized in much the same way — a menu of expressions for cartoon characters, abstracted into character sheets for animators, a few key expressions, mostly the character at three-quarters pose, because that is the easiest to animate. All these together fix the (usually male) character into the routine. They make him unchangeable. They trap him in a struggle against the motion picture machine; a struggle that continues even after sound is added. And yet, so much anarchic energy is possible.

The various ideograms are part of the visual war of surface against object, the hypnotic appeal of hand-drawn animation. This has its parallels in Russian cinema of the twenties, in the way image and text play against one another, as linguistic fantasy (as ideogram). Eisenstein began as an architect, became a visual artist, then moved into theater, before making his first feature film. He brought the architectonic theater space with him. He was thus very alert to the visual conflict within the ideograms, as they combine within a single shot or disrupt each other in a sequence of shots. In his work, the arena of battle became in great measure the flat screen itself, signifying the struggle between classes or opposing categories. For him his films were graphic art, "my constant passion [for] the dynamics of lines and dynamics of moving on":[3]

I shall always love Disney and his heroes, from Mickey Mouse to Willy the Whale. Their agile figures are also animals, also linear, and at their best without shadows or shading, like the early creations of the Chinese and Japanese — made up of real running lines of contours!

The fleeting lines of childhood, delineating the contours and forms of animals in their flight, come to life again in the real flight of real lines in the outlines of animated cartoons. And maybe it is because of these childhood impressions that with such relish and gusto I draw incessantly with chalk on the blackboard during my lectures, engrossing and amusing my students by my sketches and striving to instill in them a perception of lines as movement, as a dynamic process.

For the print-oriented twenties, the last decade of the silent cartoon, these principles are particularly apt. Cartoon story was dominated utterly by graphic references (which would change once the movie industry took more control). Felix converts question marks into skyhooks. The titles become story objects for Messmer, like Eisenstein's architectural phalanxes, the crowds. They are stories about something other than motivated characters, as we shall see.

They are visual labyrinths about an unreliable space, where the animal fable (rural nostalgia) is pitted against the electronic beam (ink, surface, industrial chaos). Who shall master whom? Who runs the machine? When Felix is attacked in his sleep by the city of New York (*Felix Dines and Pines*, 1927), Manhattan turns into a spiralling set of lines, where solid and empty are barely separated. Buildings bend like bamboo bridges. The time it takes to cross the street (perspective) and the street itself turn into grillwork, with only an ink spot in the middle — Felix's body.

As an ideogram within this grillwork, as the changeable ink spot, Felix usually does what he pleases. Starting from his feline character, he can turn back into an inked letter. He can contort his tail into a question mark. Messmer's visual gags emphasize the ideogram as Felix wrestles a letter or a line into submission. Titles and characters become interchangeable, like workers on an assembly-line in a Ford factory of 1916, or Russian immigrants trapped in sweatshops at their sewing machines, in New York's garment district in 1916.[4]

As social or political dialogue, characters who are ideograms have advantages over those who are simply animals of some kind. Eastern European animation in the sixties and seventies often used ideograms. In Jan Lenica's cartoon *A*, a letter from the alphabet haunts the flat, oversimplified lead character (locked, by the way, in broken hachure, which resembles nineteenth-century wood engraving). The letter "A" is far more exotic than its printed human enemy, far more durable; it even concatenates, by bringing on, with its death, a far more frightening letter, "B," and the suggestion that the narrative will be a chamber of horrors arriving by order of the alphabet. (In this sense, ideograms suit the spirit of the Theater of the Absurd; the cartoon was adapted from a story by Ionesco.)

In American cartoons, however, once sound arrived the emphasis on ideogram had to be set aside — at least for cartoons that were acceptable to big movie chains. Before sound, Felix lived in a fantasy world, which was literally made up of parts of speech and punctuation. After the introduction of sound, he became clumsy and sugary.

Felix did not survive well after 1928. His graphic tricks lost their importance when they had to synchronize to clangs and thumps, or harmonic strains. But there were other reasons for his failure. Most importantly, Messmer was not allowed to take the character into sound. Pat Sullivan, who owned Felix, drank too much, was haunted by his wife's tragic death (an accidental fall from a hotel window), was finally quite ill himself, and died in 1931.[5] But Felix's dilemma goes beyond Sullivan's problems, even his conviction that sound would not last, so why risk a good thing?

1928: SOUND ALTERS GRAPHIC NARRATIVE

Disney succeeded where the Sullivan Studio had failed. With very little adjustment, Disney translated his version of graphic narrative directly on to sound. To explain what I mean, I put Disney's *Plane Crazy* on the projector: Mickey flies a plane in the barnyard, runs into calamities, loses Minnie's favor, and winds up defeated, sitting beside the wreckage of his aircraft. Made as a silent in 1928, this cartoon succeeded best after the soundtrack was added. I begin rolling the cartoon, but a few minutes in — suddenly — the speakers cut out. We watch the cartoon as a silent again (even more silent than in theaters of 1928, when a piano player would accompany it). The web of thick lines changing into images is charming, very nimble, but frankly a bit like watching a coin fall down a deep well. It does look more rounded, with more perspective than Felix falling, as he does in *Felix Dines and Pines* for example, which was made at the same time. In lectures, I mention that Disney's chief animator, Ub Iwerks, was already interested in a kind of movie space that was deeper than the Felix shorts, with character movement that used more joints, more like a mammal. I add that Disney pushed for this variation in the late twenties in conferences with his staff. Still, it is a relatively slender difference compared to what follows when sound arrives.

Three minutes later the sound goes on again, and the audience comes to life. I have tried this on various occasions, and the result is always the same. Something in those caterwauls enhances the gags tremendously.

Here lies the central question for this introduction to the talking cartoon: why is it so easy for animation, yet so painful for live action? In the early thirties, Disney was acclaimed by critics as the wizard of sound, "the one great genius of the talkies, just as Chaplin was the one great genius of the movies."[6] Naive as many of these tributes were, they reflected the enormous interest in these cartoons at that time, far beyond the fame of Felix. Eisenstein visited the Disney Studio in 1930, virtually as a fan; then, ten years later, wrote praising the lyrical power of Disney animation (probably at the time when Eisenstein was thinking through the change in style which later emerged in *Ivan the Terrible*).[7]

During that decade, Disney sparked so much elaborate study, even in unlikely directions, world-wide. What problem was Disney solving? Not the introduction of music in 1928. Nor of clangs and hoots. Even in the Wurlitzer organs, there were noise attachments to simulate a fall or a screech.

Movie music was already a well-established business. Chaplin had written numerous scores for his silent comedies. Count Basie started his career as a piano player at a movie theater.

No, it was not music but the human voice that was the novelty — and the dilemma, most perplexing and hotly debated. Was voice reproduction too scratchy? Eisenstein (and later Gilbert Seldes in America, and various writers, like Roman Jakobson in Prague)[8] agreed that bad sound was not a problem. Voice should be contrapuntal or autonomous.

Meanwhile, the studio heads were terrified that foreigners would never go to a movie where an American spoke English (even with subtitles). Yet for the mouse's voice this presented no problem. Cartoons were embraced world-wide very quickly. In Paris, Jean-Paul Sartre, then a college student, combed the cinemas for Fleischer's Betty Boop cartoons. In Frankfurt, Theodor Adorno was also a Betty Boop fan.[9] Even during the Nazi period Boop cartoons were shown in Germany, with Max's name Aryanized to Karl.

But Mickey was the most famous by far. "In spite of differences of humor existing in various nations, the mouse became an international success," Fritz Moellenhoff observed.[10] In London, E. M. Forster wrote that Mickey was worshipped as a god by the British Film Society. Members "cease despising" each other as soon as a Mickey cartoon appears.[11]

In the period 1929–40, more was written on animation than at any time after for nearly forty years. And the thirties literature emphasizes how different the cartoon was from live action, how it came from different roots, particularly the Sunday comics. The art of these cartoons grew on a different, faster trajectory, yet as the art critic Erwin Panofsky wrote: "Within their self-imposed limitations the early Disney films ... represent, as it were, a chemically pure distillation of cinematic possibilities."[12] The British film critic Huntly Carter went even further (1930):[13]

The Cartoon ... is in some respects the best medium of cinema expression. The human atom and its belongings undergo whimsical changes that cause a continuous stream of images to form in the mind, and that throw an abundance of rich crumbs to the imagination ... an elastic line in evolution. Shapes grow out of it with which we are familiar even though they are distorted and battered by a sort of recurrent earthquake .... [Cartoons are] a line with the elasticity of gas. It shrinks and expands, collapses and recovers, behaves like a spring winding and unwinding, and at the same time assumes the shapes and characteristics of human beings, animals, insects, of animated things, and inanimated things made animate .... [Cartoons] outdo even an india-rubber ball in diversity of shapes, that speed through space with a velocity that has no parallel outside the Cinema.

[Cartoons] have a distinct sociological value. They exhibit man in society caught in a network of events ... trying to escape the consequences. They are in fact a comment, a very witty, instructive and biting comment on the absurdities of Man and other living things seen in the light of materialism. At the same time they are human, tragic and comic.

There was indeed another equation at work. Within two years of the sound era the cartoon industry came of age, still using systems of graphic narrative from animation, but adding sound in ways that merely enhanced their effect. As Kenneth White explained: "The immediate possibilities of sound and music were so quickly explored, once they were added to the cartoons (and resulted in two fine Silly Symphonies, *Spring* and *The Skeleton Dance*) ... further experiment and manipulation seemed unnecessary."[14]

The change for Disney was the most astonishing in every respect, but the financial change is the easiest to describe. His studio began in a tiny office in the Los Feliz district of Los Angeles, just west of Griffith's studio. By the mid-thirties, he had expanded considerably. And in neon above his office, with no other sign needed, was the most recognizable face in the world: Mickey Mouse. By 1934, after the success of *Three Little Pigs* (and lucrative advances in color animation and product merchandising), he moved to an even grander studio on Hyperion Boulevard, further East from Hollywood. So famous were his images by then that a nearby real estate developer built a court apartment complex that resembled Three Little Pigs houses, the brick kind that wolves never blow down. The roofs were thatched, in a twisted pattern, the façades artificially chipped; the crooked doors were crudely hewn to resemble oak; and the steepled fireplaces stood as if from a medieval hall. Cartoon fantasy became architecture. Throughout the Los Feliz area, single-family Disneyesque cottages appeared, with "aged" chipped stucco showing brick, painted in clean primary colors, just like the cels for the *Three Little Pigs*. (The style was also known as "picture-book" housing; as Dave Smith, the Disney archivist, states, Walt Disney had nothing to do with these.)

Even business magazines published articles on the new Carnegie of cartoon, or about Mickey as the only "unpaid movie star."[15] While the major studios were facing bankruptcy, Disney found a world audience (and, as we shall see later, a business organization) that was as depression-proof as those brick houses. It began with *Steamboat Willie*, the first Mickey designed for sound, and was followed by sound added to the earlier *Plane Crazy* and *Galloping Gaucho*.

Sound could not damage the integrity of the story in a cartoon. Quite the contrary. The cartoon was already a fractured narrative. Instead of the shot or the motivated character, the atomic unit was the gag — and the flimsiest excuse justified a gag. Sound enhanced the broken narrative within the cartoon. The characters could be

10

stopped in mid-crisis by a shift between voice and music: a sort of Tin Pan Alley alienation device. The false note was more important than the true. There was tinny music (later called Mickey Mouse music), as disembodied voices, creaking stairways offscreen, ghoulish laughs, squawks, boop-boop-a-doops.

New visual gags were possible. Inanimate objects could not only look alive, they could sound alive as well. Animals became as versatile as Felix's tail. A turtle was sprung like a couch; trees could mumble to each other in the wind; skeletons could tap out xylophone music; knees could shake rhythm to a tinny rag. On the other hand, some advantages of the silent cartoon were lost. Music replaced text as the ideogram. The cartoon moved away from what the Russian artist Lissitzky (discussing typography) called "the continuous page sequence — the bioscopic book."[16] Felix could no longer turn a question mark into a skyhook with the same effect, or tip his head or turn his tail into a valise. The graphic ideogram was replaced by syncopation. This is a considerable loss, though the principle of *graphic narrative* would reappear generations later.

The use of line itself changed. In silent cartoon, line was still the governing principle for gags. Animators ran into trouble when they attempted much beyond the linear. Like pancake makeup in live action, thick outlining was the only effective way to produce a readable character. The film printing was very limited. By necessity, the characters had to be inked outlines, particularly after Felix replaced Krazy Kat as the most popular cartoon character.

By the end of the twenties, however, even before the introduction of sound, the graphic look of cartoons had been altered. Felix had become less angular, more streamlined and rounder. Paul Terry's *Aesop's Fables* began using more complex backgrounds. At Disney, as early as 1926 (*Alice's Mysterious Mystery*, animated by the magnificent Ub Iwerks), smoke rings become organic matter like donuts; trucks sniff like dogs. In Walter Lantz's *The Lunch Hound* (1927), the ideogrammatic Pete the dog (nose into question mark) is lost inside the organic pliancy of a sausage factory. More essentially, the line figure was replaced by the rubber-hose character.

Ub Iwerks, the designer of Mickey Mouse, was a master of volume. From his pen, airplanes squirm like horses; trains breathe and sigh. The entire inanimate world is alive, and Mickey is its shepherd. One can see how sound assists in the squashing and stretching of Iwerks' silly protoplasm. Linear movement, with an essentially sketched background, is replaced by a *multimorphic* style, which dominates the cartoon world for two generations. Another comparison: when Felix is looking for an airplane, he converts two exclamation marks into propellers. Mickey, on the other hand, fancying himself a rodentile Lindbergh, builds his airplane into a puffy substance which resembles a doggy sausage.

Sound cartoons literally have a gravity that silent cartoons did not. Felix the Cat has no weight. His world is a moving hypothesis of lines. His obstructions are linear. But in *Plane Crazy*, with volume as the central trick (and perspective not as important as it would become later), sound can do for a chase scene what it did for a gangster movie (the loud, rattling tommie gun). Gravity is a sound, a thud, a crash.

Thus, when an audience sees the "silent" *Plane Crazy*, Mickey is flying an airplane not subjected to the force of gravity, with disconnected gags that could only be read graphically. With sound, the airplane is a skittish creature fighting gravity: the spinning descent of the plane at the end of the cartoon feels more like a satire of a steeplechase ride than an optical joke.

Before the mid-twenties, characters had moved on a linear grid, somewhat like a video game (a very important similarity, and one we shall return to). Then the grid dissolved into characters. The air became substance. Increasingly, this cartoon plasma is sapient and has a personality (except when it suits the animator to make it an immovable object, like a door smacking Dopey or Doc in the face, or a boulder crushing Wile E. Coyote). Meanwhile, the Roadrunner buzzes down the spiraling mountain road. With the coming of sound, a multimorphic world can sway to music, bend, arch, and tap its tree roots. If music washes over an audience, it helps when music also washes over the screen.

Music replaced text as an accompaniment. The relationship between the cartoon and the printed sheet weakened. In fact, a two hundred-year tradition of book illustration was in decline as well. Many welcomed the shock to book design and graphic narrative. In 1923, Lissitsky wrote: "The printed sheet, the infinity of the book, must be transcended. The Electro-Library."[17]

Despite the popularity of cinema, the twenties was an era dominated by print imagery, in home entertainment, in the way information was recorded. The centuries-old tradition of line as story was much more familiar to audiences in 1928 than it is today. That is what I identify as "graphic narrative."

From our film culture vantage-point, we forget that the twenties was still an era of book imagery; but not books that we associate with literary modernism. Proust's death six years earlier left not a ripple in the cartoon world, to say the least. For animators in 1928, the primary visual source was popular illustration: the cartoon in the old *Life Magazine*, when it was a wood-engraved comic weekly; the Sunday funnies; the cinematic vistas of Gustave Doré; the Tom Nast political cartoons for *Harper's Weekly*, from the Boss Tweed series to his Christmas Santas; the illustrators for comic fiction, some of whom actually drew in animated continuity by the 1870s (A. B. Frost, Caron d'Ache, Frank Bellew);[18] the photographic albums of Muybridge; the swashbuckling photo-lithography of Howard Pyle and the Brandywine school of illustrators (Wyeth's cowboys); the British fantasy illustrators, from Dickie Doyle to Arthur Rackham; a sampling of nineteenth-cenutry painters — all of these seen in books; always Michelangelo, who was somehow transformed into the ultimate Victorian painter; and much more.

This may sound odd at first, but illustration was the central visual medium of the nineteenth century, at least for popular audiences and animators. From *Charivari* in France to *Punch* (called the *London Charivari*) to Frank Leslie's comic magazines in America, satirical illustrations defined how a joke was composed visually. The animators Reynaud, Méliès, and Emile Cohl (as a very influential member of the so-called Incoherents)[19] all began as comic illustrators, essentially of satirical portraits — distant ancestors of the cephallic figures drawn for the *New York Review of Books*. One of the masters they copied was André Gill, a quixotic spokesman/illustrator for the republican left during the Second Empire, and well known in Parisian literary circles. When Rimbaud ran away to Paris, the first man he visited was Gill, hoping that the artist who drew those marvelously biting satires for *La Lanterne* might help an aspiring poet.

Winsor McCay began as a cartoonist, as did Earl Hurd and John Bray.[20] Paul Terry worked on San Francisco newspapers alongside Budd Fischer (Mutt and Jeff) and Rube Goldberg; Terry designed car cards for the New York trolleys and did a comic strip for Hearst before trying his hand at animation. Max Fleischer was a magazine art director. Dave Fleischer trained for a while at an engraving company. Disney worked as an illustrator in Kansas City; as did Friz Freleng, along with Harmon and Ising. And many painters, particularly from the Ashcan School, worked as illustrators. Walter Lantz's first job was to clean Winsor McCay's brushes at the *New York Herald*. Grim Natwick had produced over 400 covers for sheet music and worked a comic strip before being brought into animation in 1919 by Gregory LaCava. The list could fill the page. In many ways, animation became a second choice for illustrators who couldn't sell a strip or get work in sheet music or newspaper

Courtesy Standard Oil Co.

QUICK MAMA, THE FLIT!

Ad for Flit insecticide (1929), showing the continuing influence of Winsor McCay's Gertie the Dinosaur (1914), even in print advertising.

cartoons, like Tex Avery, who tried all these, and failed, before going to Walter Lantz for a job in 1929.

In the nineteenth century, the early toys that created the illusion of motion were designed by illustrators — the moving panoramas and phenakistoscopes in England during the 1830s, zoetropes, and so on. Many early photographers, like Muybridge, who influenced animators, were seen in their era as adjuncts to graphic narrative. The flipbooks that intrigued so many early animators were features of illustration, and were sold as bonuses for subscribers to picture magazines, or at shops where Currier and Ives lithographs were sold, or *Puck*, the German-American Punch from New York.

An example of the rubber-hose style popular in animation and illustration during the twenties.

The saturation of printed images was extraordinary. From the 1840s on, the illustrated magazine defined the look of many popular genres, including historical fiction, travel or exotic adventure, sentimental romance, or the Western; from redskins and Buffalo Bill, to sepoys and Arabs, wood engravings took readers to the outer reaches of European and American imperialism. Generations later, Hollywood studios would have research archives of these illustrations, runs of the *Police Gazette*, or topological books on the old abbeys of England. The sets of King Kong were taken from Doré's illustrations for Milton's *Paradise Lost*.[21] Every version of *Oliver Twist* borrows from Cruikshank's steel engravings.

From 1840 to 1885 many novels were illustrated, either when they were published serially in newspapers or in separate volumes. The influence on film is difficult to calculate. As many as five hundred wood-engraved vignettes were printed within the text of a single novel, like a miniature screen accompanying the story.

Even before animation, illustration was tried on every imaginable kind of print medium (like rocaille porcelains copied from Watteau a century earlier). In 1851, the publisher Philipon offered comic wallpaper, featuring the illustrations of Daumier. I have seen one of these unfortunate rolls — a locust of cartoons that must have been very unnerving on the wall.[22] They were advertised as perfect for a gentleman's billiard room or a lady's parlour, and looked very much like prototypes for animated cartoon cels, layers in horizontal friezes, and further complicated by a wraparound screen. They were apparently laid on the rooms of room dividers. Cartoonists like Cham spoofed this overpowering wallpaper: a couple, eyes bloodshot, stay up all night reading the captions and animated drawings on their bedroom walls.

By the 1890s, this complicated tradition, which I call graphic narrative, is continued in the Sunday funnies, and ultimately in animated cartoons. By the end of the nineteenth century, it had acquired a peculair flatness and precision, which the illustrator Walter Crane called "the cult of the line."[23] Over a half-century of mass printing had abstracted the line in many ways. For example, the background was often whitened out or faintly outlined. Even the border itself had become story, as overgrown trellises invading the text (Romantic solitude, etc.); walls of line trapping the prisoner; or doors emptying from one page into the next. In a sense, to paraphrase Barthes, the image became an object in itself, within its own fantasy boundaries.

This autonomy seems to be what most separated animation from live-action film. A drawing was free from the denotative illusion of a photograph. What is more, it told its story in line rather than representation, as an episode rather than a novel. The stories even had conflicts based on the flat page itself, like Hogarth's etching of false perspective; Grandville's mole watching an art gallery where real birds escape from painted landscapes and fly into the room; or paintings of Arab horsemen crashing through the wall, horses' hooves kicking dust on to the floor. For contrast, we roll a scene from a Fleischer cartoon. Koko and Bozo are stopped in mid-cel (*Koko*

15

"Fish Fishing for People," in Grandville's *Metamorphoses of the Day* (Paris, 1844), adventures in which "Illustration and Fantasy" leave this world for "another" upside down. From chapter XI; "April Fool" (playing on the French, *poisson d'avril*: April fish).

the Cop, 1925, among others) and returned to pen and ink. The screen is transformed into panels of celluloid. A live-action scissors held by Max Fleischer snips the film and the boys are retrieved, their escape cut off, literally.

Even today, we see the principle of line used in much the same way. In 1983, the BBC ran a television serial entitled *Portrait of Jane,* based on a forties comic strip. The story itself was elegant kitsch, like movie posters in an expensive luncheonette. A nubile young woman-detective is constantly finding herself disrobed in voyeuristic ways as she hunts for spies. In the end the spies are always captured.

The gags are generally built around her being surprised in a flimsy slip, while the man guffaws nervously. She plans strategy while in the nude, her silhouette lit behind a shade. Jane lives entirely inside hand-drawn panels matted in behind her. Like a comic strip, the action runs from left to right, crossing the borders of various panels.

In one scene, the borders were used as a bannister, where a rival vamp laid her hand directly on the lines. The director particularly liked that effect, emphasizing the autonomy of hand-drawn film. As a comic-strip story oozing cute nostalgia, *Portrait of Jane* announces its freedom from live-action narrative.

Returning to origins, we are reminded of Winsor McCay in his many vaudeville tours. At the end of his act, his body is presumably transformed into line and placed on the back of Gertie the Dinosaur. No longer a living performer, he rides a flat surface, before a simple, white background. He waves to the audience as Gertie takes him away, and the cartoon ends.

This freedom from the denotative photograph or film is essential to the cartoon, and often noted by animators, viewers, and critics alike. When live action becomes the model instead, the freedom is reduced almost immediately, as we shall discover. This is not to say that live action and cartoon cannot be held in tension together, as in the Fleischer Out of the Inkwell series and numerous others (including Disney's first cartoons in Los Angeles; and more recently, in many American special-effects adventure films from 1977 to 1990, as part of what I call The American School of High Suburban Cinema). Rather I am emphasizing how this freedom within animation worked as line and surface in 1928. We should remember, as Donald Crafton and others remind us, that 1928 was the conclusion to a tradition of graphic narrative, an end as well as a beginning.

As I explained earlier, the cartoon is a moving sketch, with a frantic life of its own; it is the Sunday funnies with filmic continuity. Koko refuses to take orders from the inkwell. Gertie balks when the drawing board tells her how to behave. The hand-drawn image becomes a mock conflict in itself. In the early cartoons, Pinocchio could never be transformed into a "real boy," not as a drawing that becomes "real," because the flat medium would not permit it.

Even financially, the animation of the twenties was tied to the funnies through elaborate deals between studios and newspaper publishers like Hearst, for syndicated funnies like Krazy Kat, Katzenjammer Kids, Mutt and Jeff. King Features, originally a comic strip syndicate, owned the rights to many of these silent characters for generations, including Felix, the Little King, and even many from sound cartoons, like Popeye and Betty Boop.[24]

But by the early thrities, Hollywood studios had completely replaced all areas of the print industry as the powerbrokers for cartoon distribution. In the same sense, film glamour and photo advertising put an end to the tradition of illustration. Even during the economic stagnation of the Great Depression, the consumer culture of the twentieth century was replacing that of the nineteenth. And with new masters, story and line in cartoons changed. Instead of complaining to the drawing-board (or the inkwell), Betty Boop (or even Elmer Fudd) makes peace with the studio boss, or, in the Boop comic strip of the mid-thirties, is completely involved in movie-studio life. In much the same sense, at Warners, Elmer furiously pastes his torn contract back together, and says: "I'm sowwy, Mr Warner. Can I have my contwact back?"

The audiences for cartoons change also, but not entirely during the years of transition, 1928–34, when the two centuries meet in the seven-minute cartoon. Considering the enthusiasm, even the lopsided "unity" of these cartoons, they meet rather amicably. Characters scramble like vaudevillians breaking in a new act. The more print collides with movie space, the more these teeming cartoons require new systems.

CHAPTER TWO

The Gag

Movement in cartoons borrowed primarily from gags in live entertainment, far more than from silent film comedy. The cartoon and comic theater share a long history, from footlights to fairground, to Coney Island. Audiences still went to the theater often enough to know the settings very well. Disney himself was a great fan of the vaudeville.

In 1979, Dave Fleischer was asked what had inspired him to create Koko the Clown sixty years earlier.[1] He began reminiscing about the Coney Island district at the turn of the century. He had worked briefly as a clown in Steeplechase Park (more like an open "carny" than an amusement park today, particularly after the big fire wiped out Dreamland in 1912, signaling the decline of the enclosed parks there). Coney Island in 1910 was not as rough as it had become by the fifties when I grew up there (cautiously, I might add), but clearly the boardwalk and the area around the old Surf Hotel had always serviced numerous saloons, some dance halls, gambling, as well as penny arcades, various rides, and the freak shows.[2] And then there were the camp followers: grifters (or conmen), pickpockets, and whores. Even a young boy could notice all this, without participating at all.

The flow of traffic in Fleischer cartoons, the errant details, remind me a great deal of Coney Island; of the images that stay most in my mind, a sense of its anarchy, sometimes sad or frightening, more often a comic agony. The style of leisure around

How to draw a pig getting hysterical (1940), in the "fuller" style required by the late thirties — more mobility in the eyes, mouth, and jaw.

Nathan's had very little of the domesticity of a Disneyland packaged at both ends by gates and guards. This is a primary difference between nineteenth-century popular culture and the electronically reproduced mass culture.

The crowds in Coney Island were more like the backgrounds for jokes in illustrated magazines from 1910 than a consumerist entertainment place today.

One image from the fifties stands out in my mind most of all. There was a game called "broken dishes" (more or less). I remember watching sailors line up at a long counter. For the famous "thin" dime, they were given three baseballs and invited to throw them at a wall covered with hanging dishes. I do not recall there being many prizes, merely the opportunity to break as many dishes as possible in three throws. In some curious way, like the barker's promise, everyone walked away a winner. "Breaking dishes" has always reminded me of the way violence works in cartoons. At the time Dave Fleischer went to Coney Island, after the great fires, as urban decay descended rapidly upon it, the scarred spaces must have resembled the spirit of anarchy even more than earlier.

From 1916 to 1930, Fleischer would dress up as a Coney Island clown and have animators rotoscope films of him as Koko the Clown. There lies the cartoon gesture. For comic timing, he borrowed what he had learned as an usher at the Palace Theater in New York, watching vaudeville acts, particularly Timburg and Rooney, or Weber and Fields. While these skits ran twice the length of an animated cartoon, they used gags in much the same way as a comic short. The narrative was associative, one joke suggesting an entirely different subject; what in television today is called the blend.

By 1910 in New York (and in most industrial cities in America) the vaudeville gag had been transformed. From the knockabout routines of, say, the Keaton family (before Buster entered the movies), the humor had shifted to verbal dialect, or two-acts. In a sense, the two versions of gag could conflict with each other, like the rural culture of nineteenth-century popular entertainment (its pratfalls and droll stories) fighting against the polyglot industrial city.

Disney and most animation studios continued the older knockabout versions of the gag (the look of 1890 more than 1910). In essence, their gags sustained the tradition of nineteenth-century popular culture: railroad-centered, traveling minstrel shows; dime novels about the frontier; latterly, the wry humor of George Ade or even Mark Twain.

The Fleischers (as I shall show in chapter 5) were practitioners of the New Humor coming out of the ethnic vaudeville skits in Manhattan. The timing and rhythms of each were noticeably different (again, an issue I will develop later).

Cinema gags in the twenties were often received by audiences in terms of vaudeville and other forms of live entertainment. We know that silent slapstick certainly comes directly from vaudeville. In 1977–78, I interviewed a man who still lived across the street from the old Mack Sennett Studios. As a child he used to sit in his downstairs porch, watching Mabel Normand, Chaplin, and the Sennett beauties cavort along the steep hill (torn down in 1989) just west of Lakeshore Drive in the old Edendale area. "I would wait in my chair early in the morning," he told me. "I'd watch them setting up for a gag. One time, they spent a few hours digging a deep hole, maybe five feet. I couldn't for the life of me figure out what they wanted the hole for. So I was ready early next morning. At 7 a.m., a man ran into the hole. He had a big miner's hat on, with a torn brim. The cameras started rolling. Suddenly, he jumped out of the hole, and screamed 'Gold!'[3]

"As far as I was concerned, we didn't need to go to one of those ten-fifteens [vaudeville houses along Main Street and just north of downtown]. It wasn't so easy for kids to get in anyway, but we had our own theater across the street. Some of the [Sennett] characters even dressed the same [as in vaudeville]."

For generations, the movies competed with vaudeville, began in fact as a music-hall stunt, and continued to "steal" vaudeville talents. At least one of the film moguls, Louis B. Mayer, started in the movie business by converting old burlesque houses in the Haverhill area near Boston. By the early decades of this century, at presentation houses, vaudeville and two-reelers mixed on the same bill. Even into the thirties, one of the Fleischer animators, Dave Tendler, remembers that "almost every movie shown in the Bronx, where I lived, was headlined with five acts of vaudeville." Each act was approximately the length of an animated cartoon. Audiences for cartoons were intimately familiar with that mix, which is evident in McCay's *Bug Vaudeville* (1915) and still evident even in Chuck Jones' *One Froggy Evening* (1957). When I asked Jones in 1985 about the frog, he agreed immediately that the character was "a little vaudevillian."

At the top of the cartoon industry, virtually every producer and distributor from the twenties into the thirties had worked in vaudeville in some capacity, either as a booking agent, or in art direction, advertising, or simply drawing or providing show cards.

Speaking even more broadly, there seems little doubt among film historians that movies were often perceived as an extension of vaudeville as well. Movie comedians were even distinguished according to whether they came from vaudeville or from burlesque, as late as the forties. References to the names of vaudeville gags were still evident by 1940, particularly in the Hope/Crosby Road pictures, but also in numerous screwball comedies, musicals, and in Andy Hardy films. There was no lack of experienced entertainers to flesh out such sequences or be hired by Disney to perform stunts that Walt or others liked; gags that involved very long tongues or silly pratfalls — for the Dopey character in particular (very clearly a composite vaudevillian). Similarly, when Tex Avery used the vaudevillian Joe Penner as one model for the Egghead character, Avery and his unit were copying more than the radio voice; they borrowed the body type, the way Penner moved his head and neck, and the sluggish imperturbability that so many in the audience still knew from live performances.

This type of borrowing was a well-established custom. For generations, cartoons

21

had been marketed as a variation of the vaudeville or the circus act. From 1892, when Reynaud set up the Theatre Optique (eventually seen by over a million people) the animated film rapidly appeared throughout Europe and the United States, in Cohl's Incoherent Cinema, Méliès trick films, and trick films from Vitascope.[4] By 1900, animation had become known as a "specialty" act, like magic or animal acts — hand-painted images projected on a screen in a setting that resembles the fairground or the entertainment stage. It was illusionary display, not unlike Epcot today. It was understood essentially as another version of the painted panorama exhibits so popular by the middle of the nineteenth century. Panoramas were wrap-around murals inside a large building — a full-scale illusion of a famous battle scene or a harbor. In current jargon, animation was a kind of virtual reality, like being inside a full-sized diorama, trapped in the natural history museums we all visited in grade school, and were just being built when Fleischer was a boy. This market had taken a few generations to establish. Panoramas themselves were not well known until about 1840. The variations, in stages, came later. As early as 1867, Gustave Doré's publisher, Hetzel, received a strange letter about a kind of panorama that was not known at the time, only imagined. A man named Temple asked for the rights to project, inside a theater, magic lantern slides based on Doré illustrations. This promoter sensed that Doré's wood engravings had a peculiar monumentality, like a panorama. (Indeed, Doré himself transposed some of his plates into massive paintings, on a panoramic scale — a kind of theatrical chiaroscuro, dull but lavish.) But Hetzel could not see the connection between illustration and large-scale theater projection. He found the request too strange to take seriously, and failed to answer the letter. Lantern slides had been used primarily in small parlors, not in theaters. Edison's motion picture machine had not yet been invented as a way to take illustrations seen in the home and transform them into a form of illusionistic theater, flat as a page, with the hand-drawn image, but somehow as deep and illusionistic as theater sets. By the 1890s, however, with Reynaud, illustration had entered the phantasmagoria of light. The market was ready even before cinema was. What created the market is not so easily summarized here, except to say that it involved considerably more than Edison's invention of the moving picture, and clearly influenced the look of animation for generations.

One point bears repeating: animated space suited a style of three-dimensional exhibition common to the late nineteenth century. Even though it was merely light on a screen, it made solid the look of mass illustration. It put Doré's giant folio plates into a real space. It transported wood engravings from a double-page spread in journals like L'Illustration onto the walls of theaters. It was a great variety act. In other words, animation began as a form of illusionistic theater similar to magic acts and panoramas. Most importantly, it began as something other than drama. It was not a story in three acts; it was a singular event, like an implausible trapeze act flying through an unlikely ceiling. In 1900, Méliès performed his magic at the Paris Exhibition, and his later films reflect that spirit. Winsor McCay was on the vaudeville circuit often from 1906, blending his circus background with his comic strips.[5]

This is not to say that cartoons needed giant hippodromes to make their point. Animation was also a fairly intimate parlor act, called the Lightning Sketch in its earliest form. After 1900, over a ten-year period, lightning sketches were practiced cinematically (and "live") by Stuart Blackton, Emile Cohl, and, of course, Méliès and McCay. In fact, the Fleischers' earliest work at Bray Studios, as late as 1917, was specifically Lightning Sketch cartoon. The formula was simple. A cartoonist would come out in tails and draw furiously. Seasons would change within the same sketch, before the audience's eyes. Faces would age; dogs become cats. Called *dessinateurs express*, or the "magic paint brush," these variety acts were based on a principle that has remained essential to animation ever since — metamorphosis. A picture changes into something impossible, but too quickly for the eye to see how.

In cartoons through the twenties, the animator was often still shown performing this sleight of hand. It was an illusionist's trick; the more deceptive the illusion, the more fantastical the result. The impossible picture was brought to life. This is quite the reverse of the photographic recording of the world. Instead of photo naturalism, the metamorphosis is supposed to defy gravity or solidity. It was a specialty act that looked out of place ouside of the vaudeville theater (or the circus, the fairground, etc.). In American cartoons, even into the fifties, the uptown theater or the concert hall is barely mentioned at all, except in occasional parodies, like *Mickey's Grand Opera*, *Rabbit Rhapsody*, or *Magical Maestro*. The stories within these cartoons suggest the distance of cartoon vocabulary from the concert hall. Usually, a snooty musician is upstaged by a cartoon vaudevillian — revenge against snobbery.

There are, of course, animation shorts that do indeed operate within a more symphonic model, by Oskar Fischinger among others. These influence character animation in the forties. For the most part, however, the American cartoons made for the mainstream studios were kept clear of that. The few exceptions — *What's Opera, Doc?*, or even *The Sorcerer's Apprentice* and *Dance of the Hours*, for example — still operate like vaudeville parodies. It took almost thirty years before audiences accepted Disney's *Fantasia*.

Character animation, as opposed to other forms of animation, was built around a vaudeville vocabulary, and remains a graphic trapeze act even today. This should not be seen as a curse that must be overcome. I admit to loving that vaudeville spirit, and find attempts through melodrama to remove the slapstick a bit maudlin as a rule. Why eradicate a glorious heritage? Vaudeville came out of a brilliant tradition, dating back systematically to late medieval theater, then the Commedia dell'Arte, and farce. As a category, it represents the narratives of the carnivalesque rather than drama.

I know of only one anecdote that clearly links the cartoon gag to the narrative code of the legitimate stage, and it's not a very flattering one. Dave Fleischer designed a plot chart based on *Abie's Irish Rose*. In this miraculous schema, abridged to a single page, every wrench of the heart or pie in the face fits into a countdown of sorts, down to seconds, it seems. He also compared his all-purpose plot remedy to vaudeville. All the anecdotes return to that, at least until the thirties. *Abie's Irish Rose* was merely an extension of ethnic humor and vaudeville one-acts anyway. In the thirties, there would be a noticeable shift away from vaudeville toward theatrical narrative in cartoons (as chapter 11 on melodrama will show). But not before, not in American character animation at any rate; and even thereafter only with great difficulty. It would be like Prince Charming playing Hamlet in an exploding suit.

I have searched for exceptions, but even these seem to reinforce the obvious. For example, cartoons also borrowed from the elaborate sets in operettas. However, operettas had been translated into vaudeville in America, as were virtually all versions of nineteenth-century popular entertainment by 1900. The heritage is impossible to shake. Cartoons, like all silent film comedy, resemble the vaudeville specialty act, or the circus and fairground stunt which are its source. Let me use one example to suggest many. In *Safety Last* (1923), Harold Lloyd uses four brick buildings in Los Angeles, as well as the Second Street Tunnel and a prop clock, to create what surely can be compared to a fairground aerial stunt. We find even the audience itself watching in awe below (the crowd gathering in front of the department store in Broadway, probably the old May Company, then called Hamburgers). The narrative is the stunt itself, a contest to sabotage gravity. The slim fable behind it, about the country boy who rights himself in the end, is essentially the fabric that the stunt tears ever more incredibly, as Harold climbs higher off the ground, hops a flagpole, or the arms of the clock. Here, to borrow from Viktor Shklovsky, the plot sabotages what little story there is, leaving only the stunt itself.[6] Within the dizzying confabulations of the stunt is the animated cartoon.

Increasingly, vaudeville theaters in Europe too were turned into presentation houses, where films were added to the bill (usually features, sometimes cartoons, but not always). Both live action and live theater shared the same hypothetical space, with outrageous results. Marinetti wrote of the European presentation houses:

> The Variety Theater is unique today in its use of the cinema, which enriches it with an incalculable number of visions and otherwise unrealizable spectacles (battles, riots, horse races, automobile and aeroplane meets, trips, voyages, depths of the city, the countryside, oceans and skies).[7]

Like the flat surface of an illustration, the stage transformed into what Panofsky (discussing graphics) called the "dematerialized page."[8] This was very much the spirit of Paul Terry's *Aesop's Fables*; backgrounds move like rotating drums, until the characters seem afloat in virtual stage sets. This turned characters into cheerfully disembodied cyphers, wiggling ghosts.

The same was true of vaudeville. Each act tended to have its own sets; as a result, the variety could be utterly disorienting, except for the overall timing — to build toward the headline act, etc. The single spotlight rarely adjusted to mood, as woodland parks with French touches appeared for a skit, then suddenly vanished. The curtain dropped: a stage card on a lonely easel marked the next act. A millionaire's drawing room might be followed by a policeman on his beat. Neighborhoods on curtain scrims dropped or rose to the music. In came the acrobats or the animal act (often opening the bill). Then, with a pause as the curtain fell, out came the soubrette, or the "class" act (adagio dancers: class was "high class," meaning serious, high bourgeois, uptown dancing).

The gags had to fit inside this format or montage. (This reminds me of an early Eisenstein theater set, from 1922 in Moscow, where the capitalist wore the stock exchange as part of his costume.) Sign and social code, like stage cards, were immediately identifiable. There was no search into the depths of character, but rather an obsession with timing, with disassociated sets, and the orchestra swelling at key moments. (But this should not be understood to mean that this format was shallow; more on that below, p. 32.)

Popular operettas might be condensed for vaudeville, *The Student Prince*, for example, shrunk down to half an hour. Potboiler fiction (dime novels or sentimental romances) might appear as one-acts, with titles and characters disguised, to avoid the copyright.

A very similar abbreviation of story appeared as avant-garde farce in Futurist theater-pieces running 4—8 mintues and called *sintesi*,[9] or, to suggest the animated cartoon, "cinematic poems." They were filled with impossible gimmicks, like a man shooting himself "half to death" — literally — or turning his stomach into an aerostat and flying out of the theater. Such gags could only be performed as trick films or cartoons it would seem; they were hypothetical theater in a dematerialized space. The stage itself became a graphic narrative.

A rowdy audience enhanced Futurist theater, enhanced the spectacle. Marinetti enjoyed the way variety shows were interrupted by hoots or cigar smoke from the front rows.[10] In pre-First World War performances, the Futurists liked to overbook the theater, so that screaming patrons fighting for a seat could interrupt the show. Marinetti called variety theater a school of sincerity where none of the tricks of naturalism was allowed. Traditional storytelling was ridiculed, as he felt it should be. Anything from the sublime to the raucous might intrude inappropriately, to keep the audience on the alert.

Needless to say, Brecht wrote about the cabaret in much the same way, as an honest relationship between audience and performers; its fractured rhythm was another way to present a story.

This chapter reviews just such an alternative form of story, as seen from many angles, and differing from one generation to the next. I focus on the period 1928 to 1934, when the gag as allusion to live entertainment begins to fade in the cartoon, much the way graphic narrative does. During that period of overlap, however, the rudiments of the sound cartoon are laid, both line and rhythm, with implications for video graphics and special-effects editing today.

Even many of the sounds in cartoons resembled the vaudeville manner. Not only did movement emphasize that these were non-naturalist stories; the sound was also used as an autonomous object. For example, in vaudeville, pratfalls were often accompanied by a sour roll of the drums off-stage. Movement and sound were separate from each other to enhance the effect, like medieval "slap-sticks" that added a loud thwack whenever someone fell rudely on the stage.

At Warners in the forties, the sound of a squeaking balloon could describe a body struggling through a narrow gap in a fence or Tweety using Sylvester's nose as a punch bag. Living matter sounded like indelible rubber. The loonier the noise, the more appropriate the parody and knockabout gags.[11] Disney would use collapsing bladders; Lantz would use mechanical ratchets. In the late twenties, animators were invited to try screeches and honks, which might add more spice to the picture.

In a hypothetical space (whether stage or screen), the inappropriate voice works very much like graphic narrative, like the vaudevillian skidding and bouncing against the proscenium stage, emphasizing the artifice, much the way panels do in comic strips, or borders in illustration; the early Daffy Duck bouncing madly through the closing titles of the cartoon (a Clampett gag from 1937), with his yip-yip-yip voice careening just as madly.

These inappropriate noises satisfy what Roman Jakobson meant when he wrote, in 1933: "Speech in film is a special kind of auditory object, along with the buzzing of a fly or the babbling of a brook, the clamor of machines and so forth."[12] On the other hand (the theatrical use of sound): "Speech on stage is simply one of the manifestations of human behavior."

"Inappropriate sound" was noticed and widely appreciated very quickly. In 1931, a critic for the American Theater Guild praised cartoons in particular for their "inarticulate ... exclamations, ejaculations, grunts, and whoops ... drumbeats, flutes, guitars, xylophones, bassoons, trumpets, oboes, and other musical instruments."[13] All this "becomes part of a mutual contest with the images on the screen." It also serves to "brighten, like the instrumental sound and human ejaculation ... used in Japanese theater." "Inarticulate sound has limitless possibilities for conveying satire, humor, or pathos." None of this remarkable "flux and tempo" is possible in the "synchronized film." That is why the cartoon is "the only type of American film that has consistently shown a correct application of the function of sound in relation to the visual image." Recorded noise was let loose on the world.

Categories of Gag

Both vaudeville and the cartoon engage the pandemonium of the industrial takeoff after 1870 in Europe and America, when mass culture began a schizoid process: rural nostalgia pitted against the machine-made, urban culture.[14] Matters had gone far beyond the steam-driven printing press of 1836, or the first off-the-peg clothing. Steadily, all live entertainment was squeezed out by electronic media, by the auto, by new leisure rituals (families staying home on Monday nights to listen to Amos and Andy on the radio).

In the same comedy routines, gags from one era fought gags from the moment, signifying shifts in population and ethnicity, which had been going on for generations, from 1890 or even 1870. Protestant small-town humor was pitted against ethnic dialect (rather like Bugs Bunny as urban rabbit taking on Elmer Fudd, the rural American yokel).

The Fool versus the Machine

As the classic summation of these conflicting gag styles, the yokel wrestles with industrial mishaps as they plague everyday life. He may be as shrewd as a Warners sheepdog or as gullible as a bloodhound. In the comics, he was a Barney Google, Popeye, or Lil' Abner. He was also Goofy, Clarabel Cow, Horace Horsecollar (often Mickey himself), Bosko, Koko, Flip the Frog, Yosemite Sam, Wally Walrus, Droopy the Dog, Wile E. Coyote, Slow Poke, and countless more. The walk and manner of the yokel became crucial to the rhythm of the cartoon, much as it had been in vaudeville humor since the Civil War, in essence, since vaudeville began in America.

Gag Dialectics

Thus, the gag is a hangover from pre-industrial rituals, as well as a re-enactment of social (and narrative) dislocation. The two are held in tension, as partners: nineteenth-century animal humor and twentieth-century chaos, like a barnyard mouse building a floppy airplane. These conflicting gags defamiliarize story and natural movement in much the way that graphic narrative lives on a flat surface. And like the city confusing the country boy, this surface is impenetrable. He is always left waiting on the surface.

Indeed, gags are more than random snatches of comic relief. They use the narrative code of late nineteenth-century popular culture. They are fables about surviving in an industrial world when the mind is still trapped inside a rural community (translated as the cartoon village caught inside the motion-picture machine).

A plot of this sort, fractured by a variety of gags, has a unity based on dialectical confusion. The potential for hazards is never resolved, only examined, in chase after chase, disaster after disaster. Once again, the gag is similar to Modernist theories from the twenties, on narrative, on epic theater, or defamiliarization. It is the Theater of the Absurd: in 1952, Beckett's two clowns in derbies play against each other on a barren stage. The gag is abstracted down to its acme of meaning: killing time while the surface of life refuses to answer, the act of chasing in place.

And now to 1928: with the arrival of sound, the ties between cartoons and live entertainment change, but are not abandoned entirely; nevertheless, cartoons lose their direct link to popular theater, fairs, and circuses. Parody and timing no longer attach fundamentally to the experience of audiences at variety theaters. The gag had meant variety arts in America certainly since the Civil War, and perhaps generally in European civilization since the satyr plays that Aristotle claimed were the source for all theater in classical Greece.[15]

This broken link resembles how the comic-strip format vanished from the animated cartoon. A long tradition faded during the thirties. In terms of the vaudeville gag, its decline followed virtually the same years as the end of graphic narrative, 1928 to 1934 (for vaudeville cartoons a few years more, until 1937, or no later than the early forties). That should bind my chapters together chronologically. And now, with the argument more or less in place, I can announce officially that vaudeville finally dies.

It is often assumed that talkies killed off vaudeville, but apparently that is not entirely true. For more than a decade before sound, vaudeville houses that did not show movies had been failing. Many vaudeville stars, who were too expensive for presentation houses, joined uptown reviews and eventually went to Hollywood (or at least gave it a try). By 1930, the old Variety Arts Theater in Los Angeles had become a private club for vaudevillians in the film business.

In the early thirties in particular, some vaudeville stars, like the Marx Brothers, Eddie Cantor, Mae West, and W. C. Fields, managed to cross over into talkies and radio very successfully. The movies undoubtedly extended their careers. They found a larger market there (and a final twilight in variety television during the fifties).

Sound cartoons alluded to many of the vaudeville movie stars. Mae West's plebeian swank shows up in Betty Boop, or as the flouncy heroine in Disney's *Who Killed Cock Robin?* Joe Penner may have been the model for Egghead, but clearly W. C. Fields, so famous in radio during the late thirties, was part of what the audience perceived in the character — the inflamed nose and the balding head. Groucho's walk and smart-aleck Brooklynese became part of Bugs Bunny.

Within a decade of the introduction of sound, live vaudeville was gone for the most part. Even the fashion for vaudeville humor in the movies had declined. New styles of popular entertainment were alluded to in cartoons, those that replaced vaudeville: the crooner, the big band, the chanteuse, the jazz club, the night club.

For a generation until 1937 (or at the latest 1940), electronic media diffused what remained of vaudeville musical styles. With the new microphones, the leathery, booming voice of Al Jolson slowly went out of fashion (a famous antique by the late thirties), replaced by the amplified silkiness of Bing Crosby.[16] Radio broadcast vaudeville songs and two-act jokes into the living room. The much improved RCA records brought the musical review into the home as well, electrically, not acoustically, recorded, with wider tonal range and much more bass. And for a time, until 1937 or so, the cartoon used the musical review format very often. The most famous examples were Disney's Silly Symphonies, but every studio had its own: Happy Harmonies, Cartunes, Color Rhapsodies, Merrie Melodies, and more.

These little cartoon operettas seem painfully maudlin today ("Depression Melodrama"). Filmic story is turned into a sentimental interlude, similar to vaudeville singers who came on between comedians or the one-acts to sing about broken hearts and happy reunions. Most of these musical cartoons were devoted to interpreting the music and little else. They toss in an endangered hen house, or evil creatures in bookland, but it is mostly to hang the crescendos on, and rather elliptically at that. One can expect a kidnapped chick somewhere, or an affianced girl bee carried away like Lindbergh's baby, and so on. Then the hive rallies, kicks the varmints out, and saves Sue Bee, all to a rousing symphonic finish.

Despite these weaker examples, the cartoon seems to transfer vaudeville music effortlessly into sound, years before Busby Berkeley's best work. One cannot compare the early Eddie Cantor films to the inspired madness of Mickey Mouse, not without wincing at any rate. Betty Boop sways to Helen Kane songs or to jazz from the Cotton Club; the entire frame is syncopated, even the walls and the furniture. As I explained in the previous chapter, music replaces the ideogram.

As overpowering as full orchestras were in the twenties popcorn palaces, they could not merge gesture and movement the way Mickey Mouse could when he turned a goat into a musical Calliope. In Disney, the buttercups on the screen could literally "swell" with the orchestra. This was a quantum leap over the bouncing ball cartoons from Fleischer five years before. At Warners in the late thirties, musical entertainers are still "burlesques," like Eddie Cantor in *Billboard Follies* or Fats Waller in *Tin Pan Alley Cats*. By the early forties, at MGM, Tex Avery was satirizing a new version of the carny or the music hall. In cartoons like the brilliant *Red Hot Riding Hood*, Avery selects the night club instead: a cartoon world of voyeuristic nonsense — the evils of the city.

But we have to look beyond the place where the music was played, and beyond the type of music as well. In the end, whether it was a rhumba, a brass band, or hot jazz was not very important. A touch of Mae West here or there, or Durante doing a sly *sprechtstimmer*, did not alter the form of the cartoon crucially. What cartoons borrowed most from vaudeville was its fractured use of story. Within the license of the burlesque stage, the gag was its own montage (naked or otherwise, like pants dropping in a crisis, or dresses blowing away).

Even by 1918, this bouncier style of vaudeville had given way to what George Jean Nathan called "the new classic vaudeville," copying the pretensions of uptown theater (in one-acts during the First World War).[17] Even before the coming of sound, when the vaudeville houses were still packed, the narrative style of the music hall was fading: "As vaudeville has acquired this atmosphere of smartness, this *recherché* quality, there has coincidentally departed from it its old bounce and gusto." Nathan remembers "the little green whiskered Irishman [who] fell onto the stage backwards through the swinging door and, colliding with the fat blonde in the red satin *decolleté*, caused the latter to land upon his stomach with a resounding kerplunk."[18] Gone is "that palmy and inspiriting day when the sensitive, artistic sister act in short green skirts with red linings meandered out before the drop-curtain embellished with Beeman's bald head and hook-and-eye root beer ads, nonchalantly scrutinized the dressy old boy in the stage box who had sneaked away from the office to be taken in the matinée, and then went at 'My Gal's a Highborn Lady' like twin gold-toothed contralto siege guns." "I seem to grow sentimental," he adds. "but the scent of rosemary lingers in my nostrils and the memories of that lovely day will not be dimmed."

Cartoons kept that spirit of rosemary for only a few years. By 1934, Disney had decided emphatically to move away from gag storytelling. As a sort of papal dictum, he "announces" his plans in *The Band Concert*. Mickey's orchestra is overcome by a tornado that blows hippos and cows high into the cartoon air, where they keep to their posts, do nothing lewd, hold tight to their tubas and violins. In a magnificent revolving flourish, synchronized perfectly to the conclusion of the *William Tell* Overture, they all land on a tree without losing a note. As the conductor, Mickey

Disney's *The Band Concert* (1935, color: "Disney Nouveau," dir. Wilfred Jackson). First Donald intrudes, then a tornado, but Mickey stays on the beat. © The Walt Disney Company.

THE GAG

had led his band through the wilderness. He has saved the mail (or the airmail, as in another famous short), and brought his orchestra from the vaudeville gag to a formal piece of music.

In Disney, by the mid-thirties, the ragged montage has become considerably more fluid. The music-hall skit is no longer the model for the cartoon. Finally, Disney transforms the vaudeville barnyard into the symphony hall, in *Mickey's Grand Opera* three years later, and, of course, *Fantasia*. The Disney cartoon leaves its Grub Street, or Tin Pan Alley, and moves uptown (or into the suburbs of Burbank). Aspects of the fractured narrative — or musical review — continue at Warners in particular: *Bosko in Person* (1933), *Buddy's Beer Garden* (1934), *Buddy's Showboard* (1934), *Shake Your Powder Puff* (1934), *Dog Daze* (1937). But for the most part, when vaudeville ends, a kind of vaudeville cartoon goes as well.

A transitional example from Warners might be Avery's *Hamateur Night* (1938), a spoof of the radio show, *The Amateur Hour*. With a lot of small-town sawdust and tinsel (and Egghead floating through now and then), the yokels audition before a laconic hound, who drops them through a trap door, while he spouts nasal witticisms, like a character actor from a screwball comedy. Instead of live entertainment, radio and cinema are the models. More than any other cartoon studio of the thirties, the Warners' animators exploited radio, beginning with a homage to the medium, *I've Got to Sing a Torch Song*, in 1933.

As a concluding vaudeville image (like a specialty act), we observe Mickey Mouse playing in *Steamboat Willie*. He is confined to the mess below deck and decides to entertain himself. Besides attacking a rueful parrot by flinging a potato at its head, he uses the teeth and backs of various animals to make music.

Similarly at Warners, Bosko tortured animals until they made music, borrowing from that early Disney style. In the third of the Bosko series, *Hold Anything* (1930), he uses a mouse to make music on a saw, then decapitates it on the beat. It's raw and unpredictable; but compare the energy and invention of any of these to the tedious musical interludes in a Marx Brothers movie and one can see why Eisenstein admired Disney for his use of sound.

In a sense, sound brings vaudeville even more thoroughly inside the anarchy of the cartoon, for a short time. The musical cartoons of the early thirties became one of the replacements for the vaudeville which had been declining, but was still well remembered. However, this was only part of the transition that took place between 1928 and 1934. Like the print era described in chapter 1, vaudeville continued to vanish. The need to refer to it finally disappeared. Two traditions — one for the drawing surface, the other for movement on the stage — keep losing ground, particularly after talkies came in.

31

CHAPTER THREE

Story

Let me begin by reviewing where we have gone so far, before discussing the Disney approach to story. I have introduced two "first principles" for the cartoon: first graphic narrative, and second the vaudeville gag. What sort of story can survive these two?

In animation, story is often defined by both, before the first blush of motivation: by graphics and by the gag (timing) first. Character will adapt to whatever these two dictate. Disney redesigned both in the thirties; and thereafter, the older use of story, what I defined as graphic narrative, was no longer appropriate. Disney was aiming for what he considered bigger game — a cartoon version of movie acting.

The best model for introducing this change is the multiplane camera, designed by Ub Iwerks in the late twenties, but not used until 1937. It became a sort of initiation chamber into Disney's new depth of field, which is the formal end of graphic narrative: layers of painted glass. The camera could pan and zoom just like a "real" camera. The replica of life had replaced the flat surface. Iwerks was not the first to try cartoon deep staging: Fleischer had tried something like it in the thirties. Miniaturizations were a standard part of the trick films, by Starevich in Russia, by Willis O'Brien in *The Lost World* (1924), then at Disney, whether from their special-effects department or their sculpture department. Cartoon deep focus *would* become a significant part of the whole, but not immediately.

In 1928, the rules were not yet appropriate for deep staging. I am convinced that the older graphic narrative with its shallow vaudeville foreground still applied in surprising ways. Of course, graphic narrative does have many comebacks; it has become crucial today with the impact of video and computers. But that is best left for the Conclusion. For now, I will define character *c.* 1928, as it had to behave when flat surface governed the hand-drawn film: autonomous lines; and asymmetrical rhythms (gags, surprises).

I will define by contrast, with two versions of asymmetry: Beardsley's illustrations of Oscar Wilde's play *Salome*, and the special-effects movie *Tron* (the forerunner of "VR" films like *Lawnmower Man*).

In 1893, when Beardsley illustrated *Salome*, he incorporated a Japanese style of line and gesture, borrowed particularly from Utamaro. His figures and absence of background are highly distressed, with many references to popular illustration. Beardsley was perhaps the first illustrator to make allusions almost completely to illustration itself. Until then illustrators had alluded to sculpture, theater, the novel, and others. By 1893, the language of illustration had been absorbed by three generations of book and magazine readers. It was its own world, a self-contained syntax.

Ironically, Beardsley is virtually the last to use illustration as its own allusion. Soon after, the unraveling of graphic narrative began. But briefly, we see every twist of line as a syntagm[1] from Dürer or from Burne-Jones. As Salome scrutinizes the head of John the Baptist and prepares to kiss it (the gesture that most offended theatre audiences), blood, ink, and a gnarled, spiraling, thorny growth combine. Rococco line, Symbolist illustration, and what was called animation (suggestion of motion) wage war against each other. The blank space becomes a painful ellipse, emphasizing Salome's distorted body.

Thus, autonomous line and asymmetrical use of gesture isolate the character in a contemplative madness. (It was too stylized for Wilde's taste, I might add, who wanted the illustrations to allude to theater in some way, to appear more ironic, as a commentary on a world lost in its foolish conventions.)

Now, we turn to the film *Tron*. It is clearly a failed film, which suggests enormous potential for computer animation. It is generally agreed that, more than the effects, the script was disappointing. In one scene (followed by many), Jeff Bridges finds himself zapped quite suddenly into the hypothetical space of the computer byte. The fluid, but flat images (in gaudy technological colors) seal him off into a world made completely of surface and whizzing motion, like an electronic video of a speedway.

What kind of story belongs in this word? The art direction and cinematography are dominated by video memory and computerized replacement of live action with simplified graphs. As a result, two forms of narrative come into direct collision on the screen. Jeff Bridges complains that he is a "user," a live-action character, but he is constantly reminded by others that he belongs to an animated world, with no real space, except on the surface.

Clearly, this animated cosmos demands something other than a live-action story. But what alternatives exist in the trunk of Hollywood formulas? Only in the eighties did the movie industry begin crossing into films about video nostalgia, from *Star Wars* and *Flashdance* to films by Spielberg, Dante, and Zemeckis: journeys into the future/past of television memory, most notably *Who Framed Roger Rabbit?* but also the *Blade Runner/Robocop* genre, what I call "cyber-opias" (cybernaut operas); and finally, horror films spiced with a few video nightmares: "brainstorm" scenes, poltergeist gags, and Freddy Krugerisms.

From all of these, I can identify some basic problems in story when computer-assisted video effects are added. The more the pandemonium looks graphically flat, the harder it is for the audience to believe in the character in the normal dramatic sense. Something too visceral and obvious intrudes. The guidance system of drama in film is altered when characters move along an electronic surface. In fact, producers are now rather spooked by a film like *Tron*. Something goes wrong with the story.

Tron failed in precisely the area where Beardsley succeeded. At the time that *Tron* first appeared, computer surface was still nothing more than a novelty effect. It is far more than that now, but not yet as defined as graphic literacy was in 1893 (for the audience, above all). As a result, the characters in *Tron* are not defined — as they should be — by the animated medium. *Tron* looks more like a cartoon (flat, linear) than traditional live action. It requires a graphic narrative. I would suggest that any form of hand-made film where the graphic narrative dominates must treat character irretrievably differently than in a detective or suspense film.

So we return to an earlier question. What is story in an animated cartoon, when the graphic medium and the unnatural rhythm (unlike live action) define what a character can do?

Obviously, there is great unity in the seeming randomness, but let us not simply argue for coherence. Let us try to identify meaning (how it works).

We start modestly, with a rather oversimplified Cartesian introductory statement. Cartoon characters were highly anarchic. This was so in silent cartoons, and the coming of sound did little to restrict this anarchy, as of 1928 or so.

First, the medium they inhabited was anarchic, as Creighton Peet wrote in 1929:[2]

Unhampered by any such classical limitations as dramatic unities, or even such necessities as the laws of gravity, common sense and possibility, the animated drawing is the only artistic medium ever discovered which is really "free."

Peet adds other tributes: "pure cinema, visual flow, graphic representation, the freedom of the cinematic medium." Let me narrow the focus of this freedom for a moment. Cartoon characters had to synchronize with graphic narrative and vaudeville timing. Their zany behavior (like the *zanni*, the clowns of the Commedia dell'Arte) was dictated by the restrictions of life on a flat surface and by jumps in coherence due to gags (the emphasis on comic rhythms).

That does not seem to leave much — just a few inches of character. And yet, we have a very complex package. When the graphics, gags, and characters play against each other elegantly, they set up a cartoon state of war, with no holds barred. Any line or jump in movement can become a weapon.

It was, to coin a phrase from Thomas Hobbes, a war of all against all. But they integrated like the gears of a machine. All these are issues that will be developed in the following pages. Here, we focus on what this *anarchy* in character means.

It means antilogy: in the very qualities that cartoon story lacked, there was unity. It lacked motivation and logical sequence of time: once upon a time would do. Its signature was graphic narrative rather than character narrative.

Peet emphasizes how free it was of phoney melodrama and moralizing. Anarchy is amoral: "The cartoon comedy seems to be the only pungent, impertinent, and sudden thing that ever reaches the average screen." On movement and medium: "[Felix the Cat] bouncing about in his fantastic cosmos adds one of the few sparks of vitality in a world of insistent proprieties."

A separate cosmos also suggested a god, just as naive irreverence (amorality) suggested folk tales. Thus, not surprisingly, cartoon characters are compared to folk gods. Jean Charlot writes: "We bow to this newly created pantheon of animal godlings, Mickey Mouse et al., for they are different from us, godlike and irrational."[3]

In 1934, E. M. Forster follows much the same logic (or anti-logic). First, on irreverence, he writes: "[Mickey Mouse] is never sentimental, indeed there is a scandalous element in him which I find most restful."[4] Then he compares Mickey to various animal gods, particularly the Egyptian god Bes (an arcane reference taken from Forster's trips to Egypt, and his fascination with folklore as a style of fantasy, meaning a form of story that is free from the restrictions of conventional character development).[5] Bes was a bandy-legged, playful, part-lion demon, worshipped for his love of music, sex, and childbirth. He was usually drawn naked, with a huge phallus, and often wore a row of feathers on his head.

Bes is not a bad patron saint for the thirties cartoon characters, who were very sensual in their anthropoidal way. Flip the Frog had a roving eye. Betty Boop had every roving eye after her. In one mock interview, she hints at having affairs with extras in the Fleischer menagerie: giraffes and the like.[6]

Sound apparently made these libidinous touches even more vivid. The sexuality in cartoons was a lively issue among film reviewers (and conservative women's groups, I regret to say). As always, since the birth of bourgeois censorship, the argument was not so much about violence or sex, as about amorality, losing control, not teaching children that evil is its own reward. The vast majority of critics applauded the sound cartoon for its irreverence. Kenneth White writes in 1931:[7]

There is a further enrichment in the animated cartoons that seems not to be found in any other place: their humor tends to the frankly bawdy. Not so long ago, the coy rhythms of Carolyn Cow troubled the censors, the umbilical emphasis in the clogging that so perpetually occurs in the cartoons continues, and villainous animals' pants, in full view of the public, are taken down and the exposed area spanked by an angry populace of flames. It is, undoubtedly, these irate flames, and startled trees, heartbroken hydrants, dancing piano stools, and helpful pianos, and all their perversities, reluctances, and contributions that make cartoons the hilarious fantasies they are.

White was talking particularly about Disney's use of line — and libido — in the early thirties. That multimorphic world in Disney cartoons could get a trifle scatological or sensual. (Until 1932, physical gags showing flesh were often used at Disney.) Most importantly, Disney perfected yet another gimmick for the cartoon war of all against all. And it was a very tactile gimmick at that: volume. Volume became as flexible as line. Like an animistic folk tale, spirits played pranks with rocks and trees.[8] Anything could spring to life. Trains could be tickled. The sky could be fleshy. This made Disney seem a little racy to some viewers. The multimorphic gags lent themselves quite well to a polymorphous perversity. Any object might get its backside smacked, its breasts fondled, sprout naked feet, drop its pants, grow feminine hips.

I feel I should break the text here, to help the reader. I am about to summarize many crucial features, which eventually vanish from cartoons, only to reappear, from one generation to another. I was considering calling this chapter "The Life and Death of the Cartoon Gag Code," but it sounded too much like an essay on the Russian novel. After all, my subject still remains the form and politics of whimsy. As a second alternative title, how about: The Narrative Structure of Whimsy; or What Happened to Irreverence in Cartoons?

We will jump from Disney's use of the cartoon gag code of the twenties to what had replaced it by 1935. In the chapters that follow, I discuss why Disney turned Mickey into a logo; and how Fleischer used ideology in Betty Boop, Popeye, and Superman cartoons. Then we watch Fleischer go under; after which, we enter the worlds of Warners and UPA (United Productions of America) during the forties and fifties. Finally, we observe their demise by the sixties, and their revival in comics, merchandising, special effects and video.

But in each case (or cycle), the essential elements of making cartoons remain much the same. It is remarkably simple on that level. The animator at the drawing-board struggles to coordinate graphics, rhythm, and character in a way that is both whimsical and sustaining.

And having said that, I return to the analysis of the cartoon character.

We begin once more, as in chapter 1, with a mouse. But not Mickey Mouse yet. We stand up a poster designed by Hugh Harmon for Disney in 1925. Here, clearly, is a lexicon of the twenties gag code, and particularly of mice. In photo-collage, two live-action characters flank the center of the poster. Walt himself, in the director's chair, wearing his rakish hat and knickerbockers, plays a younger Max Fleischer. And a live-action Alice is suitably blond and Victorian, down the rabbit hole.

Everywhere else in the poster we encounter hand-drawn cartoon characters, all properly encoded, because the twenties story required very simplified costumes for its cartoon animals, much like the masks for the Commedia dell'Arte. A Felix character is living inside a roll of paper (how suitable for an ideogram); he is also riding a linear horse and twirling the lines of a lasso. A hoodlum wolf is leaning menacingly, with his evil snout. A gullible basset hound is being led astray, taught to shoot craps by a small black mouse.

In fact, there are black mice everywhere, at the four corners of the poster. They are snipping off lines, and seem permitted any degree of nastiness. Their sign is firmly catalogued: a black mouse is usually homeless, possibly a scavenger. He is a nuisance, cute or otherwise. And he is quite possibly a black man, from the farm if in overalls, from the city if in tattered fedora, and so on. Mickey, as we shall see, is clearly a black mouse: he is an ink spot with *black strokes for feet* (barefooted; the button shoes were added later). In 1928, Felix meets just such a mouse in *Felix Dines and Pines* and tries to eat him. But this little mouse is a rugged survivor, like the street toughs Ub Iwerks drew for *Alice is Rattled by Rats*.

All these rodents are descendants of Ignatz, the snide line mouse, who was usually found happily thieving or womanizing (in one cartoon, he is hippo-izing). At the end of the cartoon, he would hit Krazy Kat with a brick, but was never punished. However, once the Krazy Kat series waned, Ignatz was forgotten. (There were some weaker Krazy Kat cartoons from Columbia in the thirties, and a revival in reprint of Herriman comics in the seventies.) The point is that no rodent was used as a lead character at this stage. By 1927, the rigid gag code required that leads be designed to look like Felix (the black outline, the saucer eyes). Paul Terry, Walter Lantz, and Disney all had Felixes, had them already in stock, so to speak. Mickey's immediate predecessor, Oswald the Lucky Rabbit, was certainly a "Felix."

If a character resembled Felix, he was granted a considerable range of roles in this cartoon state of war. Not only was Felix a clever diamond in the rough, he was also allowed to change the rules within the cartoon to suit his whimsy. He was what I call the *controller* character in the cartoon.

A Felix character could also double as the *over-reactor*. (I shall return to these terms below, pp. 38f.) He can discharge his infantile rage without fear of punishment. Like Felix in *Felix Woos Whoopee*, he can "murder" the cuckoo clock simply to release tension, and to refuse to get up for work at six in the morning. In the same sense, to repeat a gag that I mentioned in the last chapter, Mickey clobbers an annoying parrot with a potato and sends the bird through a porthole, again to clear the air. The over-reactor is as essential to the cartoon power-struggle as any other role.

Finally, there is the nuisance role (of mice, or the "bad guy," Pegleg Pete, Bluto, the wolf, Elmer out duck-hunting, Yosemite Sam).

Thus, there were three essential roles which evolved within the cartoon, and each was allowed certain moments of uncontrolled violence (or license). To review, they were the *nuisance*, the *over-reactor*, and the *controller*. Each character dressed in a definable way and was easily identified by the audience. These three roles would evolve considerably after the coming of sound, but one key issue held them together — freedom from restraint. Eventually, the controller would become a more cautionary fellow, rather like a censor. But initially he came out of the notion of lightning hand, where the animator puts his pen directly into the screen or can erase a character that misbehaves. In a sense, the controller's role always stands in for the animator himself, sketching on the flat surface.

The *controller* is usually indestructible in a cartoon: he may feel anguished, but he hardly ever gets hit.

By contrast, the *over-reactor* tends to take the lumps, like the fall guy in a slapstick comedy. Someone has to dish it out; someone has to take it. Someone has to, shall we say, take charge of the tricks of graphic narrative. Another has to guarantee a fractured gag-line (the chase, the insult, the obstacle). To get the cartoon past the opening credits, who shall cast the first stone? Who starts the trouble, and who takes it from there, past the insult into a chain of gags? The *nuisance* usually starts off the cartoon by annoying the *over-reactor*, who then keeps the gags flowing. This is the general formula, because attacks free of motivation, without moral or psychological baggage, keep the rhythm frantic. Any of a thousand, simple, heartless acts of effrontery can start the chase, though usually the audience knows who wants to eat whom, and they're off. It begins immediately, like a key in an engine.

That makes the *nuisance* particularly useful. He is more like a force of nature than a character who thinks at all. He can save a lot of time. He simply furrows his brow and the mischief is on its way.

Who guides the cartoon along, giving it a build, even a certain choreography? The *controller* does. He is the one who defines the others. He lets the audience know how far the others can go, whether they can be amoral, strike each other at will. He decides when the mischief will end. Will it end just as it begins, or long after that? Above all, like Max Fleischer introducing his own hand into the cartoon and lifting up Koko by the seat of the pants, the controller identifies which way the graphic narrative will be used. Will gravity intervene when the character walks too far off the cliff?

More often than not the hero is the controller, the one who is given the initiative. In twenties cartoons, Felix usually *controls* gravity, line, shapes, distance. By the fifties, as the use of ensembles becomes more complex, Bugs Bunny plays the controller over the others, driving Daffy or Elmer or Yosemite Sam into insanely hopeless acts of vendetta — that "wascally wabbit."

Often, characters may be allowed the controller role for only part of the cartoon, as in silent Inkwell cartoons, where Bozo the street dog turns a rock into a door to escape from Koko (as if Bozo could sketch in a perspective whenever he needed it). Before long, Max will force his hand inside the screen again to stop all this rowdiness.

Characters trade off controller roles (typically in Tom and Jerry or Woody Woodpecker cartoons). I will be returning to these issues throughout the essay: nuisance; over-reactor; controller. For now, let me emphasize a larger, related point. In order for these zany characters to sustain a chase, or a slapstick give-and-take, they must be free of novelistic uses of character (emergent remorse, guilt, deepening depression, moral crisis — a list of that sort). Instead of rules about motivation, they live by a limited cartoon version of the Geneva Convention — rules on how to conduct war on a flat screen. And these rules usually emphasize the medium, not the story. For example, in *A Feud There Was* (1938), Egghead is allowed to walk through a feud between two hillbilly families. As he passes, there is a silly pause. The guns stop blazing. But he cannot actually reduce hostilities until 30 seconds before the cartoon ends. Why? Because Warners cartoons were six minutes long, and the gags had to sustain for $5\frac{1}{2}$ minutes before the final punch line.

When Mickey or Bugs is a nuisance, over-reactor or a controller, that is a very different use of character than in drama. It is more like the narrative structure of fairy tales. Cartoons are not story trifles; they are folklore about the rituals of daily life, in our case about consumer life.

The reader is undoubtedly aware that this abstracted structure resembles the story lines in fairy tales (also the constant use of fairy-tale formulas in cartoons). Perhaps the reader is familiar with Vladimir Propp's analyses of fairy tales (victim, donor, etc.). Writing in the twenties, Propp had a profound influence on theories of defamiliarization, anti-story and epic theater, and on too many critics, artists, and film-makers to summarize in a sentence. Instead, I will summarize a keynote from his work that can be useful here.

Just as in fairy tales, Propp emphasized *function* rather than motivation for a character.[9] This is a vital narrative alternative. When medium is abstracted down, and nakedly visible ("once upon a time"), characters function purely inside a linguistic power-struggle. Fairy magic is a sort of flatness of surface, which requires mythically flat characters (at least compared to a novel).

Much has been made of the psychological advantages of *function* in fairy tales; it presumably enables the listener to externalize deeply felt anxiety. It reifies forgotten moments in a person's intimate development (stages in childhood; family crises; sexual fears), or the social meanings of taboos in a community (like kin or incest). *Function* penetrates forgotten fears. In that sense, Bruno Bettelheim criticized Disney for giving the seven dwarfs separate personalities (and others have criticized Bettelheim for simplifying his sources, and for his narrow, patriarchal reading of Freudian theory).[10] Bettelheim believed the dwarfs should be anonymous, undefined, phallic creatures. Ironically, though, the distinct personalities of the dwarfs are often seen — by both audience and critics — as the great achievement of story in *Snow White*.

In turn, fable and fairy tale have been compared to dream content. In 1913, Freud wrote a short essay about patients who dreamt in fairy tales, apparently to displace guilt or repressed anger.[11] The literature on this subject is vast. Many studies have indicated that this abstracted use of function makes the psychological effects of fable possible.[12] Since I will be discussing animation as folklore in the Conclusion, we need not dwell on this point here. The idea of *function* will do.

HOW DISNEY ALTERED THIS FAIRY-TALE STRUCTURE

In the thirties Disney decided to adjust function into motivated character. He softened the horizontal story (power-struggle abstracted into graphic narrative) to vertical story (self-discovery, character change). Here again, as so often in the history of character animation, the older style overlaps into the newer for a decade. Story codes mutate rather than transform. Once again, the decade of this mutation was the thirties. I am not convinced by the dates usually given for this shift; they seem more the critic's choice than a review of evidence. The period from *Snow White* to *Bambi* (1937–42) is made too sacrosanct, or simply attacked as too corny.

I prefer to begin considerably earlier than 1937 — and considerably simpler. First of all, Disney always used story differently than other studios (particularly Fleischer or Sullivan). The over-reactor role was exploited in a different way, to lengthen the central gag into a more coherent story. In *Mickey's Exciting Picnic*, for example, Horace Horsecollar over-reacts to being stung by a mosquito (a bumptious youth, as nuisances often are) and smashes him viciously. The wounded insect calls for help from the mosquito tribes and a mock Indian war follows; they attack in droves. Mickey, Horace, and others make a circle inside the picnic wagon. Once again, Mickey plays the general. He works up a plan to defeat the mosquitoes. They are lured into a vacuum cleaner, with a burlesque house advertised at the nozzle, and then sucked into the bag. As they squirm inside, Horace gets his last kicks in. He pounds the helpless mosquitoes and gives them a final, toothy horse laugh.

This is a far more continuous story than in many cartoons from the early thirties, where gags often came and went with little dramatic build. And in twenties cartoons, over-reaction (or infantile rage) served primarily to emphasize the anarchy of the character, a little spice, even a so-called spot gag, not a brick in a wall, added to tighten the vertical story. Disney was already on another track.

We will examine the results of this in a moment, but first let me generalize about the fairy-tale, function-oriented style of story, from Disney before 1932, and in the chase cartoon from 1937 on. (More on the chase later.) There were many variations, but the basic function-oriented story was followed, for the most part.

What was the aim of this kind of cartoon story? The resolution of "conflict"? I would say essentially to stop the nuisance dead in his tracks; to end the chase. To stop the nuisance, the controller might have to resort to desperate measures, like snipping away a cel that offers an escape route, or suddenly turning the borders of the screen into a wall (very much in the tradition of graphic narrative).

Certain gags became useful to keep the function-oriented story moving. By the mid-forties, at Warners and MGM, collision gags become almost limitless in this form of story — anything to add surprise to the chase. Anything might include a miraculous escape, followed by dauntless blunders, ruthless tricks, misguided attacks, zany reprisals, and finally — back to basics — a well-placed crack on the head. One can even force one's enemy into another cartoon, as when Jerry Mouse wakes up Spike the Bulldog, who immediately punches Tom Cat around the block a few times (*Quiet Please*, 1945; with parallel formulas in *Cat Napping*, 1951, *Hic-cup Pup*, 1954, *Royal Cat Nap*, 1958). The key is Jerry using Spike to change the balance of power after peace has been destroyed. Once Spike is showing his canines, Tom finds himself trapped in a completely different cartoon, one in which he is the weak cat. Then, in *Quiet Please*, Spike is given a huge dose of sleeping pills. He's out cold. Like entropy, his bulldog laziness takes over, and Jerry loses an ally. With Spike out of the picture (except as a carcass to poke at), the original cartoon comes back where it left off: Tom chases Jerry until Spike wakes up and beats Tom into submission. This is a typical formula from Hanna and Barbera during the forties, considerably truer to the anarchic story than their television shows, to say the least. Their limited animation for TV has numbed fans to the best of their earlier work at MGM, though a few new coffee-table books on Tom and Jerry indicate a revival.[13]

I want to emphasize that this anarchic story format (nuisance, over-reactor, controller) can be very flexible. In all cartoons, there are degrees of these functions, like a pigment added to water. In some it is faintly visible, in others utterly dominant. For example:

Anarchy Faced with Occasional Moments of Drama

What does the anarchic character do when dramatic conflict presents itself? In *Felix Toys with Time*, an earlier example, the intrepid Felix asks Father Time to send him back to prehistoric times. There he might get a little more to eat, instead of the scant pickings in the city garbage pails. Predictably for Felix, he finds life even more difficult there. Finally, he asks to go back to the present-day world, now willing to enjoy less. At the so-called obligatory scene, he is chased by a rather dog-like dinosaur. He runs to the edge of a cliff. Facing fear and raging waters below, Felix does not undergo a peripety at all. Instead, he simply changes his mind. As the dinosaur threatens, Felix throws a rock made of lines into the river below and summons up a parachute made of lines from the splash, as it rises and falls. Then he floats down to safety.

This does not mean that Felix controls his destiny, any more than Chaplin or Stan Laurel does. But when Felix voodoos gravity, he can go unchastened. Compare this to Disney's version of the controller in *The Sorcerer's Apprentice*, where Mickey is utterly chastened, even humiliated. Omnipotence over the forces of gravity and volume are beyond Mickey, and he learns his lesson. Felix learns very little, only what he can, or cannot, eat. When guilt threatens, Felix can subvert any crisis that might change him. Just at the moment of dilemma, he is permitted to use graphic magic to free himself. Surprise (as in the magic trick) is the criterion for a great gag, not a character reversal. Does a magician in a variety act go through Aristotelian character change? Or is he expected to subvert fear and mortality? To rephrase Coleridge, the cartoon is the *graphic* suspension of the unbelievable. Everything can be sacrificed to improve the timing of the cartoon (and should be, perhaps).

Let me try to invent a little history for this process (hopefully, not entirely invention). What examples of this style of character come from popular theater before the twentieth century? Certainly, these Felixes and Mickeys function like the disruptive monsters or clowns (the so-called "antics") of seventeenth-century English masque, particularly plays by Ben Jonson.[14] But even earlier, antics (intruding actors) were contrived as a prelude to the dance; dancers would then push the antics away and begin the formal masque. With Jonson, this prelude came to be called the *ante*-masque (meaning before the dance), or *anti*-masque (a subversion of the dance). Essentially, antics were contrived to keep the dance surprising, not to reveal the problems of the soul or mortality. They became a step in defamiliarization, in "once upon a time." Their function as story elements far exceeded their meaning as motivated characters. Like cartoons, these clowns presented a theater about chaos, a form of allegory so exaggerated it became burlesque.

Masque is part of an antic tradition that is very strong in English and American *variety* — or music hall — theater (originating, in part, with the snarling leather masks of Commedia dell'Arte). But we must remember that animators in 1928 had grown up at the turn of the century. There were a few new bumps on the road. By then, vaudeville came, above all, to engage the crisis of what Albert McClean, Jr, calls the New Folk — the anarchic city life in its raw, early twentieth-century conditions.[15] Violence in the cartoon reflects that source, but it still remains only an updated version of the anarchic (or antic) burlesque of Chaos. Four hundred years of burlesques had done much to make a knock on the head or a pratfall something of a science.

THE TWENTIES NUISANCE

There was a science to beating up somebody on stage. There was not much morality or justice to it, but it had its subtleties. Like an old plumber's helper, it was essential to the kit. Therefore, animation formulas for the twenties characters were built very much around ways to bludgeon somebody on paper. E. G. Lutz summarized comic violence very systematically in *Animated Cartoons* (1920), a standard text for animators into the thirties:[16]

It is indispensable, for the sake of an uninterrupted animation, that it should have a succession of distressing mishaps, growing in violence. This idea of a cumulative chain of actions increasing in force and resultant misfortune is peculiarly adapted to animated drawings.

Lutz recommended using "primitive practical jokes," like smacking a man's hat off with a stone. For crowning a man directly on the head with a club he advised "radiating 'dent' lines [to] give emphasis to the bludgeon blow." How much more obvious can a *nuisance* get?

As I explained earlier, none of this was lost on Disney: the thumpings, the ass jokes, the flesh gags. When young Friz Freleng was hired to work for Disney in Kansas City in the early twenties, he used the Lutz book to learn on the job. These were standardized formulas very early on.

In the first Mickey short (*Plane Crazy*) a barnyard black mouse, who also looks like Felix, tries to comb his hair to look like Lindbergh. Then he builds an airplane of the rubbery multimorphic type. He offers Minnie a ride, coaxes her into the plane by shoving her buttocks over the door. Then, as they float 100 feet over the barnyard, he attacks her, demanding that she smooch or else.

Minnie says no, and jumps out. Mickey is a guilt-stricken cavalier as he watches her dive into free fall, looking remorsefully at the camera the way Chaplin did so often. Luckily, Minnie's bloomers open into a parachute. But she does not forgive Mickey, and nor does the cartoon screen. At the end, a horseshoe boomerangs on Mickey, striking him for his rudeness. But he laughs anyway, and the iris closes.

Like a character in anti-masque, Mickey was a force of nature, puckishly undidactic. According to one description, he had only two expressions: happy and not so happy. Clearly, his facial animation is far more complex than Felix's, simple as it may seem: more parts of his face move at the same time, etc. He is less of a "mask." And yet, in the early cartoons, his motivation can be just as erratic (it is still more function than motivation). The obvious example: Mickey discharges his infantile anger often, clobbering ants with a hammer, knocking a parrot with a potato. At various moments, Mickey will attack defenseless creatures, destroy automobile parts (particularly tires), then laugh heartily, displaying sharp rodentile teeth. In the same sense, when Felix "kills" the cuckoo clock, he grins at the audience.

A few years later, Mickey is given "motivation" (and much more baggage than that). He is altered in many senses of the word: he loses his sexuality, gets more docile, plumper. By 1933, the rowdy barnyard jokes have been eradicated — no more cruelty to other animals. Most importantly, his behavior is no longer anarchic.

Radiating "dent" lines give emphasis to this bludgeon blow.

A chase around some object is a never-failing laugh-provoking incident in an animated cartoon.

Pictures of this sort can be presented on the screen more vividly than in this simple graphic sketch.

Lutz's manual (1920) was studied widely, particularly by trainee animators in the twenties, like Friz Freleng at Disney.

His role as part-nuisance, part-over-reactor (occasionally controller) was given to Donald Duck. In *The Band Concert*, Mickey's replacement takes over as the instigator of the gags. A snide Donald, with gawkier bill, interrupts constantly. He forces Mickey's orchestra to play "Turkey in the Straw," instead of the *William Tell* Overture. "Turkey in the Straw" was Mickey's theme song in *Steamboat Willie*, where he played the tune on a cat's tail. Donald, as the new nuisance, seems equally unperturbed. He squawks endlessly, but recovers very blithely, enjoys his snideness — and was found to be very endearing to audiences. (As an aside, consider also that Donald is dressed in a little boy's sailor suit, and has an infant's squawk. His persona too changes over the years to more of an all-suffering, over-reactive character. Our focus here, however, is Mickey.)

Mickey is translated almost entirely into a controller character (but not in the sense of *function*: he can rarely subvert story). In the Disney "motivated" cartoon, the controller transforms into a censor (not only for the moral order, but also, like the old Roman office of Censor, the keeper of the census, a presiding official).

And of course, there are varying degrees of censor after Disney makes that element popular. Grandma is censor to Sylvester. Pinocchio's censor is his nose. Sometimes the censor is the girlfriend, like Daisy to Donald in the Disney comics

Plane Crazy (1927). In his first appearance, Mickey is very much a barnyard rodent, a nuisance with a strong libido. © The Walt Disney Company.

done by Carl Barks. By 1935, Mickey becomes more of a managerial censor. He keeps his little band of motley men working together. He is a multimorphic voice of reason. Mickey changes noticeably. He get younger (or much older). The pubescent high jinks are gone. As an impressionable boy, Mickey can no longer act up (and yet he can be a sort of adult, like Laurel and Hardy polishing an apple shyly). He can be responsible, yes, run small companies beyond a lemonade stand, but an impressionable boy could not be bawdy, ever. Nor could such a boy be amoral, blow up what he pleased, or grab Minnie in unpardonable ways. No random sex, no unpunished violence.

According to the Disney Studio handbook of the late thirties:[17]

Mickey seems to be the average young boy of no particular age; living in a small town, clean living, fun-loving, bashful around girls, polite and as clever as he must be for the particular story.

In some pictures, he has a touch of Fred Astaire; in others of Charlie Chaplin, and some of Douglas Fairbanks, but in all of these there should be some of the young boy.

This formula was not entirely fixed. As Ted Sears advised in a studio memorandum from the mid-thirties:[18] "Mickey's age varied with the situation . . . . Sometimes his character is that of a young boy, and at other times, as in the adventure type of picture, he appears quite grown up." But the direction is unmistakable. As Mickey evolves, he takes on more responsibility, in *Mickey Plays Poppa*, *Officer Mickey*, and as the embodiment of bourgeois initiative, Robinson Crusoe in *Mickey's Man Friday*.

The relationships in Disney's world follow the laws of nineteenth-century liberalism, as one might expect. Instead of a defined class structure (except in the comics), there is a zany chain of command, based on initiative and natural intelligence. The word "dumb" takes on a specifically critical meaning when designing characters; it suggests how well a character handles cartoon dilemmas. The dumb character fails, because he is a bit of the vaudeville, old-fashioned, beat-em-up clown. For example, "Mickey is not a clown; he is neither silly nor *dumb*" (therefore, he is capable). On the other hand,

Pluto is best appreciated when he is not too smart. People love to see him get into trouble through his *dumb* inquisitiveness . . . . In pantomime, his *dumb* one-track mind is similar to that of Stan Laurel's. Pluto's *dumb* thoughtfulness or reasoning is also funny . . . [In *Playful Pluto*] his dumb fright, startled at seeing his reflection [in the mirror] . . . [is] characteristic.

Pluto is absolutely incapable of "self-reliance"; this amounts to yet another characterological term, rather like dumb. The self-reliant character does not tumble into his own problems, but needs instead a nuisance like Donald to make matters worse (or Pegleg Pete kidnapping Minnie again). Mickey and Pluto stand on opposite extremes of this issue. Unlike Pluto, Mickey is loved for the way he "[accomplishes] things under pressure":

Mickey is at his best when he sets out to do some particular thing and continues with deadly determination in spite of the fact that one annoyance after another, or some serious menace, tries to impede his progress.

Donald thinks he can handle it, but cannot. Not only is he not self-reliant, he is not particularly smart. Specifically, he is not a team player; therefore, he is either the nuisance or the over-reactor:

His best features are his cocky, show-off, boastful attitude that turns to anger as soon as he is crossed; his typical angry gestures with which the audience is familiar, especially his fighting pose and his peculiar quacking voice and threats when angry.

The Duck gets a big kick out of imposing on other people or annoying them; but immediately loses his temper when the tables are turned. In other words, he can "dish it out," but he can't "take it."

The motivation of each character within a Disney ensemble became increasingly important, certainly more so than at Fleischer or at Paul Terry (who remained the last holdout in virtually every area in the industry, including unions, sound, and full animation).

Clearly, the Disney ensemble became the model for many new characters at other studios. There seems little point in cataloguing these similarities; so many of them came from former Disney employees, who knew Walt from his days in Kansas City. In one case, Harmon and Ising (and Freleng's) Bosko and Honey was so like Mickey/Minnie it nearly brought on a copyright suit from Disney. And after 1935, the similarities with Disney story and graphics grow throughout the animation industry. Suffice to say, characterization grows more central to the cartoon, not always at the expense of graphic narrative, but clearly a new model for the cartoon evolves.

I will discuss this model later as domestication and full animation come to the cartoon. For now I can summarize in this way, a little historical simplification, to keep the material clearer:

- Nuisance (generally in the twenties mold — fast, ruthless).
- Over-reactor (more a product of Disney animation after 1928).
- Controller (the key element to watch, in deciding how the cartoon is timed, how the gags operate, how amoral or anarchic the story will get. This will change constantly at an animation studio, according to management, or popular taste, as expressed through pressure from exhibitors).

1934: "DRAMATIC" CHANGES

In the period 1934–c. 1938, before the best at Warners and MGM, before UPA, the cartoon goes into a hiatus, a kind of decline and recovery. As far as story goes, the

46

controller persona increasingly had to speak for justice and perseverence, rather than graphic narrative. The easiest example to cite is Mighty Mouse "come to save the day," like a cartoon New Dealer damming a flooding river. It seems that cartoon characters were no longer as free to confound the plot as they once had been. Briefly, in terms of domestication, they no longer took charge of gravity and linear perspective, but rather were running a household, a rabbit hole, a family.

Cartoon characters were given more stable relationships and lived by irreversible rules of behavior. These even include parodies of work and business, particularly at Warners: Sam Sheepdog and Ralph Wolf "take breaks" at lunch time, pause, then get back to the chase. Elmer, Porky, and Daffy interrupt the cartoon to "ask" for better roles (in effect, a satire on studio contracts). The allusions to contract players in a story formula are an extension of what were called blackout gags or spot gags. They were used to replace twenties tricks on the flat page (until such tricks return in the late forties).

After 1934, however, the threads of graphic narrative are relaxed. There are numerous financial and cultural reasons for this change, which I will discuss in chapter 9. As for the characters, they go through a very obvious transition. Even though in the twenties characters are made to move like movie comedians, they are still essentially like comic strips. It is not surprising that this changes in the thirties. Character designs now borrow far more from live-action movies. We are observing a larger process, beyond animation. Visual literacy was translating into cinema. As always, cartoons restate the audience's preferences. Today, cartoons look like special-effects movies, and as the juvenile film market adjusts to the rock video, cartoons begin to copy the mattes, jumpy intercuts, studio lighting, and fast zooms of MTV. Even Disney's *The Little Mermaid* had musical numbers cut like a music video.

1934: VICTORIAN REVIVAL

That still leaves an odd conundrum: since the cartoons of the early sound era were extremely successful, why did the animation industry dismantle that style so completely?

Can we suggest a miniature Victorian revival after 1934? It was not a Victorianism as rigid as starched linen. It was Victorian like Shirley Temple movies, where children are powerful enough to force adults to stay moral; keep to the straight and narrow. Shirley often takes control of the problem and is permitted freedoms that mature actresses are refused (to tell men where to go, etc.).

That gives her a certain edge, though it is a little ornamental, like a ribbon on a puppy. She looks very precious when she tightens her jaw. It was part of the new Hays Office method, sent down by the chain of command in Hollywood. Many in the industry came to assume that the "family" market would always make money anyway: make movies that a seven-year-old can enjoy, and the whole family will accept. That belief filtered down to the cartoon very quickly, mostly by way of exhibitors. (The moguls in the big studios saw cartoons more or less as concessions to exhibitors and let that end set cartoon standards, if it cared to.) The effects were made public often enough. Schlesinger, who always knew what was expected, made unctuous speeches to the newspapers. Disney still fielded complaints about his morality from letter campaigns and conservative organizations.

It was all part of how the film business dissolved what little autonomy the cartoon had, and how the animation industry responded — in a variety of ways, from obedience to annoyance. But initially, speaking of 1934, they responded with a very different structure for cartoon story, following Disney's lead. The new structure had its advantages and its limitations. For our purposes here, it marks the end of the cycle 1928–34. That earlier anarchy does return, eventually. The cartoons from 1934 to 1937 by no means erase it, with its three central loci: graphic narrative, vaudeville gags, and antic characters. However, for a few years, anarchy is very muted.

PERSONALITY ANIMATION

In setting up the alternative style, Disney had an advantage over all the others. By 1930, Disney was already beginning to move away from the "slam bang" action of twenties animation, away from graphic narrative. The date is early, but by 1932, a new program is laid out, built essentially around dicta like the following from Walt:[19]

Until a character becomes a personality, it cannot be believed. Without personality, the character may do funny or interesting things, but unless people are able to identify themselves with the character, its actions seem unreal. And without personality, a story cannot ring true to the audience.

By 1937, in "Tips to Remember When Submitting Gags," there were "a few traditions that have developed during the past few years," a few rules.[20] For example, some painful gags were funny, but others were definitely not: "When a sharp pointed stick is used as a prop, it should never pierce any living character." Arrows, knives, or thorns can poke the flesh, but must not remain stuck to the body:

Exception to this might be porcupine quills, etc., but only when used upon the posterior of a character, which after years of cartoon tradition has been established as the least sensitive zone.

Here is our answer to — or defense of — torturing the buttocks in Disney cartoons. Like a syringe injecting serum, the quill is finding the most padded place.

Characters cannot be touched by flames, nor can they step on a sharp object. They can still be hit in the stomach or the head ("a common gag"), "but we usually make use of mushy objects if a character is to be hit in the face":

No living creature (even a worm) should be eaten, dismembered, or destroyed in any manner. Even if a fly is swatted it should act punch-drunk rather than dead. In a realistic scene a hen might swallow a worm, provided there has been no closeup of the worm establishing a face or other comic characteristics.

The right to life of eggs is carefully preserved: "The eggs of any bird should not be broken unless for hatching purposes. The exception to this is the good old hen's egg, which will always be a good throwing prop."

And finally, "the use of bedroom crockery has become taboo. This also applies to outhouses, even as scenic props."

These cautions remind me of the Victorian code on the picturesque. In 1874, one English traveler wrote that poor people dress in a very picturesque manner, far more so than the other classes; however, one must never draw a poor person close up or they lose their appeal.[21] In essence, one identifies with their suffering, and they no longer can decorate the chipped brick of a medieval wall or the sun rising over the Escorial. As Barthes wrote of this code, "the human life of a country disappears to the exclusive benefit of its monuments."[22]

When Disney launched the program called "personality" by those at the studio, he set up a school for animators, a sort of in-house Beaux Arts. An arts professor, Donald Graham from Chinouard Institute, was brought in to run it. Other teachers, Phil Dike, Rico LeBrun, and Bernard Barbutt, were put on staff. Animators had to attend classes two or three nights a week, work from live models, study life drawing, learn musculature, composition, quick sketch animals of all kinds, and study techniques and action analysis. They also attended classes in character analysis, with mimeo sheets as text;[23] and studied the styles of famous illustrators and painters, among them Daumier. As Frank Thomas wrote: "the animator was stimulated by the strong attitudes in the drawings of Honoré Daumier."[24] By "strong attitudes" Thomas meant the characterization, the gestures, the way Daumier's characters responded to each other. Daumier was very much a master of group dynamics, of the social tapestries known in the 1830s as "physiognomies" (in albums collected from lithographs in magazines).[25] Daumier's characters face off together in a shared rhythm which can be translated into animation, or so the Disney animators found.

There were classes too on Holbein, Degas, and Leonardo, always with the focus on the drafting process, on "character analysis" (with mimeo sheets as text). When Thomas eulogized his friend Milt Kahl, he compared Kahl's sketches of Madame Medusa yanking off her eyelashes to Daumier's *Sketches of Expression*.[26] (Speaking of graphic narrative again: it was very common in the nineteenth-century magazine to print "character sheets" on how to give personality to illustration; Disney used some of these as though Daumier were on his staff.) As animation fans know, the precision in character movement became Disney's hallmark, along with astonishing syncopation to music and balletic gags involving many characters at once.

The training in the great masters resembles to a marked degree the Golden Mean in the nineteenth-century tradition, where tragedy is defined as sentimentality, and staging must be picturesque (to inspire soulful release and highlight the state of mind of the observer. I might even add "irradiate" the soul, given the colors often used, in diluted versions of early German Romantic painting). The entire sense of the cartoon had to reinforce the character, who was in turn carefully designed (excruciatingly so, given Walt's care with story). The cartoons needed what was called "personality buildup." Character point of view could alter the way Nature looked, like trees threatening when spooks were nearby (an old gag, but used to virtuoso effect in numerous Disney cartoons, and then in the features). The ominous tree was a theatrical form of foreshadowing which was very common in nineteenth-century Academic painting, even in American genre painting. Nature was subsumed beneath the mood of the character. It was not a gothic Nature, a moody, unpredictable force, but a synchronized Nature, a linear framing for the character, more the graphic affirmation of the character's ego and trials.

In this sense, Disney borrowed a theatricality from the late Romantic tradition of graphic narrative, similar to what D. W. Griffith had taken from the nineteenth-century stage or the popular novel. Only recently have the Disney animators been asked to experiment with optical light as the Impressionists did, much less with twentieth-century Modernism (a few flurries in the fifties, and that's about all). The fact that Disney began more within the twentieth century than he ended up is part of the irony of cinema, the inevitable return to the glowing landscapes of Academic painting. These landscapes provide a soothing sense of bourgeois ease and glamor — time to observe without being threatened, like a hardy English tourist visiting the Alps in 1850, with his walking stick, good quality woolen clothing, and an English-speaking guide. We are the master of what we survey. For Disney, this translated into a sense of home and family, of warm flannel and good cheer on a winter's night.

Disney took the multimorphic world and gave it mechanical laws, which are still followed in the animation industry today. Most important of these are squash and stretch, as Frank Thomas and Ollie Johnston explain in *Disney Animation: The Illusion of Life* (still the most thorough survey of "personality" available). The volume of a character is an absolute quantity, like the volume within a container; no matter how much is altered, the volume must remain constant. This means, for example, that a neck can only stretch so far before it becomes as thin as a rubber band (and thus destroys character). The necks of Fleischer's seven dwarfs in *Snow White*, the Betty Boop version, would not be acceptable, pushing outward and into the windows of their house, without regard to volume.

Most of Disney's graphic innovations involved dramatic structure, like anticipation, exaggeration, or appeal. The studio was, in effect, rediscovering the principles of Aristotelian narrative. All scenes had to develop the "story point."

Disney was also very aware of the differences between the twenties graphic narrative and his own — and would exploit both. In what was called "straight ahead action" (Norm Ferguson's approach), the animator sketches as much as he pleases, following the scene image by image — action story drawing. (I suppose, considering the analogies in that era to Surrealism — no influence whatsoever — this might be called cartoon automatism.) "Both the drawings and the action have a fresh, slightly zany look, as the animator keeps the whole process very creative."[27] This clearly lent itself to fractured story, and Disney might be able to translate the surprises it brought into the generalized studio look.

Pose-to-pose was more obviously in the Disney mode. The animator would plan scale and story development within a scene, and let the assistant follow through with the agenda. Here there are few surprises, but all the right buttons are pushed, if the story point were fresh enough. Pose-to-pose merely guaranteed that the action moved story along smoothly.

Of course, by definition, the characters and graphics of pose-to-pose were rigidly encoded, with a list of at least twelve basic rules of story. Understandably, with pose-to-pose, the cartoon tended to avoid anti-masque and settle more comfortably within the crimson sunsets and easy platitudes of nineteenth-century drama. But I must emphasize that Disney was clever enough to appreciate this problem and opened up story conferences a great deal, giving animators room to play. In the thirties, he was a master at holding the two worlds of antic and domesticated together. In many ways, the struggle between these two worlds becomes the running theme in many Disney cartoons, as in *Moose Hunters*, where Donald and his friends use aphrodisiacs to lure the bull moose, without, of course, killing him. Or Mickey tricking the Giant, or protecting the community as *The Little Tailor*. Like a cartoon Frank Capra, Disney could be both cynical and sentimental about community and order. He was as much a master of the screwball comedy and a satirist of the film medium itself as Preston Surges (who, incidentally, praises Disney on film, as many filmgoers may remember, in *Sullivan's Travels*. What they may not realize is that the Pluto sequence highlighted in the film was precisely the one that initiated personality animation, more than any other, Pluto in flypaper in *Playful Pluto* [1932, Ferguson]).

In some ways, it was merely the extension of the multimorphic into a sort of mammo-morphic, to move like people and animals. In 1929, Friz Freleng, who had a very unpleasant year working at Disney (and quit before he was fired), managed one glorious moment when he animated an object climbing out of a tub in the way a puppy might, with hesitating movements backwards. Walt pointed this out very emphatically to the other animators, as if here was an exotic possibility not quite worked out, a certain switch in gears that made possible a bit of sentimental drama inside the cartoon. But it would take a lot of money and business pressure to complete this switch. The multimorphic gags of the late twenties — making objects move like puppies — transform into the first stages of personality animation by 1932. And with the switch came a host of new problems.

A balance between cartoon anarchy and moral storytelling is very fretful to maintain. The bawdiness was not censored away simply because Walt became more conservative. The problems were more practical than that. In animation, styles calcify for reasons that go far beyond the individuals who shape them. Disney had to survive in very difficult financial circumstances — that must always be appreciated. The change was forced as much as desired. Otherwise, we can study the history of consumerism and mass culture for the next two hundred years and not get a sense of why censorship develops. The process is awesome for the entrepreneur trying to maintain quality in the product (not always to be interpreted merely as "pretty" or "expensive"). Even the most passionate crusades for quality can get twisted under the endless struggle to meet bills and overcome debts.

CHAPTER FOUR

Marketing: Mickey Becomes a Logo, 1930–34

Disney as film-maker could never make high profits. Distributors during the thirties were endlessly leeching away the massive grosses from Disney shorts.[1] Patrick Powers, the first distributor for Mickey, drew 90 percent of the gross from the Disneys. Columbia Pictures bought off Powers, but in the process threw Disney into enormous debt, keeping the right to rent many of his cartoons very cheaply for years afterward. United Artists underwrote Disney's debts, but never paid cash to cover them. Throughout the thirties, Disney was endlessly in debt — often three films of debt in arrears — waiting for box office receipts which always lagged behind interest payments. To compound the problem, film shorts always rented for phenomenally less than features.

Imagine the excitement in 1929, under this avalanche of indebtedness, when Walt was given $300 to release Mickey as an endorsement for a pencil tablet. Roy and Walt took it from there.

By 1932, Disney was financing much (if not most) of his film production through endorsements. *Forbes Magazine* in 1934 confidently stated that the new buildings at the Disney Studio on Hyperion Boulevard, costing upwards of $250,000, came primarily from tie-ins.[2] *Three Little Pigs*, the most expensive animated short made up to that time, was financed with profits from tie-ins.

Here is a sampling of Disney products endorsed as of 1934, primarily through Mickey, "the biggest unpaid movie star" as he was described in *Fortune Magazine*:[3] designs on the buckles of boys' belts, figures on the bottom of porridge bowls, ice cream, chewing gum, school tablets, dolls, books, jewelry, swimwear, dresses, soaps, caps, neckwear, watches ... these are just a few of the products that attest to the merchandising power of Mickey Mouse, and as such provide a major source of income to its creator, Walt Disney.

By the mid-fifties (this was *before* the Disneyland explosion) Disney endorsements had sold $750 million of products, some 3,000 different items (that is probably a low figure). Was this already a conglomerate, if not formally, then informally?

Mickey effectively became a moral institution when the education division began in 1941. Random, amoral, and raunchy do not fit an educational toy, and Mickey ultimately became the official babysitter through the Mickey Mouse Club. But what of Mickey Mouse Clubs in 1929 and later (reportedly over a million cherubic members during the thirties, handled by movie theaters)?[4]

The theater experiments with Mickey Clubs were modest, mostly for promotional purposes in 1929, with papier mâché Mickeys guarding the lobbies of movie houses, to guarantee quality for parents and excitement for children. Membership cards were issued — a spoof of social privilege. Heavy promotion emphasizing the children's market developed throughout the early thirties. While these clubs did not draw much energy from the Disney organization, here clearly was a direction completed later on.

This crucial shift in the meaning of the Mickey graphic (and character) is extremely important for the history of twentieth-century popular culture. We must remember that Mickey Mouse may be the primary emblem of America worldwide. Only Chaplin's Tramp ever rivaled him as the world's most recognizable face. In Latin America, there are kachina dolls of Mickey. According to *Time Magazine* in 1952,

The Disney Studio, *c.* 1933, in the Silver Lake District east of Hollywood. Still a small business that has recently expanded into adjoining buildings.

"African witch doctors" were seen dressed as Mickey, as though his face had the religious power of an icon.[5]

But from the mid-thirties on (if not earlier), Mickey was also a corporate logo. This is long before even the first Disney stockholders' annual report in 1940, where he is displayed like a miniature Horatio Alger character who managed somehow to enter the family of Wall Street. Today, he banners all Disney stationery, "edits" the corporate newsletter (even "runs" the help-wanted in the classifieds). He is the beaming host for Disney ads, the blithe little doughboy holding the curtain to show us Disney products, to announce Disney events. He is Mickey showman, and has the right to feel like a showman. He is unquestionably the most broadly marketed film image of the twentieth century. In the seventies, the permanent rights to Mickey were priced at $750 million, more than the total assets of many of the Fortune 500. One would have to double that figure in the nineties.

This was Disney's leverage against the major studios. Throughout the thirties, Walt and Roy used it superbly, plowing the money back into film production. (Though they still went into debt with very ambitious animation; Disney was virtually the only animation studio that "overshot" as standard practice. When America entered the Second World War, Disney was still in debt by over $3 million, even after the success of *Snow White*, its receipts long since spent.)

During the war, plans for diversification, including a theme-park, were already in place, but had to wait. Walt visited Latin America during the war, planned new projects there, but even many of those had to wait a few years. Worldwide markets had shrunk. Toy production was down as well. Disney barely stayed solvent, and had to rely on government contracts for documentaries. Licensing continued, but at a slower pace than in the thirties. Even after the war, advance financing was

Russian director Sergei Eisenstein visited Disney's studio in 1930.

slender and not enough to mount a three-year animated feature project. Only packages of longer cartoons were released. Then Kay Kamen, who had run the licensing division for decades, died in a plane crash in 1949. Disney took two years to regroup and work out a licensing system for the next decade. By then, *Cinderella* had been released, after a gap of almost a decade without a major animated feature to promote.

Disney geared up again for a series of cartoon features (*Peter Pan*, in the works since the thirties; *Sleeping Beauty*; *Lady and the Tramp*). Walt was now in the vanguard of high consumerism, preparing to enter family tourism, sensing the expansion — with the help of such novelties as the credit card — of disposable income. The whirlwind that heralds international Disney began again, leading to Disneyland and the television series in 1954. In the fifties, profits were divided equally into thirds: films, licensing, Disneyland. By the seventies, film rentals represented only about 15 percent of the net profits. The rest came from the parks, television, and merchandising. The Eisner era (since 1987) has changed that percentage somewhat with Touchstone movie hits, but ultimately not much. The expansion, or addition, of Disney parks in Anaheim and Orlando, as well as EuroDisney, will bring that ratio back to where it was. In the thirties, the financial source was easier to track; merchandising accounted for about half the profits.

Many of us still remember the plumper, pre-pubescent Mickey of fifties television. In his tee shirt (with a child's belly), he represented the plain style in high consumerism. Indeed, he spoke for so many things about family entertainment and the leisure ethic that, rather than try to list them all, I will summarize in a sentence or two. This fifties Mickey is a consumer mytheme, the picturesque at a shopping mall or at Disneyland. He has come to mean tourism for children, a place shared by Peanuts characters, Ronald McDonald, and others. Above all, he is the index of the child living comfortably in a broadacre suburb.

Disney plays off four generations of film fans. In the nostalgic gift section of any department store, when adults shop for items that signify childlike innocence (translated as security), Mickey Mouse is the standard graphic, a cherubic little Apollo. From Warner Communications to Lucasfilms, the Disney style of marketing has been adapted to numerous film characters. What is the color of childhood nostalgia? Bright umber, as in *Pinocchio*. The metallic gleam of R2D2 and C3PO from *Star Wars* had a similar resonance for a while, until the full effects of video fantasy in the recession of the nineties seemed to nullify that.

Audience culture eventually turns signifiers into a sort of signified, primarily because audience experience is so overwhelming a ritual in our culture, where history and marketing become utterly indistinguishable.[6] We experience this fluidity (and yet identifiable syntax) in its maturity, then look back at its process over the past sixty-five years. We observe that its impact on the seven-minute cartoon has been crushing.

Various Disney video tapes have re-released one of the first sales pitches for

Mickey, the cartoon *Mickey's Follies*, to promote a song ("Minnie's Yoo Hoo") that had some success in 1929–30. The squeaky singing and tedious romancing obscure how similar this form is to a music video. Instead of late-night television, the model being defamiliarized is the vaudeville stage.

Here I must pause briefly: the odd use of cartoons in music video is very relevant to the subject of this essay.[7] Cartoons are part of the cultural memory that has created a video literacy at the end of the twentieth century. I suppose I may have to admit eventually that there is profundity even in the story formulas on television, in the glamorous repetition of marketing in our culture.[8] If so, the cartoon will become a lexicon for writers and film-makers involved in video, not only for its martyrdom to consumerism, but also for its use of musical syncopation and allusion.

(There is very little likelihood that seven-minute cartoons will come back to movie theaters, not as antic, anarchic experiences, at any rate, even after *Who Framed Roger Rabbit?*, because cartoons will never flourish when they are made by corporations involved in heavy merchandising. Only an entrepreneur like a Disney or a Lucas can weather this pre-marketing for long, but the pressure is difficult, almost impossible, to withstand. Eventually the film product becomes part of the marketing itself.)

By the mid-thirties at Disney, characters were brought along like contract players at a major studio. Product lines, international fame, and interviews were handled with increasing deftness, to make the characters pay off (Mickey Mouse as "the unpaid movie star"). A Hollywood shading was added to Mickey's persona.

Originally, Mickey was another hayseed — but not for long. The first Mickeys were drawn at the small Disney workshop, behind a real estate office on Kingswell Avenue, and Vermont. The farm references lingered through the first two years. He resembled the poorer folk from the Midwest who arrived in the East Hollywood area during the twenties. They came in such numbers that they turned Orchard Avenue with its orange groves and pepper trees into Hollywood Boulevard within a decade, and also created a mix of classes that the earlier, much more restricted Hollywood would never have permitted.

By 1933, however, Mickey was a million-dollar celebrity, the apex of a pyramidal merchandising empire, and the alter-ego of a "genuine" American hero, Walt Disney. In a peculiarly American vision of the artist (before the language of the avant-garde reaches the popular media a generation later), Walt was a technological wizard, a business magician, a pioneer of industrial whimsy, even the spirit of how Americans could rise out of the Depression. Mickey became all these as well (eventually all too much), but in the thirties this mix of capitalism and fantasy signified as the movie star at the première.

In *Mickey's Gala Première*, we begin to see an incremental change. It was released in July 1933, a little over a month after *Three Little Pigs* had opened to a success never possible before for a cartoon. Mickey becomes a trifle more sure-footed, even capable of a professionalism, like a shy, plain-speaking, pint-sized Gary Cooper. In the end,

Garbo's kiss turns out to be Pluto licking him as he slept, but Mickey is honored nevertheless by stars like Wallace Berry, Clark Gable, and centrally by Chaplin himself (they pause in mutual admiration).

Mickey was often compared to Chaplin, by Gilbert Seldes and others.[9] Carolyn Lejeune would write that Disney was the only genius of the talkies, just as Chaplin was the only genius of the cinema.

It is the beginning of seeing Mickey in tails, clearly playing the star in a role. It also reflected the crisis of where to take Mickey next — out of the seven-minute cartoon, but into what form of cinema?

By the late thirties, it became even more difficult to make those seven minutes pay for themselves. Although the quality of Disney cartoons remained astonishingly high throughout the thirties, no independent studio could afford to rely on shorts alone, not without theater chains or major studios to buoy them up. By 1937, the double bill had become standard, and cartoons less essential, more like a filler. Rental prices showed no signs of increasing, they even threatened to drop.

From 1934 on, Disney became obsessed with the idea of a cartoon feature. He was fascinated when *Three Little Pigs* appeared above Gable's name on many marquees. The Disney strategy would have to change. Characters like Mickey Mouse were not designed for cartoons of an hour or longer. As far as antic madness, the studio declared that "Mickey is seldom funny in a chase picture, as his character and expressions are usually lost."[10] The animator/story man Marc Davis was assigned to Mickey to find a new strategy for the character. Finally, as adjuncts to the *Snow White* project, Mickey was given expanded fairy tales, with familiar live action plots: evil ogres, nasty dragons, sentimental Minnie heroines, fussy kings, girlish magic harps. Instead of exploiting fairy tales purely as allusions to graphic narrative (for example, *Felix in Fairyland*, Betty Boop's *Poor Cinderella*, or *Snow White*), these new Disney efforts rescripted the original texts, and tried to recapture the spirit of nineteenth-century children's literature.

Finally, in many ways, Disney technicolor marked the end of an era (again, by 1933–34, though the first three-strip technicolor Disney cartoon was produced in 1932). Color allowed water to ripple, wind to blow and painterliness to enclose the character. From the layers of color cels, to the stories pinned up on boards — to the new glamor given the characters — the antic qualities were overwhelmed by the sheer virtuosity of the Disney style. At last, the seven-minute cartoon was hardly enough. Those little burlesques no longer suited the master plan.

CHAPTER FIVE

Fleischer: Cities, Machines, and Immigrant Life

The rival to Disney in the early thirties was unquestionably the Fleischer Studio. Larger than Disney in 1930, they were known as the "Edisons of animation." In addition to developing rotoscoping and the first sound-on-film cartoon (in 1924), the Fleischers had produced the first feature-length animated film a year earlier, on *The Einstein Theory of Relativity*, of all subjects, as well as another feature on science, *Evolution*, in 1925. Max had worked as art editor for *Popular Science*. Dave was something of an inventor.

Their cartoons displayed a gymnastic fascination with the illusion of motion, and often referred to the technology of film-making itself (particularly with the thirties character Gramp, who comes up with strange, Rube Goldberg inventions). One might say that they motorized the lightning hand concept, first with the Bray Studios in 1915, then for a short time with Paramount, and finally as an independent from 1921 on (though constantly in debt).

Cartoon Factory (1925) is a motorized précis of their state of the art: Koko is caught between a crane device that draws characters and another that erases them, both run by Max. Finally, Koko takes over with a motor of his own. He begins printing soldiers who all have Max's face, and tries a coup against Max, only to be plunged yet again into the inkwell.

The Fleischers enjoyed beginning their cartoons with live action, then turning them into animation. Even the bouncing ball shorts were actually live action (with some animated trimmings). The ball was actually the light at the end of a pointer. It is an irony peculiar to the Fleischers that they used illusion and live action to emphasize the autonomy of the screen, rather than to evoke a nineteenth-century Academic pastoralism as Disney did.

Eventually, even the Fleischers would "Disneyfy" their cartoons. By the late thirties, the illusionism had indeed become a cartoon naturalism. In their first color feature, *Gulliver's Travels* (1939), a fluorescent and rotoscoped Gulliver looks like a relative of Snow White. Bucolic settings were not their specialty. In their Superman cartoons (1941), the granite-jawed man of steel flashes across the screen like a sequence in a Boccioni painting of the Forces of a City Street. That is their territory. Even in their adjustments to more coherent, sentimental stories, they generally chose the city for their cartoons, with skyscrapers, elevators, construction cranes — and, of course, Popeye's biceps turning into the wheels of a dynamo.

Throughout their best years, the Fleischers kept their studio in New York, not far from where the Sullivan Studio had been, near Times Square. I once asked Grim Natwick (Betty Boop's creator) what the Fleischer animators in 1930 did to relax off the job. Natwick's neighbor regularly gave him free tickets to the Ziegfield Follies or to Earl Carroll's Varieties, which Natwick shared with others at the studio. He also remembered long Friday nights which included bowling, card games, the burlesque in the Bowery, the fights. Betty Boop was modeled in part on a hoochie-coochie dancer, the garter at least, maybe her body too: "She was a little brazen, a little bit forward." The face certainly came from Helen Kane, a popular singer. Natwick also remembered clubs in Harlem (though Harlem musicians also appeared regularly on talkie one-reelers, even before Fleischer employed Cab Calloway for Betty Boop cartoons).

These lively memories more or less tally with what Shamus Culhane wrote about Fleischer animators gathering on many Saturday nights "for sex, drinking, and bridge

Max Fleischer, Koko, and the Inkwell. Max's brother Dave was rotoscoped as the clown.

A children's paperback of the Fleischer cartoon feature *Gulliver's Travels* (1939).

playing with a bevy of whores from the local bordello."[1] Also, "an extra fillip of stories about the seamy side of Harlem." "The animators and story men who worked on the Betty Boop cartoons had the earthy humor of New York street kids."

Fleischer gags are built on urban and industrial experience, a fantasy world of neighborhoods, sweatshops, pool halls, Coney Island rides, and most of all Manhattan vaudeville. From Koko to Betty Boop (and often Popeye), the backgrounds are inspired by vaudeville. Painted scrims drop behind characters. Curtains appear suddenly on blank walls.

Paramount, Fleischer's distributor, specialized in films that used vaudeville and burlesque stars, and may have pressured the Fleischers to take on Betty Boop (as they did for Popeye as well). Harvey Deneroff believes that Fleischer executives may have provided the Helen Kane portrait, on sheet music, which Natwick used for his first sketch of Betty Boop (the doggy ears and model sheet were added afterward by Ted Sears). At any rate, the vaudeville emphasis suited both Fleischer and Paramount very well.

Dave Fleischer was a vaudeville fan, and had worked for a while as an usher at the Palace Theater. Many of the acts he preferred specialized in immigrant humor. One favorite of his, Weber and Fields, were dialect comedians who spoke a sort of immigrant lingua franca, blended from German, Jewish, and Irish. Very old-timers by then, they had practically pioneered that "Dutch" dialect over thirty years before.[2] Their routines were very much in the spirit of what was called The New Humor, centered in New York. The jokes were delivered quickly, pungently. There were many rapid-fire one-liners and swift badinage, quite different from the laconic tall tales featured in minstrel shows and older variety theaters outside of New York.[3]

In time, the New Humor would represent much of Hollywood comedy as well, inherited through Eddie Cantor, the Marx Brothers, and many others, even Bob Hope (the New Humor in reverse, the city boy lost in the vaudeville circuit, out in a small town; this was central to the Hope persona). As for the animated cartoon, the Fleischers exploited the New Humor earlier, and more exclusively, than any other studio.

If I had to select one generic New Humor scenario, it would be the travails of the rube. A hick has just come to the big city from the farm. He is either a yokel from rural America or a greenhorn just off the boat from peasant Europe. He will be hoodwinked regularly. And he will always catch on too late. (As a personal note on greenhorns, I remember my father telling me that after he first arrived in America, he got a job at General Electric in Pittsburgh. As the Hungarian, or Hunkie, peasant, he was sent off to ask strangers for a "knuckle sandwich," until someone nearly punched him.)

The rube cannot get the handle of city leisure or American ways of gambling. As in the famous Weber and Fields routine, he does not know how pool is played in New York. But his greedy partner does, and will hoodwink him as much as he can.

The Popeye and Bluto cartoons run much the same way, with Bluto as the uglier, more vicious partner. Abbott and Costello, coming from burlesque, worked in formulas borrowed from the likes of Weber and Fields. The tall, greedy American slaps, cheats, and outmaneuvers the short, plump dummy, who inevitably plays the sap, and endures most of the punishment.

In cartoons, the New Humor was far blacker than anything Disney used. (Disney preferred vaudevillians like Joe Jackson and his bicycle, Willie West and McGinty.) In the New Humor, there are no Protestant heroes, nor cheerful mice achieving impossible goals. Instead, the rube — or the immigrant — is ruthlessly exploited and is always being chased. There is great confusion and a paranoia that builds in rapid-fire gags, the world of the immigrant.

The Fleischers were themselves the sons of Austrian Jewish immigrants and grew up in the Brownsville district of Brooklyn, the same neighborhood Alfred Kazin describes in *A Walker in the City*.[4] They seem to have invested their cartoons with much of the fatalism and xenophobia that were born of the experience of the Jewish ghetto (along with little Yiddishisms, a character screaming "lansman" [i.e. kinsman], etc., a gag about finding a Jew in an alien world). In many chase sequences, mobs of ghouls attack without any motivation whatsoever. I cannot help but liken these to the fears instilled in Jewish children in the ghetto: "Some day they'll know you're a Jew, and you'll wish you'd stayed with your own kind." Betty Boop is often intimidated at random, while she is out on the street. She seems to look out of place, or too delicious to pass up, and has to flee from male monsters.

In *Minnie the Moocher* (1932) she is a Jewish girl whose father screams at her to eat. His mouth turns into a victrola. He rants in an Austrian Jewish dialect (there is more Germanic than Russian Yiddish in the accents). In desperation, she runs away from home, turns up with Bimbo the dog (a goy?), but is trapped by ghouls. In a nightmare cave, she witnesses the many ways one can be publicly executed, a cartoon pogrom for the girl who leaves the neighborhood.

Of all the cartoon series the Fleischers developed, none was more packed with urban imagery than Betty Boop. Sea monsters have industrial smokestacks honking chase music from their snout. In *Alice in Blunderland* (1934), when Betty falls down a rabbit hole, she enters a cavity of windows, with a ribbing of clothing drying on the line, much like the apartment complexes I remember from my own childhood. I would hear nearby families arguing into an echo chamber, from windows facing complete shadow. Then, at last, Betty lands on a New York City subway platform. In another Manhattan cartoon, a toy factory is wedged inside the Lower East Side business district, as part of the light industry that has passed from Manhattan in recent years, but was so essential to the mood of the island in the thirties.

In *Betty Boop's Snow White* (the best of the series in my estimation), urban contrasts are used brilliantly, particularly in the Coney Island ride into the underworld. Betty as Snow White is condemned by her evil stepmother, who says "Off with her head!" while her fingers turn into a guillotine. Betty is sent to be murdered out of town, but Koko and Bimbo haven't the heart to kill her. A friendly tree covers for her by lifting off her garter and placing it like a funeral wreath on a phoney grave. She is free, but not for long.

As always, Betty is caught unawares. While looking behind her, she falls head-on into a snowdrift and is frozen into a cake of ice. Enclosed, she slides like an amusement ride into a tunnel of cartoon horror. Leading the mourners as Betty rolls along (including the seven identical dwarfs in a brief appearance) is a rotoscoped Cab Calloway, who sings "Saint James Infirmary" while reversed/transformed into a death shroud. Behind him, as he moves along, a *danse macabre* plays on the walls of the cave. Among the grotesqueries are a nightmare globe, a skeleton dressed as Napoleon, the dead playing craps, and a hippo playing whorehouse piano to an audience of skeletons. The wall reminds me of the *dia de los muertos* in Mexico, a revelry in honor of death.

Meanwhile, the evil stepmother realizes that Betty is still alive. Entering the cave, she freezes all life into toy megaliths. Then she runs the magic mirror, like the loop that children use for soap bubbles, across her body, and transforms herself into a musical dragon, with a snout that plays like a pipe organ. To give the audience a few extra goose bumps, she hisses in closeup at the viewer, then sets off in pursuit of Betty and friends. She chases them, in an oddly flat, hamster-run fashion, still very much an heir to twenties animation or to vaudeville gags of running in place while the background moves, until at last Bimbo kills her by turning her body inside-out. He reverses her skin like a sock, and leaves her a skeleton. With a final musical flourish, Bimbo and Betty dance for joy as they leave the cave — a journey inside-out for bodies and spaces alike.

That death wall with Cab Calloway singing is particularly striking (and often lost to inky darkness on video tapes or bad 16 mm prints). Three levels of urban imagery are laid one upon the other: first, Cab Calloway, who was a perennial at the popular Cotton Club in Harlem (and remembered as the star there in the Coppola film from the eighties); second, the Coney Island ride itself, and its graffiti from everyday life, particularly black life; and third, the song itself, which is interpreted "inside-out," through *metamorphosis*.

METAMORPHOSIS

Here is a quintessential example of how the Fleischers used metamorphosis. In the underground sequence in *Snow White*, Cab Calloway turns into a twenty-dollar gold piece to illustrate the lyric. This is the Fleischer signature: an image transmutes, as if by alchemy, into many others; its atomic structure seemingly comes unglued.

As a device in animation, metamorphosis began in the trick films of Méliès and Emile Cohl (also in lightning hand, even in the *Metamorphoses of the Day*, and other such illustrated series from Grandville).[5] As an extension of graphic narrative, it

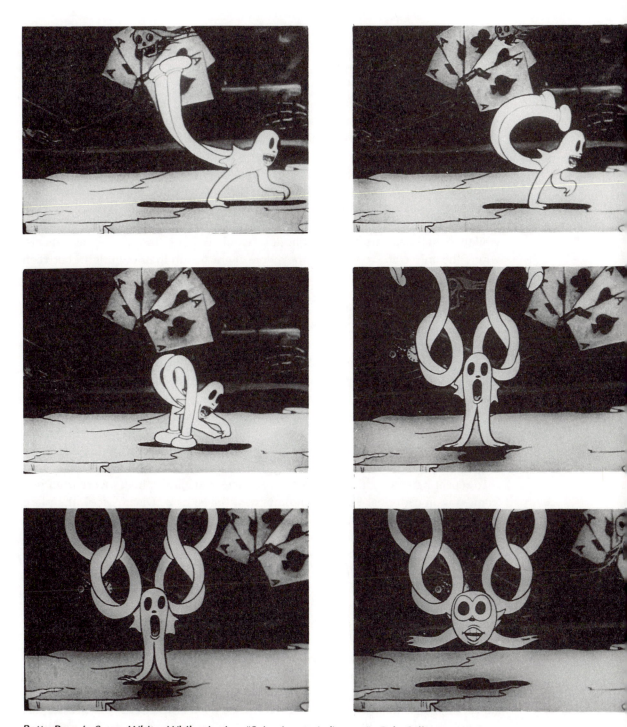

Betty Boop's Snow White. While singing "Saint James Infirmary", Cab Calloway (as ghost) turns into "a twenty dollar gold piece."

is also very similar to what Eisenstein meant by "intellectual montage," but without separate shots, more like a linear version of lapse dissolves.[6] Norman McLaren often referred to metamorphosis as the essential problem in his work, and for all graphic animation.[7]

Metamorphosis is a common cousin of both horror movies and the cartoon, both stemming from the trick film, but ever expanding in its applications. Since the seventies, through improved object animation and the bladders and appliances for special effects — and now with computer effects — metamorphosis can make a gruesome impact far beyond what was previously possible.

But in cartoons of the twenties, its possibilities were already understood. Metamorphosis lent itself very well to a nightmarish humor, as well as drunken hallucinations. In *Felix Woos Whoopee*, lines on the screen knit optically into monsters, while Felix takes his drunken walk home. I would call this "linear" metamorphosis, where the lines come to life, as if they were characters in their own right. Between the lines, the objects changing have very little solidity; they are more like a map out of control than a landscape. These webs of changing lines can work as transition also, a very common device in the Fleischer Out of the Inkwell cartoons of the twenties, where the drop of ink "metamorphoses" into Koko, or makes an obstacle, from one scene to the next — like a new act coming on. Or the pen changes the shape of a character as it runs on the screen. In *Koko the Cop*, a rock "metamorphoses" into a doorflap, like a stage scrim helping Bimbo run away from Koko. That gag was possible because the rock was essentially only a line drawing, so why not a flap? This sort of linear transformation worked best without sound effects, before sound made the change more complicated, giving the object the weight it lacked before. Linear metamorphosis survived only a short time after sound, particularly at Fleischer, and at Harmon and Ising (for Warners, 1930–34).

To repeat here: steadily, after 1928, these linear metamorphoses were used less frequently in cartoons. Rubbery multimorphic gags, as at Disney, took the place of graphic narrative. Then, after 1936, many other kinds of cartoon metamorphosis were added, particularly in chase cartoons, where the action often has to outstrip the eye, make inconceivable jumps, almost elisions — also as "fugue states,"[8] where dreams or hallucinations open into metamorphoses, typical of Clampett (*Porky's Hero Agency, Porky in Wackyland, The Big Snooze*); but also in Popeyes like *Wotta Nightmare* (1939); and then agile transformations in *A Dream Walking* (1934: arguably the best Popeye cartoon, with a ballet of industrial near-disasters similar to the superb Goofy dance in *Clock Cleaners*, or the best of the Magoos in the fifties), and *It's a Natural Thing to Do* (1939), or *Morning, Noon and Nightclub* (1937).

Fundamentally, the Popeye story — where first he is bent out of shape by Bluto, then, after eating spinach, bends Bluto out of shape — requires one metamorphosis after another, like rolling traumas. Tex Avery used metamorphosis as a form of hyper-schizoid collapse; he liked his characters breaking to pieces in hysteria, with a claghorn sound behind them — the extreme double-take taking the body apart.

The most vital use of metamorphosis after 1936 was in the way space could be shrunk or stretched: Clampett's doors stand without walls, in the non-space of Wackyland (1938); Avery's Wolfie races across a hopeless world where time seems to collapse on him like a can crushed by a vacuum. Wolfie is haunted by the omnipresent Droopy, or the lecherous fairy godmother, who exists in all times and spaces at once. This shift has much to do with the impact of movies on the cartoon (more on that later), where cartoons begin to look more like a Keaton film and less like a burlesque of the comic strip.

After 1936, the rules of personality in animation required that metamorphosis be used more to show emotional violence than the violence of the animated line. But even here, the exceptions are notable. In the most famous fifties cartoon using metamorphosis, Chuck Jones' *Duck Amuck* (1953), the transformations destroy Daffy's life, as though Daffy were a tortured film noir anti-hero, destined to suffer one change after the other.

From linear to computer graphics and back again, however one classifies its variations, metamorphosis remains crucial. I have to admit that I use metamorphosis as one way to determine whether the animator is using the medium more fully and more effectively. Too often, under the impact of full animation, the possibilities of metamorphosis are forgotten. The characters become actors too completely, and a whole range of eye-popping continuities and happy brutalities are lost. That is why I am highlighting metamorphosis in Boop cartoons.

In *Betty Boop M.D.*, Betty plays a traveling huckster for a Fleischer version of the old medicine show. Instead of allusions to the old West, we find typically the city and Prohibition. Koko and Bimbo are selling a phoney tonic called Jippo (in reality hydrant water). Through metamorphosis, it transforms people into precisely what they do not need. An old man teetering on the brink of death drinks a glass of Jippo and transforms into a squawling infant; the baby he was carrying changes in the reverse direction, withering into an old man. In the final gag, to cap the others, an innocent toddler slowly turns into a werewolf. It grins with canines flashing, just as the end-titles appear.

CHAPTER SIX

The World Upside Down:
1930–33

Allegories are, in the realm of thoughts, what ruins are in the realm of things.[1]

Walter Benjamin

Through such devices as metamorphosis the Fleischers bring to an extraordinary effect a vital element within the cartoon: allegories or fables about the world upside down. It is an old device like the English rhyme *The World Turned Upside Down*:[2]

To see a cat catching a mouse — is no news;
But to see a rat building a house — is strange indeed!
To see a beau at his toilet dress — is no news;
But to see two horses playing chess — is strange indeed!

In old French rural woodcuts of "the world turned upside down," people pulled the wagons while the horses sat at the reins, or women wore pants while the men nursed the babies, or the rich in aprons served the poor. Roles are out of place. The inanimate fight back, like Grandville's illustrations of vegetables refusing to be eaten, and organizing into revolutionary cadres.

And when Betty runs for President (1932), she offers pissoirs for dogs (screens around hydrants), and other ludicrous campaign promises on the "beer" ticket, running against Mr Nobody.

Politics and morality are upside down as well, a pilgrim's progress down the rabbit hole. But where does the rabbit hole head? These are not moral fables, a *Persian Letters* making relativist commentary. Morality is simply upside down, like a Jabberwocky. The profundity lies in its complete nonsense, a pointed escape from logic.

It is a pleasure principle about pain. Gags that are specifically upside down describe displaced pain, for what feels cruelly out of place in the world. In a broader sense, just as the old French woodcuts complained about the dislocation in the countryside

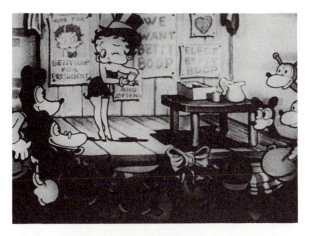

Betty Boop for President (1932). Betty is running on the "beer ticket" against Mr Nobody. She promises to make electrocutions more like visits to the beauty parlor, where hardened criminals are rehabilitated after finding their feminine side.

during the seventeenth century, these upside-down gags have fun with the dislocations manifested from the twenties on. They take the images of Prohibition and lay them against the unspeakable — the hints that the Depression was deepening. They use Prohibition imagery to hide the other, economic crisis. They are cathexes more than analysis — the knee-jerk reaction that involuntarily kicks back. Setting aside the metaphors: they are whimsically inverted images about social displacement. That is the mood of Fleischer cartoons from 1930 to 1933.

I would separate these gags about Prohibition upside-down morality into two categories: those that hint at the Depression becoming entrenched and those that seem to continue in the twenties mood, until booze is finally made legal, Roosevelt is in office, and the thirties movie culture more formally begins.

THE BOOZE HANGS HIGH: FUN MORALITY

In the old woodcuts, famine or plague has left farm animals roaming unattended in unplowed fields. Foreign armies have turned the world into a barracks. Sheep herding has destroyed feudal communities, and left families to sleep around looms and spin and weave for some distant master.

In the period of Betty Boop cartoons in particular, during the first shocks after the Crash of 1929, the social displacement seemed easy enough to catalog. Millions of peasants, coming in waves of immigration, had rebuilt their European communities as city neighborhoods, very often in a desperate attempt to sustain a traditional culture in a frighteningly erosive world. Throughout America, unemployment had rocketed until entire towns sat as unattended as the plowed fields did after the Black Death. Increasingly, this economic disaster was surpassing anything in living memory. It was not a cycle, not the Panic of 1893, bad as that Depression was. It was an economic Golgotha.

But the realization of how bad it was came slowly. The year 1930 was not yet perceived as Depression; it was late Prohibition sinking into the mire — Hooverism — like the spirit of America in the late 1980s, before the Gulf War, with Bush as President, sitting uneasily in the Reagan nest. Or shoppers at the malls in Los Angeles, unaware of the riots in 1992.

Before October 1929, before the Crash established that cloud of doubt, the so-called "revolution of manners and morals" had identified a series of dislocations that were much more about personal liberation: the shifts to the city; errant husbands; the vamps. Fun morality was "destroying" the American family and homespun American democracy. The historian Lary May identified many of these themes in the films of DeMille in the twenties, or in the celebrity and star vehicles for Pickford and Fairbanks.[3] Similarly, Felix will tipple away from home and find excitement with felines other than his wife. This continues into the early thirties, with boozy Flip the Frog at the black cathouse piano, or dancing little black Bosko; or the bawdy squeeze of Minnie's rump or Betty's chest — the "new" morality upside down (with dancing chairs and drinking furniture) oversimplified, speakeasies gleefully bouncing along, without versions of complicated cartoon divorces and adultery — only raucous suggestions of barnyard sex.

Cartoons about getting drunk also refer clearly to Prohibition. Rules about how to draw drunkenness had been set up fairly standardly in the twenties throughout the cartoon industry. The drunk was usually shown inside a nightmare, with lots of spinning and loss of balance. Often it was a whimsical hell, and this was still the rule in cartoons made in the forties, like Dumbo's dream of pink elephants: lines metamorphose into spectral volumes.

In Fleischer cartoons, liquor gags often suggest the age of the flapper. Bimbo stirs the hootch while Betty goes through mad (flapper) extravagances in *Betty Boop's Penthouse*. But alcohol often suggests something much darker as well, clearly it is not only about Prohibition. When Betty is selling to the rubes, her Jippo milk turns infants into werewolves. What a grim joke about motherhood and free enterprise, each disintegrated into hallucination.

DRINK AWAY YOUR ECONOMIC TROUBLES

After the Crash, however, the same images — labeled as "fun morality" — took on a displaced meaning, which was far more about what was rotten in the economy. Flappers and hootch stood for what many regarded as a prime cause of the economic downturn — consumer industries. The 1930 version of Prohibition as a fable about the world upside down could be summarized differently: the nineteenth-century economy, where wealth was the result of production not simply exchange (or so the mystique went) had been vanquished in some ineffable way. Instead, there was a world of sterile money, of speculation, of leisure industries like the movies, a world that many felt was encouraging broken families and changing the traditions of courtship and propriety.

Instead of movies about errant husbands, about life as a floating crap game, the jeremiads are different. They tend to blame the sumptuary madness of the Jazz Age for the collapse after 1929. Too much fun passing for hard work: a world turned upside down, where crooks are in business and businessmen are crooks — like the gangster films of the early thirties. The Prohibition references also reveal the insidious impact of the Depression, movies where executives commit suicide, wealthy families go bankrupt, playboys are afraid to leave Europe and return home. It is a world caught in between. Here we go from intoxication to darkly funny hallucination. Fleischer villains are often hallucinations, more or less. Disorientation is made very literal. The villains are drawn from another substance altogether. Snow White's evil stepmother is enraged and turns her body inside out, like a sweater. All at once, she is not only a dragon with horns, but drawn like the infernal beast in Dürer's

Apocalypse, a bizarre contrast to the other characters (though she is softened by two geese honking a tune from her horns).

In *Bimbo's Initiation* (1932), the ghouls have no bodies at all. Incorporeal laughter and lightning metamorphoses become characters: they are villains from an unnamed bundist organization trying to frighten Bimbo into joining.

These were exceptional, cranky gags — hallucinations about the instant when death strikes — hardly a standard in American cartoons of the thirties. In *Snow White*, when the evil stepmother screams "Off with her head!" the top joint of her index finger drops like a head into a basket. In other cartoons, Betty faces electrocution and infernal beasts of all kinds. In Snow White's Mystery Cave, as she floats in her block of ice, Cab Calloway turns his body inside out (again, like a sweater), and loses it, becoming a ghost who howls "Saint James Infirmary" as a funeral dirge.

After 1933 or 1934, this imagery virtually disappears from the Fleischer repertoire, and the hallucinatory games get calmer. Anyone writing about the Fleischer work is compelled to offer a theory as to why these unnameable fears appear as gags at a certain period, and not after. Beyond the obvious reason — that censorship from the Hays Office toned down the Boop cartoons — I cannot resist the sense that these floating anxieties belong to a very short era — the years when the ax was continually falling. The immediate effects of the Depression were being felt, but the long-range problems were still inconceivable. The world of the twenties still seemed to persist. As late as the winter of 1931, the stock market rose for a short time, and President Hoover was not alone in declaring that prosperity was just around the corner.

The Fleischer cartoons share in an hallucinatory code that is also central to the gangster films of that era, like *Scarface* or *Public Enemy*. Along with Betty Boop, these gangsters and the fantasy city they inhabit are censored after 1933 (by the new film code, even by the public obsession with the Rackets Commission). The look of high urban decay in these films resembles cyberpunk or post-apocalyptic imagery of the eighties and nineties: a nightmare carnival about emerging disaster.

While the theme appears to be Prohibition, by 1930 or 1931, the imagery has expanded far beyond a Fitzgerald novel or a DeMille film from 1925. Prohibition is already being treated as an historical moment. The fantasy city refers to a history of what went wrong in the late twenties; it suggests an industrial world about to crash. Portents of this imagery appear in Dashiell Hammett's stories: the city as a long drunk, as faded memories and lost freedoms.

Once the full effects of the Great Depression are felt irrevocably, these mythic hangovers become even more convoluted. At the beginning of Chandler's *The Big Sleep*, General Sternwood has barely survived a complex, boozy collapse. He lives in an enforced temperance, unable to drink, trapped in his Pasadena mansion. He is the shell of an uncontrolled capitalism now grown feeble. Even speakeasies and loose women are rheumy-eyed memories to him. As for the plot, all we are told is that Sternwood used to drink a great deal, and drank fashionably, but now has to live as an invalid:[4]

The General spoke again, slowly, using his strength as carefully as an out-of-work showgirl uses her last pair of stockings.

"I used to like mine with champagne, The champagne as cold as Valley Forge and about a third of a glass of brandy beneath it. You may take your coat off, sir. It's too hot in here for a man with blood in his veins."

Similarly, in *Scarface*, Prohibition is an allegory of the world turned upside down. The twenties are remembered as a mad binge, ending with the Crash, a consumerist erasure of morality and of the economy based on production. Armies of bootleggers struggle for territory in a black-market fantasy. Thousands of kegs of beer are loaded into caravans of trucks. The economy is literally awash in uncontrolled speculation.

These early gangsters (without the moralizing required years later, after the Rackets Commission) are as antic as cartoons where Mickey or Betty defy gravity. They are creatures living in a world where chaotic profits have turned the power structure upside down (a hint of the Crash to come). Cagneys and Munis strut through the drawing rooms owned by old plutocratic families (like the Sternwoods, I suppose); they even seduce their daughters. The paternal guardianship of the economy falls to hoodlums. Brashness confronts the decay of a nineteenth-century world. Free enterprise is interpreted perversely as criminal violence. Within twenty minutes of the end of the film, the local hoods are vanquished ("I ain't so tough"). They were only neighborhood boys after all. Immoral speculation is put to rest. The chaotic siege is lifted. The neighborhood is left to mourn its prodigal children. As in the Fleischer use of reversed allegory and asymmetrical phantom imagery, the world is a wounded place; it is both a human comedy and whirligig.

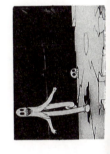

Before the Crash, the Fleischer cartoon contends more with the magic of the machine than with urban crisis. We see Bimbo loitering on street corners, but nothing like the hallucinatory breaks in narrative of the Betty Boop shorts. Those cartoons, in the first three years after the Crash, suggest unformed monsters. In much the same way, the early gangster films substitute a mystified recent history for the shock of financial and moral paranoia (what have we done to ourselves?), which came soon after October 1929.

Who is the character in conflict for fables about the world upside down, particularly its hallucinatory side? Is it the spectator himself? Who is the one sleeping?

The allusions in cartoons are graphic and literal; the unformed fear is described by a few lines, but seems to float beyond the story itself. We seem to have arrived at Goya's Sleep of Reason producing monsters — the dreamy underworld turned upside down. But it is also a political sleep. Goya designed his *Caprichos* aquatints

Betty Boop's Snow White ("flip" cartoon in margin). More of Cab Calloway rotoscoped into a ghost while singing "Saint James Infirmary." During the line "Gimme another shot of that boo-ooze," his mouth turns into a bottle of whiskey, which is poured into a shot glass, and tossed down his severed throat.

primarily as a disorienting critique of the Inquisition (standing in for the brooding sense of collapse in Spain under the weight of a dying feudalism). This is political madness as nightmare: piquant courtships with perverse rules of behavior.

Thus, the political critique in fables upside down can say much by remaining indefinable. Once the hallucinatory allusions are made absolutely interchangeable with real events, a certain tension is lost. Usually, the need for reversed allegory is less profound by then: the evil has emerged and done its worst.

Upside-down imagery probably appears more often in historical moments when the fears are still unnameable (i.e. before the invasion of Spain by the French). How can I prove that? I leave it simply as an explanation for cartoon purposes. By 1933, the Great Depression has gone beyond presentiment. By 1933, there are many ways to describe it very precisely, to give it a costume like an antic in the masque.

Disney's *Three Little Pigs* is clearly a fable about the Great Depression, and it is a seamless narrative by comparison with Fleischer (or even earlier Mickey Mouses, or *The Skeleton Dance*). Disney uses little of the ethnic experience of the city, or the reversals of Prohibition, or whimsically bizarre presentiments of disaster. His images are far more stable; for example, the figure of the *wolf*: there is nothing equivocal here. The villain is drawn precisely in terms of the Great Depression, the proverbial wolf at your door. And he owes as much to the Panic of 1893 as to the spirit of the New Deal. Graphically, the figure resembles illustrations published decades earlier: dressed animals by A. E. Kemble and others, for sardonic beast fables written by Artemis Ward or Twain himself. At that time, the baggy overalls signified the free negro or the poor rural white. In his stooped attitude, the wolf might remind viewers of the political cartoons of Tom Nast (blind greed), or Tenniel's political caricatures in *Through the Looking Glass*, possibly Sullivant's romping beats in the old *Life Magazine*. He would signify clearly as the plague of hunger and disorder blowing the house down; also as the immigrant stealing jobs (in a few gestures early in the cartoon, he resembles a Jewish peddler). By 1933, he was a common sight, the hungry drifter walking the roads.

Disney's conflict is clearly defined and tied to a graphic lineage. By contrast, Fleischer cartoons do not offer a conflict at all, but rather a paradox. The controller role stands in for a determinist universe, cartoon versions of Homeric gods. Like dark clouds in a cartoon storm, or a Renaissance map of uncharted waters, the diffuse villains stand in for crises that were too recent to define, but seemed inevitable — to the spectator, not the character.

CHAPTER SEVEN

Machina Versatilis: How the Cartoon Pays Homage to the Machine

The cartoon comes to life at the end of an end of an electronic beam in a darkened theater, as in the earliest showings of the Vitascope: "When the hall was darkened last night a buzzing and roaring were heard in the turret, and an unusually bright light fell upon the screen."[1] From the first, the effect of this machine was overwhelming: "The spectator's imagination filled the atmosphere with electricity, as sparks crackled around the swiftly moving lifelike figures."

How does this awesome technological fact change the way audiences read the graphic narrative or the vaudeville gag?[2] This is another version of the fable of the world turned upside down. It is similar to theories about the allegorical relationships betwen objects and story, for example, the meaning of the ruin in European painting, or (borrowing from Walter Benjamin on Baroque theater) the allegorical use of materials in photomontage, or environmental art, or the art installation.[3]

It also resembles the science fiction on artificial intelligence, the well-worn fable about the machine that strangles its master. In Ambrose Bierce's story, "Moxon's Monster", the gorilla-like automaton throws a fit after losing a chess match and kills its master. The audience (or narrator) notices

a low humming or buzzing which . . . grew momentarily louder and more distinct. It seemed to come from the body of the automaton, and was unmistakably a whirring of wheels. It gave me the impression of disordered mechanism which had escaped the repressive and regulating action of some controlling part — an effect such as might be expected if a pawl should be jostled from the teeth of a ratchet wheel.[4]

Like Moxon's monster, cartoons are automata that struggle.

Their graphic narrative rides that beam of light, and when it is anarchic, it suggests more than simply lines that refuse to behave or the absence of gravity. It suggests the movie projector and, metonymically, the movie camera, the editing process, and, finally, the power of film machines.

Unlike Bierce's critique of the machine, the cartoon cannot entirely disown its master or second master: first the animator, and second the motion-picture machine.

In the way the cartoon creates a parallel world, there is an unavoidable glorification of technology. Even for an animation cosmos as cynical as the Fleischers', this is so. To cite an example, we sit in a darkened theater (or living room) to watch the Fleischer Popeye cartoon *Customers Wanted* (1937). Other examples would do just as well. The Fleischers enjoyed revealing their technology as a gag, in Inkwell cartoons, in the Grampy series, in *Betty Boop's Rise to Fame*, in Superman cartoons, even in the silent feature film on Einstein's Theory of Relativity. The Fleischers were very much on what I might call the Modernist side of the debate: modeling experience in terms of the industrial machine. Their cartoons were more like art constructions, where materials replaced story, than allegorical structure, where organic caricatures refer back to nature, as in Disney. They could make fun of industrial life, but not the power of the machines themselves. By contrast, Disney made fun of the machines, but glorified the ethic of free enterprise. Fleischer characters remained like automata, while Disney gave them flesh and human impulses.

As *Customers Wanted* opens, Popeye and Bluto are rival barkers at a cartoon Coney Island. They both lure Wimpy into their penny arcades, and give him a free viewing of a flipbook machine. The rotation of the images is sped up into miniature cartoons within the larger eight-minute film. Both the history of animation, its original market (carnivals, fairgrounds), and the primary inspiration for many animators are handled as gags. We see a machine producing an image of Popeye moving furniture with Wimpy looking in. Animation emphasizes its technology far more nakedly than live-action film. In many ways, cartoons are like moving wallpaper in an engine room.

The rest of the cartoon is predictably Popeye: Bluto gets the best of him; Popeye finds his spinach and fixes Bluto. Of course, in Fleischer Popeyes, this spinach gag was played down considerably less than versions done at other studios. The Fleischer Popeyes are barely related pieces of cartoon virtuosity, like a science competition between two robots (one who grins cruelly, the other who mumbles absentmindedly).

From this perspective, cartoons resemble the theatrical machines used in the seventeenth century, particularly the *machina versatilis*, a device developed primarily in Italy, but used with phenomenal mastery by set designers like Inigo Jones (1573–1652, architect at the court of James I). For over a generation, Jones staged Ben Jonson's masques and anti-masques; it was generally a happy collaboration. In the dance, when Hercules or Jupiter cast away the antic Chaos, the *machina versatilis* worked behind the props like a horseless carriage bringing order into the world. Based on Italian themes of architecture, the Palladian façades, Vitruvian columns — and Mannerist clouds — would roll and intersect with miraculous efficiency. Children dressed as angels would rise up to ten feet along a painted sky, then descend behind an artificial horizon. In time, the audiences seemed more fascinated by the technology than the masque. In 1631, Jonson wrote:[5]

Oh, to make boards to speak! There is a task!
Painting and carpentry are the soul of the masque!
Pack with you peddling poetry to the stage!
This is the money-gett, Mechanick Age.

Jonson's meaning seems clear enough. These sets announce the end of poetry as an idealization of a courtly world. A new world comes to take its place, very much the one Jonson attacked in his comedies as well. When he identifies a "money-gett, Mechanick Age," he means the commercial classes as well as industries like iron and shipbuilding, which even by 1631 were deforesting England.

For a literary example of *machina versatilis* — the extravagant theatrical machine — I turn to Jonathan Swift, an obvious choice. During the third section of *Gulliver's Travels* he sees the flying island of Laputa. A storm three days out of Hanoi drives Gulliver's ship into unknown waters. After losing its course, he is boarded by pirates, who set him adrift in a canoe (with sail and paddle, and provisions for three days only). Intrepid as always, he manages to find an uncharted series of islands, where he forages for a few days. Then, suddenly, in his first encounter with Laputa, the sunlight is blocked by a huge man-made object two miles up in the air:[6]

The reader can hardly conceive my astonishment, to behold an island in the air, inhabited by men, who were able (as it would seem) to raise, sink, or put it into a progressive motion, as they pleased. But not being at the time in a disposition to philosophise upon this phenomenon, I rather chose to observe what course this island would take, because it seemed for a while to stand still. Yet, soon after it advanced nearer, and I could see the sides of it, encompassed with several gradations of galleries and stairs, at certain intervals, to descend from one to the other. In the lowest gallery, I beheld some people fishing with long angling rods, and others looking on.

The island is the picture of graphic narrative. It is perfectly round, as if by an artist's compass. Even the beams of the houses are beveled crooked because they resemble a diagram on a flat page, a subversion of natural perspective. Swift associates these with the idiocies of a scientifically-made world, though the galleries and hidden engine (a magnet kept inside a dome) clearly resemble a theatrical machine.

In as literal a sense as any cartoon (or the Japanese animated feature *Laputa*, 1989) we see technology lifting an island into the air, turning the logic of the earth upside down. I find this a wonderful metaphor for the cartoon: a mechanically flying island. It has a life of its own, but that life is controlled by gears. And the kingdom of these gears must be announced, like the flatness of the screen.

These gears contrast severely with the hand-made image. They become a montage between medium and surface. The cartoon, in its structure, is a burlesque of instrumentalism, of technocratic utopias of all sorts. More often than not, this "spoofery" leads to a tribute to the artificial, and therefore to the machine. Special-effects films have precisely this impact, however critical they may be of the machine world. And "virtual" reality, by its very non-nature, glorifies how the machine replaces experience. Following this logic then, it should not be strange to view Disney's early barnyard Mickey, with its gags about machines that snort like a bull, and then remember that all this leads, in some circuitous way, to Epcot — the city as pure gadgetry.

The ominous sense of technology is reduced to the charm of a toy, like those uncanny German automata from the nineteenth century, or a zoetrope, or Méliès sending a rocket ship into the face of the moon (a man's face lying in a circular tub of custard — another variation of the pie in the face).

Thus, despite all the seeming incongruities and subversive gags, the cartoon is an all-encompassing hymn to the machine world. This unifying quality cannot sustain too much cuteness and domestic calm without getting extremely saccharine. (Shall we say, too artificially sweet?) On the other hand, it balances much of the happy sadism and rueful, amoral gaiety of the cartoon.

The overwhelming charm of *machina versatilis* does make a lie out of many serious intentions within animation. It can make industrial savagery look like a wonderland. When the graphic narrative, the antilogy of the gag, and the anarchic characters are all mutually and gorgeously *out of step* together, and the audience is presented the illusion by a theatrical machine of awesome power, the effect is hypnotic. One can argue how liberating it is — as indeed I have here. One can argue that the effect is ultimately another form of narrative, not simply "*anti*-story," And clearly, *machina versatilis* is an allegory about entertainment machines turning the world upside down. That beam of light becomes the unifying experience given the audience, a nurturing warmth built out of precision steel gears, a little like Moxon's monster, but more like scenes from *Back to the Future*, cute, synchronized journeys into the xeroxed paradox of media memory.

Animation shows us how theatrical machines turn our experiences upside down. As a result, they glorify media simulation, as an extension of industrial machinery. I ought to pause on that word "simulation," so overworked in criticism these days. For our purposes here, speaking of the period 1928 to about 1960, simulation is often understood by audiences and animators as an industrial copy used for entertainment purposes. It was far more tied to industrial memory than to consumer memory, more an extension of the electrical dynamo than of advertising, or theme-parks, as simulation surely is today. That is where, historically, I would limit the meaning of *machina versatilis* — to the era when the industrial economy still dominated, and the consumer-driven economy was still a much smaller part of the whole than it is today. And for that moment in time, I assign animation a very special place, a pioneering Cassandra-like place.

Within the history and criticism of media environments, from situationism to virtual reality, animation has an enormous head start — one of many decades. For a century now, it has developed a very literal folklore about machine-made environments, and a sophisticated cinematic vocabulary to go with that folklore. The evidence left by this folklore is fairly consistent. No matter how cynical the cartoon, it never attacked movie environments without somehow paying them tribute. Speak of the devil and honor its name.

That is why the cartoon was endlessly toying with notions of the machine versus the natural, either in rural nostalgia turned upside down, or, generations later, in special-effects gags in live-action films like *Blade Runner*. Some of the sequences in *Blade Runner* are very cartoon-like: a weary scientist who "makes" friends fills his apartment with toy creatures he actually "made." They are perky and childlike, as if inside a cartoon. But in the same apartment cyborgs are dying, and want revenge against the company that built them.

Not only are cartoon characters trapped inside the borders of the screen in a whimsical power-struggle against the controller, they are also caught in a beam of electronic light. All the antics aside, theirs is an utterly deterministic world — *machina versatilis*. The more properly out of place all the cartoon elements are, the more often the medium intervenes deterministically. It is almost as if the medium steps in, not as the message but as the allegory for a conflict that continues to plague the animation business: corporate marketing dominating the hand-drawn image. That domination is certainly the ongoing crisis, and is as true now as it was fifty years ago. However, to the viewer watching a cartoon, this conflict seems more like wrestling a roller-coaster — a folklore about machines that strap us down to entertain us. We are tied down by light. The machine-made elements within the cartoons announce simultaneously their power over the audience (that hypnotic beam of light), and over the drawings that scramble on the screen.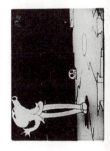

Seen another way — the bottom line — these references to machines in cartoons were also a cover-up about management. They resemble the colorfully animated graphs used to locate which military targets are to be bombed, colors that give a whimsical camouflage to warfare and to the people that profit by them. In the thirties, the beam of light from the projection booth camouflaged the industrial processes that made up the cartoon: assembly-line division of labor, from story to inking, invasions by money managers, poor pay. The cartoon seems so anarchic and cute; and yet, generally, cartoons were very autocratically controlled, as part of corporate manipulation of entertainment.

Cartoons have played with media manipulation for over a century now, with considerable ferocity and irony. They have much to show us about how machines in entertainment became user-friendly and seemingly impossible to criticize. Movies, like all consumer industries, thrive on hate, like violence in a good noir suspense film, or a fast, brutally silly cartoon. If you complain that movies are too powerful, just spell the name right. All publicity is good publicity, as long as it suggests an awesome, uncontrollable majesty.

THE ALLEGORY OF CARTOON DETERMINISM

In keeping with *machina versatilis*, what a restrictive universe the Fleischers arrange for their characters, particularly with Uncle Max interfering every so often (even as late as 1934 still tossing Betty into the inkwell). Even the characters' bodies seem an allegorical tribute to the movie machine.

While the Fleischer characters are wonderfully mobile, they look ungainly compared to Disney. Both Popeye and Betty Boop seemed trapped in their bodies. While Popeye can manage a handsome tango (his legs are far more agile than his torso), he is essentially muscle-bound without his spinach. Betty Boop may have been a twenties flapper, but the design of her body (and her persona) were as restricting as a whale-bone corset (see p. 81 below).

The machine lurks everywhere, chasing Betty as monsters. And once Popeye is finally aroused to his full fury, he becomes machine-like (his arms turn into propellers, his body into a corkscrew).

Of course, all these limitations are nothing like the interference that sank the Fleischer Studio altogether. In the case of the Fleischers, the *machina versatilis* became a many-headed monster: financial, organizational, even military.

This leaves two themes for the next chapter: first to show this determinism in Fleischer cartoons, primarily Betty Boop; and second, to show how the film business determined the way the Fleischer Studio failed.

A quick clarification: In other chapters of this book, and probably in other books, I will take this principle of *machina versatilis* further, because it is so essential to the problem of audience reception and ideology in the arts. But here *machina versatilis* will refer to the self-reflexive gag about the movie machine in cartoons.

I realize that this is something of a reverse whammy, suggesting that modernist strategies actually hypnotize rather than distance the viewer, that modernism can be something of a magician's trick, on behalf of industrial capitalism. Like Henry Adams' paradox of the Virgin and electrical dynamo, we are held in the movie machine's embrace, uncritically, as a visceral way of willingly suspending our disbelief. The movie machine is an advertisement for the industry that makes it. And this effect, properly understood, is an essential and inalienable quality to all media: film, video, and the simulated environment most of all. Animation is an artform intimately defined by this paradox and has been for a century.[7]

CHAPTER EIGHT

What Makes Betty Boop?

The story formulas for Betty Boop, such as they are, follow a very simple pattern. Usually, within the first minute, Betty gets into trouble with propriety. She runs away, is arrested, flim-flams, hooks up with larcenous men, or simply arouses the gods from a sexist underworld. Ultimately, she wiggles or sweet-sasses her way free; or the cartoon simply ends happily — and abruptly — with no clear motivation except that the ride is over, there is no more film.

Betty's motivation is extremely primitive. She always makes the wrong decision, working in a racy joint, or selling a good time, as when she runs for president, promising manicures to murderers on death row or limousines for garbage collectors. Having begun her "career" as a poodle singing to Bimbo the Dog in *Dizzy Dishes*, Betty was not fashioned for complex character development. She never had a neck. Her movements did not break down precisely into the rubber-hose mobility of Mickey Mouse. She did not stretch at all (so much for gags with volume and anticipation). She had virtually no facial expressions, except her wink, a look of dismay, and a boop-boop-a-doop.

But she was designed very well for movement to music. She could sway very delicately. Her arms and shoulders syncopated much the way performers do when singing on stage.

And she was a lovable victim, trapped somehow in her helpless body. She was often cheated, exploited, or cornered. Gaggles of spooks chase her regularly in a wild sort of action that has been called "surreal," though it clearly borrows its racy amoral, nightmarish speed and improvisation from New York vaudeville and jazz.

When the first Boop cartoons were made, there was apparently no story department (later, one man, Bill Turner, worked on stories). Dave Tendler remembers short scripts typed, then sent to animators. Al Eugster does not even remember that, "just a rough idea of what the story was about."[1] With that rough idea, "the head animator would lay out [the story], stage it, and break it into scenes. There was no control of footage. Today, we have what you call bar sheets or music sheets, and we time out one scene after the next, so we have some idea of what the overall footage would be. Here, we just sort of ad-libbed, especially when Dave came around adding gags. I know I usually ran over footage on a picture, never could control it."

Tendler calls it a "free-wheeling system," where animators were invited to add gags as they went along. Bits of business were tossed in from all sources. Grim Natwick particularly remembered Dave Fleischer leaning over his shoulder and throwing in extra jokes for the corners of a scene. There was little concern over the readability of the character. The more furious, the more improbably the routine, the better.

That gives Fleischer cartoons an extraordinary tension. The ground is never still. Gags constantly overlap: a mouse slips out from under Betty's clothing as she enters the evil stepmother's palace in *Snow White*, while dozens of miniature gags pop up (heads swinging in and out of armor, hands appearing everywhere, particularly on

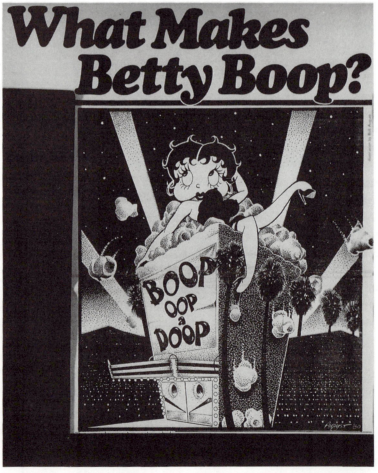

Cover of *L.A. Reader* (1980), on the fiftieth anniversary of Betty Boop.

the magic mirror). The sum of these speed along like cinematic graffiti, like the wall of the Mystery Cave at the end of *Snow White*.

In these cartoons, the Fleischers literally (graphically) broke down the screen into conflicting gags within the same frame, sometimes into fragments like a broken topology, at other times into a conflicting montage of foreground opposed to background (or a spoof of depth of field, I suppose). Instead of conflict, there was a rueful explosion of paranoic disorder. Betty had endless back luck, enough to drive Cinderella, Snow White, and Red Riding Hood to tranquilizers. In *Alice in Blunderland*, Betty sings "Always in the Way," and she is. In *Dizzy Red Riding Hood*, the chorus moans for her: "Why should they pick on the poor kid?"

Chased by a sea monster with a factory whistle for nostrils, she almost drowns in *Betty Boop's Life Guard* (1934), just managing to moan: "It all seems like a dream that makes me want to scream." Her breasts and thighs are fondled regularly. The wind blows her slip over her thighs. But she maintains her pride; that is essential to her character. As she warns the circus master who has grabbed her: "Don't take my Boop-Boop-a-Doop away."

The paranoia and decomposed screen were held together less by the story than  by the music. Dave Fleischer was fascinated by the problems of syncopation. With support (or even coaxing) from Paramount, he and Max chose big city jazz, as opposed to Disney's "Turkey in the Straw," or nineteenth-century symphonic music. Their animators tried to follow the patterns of jazz improvisation as cartoon, to use gags the way a horn plays against the piano, or to insert metamorphoses just as the vocalist holds on to an unexpected note.

Thus, we are left with a highly athleticized cartoon. The seven dwarfs' necks stretch with no concern whatsoever for volume. Tables hop and spin. And characters cakewalk to the music. (There is great detail applied to the legs and to body gestures.) Betty's dance with *The Old Man of the Mountain* follows in rotoscope the frosty spins of Cab Calloway, once again. (In this scene, Betty soothes the monster, the obligatory scene.) Once she solves her dilemma and wins over the male spooks to her side, they all begin to dance together; or like the jury in *Betty Boop's Trial*, they will change into that syncopated, musical walk. Jazz signifies the liberation of the city, while the spooks and decomposed (gag-ridden) screen identify the paranoia of city life (and the moral, social dilemmas I mentioned earlier). In its incoherent way, it is a very coherent package.

This package is expanded to include Hollywood. By 1932, Betty appears in various cartoons as a film star (i.e. *Betty Boop's Rise to Fame*, 1934, a composite from earlier cartoons, now that she is a star, 1933). Spoofs of Joan Crawford and particularly Mae West are more frequent. When West's *She Done Him Wrong* opened in Paramount theaters, Betty appeared in the cartoon *She Wronged Him Right* (also distributed by Paramount).

By 1934, very few cartoons were referring directly to vaudeville. The cartoon is now wedded utterly to the audience culture of live-action drama. Betty's persona gets the Hollywood treatment: the racy film goddess who lives in the fast lane; or great stars flutter too close to the flame. She is naughty like a Jean Harlow in spitcurls or a Mae West from the Lower East Side. More than the cartoons changing, the promotion of Betty Boop gets a bit glossier. There is even an "interview" with her, which is published in *Screenland Magazine*,[2] with naughty innuendoes about affairs with Wallace Berry and various creatures from the Fleischer menagerie. "La Boop" can "outdo Garbo" reads the boldface.

"When I first entered the movies," Betty says, "I was just an innocent young thing, unversed in the emotional ways of an artist's life. But I learned brother, I learned."

And who taught her? Max Fleischer did, with all the dazzle and crassness of an Adolph Menjou, whom Max resembled slightly. "Sure," he says, "I animated her — and boy is she animated."

Uncle Max controls her movements the way he did Koko's in the silent cartoons. To keep her from carousing, Max says he seals her in his inkwell at night. "Well, for once, she's early in bed. Always a hard time getting her to retire early — some days it's going to hurt her career."

Ironically enough, a few months after this article appeared, the Fleischers altered Betty drastically. As most Betty Boop fans will agree, the best of her cartoons were done some time before 1934. Her character continued another five years, and was closed out in 1939, but she was extremely inhibited. The sex and ribaldry, the fractured gags, and the paranoic imagery more or less vanished altogether. When the ghoulish devil chases her in *Red Hot Mama* (1934), he is melted down into an ice cream cone. Betty dresses in longer slips, and slims down until she resembles Irene Dunne more than Mae West. She is given a brother, a stable detached house (with kitchen), and a Grandpa.

Why did the Fleischers sterilize their hottest character? The year 1934 was that of sex reform in Hollywood, and clearly the Hays Office, with its new movie-code standards, put pressure on the Fleischers' distributor, Paramount.[3] But the reality of business, not morality, was mostly responsible for putting paid to Betty.

First of all, the Fleischers were not as financially independent as Disney. Adolph Zukor at Paramount kept the Fleischer Studio on a long leash. Also, unlike Mickey Mouse, Betty Boop was inconceivable as a child-safe icon (or logo). She remained a thoroughly adult character, and even market tie-ins were as much for adults as for children. She was sold as grown-up kitsch, in cigarette cases, scarves, chinaware, and the like. Even kiddie items had a satire of adult chic in them — sleek pyjamas, for instance, which had a New York lingerie look, in which a tiny miss could imagine herself doing a screwball comedy with Cary Grant.

Paramount pressured the Fleischers to tame down Betty. Why? Apparently the company was afraid of a repeat of the adverse publicity it had suffered in the twenties with the sex scandals associated with the lurid murder of the director William Desmond Taylor, as well as the embarrassing trials of Fatty Arbuckle. In 1933, when Paramount went into receivership (along with most other film companies, the notable exception being MGM), the top brass reckoned the company could not afford a moral blockage of its products or stars (which included, in addition to Betty Boop, Marlene Dietrich and Mae West).

And so in 1934, when Mickey Mouse gets a family and responsibility, Betty Boop loses her cleavage as well as her *double entendres*, and begins losing her popularity. They were forced to keep up with Disney — particularly after technicolor, in itself another shock to animation, forcing it into even more sentimentality, as well as more illusionary effects (particularly through the multiplane camera; the Fleischers had their own multiplane technique a few years earlier than Disney, actually). The Fleischer story lines become more soothing and didactic. Their Popeye cartoons remain very hectic, but nothing like the shorts from the early thirties.

Then came management problems. Max and his brothers (Dave first, then Joe and Lou) fought bitterly, with Max playing the impresario with a touch of megalomania. His animators found him lovable; his brothers were chewed out regularly.

Throughout the mid-thirties, Paramount watched Dave and Max jockey for position, as contradictory stories funneled into the Hollywood office. Were some doctors actually willing to pronounce Dave insane? How bad were Max's ulcers? After 1937 (and the big strike at Fleischers'), a cold war existed between Max and Dave. Consider the plight of Paramount — the company was bankrolling an animation house in which the principals refused to talk to each other. Despite the conflict, Paramount financed the Fleischers' 1939 move to Miami — and a grand new studio that cost $300,000. As part of the move, the Fleischers simply canceled Betty Boop and used their entire film library as collateral. Over the years, they had tried to Disneyfy their product: by 1938, most of their animators had worked at Disney and been initiated into "personality animation." Now Paramount wanted a Fleischer answer to *Snow White*, and every available dollar went into a feature of *Gulliver's Travels*. But the mixture of graphic styles in *Gulliver* reflects the confusion at the studio. The towering Gulliver is rotoscoped into a linear human being, and lit differently than the Lilliputians, as if he were laughing at a New York bistro, watching them on stage. Gulliver's shipwreck, meanwhile, is "shot" like an MGM sea epic. Lilliputians like Gabby and King Bombo bear some resemblance to the earlier Fleischer style, but also to Disney sidekicks and to the seven dwarfs. Despite the stagnant story, the animation itself was very elegant, and rather architectonic — no asymmetry, no death gags, no uncut toenails (nothing like the googly-eyed giant in *Old Man of the Mountains*). The principles of volume and cuteness were observed; overall it was a more than competent, if uninspired, effort.

Released for Christmas 1939, the film was a hit, but it barely recovered its expenses. And foreign markets were cut off by the war in Europe. They tried a few cartoon spinoffs (again, Gabby and King Bombo) without much luck. Popeye remained quite saleable, but the Fleischers did not own any of the merchandising rights (as always the key to the survival of an independent studio).

The Fleischers had been capable of brilliant satire of live-action cinematography.

Perhaps that would have been a more profitable direction to take, like their longer Popeye cartoons done in glamorous primary colors. In *Popeye the Sailor Meets Ali Baba and His Forty Thieves* (1937, Dave Tendler), Bluto is a gargantuan — and manic — Abu Hassan, the leader of a cartoon locust of desert thieves, who swarm across the crazily awesome horizon, a wonderful spoof of the use of depth of field in adventure epics. Unfortunately, in their features, the Fleischers opted for cinematic literalism instead.

They did return to a clearly graphic narrative in a series of Superman cartoons, particularly those done in 1941. Paramount had, in effect, "assigned" the Fleischers to this project, to turn the adventure comic book into Saturday serials like Buck Rogers. (As a coda to nineteenth-century graphic narrative, the early Action Comics, from 1938 on, revive many of the old devices, and add one more in particular — the fantasy urban metropolis.) The Fleischers were able to play with this urban fantasy very effectively, despite the cardboard formula stories. They updated an old theme of theirs, the film screen as machine, like the Inkwell series. And they still maintained a graphic look, square axes of a comic-book panel, even down to the square jaw of the Man of Steel himself. The entire screen seems to be made of steel, like a machine housed in black, corrugated metal, with gray canyons beneath the skyscrapers, and diabolical machines instead of ghouls. In the cartoon genre, which focuses on technological perversity (leading eventually to *Heavy Metal* cyberpunk graphic novels), these Superman cartoons deserve a special place. Instead of the Coney Island ride, the underworld is the depersonalized stagnant quarters of the city, contrasted by the bursts of Superman diagonally across the sky. In the spirit of the German advances in Europe at the start of the Second World War, the cartoon begins to resemble the terrifying diagrams of aerial or tank warfare.

Unfortunately, these Superman cartoons were too expensive to make a profit. Fleischer had to pay premium salaries anyway, simply to draw people out to Florida. Heavily in debt to Paramount, the Fleischers were given, in effect, one last chance. They pinned their hopes on a second feature, *Mr. Bug Goes to Town*, an insect variant of Mr. Deeds (with spectacular "camera angles" as the insect community fights the inevitable bulldozers taking away their homes). The spoof of depth of field was less exaggerated, and the technological diablerie was avoided. Instead, the Fleischers went for a Hollywood narrative film, scripted like a child's eye version of Frank Capra. Once again, the animated effects were remarkable, if uneven, without a graphic center (not quite Disney, not quite graphic narrative). Worst of all, the film opened in the season of Pearl Harbor. With America entering the war, and Paramount refusing to promote the film, it flopped disastrously. Finally, the debts to Paramount came due, and the brothers were finished. Paramount took over the Miami plant, renamed it Famous Studios, and fired Dave and Max. Of course, Dave was already at Columbia and could not run both studios. Max considered suing, but his daughter persuaded him to wait, since she was married to Seymour Kneitel, who was put in charge of Famous Studios.

For the most part, that finished the Fleischers. As for Betty Boop, beyond suffering from cruel distributors, peaheaded censors, and the perils of her cartoon world, she was laid low by a bad business manager. For a screen goddess, that is the worst blow of all. Max as impresario was a lousy businessman.

In the process, the studio animators were left dangling too. The Fleischers regularly lost key artists. Though they loved Max (except at the picket line in 1937), they quit anyway, and not surprisingly. In the thirties, the animators suffered a namelessness even more extreme than today. They were rarely given proper screen credit and never rights to their characters. Ironically, in 1938, when Max was preparing to jettison Betty Boop, he offered the rights to Grim Natwick (her creator, now at Disney after designing the character Snow White — quite a sublimated contrast!). Max asked Natwick to "see what you can do with it." In the discussion, the subject of why Natwick had received not a penny in Betty Boop tie-ins never came up. Natwick turned him down.

Of course, the Disneys also kept their workers anonymous. Carl Barks designed Donald Duck comics for twenty years, but until his rediscovery by film historians in the seventies, practically no one knew his name. But the main difference was that Fleischer refused to move to Los Angeles, paid only comparable wages, and had less equipment than Disney. Gradually the best Fleischer animators headed west.

In Hollywood, many animation executives came directly out of the studio system, like Leon Schlesinger, who headed the animation unit for Warners. Formerly a vaudeville manager, Schlesinger was apparently quite at home in his total ignorance of animation. The satire and allusions in Warners' cartoons rarely penetrated him. Chuck Jones often tells the story of how Schlesinger first heard Mel Blanc's voice for Daffy Duck:[4]

Cal Howard ... suggested that Leon Schlesinger's lisp plus Leon's absolute belief that the world owed him a living made him a perfect prototype for Daffy. Mel Blanc saw no difficulty in marrying Leon's voice to a duck, so the deed was done, and Daffy found a new voice as well as a new personality, an acquisitiveness to match Leon's. In order to save ourselves the embarrassment of being fired, all of us were careful to write out our resignations before that fateful day when Leon strode into our production room and sprawled on the gilt throne he had snatched from some early Warner pseudo-DeMille film or other. The rest of us, still sat on beat-up splintery church pews from an early family film. The new Daffy Duck lit up the screen at Leon's courteous command: "Roll the garbage!" The cartoon played to the studio audience, accompanied mainly by crickets, prayers and silence. Then the lights went on, and Leon leaped to his feet, glared around: "Jeethus Christh, that's a funny voithe! Where'd you get that voithe?"

Apparently, Schlesinger had failed to notice the joke — he being the oblivious bureaucrat. But when this benign neglect entered the world of salary, he was another man, a very tough nut. Again, according to Jones, an animator once asked him why the Schlesinger yacht, *Merrie Melody*, remained off limits, to which Schlesinger replied archly: "You don't earn enough." And apparently never would. (The animator Phil

Monroe, however, remembered being taken out on the yacht.) But more than checking who claims to be where, the point of the story seems to be universally accepted, that Leon Schlesinger, with his yellow carnation and casual manner, was more involved in what went on at the races in Santa Anita than in the cartoons he produced; and that he was a tough negotiator, though very low on the chain of power at Warners. In the feudal hierarchy of the Warners system, he was essentially a jobber for short subjects, providing a service more for the exhibitors than for the production heads. The animation units were perceived as fill-in, not as movie-making. Jack Warner would occasionally stop by, or watch a cartoon or two, but little more. A few of the Warner actors might poke their head in to see what went on, from time to time. But according to Jones, the animation directors were rarely invited to meetings with the top brass. They were treated, it would seem, on a par with the set-builders. After many years, Harry Warner finally took the cartoon directors out to lunch and said, in the profoundest ignorance: "I really want to thank you boys for the work you've done on Mickey Mouse."

Even before the big Warner strike of 1945, the workers at Fleischer and Disney sought unionization, which the studios fought desperately. After a near-walkout at Fleischers in 1935, there was a long and ugly strike there in 1937, including police brutality, fist-fights between workers on the picket line, and a bitter period of arbitration. Many salaries had been kept near the NRA Picture Code minimum of $17.40 a week, an amazing contrast to animators who might earn over $100 a week. Many animators, however, were promoted simply at their old salary.[5] Then, after the Van Beuren Studio across the street went under, there was a glut of animators, and many at Fleischer had to take a cut or a demotion, which put their salaries below the cost of living in New York. The pay scale at Disney was also low (except for the few at the top), and attempts at union contract in 1940 brought an explosion of industrial unrest in 1941. To this day, many from Disney claim that their big strike of 1941 destroyed the heart of their animation team.

The Fleischer story — why they failed — is summarized more easily. Lacking tie-in money, browbeaten by Paramount, the low man on their studio team, they tended to shave animators' salaries even more than the Disneys did. Finally, at Miami, they had to pay over scale to bring people out.

The solution — more rationalized production — did not prove comfortable to the Fleischers. As of 1930 (according to Grim Natwick), their working methods called for an animator to produce about 4,000 drawings for one cartoon, usually within a month. If he knocked out 100 drawings by noon, he was on schedule. Each animator did more of the work from start to finish than at Disney. Dave Tendler apparently directed the last color Popeye two-reeler, *Popeye ... Meets Ali Baba*, because so much energy was put into the *Gulliver's Travels* feature, and the studio was generally not organized enough to keep track of much beyond that, particularly after the staff had more than doubled in a year. The Fleischers had trouble changing over to the new systems.

The beginnings of this change date back to the Bray Studios in the twenties, a factory style of rationalization (according to Donald Crafton); one the Fleischers seemed to handle easily enough at first.[6] By the thirties, with sound and a broader marketing system, however, the animation studios had expanded beyond these earlier limits. As of the late thirties, the Fleischer payroll had swollen to over 400 employees, from a few hundred in 1930, averaging around 170 in 1937. To monitor this horde, good business required that the work of four to six animators be sewn into a single cartoon, with storyboards, thumbnails, and pencil tests along the way (and lots of commentary on the borders of the drawings, whether in storyboard or layout). It had to be very orderly, an order that produced its own problems: the tendency to regiment the product, as I will discuss below (p. 89). Increasingly, as the pyramid of workers grew, the head of studio became the chief story man, with many bottle washers below, from chief animators all the way down to cel washers. (The latter, at the bottom of the system, were hired to scrape off the paint from old cels, and get them ready for new ink and paint.) The many stages, with so many more hands at each stage, required enormous agreement as to how the style had to survive through to the end. At least five different people would redraw and paint the very same images. The Fleischers never shifted wholeheartedly to the new way of doing things. Disney did, becoming the Ford (or even the MacDonnell-Douglas) of the seven-minute cartoon; but one must understand the pressures that came to bear. Even today, with computers to keep the in-betweening and the cycles consistent, with computers replacing cels, animation is both expensive, very time-consuming, and a very conservative process.

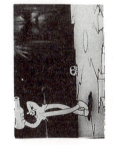

In terms of my argument here, I would suggest that the twenties system of industrial production, as "Fordist" or "Taylorist" as it was, still looks more like a cartoon atelier, much more like a wood engraving shop (graphic narrative) compared to what followed with sound and the Disney method. The late thirties cartoon factory was much more integrated into the architectonic complexities of the movie business. That took cartoon management far beyond the way drawing worked in the illustration business, in the magazine field say, an earlier influence that was no longer appropriate at all, but had been very workable a few years earlier. To clarify this difference between the twenties and thirties, I refer the reader back to 1928 — or approximately the date where I began (*Plane Crazy*, etc.). This is a famous story, often remembered:[7] Winsor McCay is being honored at a luncheon by the younger established animators, like Otto Messmer. In his banquet speech, he offered what seemed to him new technical advice. No longer did an animator have to draw every frame, he explained. One could hire in-betweeners. This was hardly news to anyone else in the room; in-betweening had been standard practice for at least seven years. The younger animators smiled wrily to each other. They knew that McCay had drawn 25,000 frames for his *Sinking of the Lusitania* (1915–17, with backgrounds added by his small staff, though not every line, of course). At the same time, they were awed by the innocence of his belief in craftsmanship. McCay could not comprehend how animation might become a rationalized factory process. But the change was inevitable and just as surprising to the Fleischers, when the systems kept growing to keep pace with Disney, as it had been for McCay a decade earlier. Within twenty years, American animation went from an artisan craft (modeled on illustration) to a corporate studio, and finally to a division in a conglomerate corporation, with licensing specialists, toy outlets, and, in time, to theme-parks, and beyond. Certainly by the late thirties, with technicolor features, there was a clean break from the production techniques left over from centures of graphic narrative workshops (and still applied even in the twenties, in cut-and-slash animation, for example, and still in silent cel animation).

The need for a clean break finished off the Fleischers. It also made any intensive production of seven-minute cartoons at Disney quite untenable. Add to this the shock of the Second World War, felt even by 1940 in lost European and Japanese markets.

Once America was itself in the war, cartoons could only be made under the wing of a major studio, except at Disney (though as I explained, Disney felt the severe pinch). Even the State Department, in its way, became a film studio hiring animators.

The war also liberated the cartoon and began another cycle. In the displacement caused by military life, the confusion and intense regulation (even at home), a new audience appeared who enjoyed a bawdier, more antic style of cartoon. To serve our boys overseas, earlier restrictions on cartoons were lifted temporarily. Also, consider that virtually no one in America did not have a relative in the war or in army camps somewhere. Within this state of mind, the antic style returned, as propaganda in *Der Fuerher's Face* (1943, Donald Duck robotized into the Nazi war machine, with touches reminiscent of Chaplin in *Modern Times*), as violent cautionary gags in Private Snafu (mostly Warners animators), as balletic chases in Tom and Jerry, and frenzied courtships in Tex Avery cartoons (at MGM), or Bob Clampett at Warners, and militant characters who evolved mostly during the war, like Woody Woodpecker, Mighty Mouse, Heckyl and Jeckyl, Tweety and Sylvester.

After the war came yet another shift, more after 1948 actually, once the peacetime readjustments of GI's and the economy had been put into motion. This shift was dominated by the UPA Studios (begun in 1943, but not in gear until after 1948). Another cycle began, where graphic narrative was emphasized more than antic character. However, this linear style was more a part of the emerging consumer world than older pre-industrial crafts, like illustration. Later on, I will be explaining how the links worked between UPA, Disneyland, the International Style in architecture, shopping centers, and the one-stop convenience fantasies of the fifties. Like other cycles, that one did not last long — about eight years — though its influence has been enduring. By the mid-fifties, with the collapse of the studio system and the shaky early years of TV management, entropy set in again. Whatever the era, the fabric of the cartoon remains as delicate as ever, as we shall see in the next chapters, going in stages from 1934 to 1940, then through the war, and into the brave new formica world that followed.

CHAPTER NINE

How Money Talks in Cartoons

By 1934, the cartoon industry was in deep trouble financially. Even though cartoons were distributed more widely than ever before, profits were weak. Animation studios had to scrape mightily to fulfill their contracts.

Steadily, the cartoon industry had grown more vulnerable, even as it seemed to be flourishing. In 1921, cartoons could rent for as high as $300 a week. By 1926, rates had dropped to as low as $2 a night and never recovered, despite the popularity of cartoons in the thirties.

Even after sound came in and the audience for cartoons grew, the money problems remained. Rental rates stayed low. Advance financing remained uneven. Every cartoon studio remained constantly on the edge; if it did not get long-range contracts, guaranteeing credit and bookings even years in advance, staying in business seemed impossible. And increasingly, as the bottom fell out everywhere, old sources dropped away.

Live theaters rarely showed cartoons anymore. Business sponsors declined. Corporations were cutting out animation ads entirely. In the twenties, cartoon advertisements for movie houses had been a thriving market, a small-time craft industry with its own homely product, not unlike the naive ads found on the asbestos curtains of theaters. In 1920, Disney started out by making just such cartoon advertisements in Kansas City, for United Film Ad Service. They were essentially industrial short films, with an eccentric distribution, including movie houses and vaudevilles. Fleischer made quite a few promotional shorts, including a quirky favorite among nostalgia buffs, *In My Merry Oldsmobile* (1930), a bouncing ball sing-along for General Motors with peeping tom gags and suggested rape. After 1930, front money from big business dropped off, as advertising budgets shrank during the Great Depression. For a time, about 1933–34, only the movie studios were ready to commit any money at all (and they were near bankruptcy themselves).

Hollywood studios had been investing more heavily in cartoons since the arrival of sound. From 1929 on, new in-house production units were set up at Universal, MGM, and Warners. Steadily, cartoons were replacing one-reeler live-action shorts on movie bills. By 1936, Hollywood studios controlled the distribution and advance financing of cartoons more totally than ever before. Independent cartoon distributors, like Powers and Winkler, were folded into the film monopoly.

Only Disney had an alternative source of income (perhaps because he had been burnt so early by Powers and Winkler over the Oswald contracts in 1927). Roy Disney worked hard to set up revenues outside of the movies — from merchandising most

The leading cartoonists to survive the pressures of the mid-thirties. From top: Walt Disney, Walter Lantz, Paul Terry, Max Fleischer, and Rudolph Ising and Hugh Harman.

of all, and even large loans from major banks, like the Bank of America. (Walter Lantz also took out loans from the same bank, then called Bank of Italy, but never on the scale Disney could.) And yet, Disney's advantage did not make Walt less concerned about the movie monopoly. On the contrary, Walt was even more obsessed than other cartoon moguls; he invested millions to produce cartoons that could compete with movies. He was determined to make cartoon shorts which could eventually achieve rentals similar to live action. (That never happened, though — another reason why Disney went to features.)

It was indeed a buyer's market on all levels. Cartoon producers operated on negative income, because the movie studios often withheld profits from cartoons until well after their release. Luckily — if that is the right word — labor was cheap and hungry. Unions were unthinkable. Salaries until the late thirties were just about the lowest in the film industry, essentially comparable to clerical and construction wages in the country at large, except for full animators or cartoon directors, who could earn over $200 a week.

And the movie studios bought cheap as well, as little as $5,000 or $10,000 for each cartoon, more like $12,000 for Warners cartoons (again, except for Disney, who might spend as much as five times more than the others). And the competition could be fierce in the mid-thirties. By 1939, many smaller, less efficient studios, like Iwerks, Mintz, or Van Beuren, had been squeezed out. In 1936, when RKO decided to distribute Disney cartoons, the Van Beuren Studio simply folded.

To make matters worse, the costs for a cartoon, from conception to delivery, had risen very fast, at least doubling between 1928 and 1935, mostly to pay for sound equipment. Then, when full animation was added, with more intensive labor costs — along with the expense of processing in color — the budget for a cartoon could easily double yet again.

Stakes were higher, and so were the expectations of quality, as the rivalry for distribution contracts intensified. To stay ahead, a certain integrated production was needed, and this tended to add new restraints on how animators could work.

The print-oriented gag was definitely out — not that critics, animators, or audiences seemed to miss it; this was very much a different era. Also, flat, linear graphics did not sell easily to a market governed exclusively by the film industry. "Flat" looked wrong in a movie theater; movie space was not print space.

Movie space needed deep-focus effects. Backgrounds were painted to resemble film mattes more than printed squares. The layout lost its panel outlines (as in comic strips); more often, the boundaries of the frame were muted now, to suggest a camera lens directed into open space. Presumably, the camera only saw part of the larger field, much the way scenes shot on a sound stage could suggest thousands of miles of ocean horizon, or a ten-bedroom mansion simply by keeping walls or natural boundaries out of the frame.

Within this fuller space, movement had to look more seamless. Characters needed more transitional poses. The jump-and-stall body positions of the comic strip would no longer work.

And the rhythm of gags had to "move" like a movie (at least as movies looked in the years 1935–37). They had to move more deliberately. A random blast of 20-second gags did not make a cartoon feel like a movie. Cartoons were being repackaged. New guidelines were set up, based on story conflict, naturalistic movement, and moral discovery.

When veteran animators remember this era, they talk about changing their style to suit color, about tighter production systems (less freedom to play with throwaway gags; more power directly in the hands of the cartoon director or supervisor), and then the race to keep up with the Disney look.

The sum of all this came to be called *full animation*, but the changes arrived one step at a time, over a period of about seven years. As of 1934–36, the issues boiled down to one industry-wide agenda, which was still rather vague: *cartoons had to be redesigned, because they did not feel as smooth as live action movies.* (And cartoons were being compared to rather sedate movies at that: it was a time when the film industry wanted less sex in family movies, as well as gags that were safer for children.)

This shift is apparent after the summer of 1933, following the success of Disney's *Three Little Pigs*. Disney imposed a new movie-centered "state of the art" throughout the industry. Cartoon story and graphics changed everywhere, even at Fleischer. More cartoons were storyboarded before going into production. Background tones and character designs became "softer," with more shading and facial expression.

To manage this new style, different drafting skills were needed. For example, in 1935, while gearing up for *Snow White*, Disney recruited many animators from other studios, particularly from New York. But even the best of them, like Grim Natwick, had to change their working habits. New York style cartoons (even LA in that style, like Iwerks) were less divided into many hands, with fewer clean-up men for roughs, fewer story conferences. The New York animators at Disney, most from Fleischer, even had problems at first in timing their drawings precisely to the beat and to the storyboard.

The animator Shamus Culhane devotes chapters of his autobiography to the differences between Fleischer in New York and Disney in Los Angeles. When he first went to work at Disney, he was amazed at the improved decors; every three animators got their own office, with new desks, upholstered chairs, and, above all, their own moviola:[1]

By contrast the New York studios had desks and chairs that looked as if they had been stolen from the Salvation Army, and everyone worked in large rooms that were separated by nothing more than beaverboard. There was only one moviola in an editing room, and it was for the sole use of the cutter. Animators never saw their work until it was a finished film, ready for distribution.

More than anything else, the animators who moved across from New York to Disney remember the novelty of the pencil test. (Of course, this is now standard at animation programs throughout the country.) At Disney in the thirties, a pencil test could bring on palpitations at the "sweatbox" (the projection room, where Walt and a committee watched and decided). Based on the final shooting script, the animator had a running reel made of a scene without color or inking (though later with some sound). Rough sketches were cleaned just enough to be readable. Some in-betweens might be added. Then it was shot.

As film, pencil tests can look very unsteady and not always flattering, though I find them exciting and vulnerable to watch. They are a record of how a scene is built, virtually from the first line. Since animated figures are sketched in arcs, numerous circles are still visible, giving pencil tests a brilliant, circular intensity. The layers of line seem to claw for life like a statue emerging out of rough-hewn marble. They remind me of a similar form in early nineteenth-century painting: the study or painted sketch that preceded the finished canvas.

But when these running reels were shown in the Disney "sweatbox," all thoughts of gentility were gone. Originally, the sweatbox only had moviolas, in what some remember as an alcove, without air-conditioning. Moviolas were noisy and could get very hot (even leave a smell like frying bacon). Eventually, as Disney upgraded, the moviolas were replaced by projectors, in rooms with air conditioning and amenities like larger ashtrays. But the name "sweatbox" stuck. The animator would sit and wait — and sweat — with or without air conditioning. A small committee watched along with Walt, but he alone would pass judgement, as the single juror, sometimes with only a brusque comment that could feel devastating.

Walt could be tough on his beloved story men as well, and the layout artists. They also went through a sweat, presenting their massive story boards, with an explanation, usually a performance, like pitching a movie today. Walt also liked the element of surprise, partly out of his own nervous energy. He tended to burst in on people at work, perhaps coughing first to warn them he was at the door; and that seemed to add consternation.

Often Walt's comments were braced with reminders of the Disney corporate mission: all talents must be sublimated toward the greater good. All hands work within a single vision, toward a perfected illusion of movie-like elegance. In other words: don't take it personally; we all knuckle down around here to make the cartoons great.

A NOTE ON HOW EMPLOYEES HANDLED THIS PRESSRUE

The studio was obviously something of a feudal manor, demanding a unique fealty. And yet, veteran animators interviewed today rarely grumble about the Disney shop of the thirties. Indeed, some found it too restrictive or exploitative (particularly those who later formed UPA, in 1943). And the pay could be discouraging. Salaries for inkers or in-betweeners were as low as anywhere in the industry (ranging from $17 to $26 a week). Also, animators were expected to donate up to half a day on Saturday, without pay, and some evenings for art classes. But morale was clearly very high indeed, and remained so until the big strike of 1941, when the vindictive side of Disney made itself known. His vengeful treatment of Bill Tytla and Art Babbitt still sparks heated discussion.

Except for the strike, however, most remember the studio as a very lively, even inspiring workplace. Walt gave animators the privilege of time, extra weeks to polish the work, with none of the hefty footage quotas required at other studios. One of the most ardent strikers from 1941, Bill Melendez, is still somethat amazed at himself when he thinks back on his youth at Disney in the late thirties. A confirmed union man, he did not chafe much at the free labor he gave; he regarded the extra night classes and unpaid Saturday work as a free education and still feels that it served in that way.

In 1987, when I walked through the Melendez studio on Larchmont in Los Angeles, I was immediately struck by its similarity to the location and layout of the old Disney operation on Hyperion. Like Hyperion, it faces a north–south commercial street, made up of an assortment of private houses and small stores. Though the Melendez studio is infinitely smaller than Disney was, it also is basically a converted single-family house, with twenties built-ins as work space and odd conversions of old bedrooms. Disney started out with a portfolio of unlikely buildings, some residential, some commercial, then steadily expanded. He bought the small factory next door, and used apartment buildings in the back. The result was a homey world, with too many doors, too many unlikely entrances, odd-shaped little rooms, bad ventilation. Melendez is the first to admit that he still tries to shape his own studio in the spirit of that thirties Disney look: a casual mix of single-family domesticity and corporate management.

Walt was indeed the beloved little father on Hyperion. Even today, fifty years later, documented complaints are hard to find. Friz Freleng hated the way Walt kept insulting him (1930), perhaps due to anti-Semitism; but few other veterans even discuss the problems, without reminding me that there also was an élan there that they have rarely experienced since. Jack Kinney wrote about an abrasive Walt, a hard-driving boss, with caricatures of his tense moments and cranky entrances.[2] Art Babbitt is still angry at Walt. I did find one startling grievance on paper, in 1977, at a memorabilia store in Los Angeles. On the wall, behind the counter filled with old comic books, a strange watercolor had been hung, left by a thirties animator from Disney. Animators often drew little parodies for each other, inside jokes, also pornographic nudes — Fred Moore's specialty — even little bawdy in-house cartoons occasionally; and drawings about the pressures of the job, the pecking order. This drawing was particularly revealing, a fairy tale about management, done up as a storyboard sketch (or possibly an "inspiration" sketch from the art department). In the background, there was a broken bed with skulls for bedposts and a wooden Mickey Mouse frowning through the molding. The dwarfs' little bedroom had been transformed into a torture chamber. In the corner, an exhausted animator was slumped against the wall. In the foreground, Walt in pyjamas was on his knees, hands clasped in prayer. The caption reads: "Please God, send me an animator who can work twenty-four hours a day."

The elaborate style at Disney demanded more than just a forty-hour week, at least for newcomers. During the early months, they often took their work home at night to polish sketches. They might wake with a start, to find they had fallen asleep over it.

Even Fleischer veterans like Natwick and Culhane, when they first arrived, had to start over (even after hours), and work as hard as beginners until they found their work rhythm. Animators at Disney needed much more life drawing and anatomy than anywhere else. Characters' bodies required more bones and hinges, cartilage for ankles and wrists and neck joints. By contrast, Fleischer still worked with characters who were boneless bendables, with clown faces in makeup, much stiffer than Pluto's snarl or Donald doing a double-take. Fleischer's graphics split the body horizontally, between printed face and rubbery body (in short: top half, graphic narrative; bottom half, vaudeville rhythm). The limbs moved with a very fluid elegance, but the heads were rather impassive, as if inked on papier mâché.

At Disney, the bodies were expected to show expressions like movie actors, not dough-babies with clown masks. Animators were asked to design characters with skin and flesh. For example, instead of wrapping Popeye's body in rubber appliances (better for bouncing), animators in 1939 had to stuff Pinocchio with protoplasm (like a "real boy"), as if there were a beating heart inside, instead of an elegant clock mechanism. In many ways, *Pinocchio* was the graphic summation of this change, from puppets and machine parts to a character with body heat.

Disney required hyper-rounded limbs (particularly in the style of Freddie Moore, who briefly dominated among Disney animators with drawings that exaggerated the fleshy volume of characters). This density took a lot of work: more shading, more pleats added to clothing, to show the full belly and the upholstered bottom. But most of all, the faces had to be extremely mobile, from frowns to smirks to horror to wonder. Between 1934 and 1938, Disney's cinematic body forms replaced the New York style everywhere. The last of the graphic-narrative look of the twenties, originating from New York, disappeared, even at Fleischer and Paul Terry.

In LA, linear animation based on print was a dead issue anyway. Once the industry came out west for good — as it had by 1936, with only a few holdouts left — there was little choice anyway. Even though most animators, including newcomers, were still trained in magazine work, where could they take that in LA? Publishing was weak in southern California. In New York, the young Joe Barbera could take a subway during his lunch hour at Van Beuren and sell illustrations directly to *Colliers Magazine*, as he so often mentions in interviews. Animators in New York might still work on sheet music or theater cards in their spare time. And in fact, "cartoon show cards" of the twenties and thirties have a rubber-hose look similar to Fleischer. As one manual on "show cards" explained:[3]

97

Exaggeration of drawing also attracts attention .... Attention can be secured just as well through the omission of lines as by the making of them. In this day and age, all non-essentials are omitted.

In New York, many animators had experience working by these rules. But in LA, one drew strictly for a movie world.

The shift to a movie style divides by generation too. The new animators entering the field had been born in about 1910 and had grown up with the movies (e.g. Chuck Jones, Bob Clampett, Frank Thomas, Ward Kimball). They were children of the twenties. They visualized cartoon timing far more in terms of movies than comic strips or vaudeville.

This change is so remarkable that we tend to forget how close the generations were in age. Even the "old-timers" were only in their thirties; it was a young man's business, with young "gals" in the ink and paint department. But in this case, ten years brought an entirely different way of making visual reference. The youngsters had grown up much more as modern consumers. The twenties had been a takeoff point in emerging consumer industries and mass media (movie studios, radio, photo magazines, the automobile, advertising agencies). The older men in the field, born between 1894 and 1900, had grown up in a world quite removed from all that — a world of horses, farms, more live theater and print illustration. Films had barely made an impact on their childhood at all. Frank Thomas remembers how Norm Ferguson, a Disney veteran, still used, in Thomas's words, "vaudeville staging," described as a shallow curtain effect, to hold the action in place. The shift from vaudeville graphics to movie graphics was very evident to the animators themselves.

Ignorance could be bliss, if there was talent and a willingness to learn. The youngsters, without old habits to restrict them, were presumably more accommodating. The new generation hired between 1931 and 1934 had different art backgrounds than the "old-timers." They were more likely to have attended art school, and studied life drawing and painting. They could be trained toward illusionistic movie effects more easily. New layout men like Claude Coates came from architecture programs or were trained painters, and were interested in adding depth, rather than shallow curtain backgrounds. Disney looked for these qualities and encouraged them, with special life drawing classes for animators, new inking techniques, more moviolas, and, above all, stories that required deeper staging.

On Wednesday nights, Disney rented movies for animators to study, even rented a movie space in North Hollywood. And every day, cartoons and films were reviewed on moviola frame by frame, or at least scene by scene, until certain key gestures could be isolated for drawing. Nothing as studiously cinematic went on at the New York studios.

And yet, as enriching as full animation might seem, it brought with it a very sharp censorship. It is curious that so much investment in animation resulted in a much tamer cartoon. The movement was more lifelike, the layouts more stunning; but something was lost. Now irreverence had to "fit in" to the character's personality. The anarchic gags were trimmed back for the sake of story and good taste. I am speaking of 1934–37, so we still do not see the blistering chase cartoons of the early forties, or the blackout gags and crash-bang that come with the chase. That would bring renewed anarchy to the cartoon. Nor do we have the opulence of full Disney feature animation — not yet, not until 1937. We find instead an interim, a pause before all the elements of full animation are put into place.

For a few years, cartoons lose a certain rawness compared to the "anti-stories" I described in earlier chapters. Random, throwaway behavior lessened. Eager cartoon youths no longer bashed animals on the head simply to keep the beat of a melody. In *Hold Anything* (1930), Bosko tried so hard to make music out of a mouse's body, he accidentally chopped its head off. The initial novelty of these musical revue cartoons had worn out, along with the market for musical one-reelers in live action.

Many gags that had been acceptable in 1931 were deemed immoral by 1935. In some cases that may have been welcome relief. Veteran animators talk about how they were glad to stop doing "chamberpot" humor. And though I admit to an unusually high tolerance for raunchy asides with a whimsical touch, even I find it difficult to argue at length for jokes about excrement and septic tanks. In 1931, cartoon pigs still wandered out of outhouses. Bosko parked his car in one. Streetcleaners scooped up droppings left by horses and elephants. It was inevitable that these would be forbidden, or found unnecessary, within a few years.

Cartoon women were not brutalized quite as much. They were condescended to instead. By 1935, Betty Boop's breasts were no longer being pawed by slobbering ghouls; Minnie was not being hoisted regularly by her panties.

Cartoon alcoholism ceased to be a jokey subject. Up to 1933, animators had visited speakeasies often, to judge by accounts, particularly animators in New York. And some of the mood of those visits transferred to cartoons, with titles like *The Booze Hangs High*. Flip the Frog or Bosko might play drunken honky-tonk piano, then grin wildly as he hopped on dancing piano stools. After prohibition, we see less piano jazz. The musical rhythm in cartoon slows down.

Courtship after prohibition had clearly grown more temperate as well. Characters abandon the speakeasy, and adjourn to the parlor. Instead of Bosko meeting his gal Honey at a saloon, with her open liquor bottle nearby, we find Porky, bouquet in hand, struggling shyly in the sitting room.

Even cartoon flesh gets more solid — heavier than air, not as buoyant as it had been. At first this makes movement more severe. Characters who look denser than pen-and-ink rubber hoses do not bounce as lightly. They are definitely weighed down by gravity, particularly Porky, who begins his career looking like a blubbery melon at his top weight, then slims down gradually over the next twenty years.

The entire cartoon silly-scape looked denser as well. As I explained earlier, once painterly touches were added to backgrounds, the characters "lived" in more of

The domesticated Bosko, with Honey and dog Bruno (Warners, *c.* 1934).

a spatial, cinematic world. When they ran away, they shrank into a much more illusionistic distance. Deep focus stopped looking linear. That means that characters no longer moved like comic strips running on a narrow vaudeville stage, dropping in for their turn, then bouncing out stage right. Deeper space implied movie acting — more complex responses and interaction.

Compare this to 1931 again. Cartoons made in that year were often set in imaginary vaudevilles or circuses, and these were raucous places indeed. Instead of dramatic story, there was cheerful incoherence; performers went up and down like yo-yos on a stage, doing their act and leaving abruptly.

Rowdy circus schtick was common, even the smells of fecal matter turned "upside down." In Warners' *I Love a Parade* (1932), the horse wears a sanitation cap and picks up droppings left by the garbage man.

The faintest story association was enough to launch a song. In *Smile, Darn Ya, Smile* (1931), songs available on Warners sheet music are virtually all that one saw. Forget the story. Warners published more sheet music than any other studio, so the animators were told that each cartoon had to include two choruses of a song that Warners sold.

Cartoons in 1931 interrupted the story regularly for shots of the audience, like performers in vaudeville stopping for applause, usually a dull-faced wallpaper of clapping animals, as in the Bosko cartoon, *Big Man from the North* (prospectors and animals), or when the vaudeville act becomes the entire cartoon (*Bosko in Person*, 1933) or when Boop offers herself as a candidate, to cheering throngs, in *Betty for President* (1932).

Sometimes, the animators themselves came in as audience: In Warners' *Ride Him, Bosko* (1933), the directors, Harmon and Ising, appear in person (reminders of Out of the Inkwell gags), checking how the action is going and deciding how to cut in. Bosko, in the first of many Warners cartoons where the characters complain about working conditions, is left stranded on the screen at the end, unable to finish the story.

In the circus cartoon *I Love a Parade*, the curtain is raised like a tent show. For an instant, the elephants and pigs in the stands pause, then start clapping. The show was stopped regularly by shoving crowds, and always a few loud guffaws at the ladies, particulary when a dainty hippo dancer lifts her skirt.

After 1934, these gags about audiences in live theater can hardly be found. We do not see manic struggles in the seats of cartoon vaudevilles. Only in cartoons about symphony conductors do characters appear on the stage, to bow, while the animals in the audience applaud. (After 1939 that changes yet again, in Warners cartoons, where characters meet in movie theaters, or Bugs tries to win an Academy Award and gets pelted with produce instead.)

Even when vaudeville allusions do start, as in Bugs cartoons of the fifties or the ironic fable *One Froggy Evening* (1954), they are nostalgic artifacts (characters in straw hats, etc.), out of the old trunk, certainly not a familiar part of the audience's weekly leisure.

Unless the story absolutely required it, gags about any theater space were omitted as unfamiliar. After 1934, cartoons were set more often in painted small towns — and relatively sedate ones at that. Some cartoon towns were brilliantly animated, like the band box in *The Band Concert*. Some were big cities dressed in a bonnet like a small town. Disney's *Musicland* is particularly striking: the Land of Symphony reminds me of thirties Manhattan at a distance, but without cars and urban tumult — an idealized cosmopolitan city, not unlike the Emerald City in the MGM *Wizard of Oz*. Equally clearly, the Isle of Jazz in *Musicland* resembles Los Angeles of the mid-thirties, particularly the Mediterranean hills of Silver Lake which surrounded the old Hyperion Studio. The dome of these hills turns into a pumping jazz club.

But many cartoon towns were rather tepid, lined with tract homes and unmemorable streets, particularly those with Betty housecleaning or running a painfully cute pet shop — which is wrecked by Little Henry, who should know better. But then he goes on to redeem himself morally; and Betty realizes that Henry is a nice kid after all.

Along with these old-fashioned towns came the old-fashioned homilies. In *Little Nobody*, Betty's dog Pudgy plays Horatio Alger and saves a rich lady's pet. Then he is rewarded. The working-class mongrel proves he is a natural aristocrat (shades of *Lady and the Tramp* some twenty years later). While Pudgy basks in the admiring gaze of the wealthy dog owner, neighborly Betty sings: "Every little nobody is somebody to someone." (In our day, we might add, borrowing cynically from Warhol: but only for fifteen minutes, until Pudgy gets sent to the pound for good.) It seemed for a time, however, that cartoons needed that moral tag at the end.

These little sermons were added for the benefit of children, who became more emphatically the target audience for cartoons by 1936. Every studio felt a need to develop a musical series about children learning from experience. Gags with children and puppies seem to multiply steadily from 1934 to 1938, climaxing in Disney's *Merbabies*, an underwater pageant done like a Victorian holiday ride. (*Merbabies* reminds me of the cherubs that the Victorian illustrator Dickie Doyle would draw for *Punch* in the 1850s. It was a favorite of Eisenstein's, by the way.) For a few years, cartoons look very much like Victoriana revisited, and are generally far more sentimental in 1936 than in 1931. Characters were stricken with bourgeois respectability, Mickey and Betty in particular.

It is tempting to label all this as censorship and simply move on. But I would blame the market more than the censor, and that suggests a far more complex problem. The Hays Office did not ask Disney or Fleischer to change their graphic style. Fuller animation was an answer to the power exerted by the film industry. And fuller, more sentimental stories were a first attempt at capturing the look of movie drama (at a conservative moment in Hollywood).

To clarify how the process operates, let us examine a few comparisons with live action and theater: cartoons of the mid-thirties undergo a change similar to what happened to Chaplin's work some fifteen years earlier. Chaplin's Tramp started out as a vaudevillian with great slapstick finesse, then, like cartoon characters later, was modified to fit the imperatives of movie-making. A distinctly different Chaplin had emerged by 1923, and that created a sentimentality very similar to what occurs with full animation.

While working with First National (1916–17), Chaplin kept refining the Tramp, placing him in more motivated plots. He also came under pressure from the National Board of Censorship in 1916. The film historian Charles Maland calls this the "refining" of the Tramp, Chaplin's response to the "Genteel Tradition," to those who opposed the working-class vulgarity of his films (who even saw this vulgarity in Mary Pickford's films). The pressure to produce work of high aspiration (which also meant genteel taste) was very strong and very personal with Chaplin. Maland found a useful quote from him in 1916, which reveals how self-conscious Chaplin was about the historical roots of anarchic pantomime — again, labeled by genteel critics as "vulgarity":[4]

It is because of my music-hall training and experiences that I ... work into my acting little threads of vulgarisms .... This Elizabethan style of humor, this crude form of farce and slapstick comedy ... was due entirely to my early environment, and I am now trying to steer clear from this sort of humor and adapt myself to a more subtle and finer shade of acting.

In response to this interview, one critic wrote that "this new Charlie Chaplin [has] burst the tawdry chrysalis of the ... English music-hall manner [in favor] of a new fame, to be built on the basis of a more delicate art." The "raffiné" Chaplin was already announcing himself in 1916. How fragile the canon that both artists and critics apply, particularly for art that began with working-class associations, and aspires to "greater" things (but still, as in Chaplin's case certainly, wants to hold on to its roots). So it was with Disney in the thirties (the myth of his farm years).

Chaplin's *The Kid* is obviously his transitional film; it took fifteen months to make. Audiences saw a new Tramp, a more melancholy, responsible clown. But in adapting the Tramp to movie melodrama, a certain grit was taken out of the gags. In his autobiography, Chaplin wrote about the slower opening, the changes in rhythm and gesture, so that the Tramp could have more than a foil to play against.[5] He wanted to add the child Jackie Coogan, not so much for comedic range, but for expressive possibilities. With the little boy at the center of the film, the Tramp would submit to love in ways rarely seen in Chaplin films before.

Changing the Tramp brought some risk apparently. Chaplin's backers were initially rather shocked when they were asked to pay the princely sum of $1.5 million for *The Kid*. This Chaplin film was not filled with as many spectacular chases as usual; it was not slapstick enough. But the film was a success, of course. I need not dwell on that. Chaplin seemed invincible at that point in his career.

We divide Chaplin into two personae: the Tramp before *The Kid*, and the Tramp after. Both Chaplins are awesome but entirely distinct, like rival forms of narrative.

The early Chaplin of the teens is another species compared to the mature Chaplin.

The same profound split holds true for full animation. It is a species in itself compared to cartoons made earlier. It emerges from different sources and to different ends. Disney's personality animation is as drastic a jump as Chaplin's *The Kid*. In fact, from 1934 to 1940, cartoon characters take an even wider turn than Chaplin had. They start out quite free of the boundaries of *dramatic* story altogether, far more antic than Chaplin. Then, under the impress of movie marketing, they are reinvented, like molecules developed in a laboratory. Characters are given more motivation, more sweetness and pathos. The change revamps an entire industry.

But it also began the problem of over-corporatizing the cartoon. A bigger animation shop needs more rigid organization. From 1930 to 1940, the average number of employees in cartoon studios grew from dozens to hundreds. It took a much bigger shop to stay in business. That brought new systems, tighter systems, to add more polish to the product. In order to keep a character consistent for that many employees, and to justify that much payroll, rough edges were smoothed away. Extra shading was added, along with more conventions about what a good story needs, or a moral ending.

Also, when production expands, continuing characters inevitably go through too many hands. They can be retraced to death. From cartoon to cartoon, dozens of animators and in-betweeners work on a single character, until it gets either more plush, more wide-eyed, or more streamlined, as happened to Mickey, Betty, Bugs, Woody, and even Chilly Willy or Magoo.

One might find a few exceptions; perhaps the late eighties *Mighty Mouse* TV series (from Bakshi and Kricfelusi), with its ornery, scattershot look, or *Ren and Stimpy*. But those are indeed rare. Even a gifted director like Chuck Jones could not overcome the erosion of character. In 1962 he directed Tom and Jerry shorts, and, by his own admission, could not capture the energy of the original.

With full animation, if the work gets too rote, a character can be turned into a dull polytextual cipher, so loaded with good intentions that the faintest surprise might look out of place. Very often, even in quality work, the more cartoon characters were polished, the less freedom they were allowed.

We can compare this censorship to "overdevelopment" in the film industry of the nineties, stories "meeting-ed to death," as the expression goes (very much what happened to Betty Boop generations earlier, I might add). In the eighties certainly, many live-action characters were worn away by sequels — censorship by over-management. The same holds true for cartoons. Popeye, Daffy, Porky, Tom and Jerry appeared in hundreds of cartoon sequels, even more than James Bond, Rocky, or Sherlock Holmes put together. One has to expect a certain erosion.

I can also cite other awkward examples where corporate fiat has damaged the freshness of the theatrical cartoon, from colorizing them to over-licensing them. But why hammer the point endlessly? To sum up, corporatizing cartoons tends to remove the elements that make the animation surprising or funny. The more steps in the production, the more the risk, unless the shop is run like an artist commune or a feudal monarchy. That seems to be what the evidence shows, from the long-term process at Disney to other studios. For that reason, I am amazed that cartoons from the mid- to late thirties survive well at all. How brilliantly those shops must have worked to overcome the endemic tendencies of full animation. For once the initial shocks of 1934–36 were over, full animation added extraordinary volatility and variety to cartoons, from Disney extravaganzas to the blaze of forties chase cartoons.

Still, it is best to end this chapter as it began, with the problem of money. That remains a primary force for change in cartoon graphics and story. Weak financing continued to haunt the animation studios, bringing on new levels of caution and risk. Not all of these crises ended brilliantly, with full animation. Indeed, of all the forms of censorship I have researched for this book, financial censorship seems by far the deadliest. By the early sixties, essentially the same problems — shrinking loans and exploding costs — finally wiped out the cartoon industry altogether.

A Summary of Where Cartoons Go after 1934

To review my argument up to this point, the animated cartoon has a complex syntax of what has been called "anti-story" (graphic narrative, vaudeville timing, antic characters, upside-down gags, and staging). During the period 1928–34, the outlines of this complicated narrative were established, with the introduction of sound, and the many formal elements continuing from the twenties cartoons, and borrowed even nineteenth-century illustration (and the comics from 1890).

From 1934 through 1936, this vocabulary went into hibernation. Perceptual changes linked to movie marketing brought profound changes in the graphics, story, and gags. Animation became far more about movies and less about the printed page or vaudeville. As a result, entirely new systems emerged around what generally has been called full animation.

But whatever the changes, I see animation (full or otherwise) as a struggle against the inevitable anarchy that makes animation effective. Full animation is a package always about to explode, always at war with its nature. That is why it remains so fascinating.

That will become clear as I proceed, also as I enter the fifties, to the world of consumer marketing, consumer graphics, and television. The sum of all these shifts over three decades will be documented along the way. I want to remind the reader that while we race from one shift in style to another, the overall importance of cartoons as historical documents should not be lost. I will not be analyzing how this evidence compares to others, how animation fits into historiography. I will occasionally insert a few paragraphs about the history of melodrama, or of variations of anti-melodrama or pre-melodrama. These are like side-bars, to remind the reader that animation is older than cinema, just as pantomime is older than drama. Animation is another example of why postmodernism may have started in the fourteenth century, when the carnival began its shift toward the Commedia dell'Arte.

I can only make these observations as they fit the central aim of the book. But I want the reader to notice that there is a secondary aim as well. I do not want that to get lost. In many ways, I am examining the history of audience perception as well as the history of the American cartoon. After 1934, the decline of print as the defining medium for audiences can be traced very clearly, in background layout, animation technology, and technique. The cartoon literally reveals a shift in paradigm, very coherently. It documents precisely when audiences turn from print-driven entertainment to cinema-driven entertainment. Then, in chapters on the fifties, cartoons respond to new consumer industries like television. There is a lot in that evidence as well.

What does the cartoon as evidence tell us about the history of media? It tells us that media must be studied by the evidence of how an audience remembers (entertainment, leisure, personal details, history, politics). At one point, much of this memory was left to print, then to film, now to video. But the record in cartoons warns us to be cautious in our carbon dating. According to cartoon "evidence," it takes quite a long while for a cycle like that. Despite the popularity of film, the twenties were still very much a print era. Only in the late thirties is there clear cartoon evidence that movies have begun to replace the way memories are stored by an audience.

Using the same approach, television through the early fifties was essentially radio with a picture for many in the audience. Its impact on how the audience "remembered" becomes much more evident by the late seventies (with *Stars Wars*, new special effects, new ways of repeating genre in cinema and TV, new forms of film and video editing with the video/computer era).

Another question: Why are cartoons such useful documents in this matter? For any number of reasons that I will elaborate as I proceed, animation must be guided by changes in perception more directly than any other area of mass culture I know, except perhaps advertising. Cartoon gags, to be read as funny, must play off the pain and embarrassment that is familiar to audiences at a specific time; and show these in terms of entertainment. The world that cartoons turn upside down must be perceptually in tune very directly with a specific year. For example, audiences today still love Second World War cartoons, though we may fail to get all the gags about rationing or whether a trip is necessary. Something in the way cartoon humor was assembled simply operates as its own code. That does not mean that humor is the international language. *Quite* the opposite. It means that humor must be lodged inside its moment to be funny.

The last paragraph forces another question: Why, fifty years later, do audiences still laugh intimately at a world they have forgotten? I believe they laugh because the humanity of the cartoon is coordinated in subtle ways: gestures, turns of phrase, characterization, they all operate so well together. The notion that Disney features are timeless has tended to obscure the crucial modernity that makes cartoons funny. They are their own brand of ethnic correlative.

Cartoons are timeless because they look — and feel — like the year they were made. They are an upside-down version of entertainment and consumer rituals popular in that season. As historical documents, they are priceless journeys into the signified.

More recently, as I will discuss in the Conclusion, this journey has taken us toward animation in architecture, special-effects cinema, TV and musical-video editing, computers for the workplace (and in warfare). The implications would make another book — a raft of books actually. This book has to be more modest — seven minutes long.

So rather than expand the text with sweeping theories about media perception, like someone trying to talk too quickly into an answering machine, I wanted to stop for a while to alert the reader to implications that are surely, but not primarily, in the text. They are a subplot. And this is an *entr'acte*.

The history of perception in entertainment has to take a secondary place (except for a few inserts along the way, inserted as modestly as possible into the basic text). My primary goal is to set up a cartoon vocabulary. I want to reveal hidden possibilities within this seemingly innocent area of American cinema and be certain that this vocabulary comes directly out of the historical evidence (interviews, films, documents, the practice itself).

The vocabulary is extremely "telling," in all senses of the word. It is the story of how an industry was invaded, of how the viewer is invaded, and how characters invade each other. Remarkably enough, this vocabulary survived under fire for generations. Its anarchic mode was remarkably durable. Despite the problems and new methods, that early system of amoral and anarchic graphics repeated in new ways from 1928 to 1960. The vocabulary, ever mutating, also left a record on the rocks, about social history and perception, about the transience of the gag.

I also want the writing style to honor that vocabulary. That limits how judicial I can get and still accomplish my task as historian. The trimmer the vessel, the more it can carry. And I am trying to keep this vessel as trim as possible, to make suggestions for future work, not to girdle the universe. I write in broad strokes initially; that is my style. Sometimes I feel as if I write with a blunt point cut by a knife. But I want to write in a way that honors the abbreviated language and the music of those I have interviewed, and their films, to maintain a literary honesty to the original texts. These are cartoons, after all, a miniature world made by gifted cobblers. One has to see an animator at work to understand what I mean. What is discarded is in itself often a marvel. In fact, at the old Disney Hyperion studio, many people, including garbage collectors, used to rummage through the trash at the weekends. Neighbors also used to toss stray cats over the fence, believing somehow that Disney would know what to do with little animals, flatten them on to a cel perhaps, and give them a funny voice. The politics of innocence can be rather perverse.

But the history of audience perception can be told through cartoon; it shifts from print to cinema and then to video. I must emphasize that somewhere. The evidence is palpable, in thousands of 500-foot reels of film. Cartoons are an encyclopedia of allusions and refractions, as I explain in the Preface and in the Conclusion. This summary is something of a coffee break between the two. Hopefully it provides a moment to check if what you are sensing about this book is close to what I am intending — a multi-leveled journey through the "anarchy" and pluralism of the American animated cartoon, 1928 to 1960, the major figures, the major techniques.

CHAPTER TEN

Transition toward Full Animation: 1936

By 1936, very clearly, the graphics of the early "talkie" cartoon were being replaced. Production techniques were changing rapidly as well. And yet the results were not even approaching what they would be a few years later. If anything, the cartoon industry looked rather stymied. Disney was pouring money into a feature-length cartoon, with no movie in sight. That was all anyone knew, at the time, and many expected disaster. MGM had stopped funding cartoon production for a while. Paul Terry refused once again to change his style if it meant more expensive cartoons. Various smaller studios were in jeopardy, like Iwerks in Los Angeles or Van Beuren in New York. Walter Lantz thought he was settled in with Universal, having run a cartoon studio there since 1929, with little change in the way he produced cartoons. Then, in 1937, Universal executives told him, quite abruptly, that they would no longer provide money for his cartoons and that he had better find his own financing. Luckily, the Bank of America (then called the Bank of Italy) gave him a loan, perhaps as one Italian to another.

In terms of what audiences saw on the screen, with the exception of Popeye and Donald Duck, many new characters looked stiff. Even the Warners cartoons from those years seem tame today. In 1933, Warners had lost its first production company, Harmon and Ising, and its lead character, a little black boy named Bosko, who was obviously modeled on Mickey Mouse. What followed after Bosko was rather uninspired. At first, the Warners units experimented with two boys named Porky and Beans; then with a dull "whiteface" Bosko named Buddy, then with an "Our Gang" duo, Porky and Beans. Finally, with the first Porky Pig cartoons, the Warners look began to take shape — but not very clearly until late in 1937.

To give a sense of what followed, by 1940, not only was the Warners style in place, but its animators were producing forty-eight cartoons a year, more than any other studio in America. The growth of Warners in those three years points toward the key trend — *the steady expansion of animation on the west coast and its decline in New York*. The move west to studios like Warners or MGM tilted the scales toward the movie industry more firmly.

For a time, the gag routines that suggest a linear style are taken out, along with much of the antic syntax, the reversed allegory, even the zanier characters. But out of all this, a new fantasy world was emerging, with new assumptions. Its code was observed by Warners and Disney alike, however different their styles may seem to us today.

The rules suggest harmony and symmetry, but they were rarely applied that way, not in chase cartoons, nor UPA cartoons later on. In one way or another, the rules were readjusted to the antic spirit of animation.

We sit through three cartoons made in 1936, from Warners, Disney, and Fleischer. To expand the list, I could add any number of highly sentimental shorts typical of that year, particularly from the Van Beuren Studio (based in New York and begun in 1930 by former Paul Terry animators). But restricting myself to three cartoons, and discussing them in some detail, will make the argument much clearer — a kind of middle style preceding full animation. I should prepare the reader by listing their titles: first, one of Tex Avery's early Porky cartoons, *Plane Dippy* (Warners), to look at character. Second, a brilliant Silly Symphony, *Musicland* (Disney, late Fall, 1935 actually), for changes in graphics and story. Third, the first Popeye that Fleischer made in color, *Popeye Meets Sinbad the Sailor*, on movie staging in cartoons.

THE PORKY STUTTER

In *Plane Dippy* (possibly a pun on *Plane Crazy*), Porky is a childlike recruit in the air force. Put to work in a hangar, he cleans a robot plane built by Professor Blotz. The plane responds to orders spoken into a radio microphone and follows them blindly.

Porky is sitting dreamily in the cockpit, when he is suddenly trapped. The plane is given the wrong commands when it accidentally overhears children telling a little dog to roll over and beg. The plane hops to life, barking and scratching. In typical multimorphic fashion, it twists through a rubberized sky, with black circles to indicate wild spins. It curls its body, dog fights, knocks down a building without making a dent, enters a cloud by a fluffy door. Finally, after it lands with a bumping screech, Porky is left in a daze. He has had enough of the air force. He decides to join the infantry instead.

What does this cartoon show us that we would not find in its ancestor, *Plane Crazy*, or even in Warners cartoons from a year before, like *Hollywood Capers*, where Beans (of the Boston Beans) runs through a world populated by vaudeville acts (barbershop quartet; a version of W. C. Fields' pool table routine)? In *Plane Dippy*, we see a deeper sky, with more painterly tones. The story is far less scattered than most earlier Warners cartoons, even than cartoons Avery would make less than two years later. In 1936, the visual non-sequitur and blackout gags we associate with Warners were not as common as they would become, not from Avery, Tashlin, or Freleng — and Clampett had not started directing yet, nor indeed Chuck Jones. We still have a fairly standard plot, for the time, not unlike Oswald on the ball field, Mickey with his baton, or cartoon kids in trouble. Like a sensible children's story, every gag helps Porky learn a lesson. A sensible boy knows to keep his feet on the ground.

Porky had begun as a little boy pig, redesigned by Clampett, and directed by Friz Freleng. Porky reminded Freleng of two fat boys he knew at grade school, nicknamed Porky and Piggy, and a comic strip he had tried to launch named Porky and Piggy. At any rate, Porky is launched in I Haven't Got a Hat. Like Donald's first appearance in Orphan's Benefit, Porky must recite, with a speech impediment, before an audience of noisy children. To make matters worse, Porky has to be animated to a stutter. (That led to disaster for the animators. A man who actually stuttered was hired to do Porky's voice, reciting The Midnight Ride of Paul Revere. But his track was filled with excruciating pauses while he fought for words, and for air. This Porky was too uneven to animate well, and painful to hear. Eventually, in 1937, the studio hired a trained voice impersonator, Mel Blanc, who could do a stutter on cue.)

But these nervous pauses remained crucial to Porky's personality. He often slows down in mid-phrase, like a small child trying to find words that catch up with his thoughts. Verbal regression was built into his character. In fact, directors seemed determined to keep him a trifle retarded emotionally as well, in a charming way of course, like an Oliver Hardy. While he played adults generally, Porky still got his laughs by reverting to the gestures of a small child — "Oh b-b-b-b-oy!" (clapping his hands). He struggled with long-winded, very adult, dialogue, usually a bit old-fashioned in its vocabulary, like an elocution lesson in a Victorian madhouse — trying to say those long words, then g-g-giving up.

DISNEY, 1932–36: CHANGES IN GRAPHICS CHANGE THE PLOT

Like Porky, 1936 characters seem stilted compared to those we see a few years earlier. A certain brake had been applied to adult gags. The stories worked essentially in this way: chaos was bad, so good guys shut down the chaos. That does not mean cartoons were simply dull. The war to rid the cartoon world of chaos could make for brilliant gags, particularly at Disney, where characters fail miserably at handling adult problems, but fail with staggering grace! Mickey, Goofy, and Donald try to run a gas station like adults, or tumble down a hill in a runaway trailer. Donald struggles at a celebrity polo match.

(I must add: polo was Walt's passion in the thirties, and various animators with enough income followed him into the sport. According to Walter Lantz, it was frightening to see them blundering on horseback. And in fact, one man on a Disney team died during a game. Walt was so upset, he gave up polo altogether.)

At Disney, from the mid-thirties on, many of the best cartoons still allow anarchy "the best scenes" before the mess gets straightened out. Chaos invades with very grand gestures, often as natural disasters. While the storm rushes ahead like a giant broom, the wind belts everyone out of their chairs. Then, the anarchy could be conquered by cartoon wizardry, by every weapon in the animator's arsenal. Often this might mean heavy artillery which was literally too heavy, cannons gasping and sagging, then reloading. Or we see cartoon soldiers who turn everything around them into weapons. But more often, the subject was domestic survival: we see a family unit clinging gracefully to each other, surviving by magic. They stay in formation, no matter how they get thrown about. Often, the central characters are not making war, but rather getting through it.

In *The Band Concert*, Mickey guides his orchestra through a tornado. In *Musicland*, war breaks out between jazz and symphony, while the hero and heroine are caught in the middle.

Finally, the chaos stops with magnificent flourish. The subject is always "the conquest of the irrational," but the war itself is brilliantly chaotic. After the struggle has been won, the heroes emerge from beneath the rubble, like stuntmen surviving a carefully planned disaster.

But overcoming disaster was not the only way to have the meek inherit the earth at the end. There were soothing devices as well — munificent rainbows and smiling skies. A kindly look melts the mean-spirited. Most of all, there was a Disney "mood."

From 1932 on, Disney began to experiment with a gentle graphics similar to early twentieth-century picture books. This meant generally a mix that we associate with Art Nouveau. It was not a uniform style, however. The figures were drawn in one style, but the background in another. Figures were rather massive, in the stylized neo-gothic of William Morris, while the landscape was floridly linear, like a Japanese woodblock.

This "Disney Nouveau" had its own sources, a different track — not the European Art Nouveau or Arts and Crafts. Disney's animators followed more in the way Americans translated Art Nouveau. From the 1880s on, beginning with Howard Pyle, American illustrators and comic book artists came up with a much sunnier version of the Gothic Revival. In a way, theirs is a more harmonious reading of Japanese naturalism than the reception elsewhere (perhaps even closer to the original Japanese than English and French versions). European composition added an asymmetry that Americans redesigned to look smoother. We contrast Maxfield Parrish's "blue-scape" with Aubrey Beardsley's decadence or with Arthur Rackham's ominous, spiraling effects. In the American version, order subdues the sky and the winding stream.

In a Parrish world, as the eye is directed toward the castle keep at the horizon, the late romantic formula is given a uniquely American statement. It is not simply a ruin looming on a crag. It is instead, quite literally, the city on the hill stripped of history, and as gentle as a daydream. Stated another way: however ornate the scroll or the landscape, the composition had to suggest the harmonious. The west would be won; the castle would be clear of turmoil. The sense of order — or "Faerie" justice — was announced in the composition, like a Bill of Rights or the laws of free trade. The diagonals were balanced, not threatening. The characters were posed at ease, more in stately control of their bodies.

In Disney, this becalmed use of Art Nouveau elements is combined with a midwest spirit of urban planning — the simple grid village (or the suburban plan for Los Angeles, but more on that later, p. 248). Trees and houses line up neatly, like a mythically clean Dutch village or a well-managed toy-store window. I remind the reader that these cartoons still have a staging that differs from the Disney of *Snow White*. The landscape is much more ornamental, to match a story that requires less personality in the characters. The background has not been altered to help us read the mood of the characters, not as it was in *Snow White*. We do not yet see the waters darkening when the witch has an evil thought, or the lighting change when goodness arrives. Personality animation has not created conflict in the background staging.

In mid-thirties cartoons, the backgrounds tended to be more paradisial. No matter how bad matters got, the world looked friendly, even hallowed, with an obvious message that could not be changed. The evenness of the background meant that goodness was inevitable. No threat could ultimately invade it, not even long enough to create much story conflict. Goodness was a constant fabric; only the story was changeable.

In short, the unchangeable staging slowed down the story, and gave the characters little to play against. The happy ending had to radiate throughout, like Dante's Beatrice spinning in her aura at the end of *The Paradiso* (as in one nineteenth-century version from Doré, where every plate of *Paradiso* tells us that God's blessings protect the story). The background was also a bit flatter, mildly foreshortened; but it was still like a rotating theater screen. That would certainly be adjusted later on, to allow for more story conflict.

Of course, some visual symbols found later at Disney were already being used. They would remain, no matter how the style changed. For example, even years later, Disney still liked to display evil as bad weather: black wind, torrential rain, or tidal waves. We all know how stunning this contrast becomes in his features or in the cartoon *The Little Mill* (1938).

To repeat: at first, from 1933 to 1936, "full (more movie-like) animation" was accomplished in a much flatter style, a kind of middle style before full animation. The Disney backgrounds were still quite linear compared to *Snow White*. Instead of painterly fullness, the trees and sky were faceted and outlined in rather dark ink, like a Walter Crane wood engraving or print advertisements for Christmas ornaments in the *Saturday Evening Post*. The solidity of each object seemed more important than the naturalism of wind or dust, which was still drawn in lines and swirls, not washes. The result reminds me of how candy is displayed at a chocolate store or trees in a quilted sampler. It is a taffy-apple picturesque, quite literally taffy in some cartoons, like *Cookie Carnival*, or glazed like porcelain in *the Chin Shop*.

Among these transitional layouts, with a more matched, slightly flatter background than Disney used soon after, I have decided to concentrate on *Musicland*. Like many

114

of the Silly Symphonies, the background here is a single graphic metaphor, similar to those I mentioned above: world as candy; world as glaze. Here, obviously, the world is music. But in *Musicland*, this metaphor is constantly being topped, as a gag building toward a big ending.

The metaphor literally becomes a drawing. The drawing virtually replaces the plot, which is too thin anyway. (I should call it cartoon metonymy, not metaphor.)

One visual conceit tells the entire story. It is an *iconographic* plot (about drawings more than character); and it goes like this. Music is so alive that it animates everything in Musicland. It even animates the background, foreground, voices, character design — the works.

Along with this dominant conceit, a small, dramatic plot sustains the characters, certainly not the driving narrative of the cartoon, but easy to find. The story is Romeo and Juliet where instead of feuding families, the lovers come from feuding musical forms. But the metaphor governs the events we see far more than the characters. Every detail, every heart string, is drawn either as coming from symphonic music or jazz. Every character is a musical instrument and speaks in short blasts of notes instead of words.

The story is still overwhelmingly based on drawing styles more than plot points. The characters are slender postcard gags taken from musical scores. Classical music (in the symphony hall) meets drawings about jazz (in the nightclub). The characters are memory stops essentially. Instead of story conflict, the plot is driven by a conflict in graphic styles. One style fights the other.

This, of course, presents fascinating problems for animators. To make the conflict readable, and somewhat dramatic (as if something were at stake), two distinctly different layouts were needed. Each form of music had to look discernibly at odds with the other. Like oil and water, Montague and Capulet, they could not mix. So the layouts had to work from extremes, like conflicting world-views. But each view needed to stand out, as instantly readable as an actor standing upstage to deliver a monologue, or posters for concerts tacked on a wall.

One might call it *graphic* melodrama, a transition toward full animation, but not the final form itself. The story "looked" (rather than "went") this way.

Near the Sea of Discord are found two kingdoms. On the coast is the Land of Symphony, a beach town with Greek columns representing classical music. Out to sea is the Isle of Jazz.

On the symphony side, the instruments are literally high strung and fussy. They live inside vertical, marbled hallways, and under Greek pediments. But on the Isle of Jazz there is a lot more hustle. It rises and pops, on a hill shaped like a jazz drum, with high-hat cymbals. The king is relentlessly jolly, something of a free-wheeling widower. When we first see him, he is flirting with an "exotic" dancer. She is a naked, brown-skinned ukelele doing a hula. Her piquance suggest that she is probably a lot younger than the king. He gives her a knowing squeeze under what might be her chin.

Life is quite different in the Land of Symphony. The queen is definitely a viola, and her daughter a well-tuned violin. But the princess is "espied from afar" by the little Prince of Jazz, a chunky saxophone with crooked derby and winning smile. He paddles across the Sea of Discord to meet her. They woo. He chases her. He tries to steal a kiss. He honks his love. Very quickly, his "pluck" or "brass" wins her heart.

Unfortunately, the matron queen sees them circling a may tree, and has the prince locked up inside a metronome, with brilliant linear touches: the shadows suggest prison bars and prison stripes. Desperate, the prince sends a mesage for help (by pigeon). The note arrives at the Isle of Jazz in the midst of constant partying. As soon as the king reads it, he stops everything and sounds the alarm.

Both kingdoms go blindly into war. From the Isle of Jazz, musical riffs are fired at the coast. From the Land of Symphony, notes stream out of organ pipes lowered as artillery cannon. Meanwhile, the lovers are drowning, while they paddle toward each other across the Sea of Discord. They raise a white flag, but the waves cut them down. Needless to say, they are saved just in time.

The conclusion of Disney's *Musicland* (1935, dir. Wilfred Jackson). © The Walt Disney Company.

116

Afterward, the young lovers are delivered safely. But the parents are heartstricken and make peace. Then, during the ceasefire, romance takes over as mechanically as bread out of a toaster. On first meeting, the King of Jazz winks at the Queen of Symphony, then grins excitedly. She seems to respond. In less than thirty seconds, the parents also fall in love. The imaginary camera cuts quickly to a wedding bower. A double marriage is performed by a cello in a priest's collar.

At the wedding, however, Disney added a curious false step, as if testing other possibilities (or thinking momentarily of what Mickey might have done). We get a hint of the characterization to come in future Disney cartoons. Just as the marriage vows are given, both grooms suddenly get cold feet. They are posed awkwardly. It's hard on a guy giving up his freedom, etc. They sweat and shake before saying I do. The brides meanwhile seem to glow with victory (gotcha!). The anxiety passes quickly though, a pause, and then love takes over. The ceremony goes ahead.

Once the wedding is over, the two contrary graphics become one. Even the men are thrilled now. The newlyweds nuzzle. The honeymoon pageantry begins, drawn in a third style (rather like the Disney Nouveau I discussed earlier). An imaginary long shot pulls back from the happy couples to a picture-book finale, very typical of Silly Symphonies. The sky looks like a church fresco, or the staging for an operetta. We see the Bridge of Harmony from a distance. All of Musicland celebrates. Jazz and classical music have been merged (perhaps into "semi-classical"). The message itself is unambiguous, of course. Soothing chords tell us that gentility — or domestication — has won, not jazz improvisation. A divine order, in picture-card colors, has altered the contrasts into a single system of notation, both music and image together.

What does this notation tell us about cartoons generally in 1936? We review both the Porky cartoon and *Musicland*. What was being added to each? Certainly, the backgrounds tend to be much more elaborate. At Disney in particular, the stories build toward a stable marriage at the end, far more ornate than Mickey getting his hero's kiss from Minnie, more like the rainbow long shot at the end of *Flowers and Trees* (1932, the first technicolor Silly Symphony, and a harbinger of cartoons to come). But even in the Porky cartoon from Warners, gravity wins at the end, all in a background much less like cutouts or ink blocking than a few years earlier.

FLEISCHER, 1936: POPEYE IN MOVIELAND

Fleischer will be our third example. Even Fleischer, who specialized in the anarchic story, moved toward this more cinematic style of cartoon — a mid-point in the shift toward full animation. In 1936, Fleischer released *Popeye Meets Sinbad the Sailor*, an odd departure from the Popeye series generally, one of three 20-minute technicolor cartoon epics Fleischer made with Popeye.

In some ways, I find the cartoon slow going. Early on, Bluto as Sinbad sings about how powerful he is. He terrorizes one beast after another, from lions to twin-headed giants (with Yiddish accents). We cruise through Sinbad's monster island, which is drawn in extraordinary detail, particularly the shadow and hatchwork of the rocks. In addition — and very telling — live-action effects were added to the backgrounds. Part of the cave is actually a color cel photographed from a live miniature. Leonard Maltin located a Paramount press release (for the cartoon):[1]

Ordinary cartoons today are drawn and the drawings are photographed. With the method which Fleischer has introduced for Popeye the cartoon studio looks like a duplicate in miniature of a regular Hollywood production camp. Sets are built and scaled down so that they will fit on a revolving turntable. This "set" is within six feet of a special lens and camera. The machinery entailed in the new process weighs some three tons. It has trusses, movable tables, cranks, steel framework, gears and gadgets enough to make a mechanical engineer dizzy

This is even more three-dimensional than layers of cels separated by multiplane. It is a diorama in real space, considerably more like a tiny movie set than the flat, animated backgrounds Fleischer generally used.

Curiously enough, live action miniatures show up in quite a few Popeye cartoons, not only the Technicolor epics, but many of the others as well. Here is a partial list of Popeyes with three-dimensional miniature sets: *Popeye the Sailor* (1933, the first); *A Dream Walking* (1934); *The Two-Alarm Fire* (1934); *For Better or Worse* (1935); *Adventures of Popeye* (1935); *Lil' Swee Pea* (1936); *Organ Grinders Swing* (1937); *Goonland* (1938). (I believe the growing popularity of Popeye allowed Fleischer to risk a few dollars more. But why add dioramic effects, except to enhance the resemblance to live-action movies?)

To return to *Sinbad*. After braying about his virility, Bluto pulls out a telescope and spies Popeye out at sea with Wimpy. We see the ship through the iris of his telescope. Then, the lens turns to the right and lingers over Olive Oyl. As in many Popeye cartoons, Olive is a parody of glamor. Her spaghetti legs dangle seductively. Her stringy hair is blowing in the breeze. We know what gag must follow now: Bluto is instantly smitten. So he sends a massive vulture to kidnap her.

All this business amounts to the standard Popeye opening. But in this version, the scale feels too Homeric. The shadows are massive. The landscape is very sculptural. We sense the bird overcoming vast distances as it approaches Popeye's boat. The usual Popeye shtick seems less relevant, though we see it all: the whimsical machismo; Olive's kidnapping; Popeye's headstrong entrances; Wimpy creeping in and out of the action as he chases a duck with a meat grinder; Popeye mumbling to himself like a man alone in an elevator (ad-libs by Jack Mercer, the voice of Popeye); and the near-misses with his can of spinach.

The usual rhythm has changed, though. The camera has to linger more to show us background. When Popeye returns from one labor after another, the rocky landscape of the cave overwhelms his little asides and actually makes this cartoon a bit leaden compared to the jumpy unpredictability in other Popeyes made at the same time.

The epic background actually slows down the story. But Fleischer will still use that over-scaled look later, and more successfully perhaps. We find some of the same wide, diagonal sweeps and high-key shadows in the two features that Fleischer made; and most effectively in Superman cartoons (where the epic style works very well with the story, in flashes of laser warfare). When the budget had to "look big," Fleischer added movie effects (big sky, small figures) and movie perspective.

Fleischer particularly favored massive long shots, as if from a movie that could never be made, except with special effects. It seems only in recent decades have such effects been possible in live action (and these often developed by animators, like those at Lucasfilms, or earlier from Ray Harryhausen). As of 1936, however, the predecessors, except for Willis O'Brien, seem rather scant. I wonder how Fleischer might have animated Griffith's Babylon set or Lang's *Metropolis*? Rummaging in my mind through the late thirties, I am reminded more of the mattes for Korda's *Things to Come*. But Fleischer's staging looks even fuller; it suggests the gloss of science fiction fantasy in picture book colors, the glamor to come, from *Star Wars* to Frazetta paperback covers, and finally to Heavy Metal and cyberpunk. It shows us, once again, how Fleischer turned at each moment toward technology; in this case, the look resembles the wizardry of fantasy movie sets, or various machine gags in Fleischer since the teens (they occasionally resemble the whimsical machine parts in New York Dada. One might call it machine humor — again *machina versatilis*).

In practical terms, it is full animation as background and staging. And its variety from one studio to the next is quite revealing — for example, the difference one senses between Fleischer's epic style and Disney's. I compare it to science fiction versus the fairy tale; industrial whimsy versus the hand-crafted consumer object.

Beware of Barnacle Bill (1935). Though he mumbled continuously, and could dance up a storm, Popeye rarely showed much stretch on his face, except when it was punched or disfigured.

119

Fleischer built their epic effects more like the Brooklyn Bridge than a painted picture book. (The only exception might be *Gulliver's Travels* [1939], but even there, when Gulliver is tied up by Lilliputians [one of the best scenes in the film], or in the various over-sized weapons and details about warfare, Fleischer still favors *machina versatilis*.) In the Fleischer style — Superman's world in particular — the setting often looks very metallic, like a journey through the old Brooklyn navy yard perhaps, ships in dry dock set against the East River. The layers are usually of stone, steel, or rock. They faintly resemble a robotized stage, more than Disney backgrounds surely, but not a very evident stage anymore. The vaudeville remnants are barely vestigial by 1939.

Full animation, when it first appeared widely in 1936, also created new problems. As with any studio that tried movie staging, Fleischer had to change their stories to match the effects. The standard Popeye metamorphoses and reversed allegories look more awkward in settings like this, and were cut back, except for the usual dynamo inserted in Popeye's biceps (dynamo gags were also common in Superman cartoons). Those slapstick gags seemed outclassed when Fleischer made special cartoons; by special, I mean, those made to look "as full" as a feature-length movie, essentially as epic parody of the big screen. (I will introduce the story formats that suited full animation in the next chapter as the next step in this process.)

Let us review what was gained and what was lost when animators in the mid-thirties started developing a fuller animation style. We turn back to the three cartoons I selected from 1936. In different ways, each cartoon has been stripped of throwaway gags. Instead of fast slapstick, they each orchestrate music and characters more like miniature dramas. Backgrounds look considerably more lavish. Characters are more restricted by their environment (whether a deadly lake, a stony island, or a guided airplane) than in cartoons from these studios only four years earlier. You will recall that cartoons earlier often had all objects made of the same all-purpose substance, a rubberized cartoon plasma. All air was rubber; the gags tried to show how many ways difference could look the same. Now, that had been reversed. Now, the table of elements has gotten much more complex. Some were harder, or softer, denser, fuller, even vaporous. Characters had to fight the elements more, be changed by the atmosphere.

Where does this complexity lead at last? Let us go forward a few more years and imagine the fully animated world in 1938; let our minds play for a paragraph or two.

Like a computer-generated journey into Toontown '38, we walk through a fully animated space. We enter a banquet room with buffet tables that groan beneath dishes filled with brilliantly sculpted fruits and vegetables. The floors look waxed and show their grain elegantly. The lighting allows for complex shadows. There are imaginary movie cameras all around.

This room is certainly an innovation over the past. It looks more like a fine hotel and less like rooming houses with inked walls. A certain permanence has been added. Instead of a world make entirely of rubbery tapioca, objects are held in place by plaster walls, inside massive brick buildings, often in full color. Outside, the landscaping is rather grand, brilliantly manicured. Backgrounds look deeper, more like mattes painted for live action movies. And the sociability is much more formal. Characters behave more like actors than dancing sprites.

Even the music is more symphonic. Characters no longer dance to a piano tinkling in the orchestra pit (like a silent movie with a sound track). At Warners, the entire studio orchestra was made available whenever the music director scored cartoons; and Carl Stalling (arriving after years with Disney) took full advantage, synching in brass crescendos and a mix of musical styles that might be called "cartoon postmodern" today — much grander than the early "Mickey Mouse" music of 1930.

Cartoons had found a cinematic style. Much of this was sparked by Disney's success after *Three Little Pigs,* but not Disney alone. Movie studios were coming to expect it. Animators and cartoon directors, rather quickly, came to accept it.

In such a world, multimorphic gags cannot work as well. Instead, the cartoon farces we saw from 1928 have been transformed into much more elaborate illusion. They have been more sentimentalized and given more spectacle.

In the next chapter, we will examine what kinds of plots were found suitable in such a world. We observe full animation yet another step closer to its final development, by 1938.

CHAPTER ELEVEN

Depression Melodrama: Story

A fuller graphics was accompanied by a much more cautious form of story. It was essentially movie melodrama, condensed to seven-minute pastiche.

To animators of the thirties, melodrama suggested *deep staging instead of flat surface*. That became the alternative to graphic narrative. Flat linear graphics would not fit in a story built around melodrama.

For the animator working at the light table (whether or not the term melodrama entered his thoughts), a melodramatic drawing was very tangible as technique. If he were a trained illustrator, he knew that a story with melodrama required more shading. Since the middle of the nineteenth century, when melodramas were illustrated in magazines and books, they tended to have deep staging and more tones, like the layered skies in the Doré Bible, which so many animators remembered from their childhood. This was the sort of sky that already looked like a movie — again before the fact — before movies were invented. To draw for melodrama one relied less on the comic strips and more on Romantic book illustration or academic painting. (Similarly, in adventure comics of the thirties, from Terry and the Pirates to comic books about superheroes, the "cinematic" style of Romantic book illustration dominated, far more than the linear composition in Krazy Kat or Mutt'n'Jeff.)

BRIEF OPERATOR'S MANUAL

The term itself, "melodrama," comes from "melody-drama" in the sixteenth and seventeenth centuries. It meant a variation of opera where the dialogue and spectacle took precedence over the music. Gradually, by 1800 or so, the dialogue replaced most of the music altogether, though the thrum of the orchestra could still be heard in many nineteenth-century productions. Even for early twentieth-century melodrama, in key scenes, the eager tenor might still sing a tragic ballad, with hand on heart.

Film repeats many of the same gestures. We see 1820 gothic melodrama in James

Whale horror films like *The Bride of Frankenstein*, or Victorian interlude when Jeannette McDonald perches beside Nelson Eddy. Caped heroes duel to the death like characters from serial novels of the 1840s, adaptations from Dumas adventures.

Most of these genres began as plays about monsters and horror. By the first third of the nineteenth century, gothic melodrama had become extremely popular, a variant of Romantic literature. Byronic vampires stalked the theaters, particularly in London. Throughout the nineteenth century, theaters on all levels carried the horror format along, in the spirit of *Sturm und Drang*, penny dreadfuls, various blends of spectacle, sentiment, and domestic conflict. Thus in all its forms, melodrama remained a mix of ghostly horror and exaggerated spectacle, with elaborate gesture, mad grieving, and a general clatter of costume. It also made gothic tragedy out of the moral crises of the age, the horror of drink, of adultery, of falling into the working class. The fall of virtue became a full-course nightmare, like the fall of Lucifer or the attack of a vampire.

These fright shows also became very lavish, prematurely cinematic. By the 1840s, the most famous stage for melodrama, the Astley in London, was so massive it often doubled as a circus on the same day that it ran plays. Such oversized dramas required special effects that grew ever more intricate, to include trap doors (for spectral visitations), forms of rear projection, and backlighting. In America, by 1905, there might be atmospheric "transparencies" to evoke the "northern lights"; or platforms on cables to make characters disappear; even mechanical grandstands, with a painted or sculpted audience on the stage itself; or a mechanical iceberg crashing into a ship on stage.[1] The competition for deep-dish effects led to an illusionism that could be so extreme, ultimately, only one medium could put on full melodrama, with all the stops. That was the moving picture.

When movies were first made as melodramas, they looked a lot like the stage plays. Even many of the effects we associate today as purely cinematic, like intercutting, have some roots in theater melodrama.[2] And the borrowings continued into the teens and twenties, even to Eisenstein's theories of "montage of attractions," taken from theater, which form the basis of his early film work.

Movies also changed how plays were produced. Theaters began to add movie screens as backdrops in melodramas, like the backlit screens in use since the sixteenth century (part of *machina versatilis*). In 1907, for example, theater patents were issued for new rear projection systems in Italy, for movable picture screens in New York.

Animated Interiors

When film was added on the stage with live actors, patents describe this as "theater animation." For example, in 1924, one play featured an "animated book." Another in 1930 had "animated objects" projected on to the stage.[3] Animation, in this sense, meant a simultaneity between theater and film, achieved through "animated" light.

The viewer sat in a theater with live actors, but the stage seemed transformed into real landscape, or into a painting or a picture book. The spectacle was supposed to look seamless, like a bower of real trees planted on a wooden stage. And plays that needed such devices often were melodramas, from theater to film.

For a story man working at Disney, melodrama also had a fairly precise code, on the story boards, in the plot. It needed a moral continuum made as graphically obvious as possible, like a color or a face poking through a door. The scales of moral justice threw shadows across a forest, or played against the faces and bodies of fully animated characters.

The plot required a very moralistic view of the state of the world. Goodness had to triumph. The audience clung to this guarantee for hope and guidance. As one melodrama from 1846 declared, in rather clumsy verse: "Deeds have their orbits, but fly off to return, and wrong its settled round, in which wander as it may, it ever comes back to its source."[4] In other words, justice holds sway over audience and characters, like an orbit. Tragic moments serve as suspense until this orbit takes over.

This orbit moves by a few obvious rules, beyond story conflict and characterization. They are as familiar to us as clips from famous movies, a drawl from James Stewart, a stare from Bette Davis. They are also basic to screenwriting:

1. When motivating your characters, keep a *moral* ending in mind at all times.
2. Be certain that characters make their own mistakes and *learn* from them (the cinematic answer to the problem of free will). And most importantly:
3. Always bind your characters inside a *moral continuum*. But make the situation seem terribly *immoral* through most of the movie. Create suspense until the continuum takes over.

Any film by D. W. Griffith could serve as a clear example of moral continuum at work. Griffith, like many actors, knew theatrical melodrama very well. He knew that in melodrama, chaos is evil on stage, even if the chaos is democratically inspired. And order is good in melodrama, as long as it is morally correct. In *Orphans in the Storm*, Lillian Gish waits to be guillotined, essentially for falling in love during the Reign of Terror. Meanwhile, Danton rides furiously to bring order to the Revoluation. Then, after Lillian is saved, as if she were the Maid of Liberty herself, morality returns to Paris. In the final scenes, anarchy leaves the streets.

For comparison, let us whistle through the final scenes in *Snow White*. The seven dwarfs chase the evil queen furiously up the mountainside. A bathos of heavy rain is pounding in front of them. Evil chaos is unveiled. At last, the moral continuum catches up with the bad queen. Of course, we knew it would. In the midst of her hoarse laughter, a bolt of lightning strikes the cliff and plunges her from the movie for good. (In movie melodrama, evil often must fall from a great height, down into a sulfur pit, crevice, or off a building.) The forest is made safe. However, Snow White is still lying dead.

We wait for the *moral continuum* to finish the movie. We pause. Snow White's lovely corpse is on display in a glass coffin. The dwarfs and forest animals mourn her. Doc weeps on Grumpy's shoulder (at the première in 1937, the audience cried out loud at this gesture).

Suddenly, the clouds part. The young prince stops by to look. In a moment of necrophilia, he kisses Snow White on the lips. She awakens, quite refreshed, and ready to get married. She says goodbye to the dwarfs. As the chorus sings off-screen (not unlike old melodrama), the *moral continuum* is underlined in silhouette: the black outline of the lovers moves toward the castle.

Snow White is thrillingly animated, but, to be honest, whatever its extraordinary power, it is also unadulterated melodrama, taken directly from nineteenth-century sources. It blends movie editing with atmospheric illustration, also mostly from the nineteenth century (see p. 143).

But what of seven-minute cartoons made at the same time as *Snow White* like those I discussed in the last chapter? An obvious example would be *A Waif's Welcome* (1935), directed by Bert Gillette when he ran the Van Beuren Studio in New York. Gillette, an extremely irritable fellow apparently — some described him as mentally unstable — had been at Disney for a time, and had directed *Three Little Pigs*. As a result, he understood personality animation very directly, but could not transmit it easily as a boss. The general level of the animation at Van Beuren was erratic, with shifts in systems almost month by month, and threats always that the studio was about to skid into bankruptcy. At its best, the Van Beuren style had an odd, ironic solidity, a doughy, almost lumpy rendering of figure, rather like characters made out of wedding cake.

In *A Waif's Welcome*, a gentle orphan is brought in from the storm, into a comfortable household. Unfortunately, a bad boy lives there, who is consumed with jealousy and torments the orphan with cruel pranks. One of the pranks goes too far, and a fire breaks out in the house. But during the fire, the waif proves himself brave and loyal, a natural aristocrat straight out of Victorian melodrama. The tables are turned. The bad boy learns to be good. Moral rectitude takes over. Now he too loves the waif.

On first viewing, cartoon melodramas of this sort look infinitely less successful than the comedies. The tenderness looks too sappy or too awkward. It works off cues that limit the gags. Like *Snow White*, these cartoons are not only more "structured" — more like domestic melodrama — they are also more "controlled." In other words, the controller function is given much less freedom to break the rules or turn the world upside down. The character is not allowed to behave anarchically (amorally).

But this moralizing cannot be blamed simply on melodrama. Some variations of melodrama can be very antic; others clearly are not. There are at least two species of melodrama used in cartoons, one more anarchic, the other more rigid. Before 1934 — that same cut-off date — the more anarchic form was used more often.

SWASHBUCKLING MELODRAMA, 1930–34

The Controller is anarchic, a swashbuckler, a moral gunslinger. He cleans up the town.

Swashbuckling melodrama came out of Romanticism and pulp fiction, identified with boys' adventure stories, known mostly through authors like Stevenson, Scott, Dumas, and through the Western. A swashbuckler fights to bring down the evil empire. A pathfinder (frontier swashbuckler) leads settlers across the prairie.

Memories from these adventure stories suited the anarchic rhythm of early talkie cartoons and were very commonly used from 1930 to 1934. The intrepid hero breaks the rules (Mickey, Bosko, Betty, Popeye). Beyond an instinct for righting wrongs, the character's motivation is barely noticeable. Action speaks louder than words. The cartoon heroine screams on an ice floe. Bosko jumps in to save her. Or the natives are cannibals with rubber lips. They chase Mickey, Bimbo, or Betty.

Mickey as lone hero butts heads with the villain, Pegleg Pete, in Arabia, in airplane dogfights, on land and at sea. In *Shanghaied* (1932), as Walt's pre-production memo indicates:[5]

Pete kidnaps Minnie and takes her aboard his pirate ship. Pluto awakens Mickey. They follow

Mickey dueling Pegleg in *Shanghaied* (1932). © The Walt Disney Company.

spoor to Pete's ship. Mickey sneaks aboad the vessel as it is about to go to sea in a huge storm. Pete has Minnie in his cabin and is trying to make love to her; Minnie screams.

Then Mickey does some swashbuckling: using a swordfish to duel with Pete (encumbered by a chair on his foot), while the ship pitches back and forth. Then Mickey overcomes the crew, and finally undoes Pete with signal rockets. A kiss from Minnie and close iris.

This was essentially musical farce converted into action melodrama, like a spoof of the dime novel. Not much "moral discovery" went on. Characters did not discover from "deep inside," as they would in Disney features a few years later. Pete grabbed Minnie. Mickey got her back, using his Yankee ingenuity. The tinny music rose and fell. In the end, Mickey enjoyed a grateful kiss from his leading lady. It was a simple track, with everyone in costume, unspoiled and racing to the music, leaving no time for Mickey to realize very much.

As action hero, this early Mickey is the *controller* character. He solves his problems through pluck and ingenuity, a cross between Edison and d'Artagnan. He always makes his way, and rather anarchically, by zany device or outright destruction. Will he tear up the town or the kingdom, for goodness' sake? Pegleg doesn't run things correctly; he runs things too much. He's bad for morale. His rules are wrong. Pegleg has locked everything up, including Minnie. Pegleg is perversely orderly, a despot. Morally correct anarchy has to make things right.

To make the world free, the town has to be blown to bits by Mickey the adventurer, who stands in for the entrepreneurial spirit. As E. M. Forster wrote, Mickey "reaches heights impossible for the entrepreneur."[6] Action heroes are like businessmen-inventors opening up new markets, but leaving a gouged moonscape where trees used to be. Chaos is progress, an ambiguous moral message at best.

AFTER 1934: MORE MELODRAMA ABOUT FAMILIES

Instead of the action hero as controller, a moral abstract controls the gags.

The domestic form of melodrama is much more sentimental and moralistic. It was very widely used from 1934 to 1938, and continued thereafter, though not as consistently. The stories in that form required fuller animation and fewer antic gags. Unlike the dashing, anarchic adventurer, the "domesticated" hero must preserve the rules, exercise great self-control. Therein we find the subdued Betty, the less plucky Mickey, and a host of peaceable others (e.g. Porky).

Background

Domestic melodrama comes out of the same roots as soap opera, from the mid-nineteenth-century arch-tragedies about family life, particularly those for the Temperance Movement in England and America. A high-gothic anxiety taken from horror tales was applied to stories about life under capitalism: families of drunkards, the sins of adultery, the shames and rewards of economic struggle, with any number of fainting heroines and cruel mortgage penalties.

The family was a temple. Any cardinal mistake left fatherless children and seemed to spread tuberculosis like the eleventh plague. Sex outside of marriage placed characters beyond redemption. Whores and wild singles died coughing hopelessly, like *The Lady of the Camelias* (a French melodrama). But virtue was rewarded. The innocent shop girl, victimized by an evil boss, would have her revenge.

Above all, characters had to exercise rigid self-control in order to make good. They had to suppress flamboyant, amoral behavior and stay within the family, which was equated with rural democracy. In addition to getting ready to start a family by the end of the story, the hero was supposed to save the frontier and the virtues of farming as well. To manage all this, he had to be mentally streamlined into a good-hearted yokel, with a simple calculus for good and evil. The farm symbolized middle-class virtue; the city was the abomination.

In *The City Slicker and Our Nell* (1893), Toby Snodgrass utters one of the grand old clichés: "She's a talkin' to that city slicker — the good-looking one with them fancy store clothes."[7] How much more streamlined can a message get, except in a cartoon? Domestic melodrama was a direct attack on urban life. If Toby expects to start a family with the right woman, the old farm truths had better be potent enough to make Nell see the city for the evil it is. The shrewd farm boy struggles to save his betrothed against the evil suitor — often an unethical businessman, with devious city ways. In the end, the simple heart triumphs. The uncomplicated is ennobled.

In Toby's fight against the moustachioed slicker, we see an allegory, which repeats for generations: hard-working men from small towns are threatened sexually by a placeless industrial job market. They lose their sense of virility and the respect of their home-town gals, but recover in the end.

To redeem such men, domestic melodrama empowers the innocence of rural life; farm ways miraculously survive attacks by business. The evil job market is translated into moral-drama, or melodrama. And yet, critical as it might be of business (many a theatrical "millowner" was shot dead by Tobys of one kind or another to the resounding cheers of the audience), heroes still had to behave according to the strict rules of the Protestant work ethic. They still had to act industriously, like a decent businessman, in order to be saved. Characters had to find an "object in life," drive out bad business with energetic, profitable planning; that was the hero's "social duty." In some stories, one's object in life was merely to know one's place in the economic system, do it well in the eyes of God, and stay an efficient millworker. One learned that class struggle was against nature.

Generally speaking, as domestic melodrama evolved in Europe and then America it was often laced with a moralism typical of the emergent bourgeois rhetoric of the nineteenth century. Business and labor were each expected to act responsibly. The laws of uncontrolled capitalism needed egoistic managers as well as loyal workers, both struggling through an obstacle course filled with dark forebodings. (Has the resemblance to the Disney ethic come to mind yet?)

Free trade was just, but business was evil. In its way, domestic melodrama was a morality play about the common man conquering social dislocation. Perhaps that suggests why the form survives so well; it offers heart-wrenching vindication for economic injustice.

Poetic Justice

But most of all, in terms of simple cartoon plots, domestic melodrama specialized in "poetic justice," that ancient story principle, as old as dramatic theater itself. In the nineteenth-century version though, poetic justice was often equated with what the economist Adam Smith called "the invisible hand" of free enterprise. God watches over profit and loss — and settles accounts in the end. Virtue is divinely protected after great trials (as in recent movie melodramas, like "The Force" in *Star Wars*). Work hard, stay pure, show some mechanical ingenuity, but still know your place; then the cosmic Fates of capitalist justice will help you rise. Or would that be The Blue Fairy turning Pinocchio into a real boy? Or Snow White and the dwarfs at work, nose to the grindstone?

The Small Town in Melodrama

Much of the Disney ethic is contained in domestic melodrama — even architecturally later, with Disneyland, or his links to the fantasy of the midwest town, which was essential to the promotional image of Los Angeles. In LA, from 1890 to the mid-twenties, the city fathers set up advertising campaigns, which they financed themselves, aimed at midwest small town folk in particular. Los Angeles was sold to the public as a rustic alternative to urban strife. Not surprisingly, Disney's cartoon town resembles the fantasy LA. It is even set in the years from 1890s to the 1920s. And it sponsors the cult of childhood and family life in much the way the LA leaders did.

Domestic melodrama spoke very directly to the Depression era, which ended with the war, about nostalgia for an age presumably of greater simplicity, before the Crash, even before the automobile; an age that suggested prosperity (not true in fact, only in fantasy). It referred to rural values from the "good old days," to social conditions before the industrial expansion of the 1870s. As it was understood in the thirties, cartoon melodrama might be likened to an old-fashioned chair with antimacassars on the arms, to an age when property was easier to own and banks were solid.

Disney animators from the mid-thirties remember very well Walt's love of domestic melodrama, in the way he discussed character coming from "inside," like a redemptive spirit. Inside meant, more or less, a childlike interior. Despite the insistence by animators that they made cartoons for an adult audience, this was the era of Shirley Temple and Andy Hardy, of the family picture, where children were often shown running an adult world, even taking over from adults. Cartoon heroes were more frequently dressed like children than they had been earlier. That includes Porky, Mickey, Oswald, even the revived Felix of 1933 from Mintz Studios (for Columbia).

By 1935, in technicolor cartoons, we see babies by the armful, cherubs and kittens and puppies, particularly from Disney and Van Beuren. And the cherubs show up in unlikely places, often as bunnies or bunny families sexually tempting the villain.

Also in the mid-thirties, the nephew and brother syndrome begins, in comic books as well as cartoons. It seems that adult characters needed more relatives, added as permanent responsibilities, like Batman adopting Robin, or Donald burdened with Huey, Dewey, and Louie. With families in place, the stories could be built around the problems of small children more than adults.

The same was true of Fleischer. In *Grampy's Indoor Outing* (1936), the story is built around Betty's little brother, who cannot go to the carnival. And in *Christmas Comes but Once a Year*, the children in a large but poor family will receive no Christmas presents — until Grampy delivers a dazzling Rube-Goldberg parade of goodies. Ordinary objects are transformed into toys — a very inventive cartoon on a theme we know all too well: bringing the department store into your house, dreaming up the consumer Christmas.

The Joy of Punishment

Melodrama about family had its dark side, though, in a few grisly cartoon melodramas. These were very uneven generally, but very revealing as well. Some of the anarchy would creep back into the cartoon in a sadistic way, never from Disney, but from virtually all the other studios. Only a few dozen of these sadistic melodramas were made, but they point out the problems for cartoons with moralistic restrictions. They taught moral lessons very cruelly, as if the older, bouncy cartoon had become perverted, and been born again pathologically. They also point toward what later develops as the chase cartoon (see chapters 19 and 20).

I would call this variant from 1936–39 "the brutal moral fable." As a story form, it resembles an eccentric genre of children's literature known as the "cautionary tale," though not even in the thirties was that term still used. Animators probably knew cautionary tales as selections from the *McGuffey's Reader* of their childhood. I would not make a case for these stories as a source however. Cautionary tales proliferated much earlier, mostly from 1800 to 1860, as little illustrated books, the most famous being *Strewelpeter* (1848; translated by Mark Twain, curiously enough, and printed in a special edition in 1932; the character also physically resembles Edward Scissorhands). *Strewelpeter* reads like the last five minutes of a gangster nightmare, or a slasher sequel, but with a whimsical sadism that children enjoy. As anyone who grew up with it will remember, the annoying thumbsucker has his thumbs snipped off by a barber with giant scissors; and a little girl who is careless sets herself on fire by mistake and is reduced to a sickly heap of ashes.

The sadistic moral cartoons of the late thirties have that same displaced anger. It is no overstatement to say they look like the return of the repressed. Punishment takes on insane exaggeration. They are cartoons about oppression, about getting the rules straight at all costs. As plots, they are as plainspoken as a mugging in the backyard: punishments dominate most of the story and they occasionally get rather ruthless, even for cartoons. They also feature quite a few examples of assembly-line torture (like the end of *Three Little Pigs*, perhaps, but more intense).

They may be the first cartoons using sound effects where a body is actually whipped or smacked realistically. The laughter of the righteous often follows; and the laughs register so sadistically to our humanistic era, many of these cartoons have become "new wave" cult favorites, shown along with *Reefer Madness*. We see how "bad thinking" takes you straight to hell. Families who are good hurt families who are bad. Bad kids are taught to be free.

More of these were made in New York than in Los Angeles — perhaps a symptom of how daily life was observed in these two cities. Once in a while, learning to be good was simply a passage through pain.

Some of the ripest of these were made at Fleischer, between 1936 and 1939, islands of the grotesque amidst the cute and frisky cartoons Fleischer produced at the same time, with Betty happy in the kitchen, or Pudgy learning to be a good puppy, or Color Classics with Hunky, Spunky, Lamby, or Little Lambkin. Perhaps someone at Fleischer felt an irresistible urge to throw in very dark humor, in the older Fleischer style, a little street-wise morality with a gothic touch.

In *Small Fry* (1939), a little boy fish plays hookey from school. His trout mother is distressed. Small Fry wants to hang out with the Big Fry at the underwater pool hall, and this frustrates his mother into the blues. She warns him by singing that popular ballad "Small Fry": you'd better stay out of the burley-cue, because you're not a Big Fry yet ("Oh me, oh my, Small Fry"). But Small Fry thinks he's tough enough, and swims away from home to join the Big Fry pool hall. There he learns his lesson. The big fish scare the daylights out of him. They throw him into an empty room where he sees monsters: flourishes of neon octopi on a dark field. Finally, he zips home to his mother's arms.

Later, in the forties, ghost cartoons from George Pal and from Warners seem to play with some of the same themes — to scare the wits out of children — but not with the same need to teach a moral lesson through cruelty.

In a later Betty Boop, *Be Human* (1936), *machina versatilis* meets domestic melodrama.

A sadistic man keeps whipping his horse for fun. The screams of the poor beast are driving Betty up the wall. The man refuses to stop when she complains; he just keeps laughing. Finally, neighborly as she is, Betty complains to Grampy, the inventor who runs the local animal shelter. With machine-like speed, Grampy builds a torture device that also serves as a gruesome ecosystem. The sadist learns his lesson all right. Trapped in a pit, he is whipped along a treadmill that helps feed pigs and swat flies. Meanwhile, as an unsettling twist on poetic justice, Betty, her little brother, and Grampy laugh while the sadist gets brutally paddled. Look, they giggle, it's his turn to suffer now. They lean over for a better look, like figures from Goya's *Tauromaquia* watching the bulls bleeding. Indeed, the Fleischers take melodrama in a strange direction, into some of the grimmest cartoons made in the thirties. One might call them revenge melodramas.

By far the oddest is *The Cobweb Hotel* (1936). This is about a ghoulish spider who ties you up on your honeymoon, like a serial killer with eight legs. The Cobweb Hotel is an old rolltop desk, run by the spider who has a long nose that doubles as a quill for unwitting flies who sign the ledger. A pugnacious young fly, named I. Fly, enters with his new bride. Immediately after signing at the front desk, the young "Flys" are interrupted by a creepy sound: the fearful screech of a trapped insect in an upstairs room. They see a little fly squealing helplessly from a bed in a corner window. They turn to look at the audience — gulp! — the melodramatic aside.

Soon after, they are both imprisoned in exactly the same way, in spidersilk, by the evil manager of the Cobweb Hotel. Luckily, the bride escapes, frees all the other flies, as well as her husband (whose wings were held in paper clips). Then the flies wage war against the spider, shooting at him with pen points and machine-gun aspirins. In the final scene, the newlyweds are carried off inside a cushioned case with a wedding ring.

The imagery resembles the ghoulish turns in early Betty Boop cartoons, but now the subject is punishment and revenge (also possibly a reaction against American conservatives who refused to get involved in the growing problems in Europe; or simply about bad hotels and pool halls too far off the main road).

In Fleischer's *The Fresh Vegetable Mystery* (1939), all the characters live in a vegetable larder. A mysterious creature, like the sinister "Shadow" on radio, kidnaps vegetable children and disappears. An alarm is sounded. Irish potato cops roll out of a sack to solve the crime. They round up the usual suspects and torture each vegetable by crushing or scraping it with a household appliance. One hoodlum, an egg with a broken nose, is dropped into boiling water. But you can't break me, he says, "I'm already hard-boiled."

Even some of the gentlest cartoons from the period have that insistent quality, like *The Sunshine Makers* from Van Beuren — a melodrama about filial warmth through inoculation. One might call it the milk cure or the technicolor lobotomy. (Many more like this were made during the Second World War as well — cartoons on how to de-program Nazis.)

But this is 1936, mid-Depression. A village of happy dairy elves, who all look related, like a family, fight the nasty blue grumpies. Every dark grumpy wears the familiar uniform of the evil fiend (again, like theatrical melodrama: the black suit with tails, and the bent top hat). To make the grumpies smile, the effervescently cheerful elves fire happy milk as artillery, or rather as anti-depressants. Once a grumpy is hit, he has to smile. The happy milk literally shakes those blue colors away, and the grim Depression gets a lift.

Lessons must be taught against one's will, democracy in vigilance. At the same time, these are grim jokes indeed: the crueler the punishment, the truer the message. I suspect that the cautionary cartoon simply evolved out of the nuisance/controller gambit left over from the twenties, and blended uncomfortably with domestic melodrama. In cartoons from 1936 to 1939 (not to mention poor Wile E. Coyote later), all sorts of devilish machines are invented to teach children a lesson. In *A Waif's Welcome* (again, from Van Beuren), the "cruel boy" learns his lesson by accidentally setting fire to his own house.

In another cautionary cartoon, the nasty father won't play with his son, so the father is tortured in his sleep. He dreams he has been sent to trial in a court run by children. The jury warns in an immigrant singsong: "You went to college but you have no knowledge." You make your son brush his teeth and "massage his gums." The father is haunted like Scrooge at midnight. A trio of witnesses chant in Yiddish accents: "Mental, dental, it's inconsequential." Finally, the grumpy father is found guilty by a four-year-old judge. He is condemned to torture. In a cross between the Inquisition and the assembly-line, he is beaten constantly by a rotating machine. With each revolution of the steel arms, he grows younger, until at last he is a squawling infant himself. The adult learns first hand about child abuse. Then the dream stops. Screaming like an infant in his dream, the father finally wakes up. And like Scrooge after the nightmare is over, he learns to be kind to kids from then on.

I imagine the entire family watching these cartoons together in 1936, between a double bill. Would the mother lean over and say: "See son, you might be tortured if you don't shape up"? Perhaps. I am a parent living in a more permissive age, tortured by books on child development.

These cartoons reduce melodrama into one obligatory scene, and stretch the message continually, like a dog barking outside all night: see how the wicked are punished. The punishment replaces much of the story, and is made very vivid, like a long spanking. Poetic justice is written literally on the body of the evil-doer. (I cannot resist reminding the reader of Kafka's frightening satire of the nineteenth-century cautionary tale, *The Penal Colony*, of Poe's fascination with the rhythm of cautionary fiction, and Lewis Carroll's objections to its messages. There is some complexity in these tiny, manic explosions of punishment.)

Indeed, the cautionary tale reduces the essential ingredients of melodrama into a simple on/off switch, rather like the nuisance/over-reactor/controller I have already discussed. We simply add another "function" — the conscience. To display morality, the graphics concentrate on the problems inside the conscience of the child, with justice correcting the child's black soul in the end. Like domestic melodrama, it is a very chastening way to tell a story. It is also obstinately rational in its way. The good characters have to exhibit (or learn at terrible expense) great lucidity of conscience. To make cautionary stories follow clearly, random gags were taken out. Other changes became equally helpful. A more painterly style of graphics suited the full poses needed for moral discovery. And while the characters still had to dance as nimbly as Mickey or Betty, they had to use nimble facial muscles as well. We have to see their inner discovery, after they are morally regenerated. After all, how can you regenerate a character whose face cannot express guilt? Linear ambiguity was too amoral, lacked personality, and therefore hurt the dramatic structure of cartoon melodrama.

Let me review where this argument has gone. In the mid-thirties, a moral element is added to cartoons, which was relatively absent earlier. In order to add moral instruction, cartoon studios turned toward domestic melodrama, which also resembled stories in live-action cinema, and made primary use of fully animated faces and gestures. A number of needs were satisfied at the same time. Of course, the shift was not always comfortable. This is not surprising when one considers what the cartoon had been like earlier. Ultimately, the antic forms of animation returned, but only after the graphics and story formulas had been radically changed, with no way to revive the talkie cartoon, nor much interest in doing so. The cartoon moved from vaudeville gags to movie melodrama, with cinematic references added. Now, audiences could see more cartoons about troubled consciences that needed mending. From 1936 to 1940, dozens of cartoons about troubled conscience were made, even with something of a vengeance. But in social-historical terms, all this was essentially a transition toward full animation, in graphics, story, allusion, and marketing.

DRAWING FROM LIVE ACTION

Disney led the way in expanding personality animation to include melodrama. In fact, even after cartoon melodrama was exhausted and was replaced by the hyper-chase cartoon, by 1940, Disney hung on. For another twenty-five years, that high seriousness rarely left his work, and only in the 1980s did it begin to cease at the live-action end of the Disney studio.

Here is an anecdote to explain how, in the late thirties, animators shifted their graphics toward movie melodrama. As the reader will recall, on Wednesday nights, Walt would show popular films at his studio, mostly comedies, to the animators in particular. Animators would notice a gesture or a gag and try it out. For example, Frank Thomas had to show Pinocchio cringing when Stromboli locked him in a cage.

Walt often assigned the human characters to Thomas, who had magnificent drafting skills for the human form. He also had a great feel for the dramatic human gesture, not as zany over-reaction, but a pose based closely on how human beings respond.

One Wednesday, Thomas saw the film *Captain Courageous*, with Freddy Bartholomew weeping in shock as Spencer Tracy is bitten by a shark. (Here is a film that suits this chapter — a full blend of all the forms of melodrama in cartoons: cautionary and domestic crisis in a setting for costume adventure.) As the boy witnesses the shark attack, his head swings back almost convulsively. The pose looked perfect for Pinocchio. The next morning, Thomas had the projectionist run through the last two reels until he found that scene again. Then he applied those gestures to the moment where Pinocchio realizes he has ignored his conscience and will never be released from his cage — that same turn of the neck and gaping horror.

DOMESTIC MELODRAMA AFTER 1940

Obviously, Disney continues to work in domestic melodrama after 1940, in a long series of features. By the late thirties, however, the vogue for melodrama was declining. Fleischer made a New Deal melodrama, just before the studio closed down. It was their last cartoon feature, *Mr. Bug Goes to Town* (December 1941). Hoppity the grasshopper (styled after James Stewart) fights urbanization and land fraud to save his gal, Honey Bee, and his fellow bugs. The story opens in a bug neighborhood in Manhattan (a sub-level small town). After a few happy songs, and a lover's date at a bug nightclub, evil takes over. Mr C. Bagley Beetle, a thick-shelled capitalist, kidnaps Hoppity and manipulates land futures. Then, with no one left to fight, and the truth well hidden, he forces Honey to marry him. Luck takes a hand, though, to guarantee poetic justice. At the climax, just as Mr Beetle is about to take over entirely, a machine crushes the altar. The "human ones" flatten everything, to make way for a skyscraper.

What follows is probably the strongest moment in the film, not as melodrama, more as Fleischer and machinery. Monstrous steel claws disembowl the bugs' neighborhood. A giant back-hoe wrenches a screenful of gravel filled with tumbling bugs. Afterward, nothing of the bug neighborhood is left. Even Mr Beetle's property is uprooted. Then the skyscraper goes up, steel eye beams in slashing diagonals similar to the graphics in Superman cartoons which Fleischer made at the same time.

Those scenes remind me of the Great Depression re-enacted: even the cruel speculators are swallowed by the Great Crash. Then an ant-trail exodus moves like a miniature grapes of wrath. At last, the refugees find a new home in a penthouse garden. (I also see allusions to decay in the old urban centers, and to identifying the future with skyscrapers and modern architecture. But I'll say more about that in chapter 22, on UPA and the fifties.) It is a cartoon about fighting urban renewal, with a weak melodramatic story.

Fleischer's Popeye, however, is another matter altogether. There is not much melodrama in Popeye cartoons. They remain as gruff as ever throughout the thirties, a confirmation from swashbuckler cartoons from before 1934. Popeye remains the sailor adventurer, who mumbles to himself in a South Jersey accent.

And in Popeye, I find elements that point towards what replaced cartoon melodrama. Popeye and Bluto take turns demolishing each other. Bluto is windmilled, boxed, flattened, and knocked generally across the screen, not unlike the chase cartoons of the forties. In Popeye, we sense how the transition might work, by mixing swashbuckler adventure with cautionary melodrama. That blend, I believe, helps explain the phenomenal popularity of Popeye from 1935 until the forties.[8] In Popeye, we can see a precursor of the chase: faster action, with more eccentric use of dialogue (his constant mumbling), and zany revenge, where characters turn into machines of war.

Also, unlike melodrama about the family, Fleischer's Popeye is utterly incapable of moral doubt, as is Bluto. They are mean machines, like chase characters of the forties, who are too breathlessly on the run to feel remorse (and too primitive for the complexities of the full-scale chase cartoon).

Olive Oyl also seems devoid of moral judgement. Unlike Disney's Snow White or Minnie, she spends most of her time making crabby demands, swooning for cheap materialism, or simply screaming for help, while her size 15 shoes kick in all directions. She wants what she wants, not unlike Daffy or Bugs. When Popeye and Bluto leave in a cloud of disaster at the end of one cartoon, she complains: "There goes the navy," but then brightens cynically, and says: "But there's always the army!"

Family is annoying to Popeye. In *Lil' Swee Pea* (1936), the baby crawls through an obstacle course of near-disasters. Finally, a wilted Popeye returns Swee Pea happily to Olive. Popeye is thrilled *not* to belong to Olive's family, and asks the audience frankly why anyone would even want a child. There's not much melodrama there.

But melodrama is not a system of absolute homogenity either. It is not nearly as symmetrical and balanced as it may seem. The illusion of life keeps springing leaks. Indeed, in early Disney features, that uneven illusionism added excitement for the viewer, not because the screen looked lacy and controlled, but because it seemed to be exploding with contradictions. *Snow White* was virtuously and impossibly overloaded, and that added life, as we shall see in the next chapter.

ADDENDUM: A NOTE ON TECHNICOLOR

In 1931, Disney made a contract with the foundering Technicolor Company, and re-made *Flowers and Trees* in three-strip technicolor. This was not the first color cartoon. Ub Iwerks had already tried a two-strip color almost a year earlier; and there had been some tinted cartoons in the twenties. But Disney's Technicolor did set the standard, even while no one but Disney could make color cartoons for four years, until Disney's exclusive lease with Technicolor expired. By 1935, color had become the state of the art. Every animation studio had to provide at least one series in three-strip color.

At first, color was used almost exclusively for musical numbers with melodramatic stories, led by Disney's Silly Symphonies, of course. In color, the cautionary fantasy took on a new moral weight and a new power.

Obviously, color adds an illusionism to cartoons that gives them a new novelty. And just as sound had initially heightened the anarchic possibilities of graphic narrative, so color enhances the miniature movie fullness of cartoon melodrama. Color gives the story a certain solidity, clear boundaries for moral discovery. It advances cartoons into the atmosphere and moral weight one found in live-action cinema.

As of 1935, however, the process was only half-developed. To explain what I mean, we return to *Waif's Welcome*. The orphan looks in from the cold, through the frosted window. Gillette has used color in peculiar ways that enhance the moral distinctions needed for this cautionary cartoon. For example, the indoors and outdoors are heavily contrasted — the frost versus domestic warmth. It is a moral tale about opposites; and these opposites are rock solid. The walls are thick, not rubbery like the multimorphic cartoons a few years earlier. Inside the house, we find yellow light; outside, variations of blue.

The fire that nearly destroys the house is revealing as well. Flames dancing across pianos or bookshelves are a very common gag for the mid-thirties (at Disney and even at Warners). It is a palette announcing the novelty of color — the shades of yellow and a range of shadows.

And yet, it is a transitional use of color as well. The flames themselves are still very rubbery, compared to what will be standard five years later. The fire bounces like custard drops, and is put out by a bluish, still inky water.

What has changed from the color cartoons of, say, 1930? First of all, the cartoon screen is framed differently, not like a comic strip at all. In Ub Iwerks' cartoons, in two-strip color, the background still looks like a comic strip panel, as Jack climbs the beanstalk (quite a contrast to Mickey climbing the lush and swaying beanstalk a few years later). In *A Waif's Welcome*, the magic square of the cartoon screen looks solid, more like pie dough than paper. It looks supported by construction lumber. It has become a "fictive stage," or should I say a fictive sound studio? Beams and bricks have replaced lines and hatching.

Obviously, the classic transition is the brick house of the smart pig in Disney's *Three Little Pigs*, the cartoon that changed the animation industry. That brick house required a volume and solidity in color that made the old graphic narrative obsolete. Also, the use of color as metamorphosis was well noted. One film critic, Lewis Jacob, remembered how "the wolf trying to blow down the house . . . literally blew himself blue in the face; ... changing hues with each of the dramatic developments."[8] Jacobs felt that devices of this sort helped convince the entire film industry of the potential of color as drama.

Color seemed to announce the freedom of cartoons from the ink and paper. So instead of a graphic narrative, one entered a simulated environment, quite a difference in gags, story, and rhythm — so much so that it took about five years for animators to find a way to accommodate to it, for melodramas and for anarchic chases alike.

But more on that later on. For now, we enter the variations of cartoon melodrama in the era of Shirley Temple, and, latterly, of Andy Hardy. We will hop from Disney to Warners, from the high style of cartoon melodrama to the "anti-melodrama" of the new slapstick chase cartoon.

For the moment, let us deal with Disney from 1934 to 1940, the power of amber light against the whiteness of Snow White. We enter the cartoon version of thunderous adventure and sensational incident — melodrama on the multiplane camera. We enter the simulated atmosphere, with light, shadow, differentiated volumes and substances. And we enter a new stage in the business end of making cartoons.

CHAPTER TWELVE

The Whiteness of Snow White

What does Disney's *Snow White* add to the seven-minute cartoon? And what does it take away? Let us gloss over the usual anecdotes: the twenty million who paid to see it in the first three months; the fortune ($1.5 million) Disney poured into the project over three years; the creation of the seven dwarfs wrinkle by wrinkle; the toyland nostalgia their happy walk brings to mind (heigh-ho).

To make the film, Disney tripled his staff and paid for at least three million working hours. Some two million cels were produced and only 250,000 finally chosen, an unheard of extravagance for animation, where the number of cels was usually predetermined before going to the camera.[1]

New cameras were designed. Production techniques were scrutinized, from layout to storyboard, to the movement of characters. The Disney art program was expanded. Special lecturers were brought in, including Frank Lloyd Wright (who apparently was not that impressive, and advised using more of the inspirational sketches and keeping roughs in the final product). Don Graham led a countrywide search for talent, though many of the new recruits came from the nearby Chouinard Institute in downtown Los Angeles.

Animators were expected to study live-action films very carefully for lighting, staging, editing. Like a Hollywood movie, this cartoon would look "real." By real, Disney meant, as was generally understood in the animation industry, the *movement* would look life-like.

Backgrounds had to look "real" as well, though that was a knotty problem. Disney wanted softer colors for the background, what we might call earthen tones. Otherwise, the colors would pull the audience away from the action. But he also demanded exhaustive detailing on the wood, the shadows, the cartoon weather.

Every painted corner was supposed to fit into the story, or the "locale." Walt was convinced, as if driven by a Kantian imperative, that he could feel what a true faerie interior needed. Rooms and forest settings were taken directly from Victorian versions of fairy tales (and from German eighteenth-century interiors themselves). In no other film of that era were period details hammered out so fastidiously, like tin plate, scene by scene.

And yet, what comes out is not an integrated film at all. Instead, one is confronted by a bewilderingly overwrought surface. In fact, that is its power, to compress shelves of merchandise inside a single store window.

These contradictions are not "flaws." They add tone and a very physical sense of entry into a "real" space. They are a syntax based on painting, and a Disney brand of architectural fantasy. They make *Snow White* a unique experience on the screen, a space ride into a Disneyland of ink and watercolor.

As soon as the opening credits pass, and the white book opens, one enters the film as if through a ride, through layers of background. The light sources vibrate like stained glass windows. And the landscape, however naturalistic, seems planted inside a vaulted room, along with rain and sunlight.

The landscaping resembles a botanical interior, designed to fit inside an air-conditioned movie theater, or even a sound studio. Later, as the dwarfs cross a bridge at dusk, atmospheric lighting and exaggerated perspective suggest a huge terrarium.

Inside that terrarium, the natural is "caricatured" (Disney's expression). Slapstick mime and Victorian claptrap collide, gracefully, like a crash in slow motion. From pulchinelles to Victorian heroines, the fairy tale in painted filigree comes to life.

Let us refresh our memories on the film, run through the first reel essentially.

A white leather book opens to the illustrated page, which becomes the cartoon. We find Snow White scrubbing the palace steps. She helps the birds. The prince comes to woo her, singing in that handsome tenor. She runs away demurely.

Meanwhile, the evil queen consults the magic mirror and is told that Snow White is the fairest of them all. The scene darkens as the queen seethes with jealousy. We intercut between gothic interiors and pale watercolor landscapes (utterly different graphic styles laid side by side). Finally, the queen calls the huntsman. She orders him to kill Snow White and bring back her heart.

We shift to Snow White alone in the woods. Suddenly, long shadows move across her back. The huntsman surprises her. As she turns he glowers like a madman, and lifts his knife. The blade glints; he seems on the point of killing her.

Then, the huntsman pauses. Stricken with conscience, he cannot go through with the murder. Instead, burying his head in shame, he warns the princess to flee far away from the queen.

Snow White is hysterically confused. She doesn't know where to turn first. She sees danger on all sides — a unique scene, one of the last times Disney used thirties metamorphosis and animism. The limbs of trees and eyes of forest animals surround her in sweeping diagonals, and jagged shapes. Cartoon lapse dissolves add to the ghostly mystery-ride effects.

Finally, in the morning, a happier movie begins. Snow White awakens refreshed. The forest has been transformed into a very hospitable version of Disney Nouveau. Animals recognize her instantly as the heroine, and make friends. She wonders where she can stay and the animals pull back bushes into a clearing.

She gets her first glimpse of the dwarfs' cottage and rushes to visit. No one is home, so she breaks in, with only the best intentions, because once she sees the mess, nothing can hold her back. She was born to clean (a simple heart in a noble body). Quickly, she commandeers the animals to help. In no time at all, everyone is whistling while they work. Tails start dusting; beaks lift clothes or stack dishes. In the midst of all this activity, one awkward turtle gets spun on his shell (he seems to be drawn in an older, more linear style, a refugee from an earlier slapstick cartoon).

Then we meet the dwarfs for the first time. They're hard at work too, syncopated along a happy assembly-line. Nature's bounty is at arm's reach, diamonds as easy to gather as seashells. In a free enterprise system like ours, it's a joy to be petit bourgeois — and sharp as a tack besides (except for Dopey, who fools around too much).

At the end of the work day, a cuckoo clock screeches (a gag we find in other Disney cartoons of the period, like *The China Shop* [1935], or, later, *Pinocchio*: the ironic contrast between mechanical toys and lifelike movement).

"Heigh-ho! Heigh-ho!" The dwarfs sing as they leave for home. They cross a bridge against an orange sunset (with vertical waterfall, one of many virtuosic watery effects). But when they arrive home, their cottage looks suspiciously clean. Also, a monster has taken up residence in their bedroom upstairs. Every dwarf shakes with fear. After a short conference, Dopey is shoved up the steps to spy on the monster (it seems to be hiding under the blankets — another very common gag in thirties cartoons).

Of course, the monster is not scary at all; it turns out to be a very "purty" lady sleeping (Snow White will regularly nod off when the going gets tough, a sign of her delicate nature). The dwarfs are stunned, but Grumpy warns: "All females is poison. They're full a wicked wiles." When asked to describe "wicked wiles," Grumpy sparks defensively: "I don't know, but I'm agin' em."

At home, the dwarfs are essentially "seven untidy children," as Snow White has guessed earlier — seven unworldly little men in need of maternal care.

Finally, Snow White awakens (cheerful as always — obviously a morning person). She meets the dwarfs formally, guessing their names one at a time. Her "gentle grace" wins them over very quickly (except for Grumpy, whom everyone ignores anyway).

The dwarfs decide to take her in, particularly after they smell the food she is cooking. But first they have to get more civilized. Like Little Rascals and Huck Finn, they need to scrub up for Aunt Polly — wash hands and face to sit for dinner. Everyone but Grumpy gives in. Finally, even Grumpy is soaped at the well, against his will — possibly the most brilliant animation of water ever put on the screen. A new domestic era begins for the dwarfs, rather like entering kindergarten or watching the first highway linking up a small town.

That ends the first reel, a suitable place to stop, for our purposes, to examine what I call the anarchic qualities of *Snow White*. The scenes look astonishingly fluid to the eye, but the graphics — frame by frame — are very disjointed. Three conflicting media fight for the same space at the same time:

1. *Live action*: The character Snow White is "painted" like a photo. She is practically a *live-action character*, not quite rotoscoped, but nearly so.
2. *Animation*: The dwarfs are "drawn" like a cel. They are entirely *cartoon men*, obstinately hand-worked, with linear, mobile faces and complex follow-through (personality animation).
3. *Shop window*: The forest is "layered" like a sound stage or a fantasy store, particularly in those scenes that use the multiplane camera. A *machina versatilis*, like a robotized watercolor, encloses everything inside exaggerated depth of field. It resembles the Disney theme-parks to come, or special-effects films of the late seventies.

In other words: the painted photograph (Snow White) curtsies to drawings (the dwarfs), between layers of glass, in some scenes inside a 14-foot metal chamber (the multiplane camera).

Disney was well aware of these contradictions. The backgrounds looked too round. The characters looked much too flat. A battery of new camouflages had to be developed; if not, the contrasts would overwhelm the illusion. Pure black was virtually removed, particularly in outlining. And the background had to be pushed forward to surround the foreground somehow. Like stage lighting, an animated atmosphere covered up the cracks, made it look whole. Otherwise, the mishmash could create a new brand of mad slapstick, as indeed it did in Warners chase cartoons a few years later. With full animation, the possibilities for anarchy are multiplied, not reduced. That is why Disney's achievement, set firmly against the grain, is so striking.

It was dangerous to make the cartoon too life-like. Animators were told to work from live-action film, frame by frame, but very freely. The live footage had to serve mostly as a gauge for timing the movement. Only the dwarfs were drawn entirely without live moviola sketches (among the principal characters); and they look it. Some vaudeville entertainers were brought in to cavort like dwarfs in front of the animators, but not studied frame by frame. One clown, a favorite from local vaudeville, was famous for his ridiculously long and nimble tongue; later, his tongue was added to Dopey's face.

The dwarfs are brilliantly *unreal*, or should I say cartoon real? They move like masked waterbags. They constantly fall victim to their sagging faces or unnatural body weight. Gravity seems to attack them more densely than Snow White, as if they lived on a different planet altogether.

But as cartoon protoplasm, no character seems more *unreal* than Snow White. She seems made of some rare phosphorous alloy. She is so much whiter than anything around her; she reminds me of glowing condensed milk. Only the evil queen is as classically white.

Snow White is so encumbered with audience memories from other sources, her body matter dissolves. No character in the film is as overcoded. Every neat wrinkle in her middy blouse seems to comment on the ideals of princesshood. She radiates her pure intentions: her fragility; kindness to little animals; maternal domesticity.

It took animators two years to design all of these qualities into Snow White (primarily by Ham Luske and Grim Natwick, with Marc Davis his assistant). In the end, she wound up almost translucent, like a frosted cameo from a Fragonard painting — the sort one might find in a Victorian parlor. When she walks through the dwarfs' cottage, with its earnest browns and umbers, her body glows like a porcelain lamp — not just with virginity, but also with her trust in the all-knowing governance of Nature. She works hard and keeps a clean house. From the first scene, she never gets uppity like a princess. We find her on her knees, scrubbing the palace, doing a happy penance. She is the patron saint of small birds who guide her and help her dust. In making Snow White camera-ready, as a final, wholesome touch, the "gals" at Inking added "real" rouge to her cheeks — blushed it directly on to the cel itself.

SOURCES FOR THE BACKGROUNDS IN SNOW WHITE: *FANTAISSISTES* AND THE CULT OF THE PICTURESQUE

As a boy, Disney had seen a silent film version of *Snow White*, based on a cycle of revisions, from a nineteenth-century German play that was translated for American audiences by Minnie Hertyz Heniger, then redone for Broadway, and elsewhere. The original nineteenth-century look, however, what we might label a Victorian picture-book style, remained the essential setting, for Disney as well.[2] *Snow White* was a Victorian pop-up book, animated like a thirties movie, with dramatic lighting from nineteenth-century painting and from wood engraving. In looking over nineteenth-century children's books, the closest model to what Disney animators accomplished was the work of the *fantaissistes*: a term applied in the 1850s to late Romantic French illustrators, particularly Gustave Doré, the master of fantasy landscape; also to the Dalziel brothers in London, who developed folio illustration to compete with theater sets used in London melodrama. These huge coffee table journeys into wood engraved magic kingdoms were designed to look as grand as the *machina versatilis* of popular theater. They were so grand, in fact, that illustration seemed no longer subservient to print, a point well noted at the time (and afterward). When I lift one of these large volumes on to a library table, and turn the pages, the images are so spatially-oriented, they remind me of congested Victorian interiors, rooms filled with knick-knacks, shrouded in heavy drapes, fractured with end tables. These books were made with such rooms in mind, as part of the barricaded quality of domestic life at the time — high fantasy for the high industrial takeoff.

Obviously, much has been written about how Victorian the Disney films can get, about his conservative nostalgia. We must remember, though, that he was working off a tradition already in place by 1850, and surviving to the present day. The term

143

that captures this tradition most aptly is *"the cult of the picturesque."* We see chapters on it in Ruskin's writing (even in early Coleridge — a very widely developed term throughout the nineteenth century). And we see it also in travel literature and advertising — how to make the spiritual in nature. Roland Barthes expressed the problem very succinctly by calling picturesque images "mythologies." In early work,[3] he defines a mythology as an artificial image posing as natural; we are asked to appreciate certain pictures simply as entertainment, food for the heart, beyond analysis. He expanded far beyond that simple frame, of course, in two series of essays on mythologies, over many years. The earlier book ranges from toys to Garbo's face, to guidebooks, to laundry detergent. Let us simply review how he discussed laundry soap. Makers of laundry detergent will claim their product is as natural as "the great outdoors," but, obviously, detergent is an odd-smelling, industrial product which removes nature. Soap cleans the dirt nature leaves. As a mythology, the whiteness of Snow White is also something of a detergent; her presence stands in for the cult of childhood innocence in the late thirties, a laundered white that we presumably accept without reservation.

Layouts from *Snow White* are also mythologies about the picturesque. But this issue is too evident to labor over for pages. Disney translated old tourist fantasies into the backgrounds for *Snow White* (many of the research sources were antique tour books of wood engravings). Eventually, when he built Disneyland, these tourist fantasies ran full circle. The fantasy layouts were reconverted into a tourist park. They were reconstructed (or returned) to real architectural space.

By now, this space has become as American as the flag, and as universally loved as Mickey Mouse. But originally, Disney wanted a mythology about Protestant childhood, about the joys that go without saying — families being tourists together, in a world that honors the shopper's dream of a rustic childhood.

Too often, Disney is simply condemned (or praised) as the prophet of fifties suburbanism, but that assumption misses the subtlety of his achievement in *Snow White*, and what followed. The atmospheric lighting of Disney epic cartoons is very similar to the reverie of shopping, to shopping arcades, even to the permanent dusk of a room illuminated by television. It takes us more to the expanded shopping mall than a planned suburb, to a civilization based on consumer memories more than urban (or suburban) locations. In recent years, of course, even old industrial cities are being planned as if they were shopping malls — gentrified, as the term suggests (made white for consumer safety, to encourage shopping fun). That is Disney's achievement, to invent consumer-scapes as an architectural idea; the city on an animated hill, like a mental postcard, lined with electronic billboards, and available also as a video game. Disney showed us how to stop thinking of a city as residential or commercial, but rather as airbrushed streets in our mind's eye, a shopper's non-scape. If we can make a city remind us of animated consumer memory, it removes the alienation of changing cities, and replaces it with a cloud of imaginary store windows.

144

Snow White was the next step for Disney after the merchandising of Mickey Mouse, from a world logo to a world made entirely of nostalgic shopping architecture — corporatized fantasy on the scale of an invented civilization. I do not believe Disney planned it quite that way, but Disney with *Snow White* began the process that eventually mixes consumer memory with urban planning. He pioneered the complete intersection between electronic media and architectural space that we all know very well today.

CHAPTER THIRTEEN

Full Animation: Putting Clouds into Exterior Scenes

The sub-title to this chapter is taken from the title of an essay written by a cinematographer with Twentieth Century-Fox in 1944. "A landscape that includes a cloud-flecked sky is far more attractive than the same scene without clouds," he explains. Movie skies are too monotone without clouds inserted. So it becomes necessary to "'dupe' in the clouds after scenes are made."[1]

Through glass transparencies, the sky is matched appropriately. This is one of many special effects developed in the thirties, for films shot inside sound studios. Consider how much of the first four minutes of *Citizen Kane* uses mattes, ending with the animated sensation of entering a glass ball — simulation through lapse dissolve — how much of the film exploited animation techniques. The Bazinian space, so often an argument for a "realism" in cinema, was also an *animated* space, in Hollywood anyway — Lumière and Méliès as a hybrid.

The importance of animated space in Hollywood movie-making of the period 1937–45 cannot be overstated. Most of the effects came directly through animation, "such as putting lights into night shots of moving objects — boats, trains, headlights of automobiles, gag shots, bullets shattering automobile windshields, animated map diagrams, flashing letters and signs, and practically everything that can not be done on the set in regular production."[2]

Traveling mattes were used to combine people and moving objects, to have buildings fall on them in earthquakes, to show forest fires. Stationary mattes, or rear projection, could put an ocean in the blackness behind a couple while they stared lovingly at each other. Storm effects involved fog and wind machines, but also dupes of photographs. If the weather in an exterior didn't behave, they could adjourn the shoot indoors, and dupe the rest in later. Miniatures allowed autos to go over a cliff or get struck by a train. Much of this was added precisely at the time that full animation was developing — a general trend toward "depth of field" or complexity of lighting and movement.

Beside animation, the lighting in sound studio films grew more elaborate as well as the thirties progressed. One might call this "optical" animation. Clearly, a "fuller"

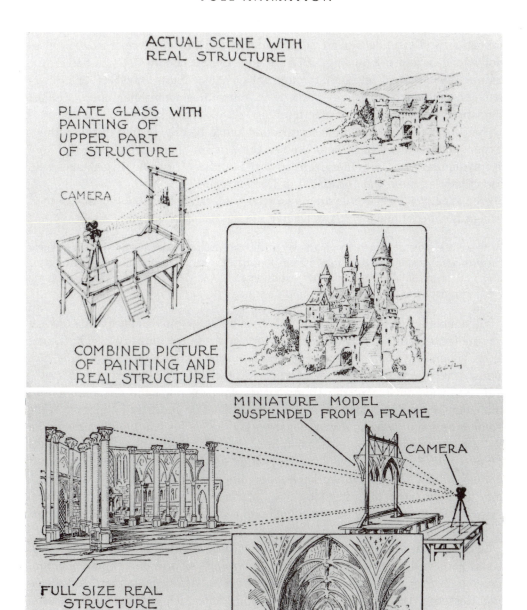

ACTUAL SCENE WITH
REAL STRUCTURE

PLATE GLASS WITH
PAINTING OF
UPPER PART
OF STRUCTURE

CAMERA

COMBINED PICTURE
OF PAINTING AND
REAL STRUCTURE

MINIATURE MODEL
SUSPENDED FROM A FRAME

CAMERA

FULL SIZE REAL
STRUCTURE

COMBINED PICTURE
OF MINIATURE MODEL
AND REAL STRUCTURE

Two examples of film mattes before the coming of sound, both similar to the layering
of cels to background in animation; or to multiplane cameras of the thirties.
(a) Glass transparency.
(b) Model shot.

animation was essential for an understanding of Hollywood cinema, as well as Hollywood cartoons. And since 1977, the look of that late thirties film has grown enormously important yet again, through links made by Lucas, Spielberg, and others between animation and live action film: miniatures, computer effects, object animation, closer to monochrome lighting.

The concept of full animation in cartoons has to be appreciated in this setting. It came out of a moment (1934–40) when the lyricism of animated space was very deeply appreciated, whether from a von Sternberg or from Eisenstein, who particularly admired the "lyricism" of Disney in 1940.

Even as early as 1936, a Yale drama professor, Allardyce Nicoll, wrote that cartoon "magic is not confined entirely to Disney's fantasies has already become clear ..."

By means of simple camera tricks a man may be shown walking upside down, striding serenely across a cloud, rising wingless into the air. Reinhardt's fairies soared aloft like aeroplanes after a little run for take-off; René Clair's spirit in *The Ghost Goes West* was at will seemingly solid or transparent.[3]

Full animation was a corollary of "full" sound-stage movie space. This linkage was understood fairly routinely by crafts people in the movie industry, also by theater set designers, by many directors in both live action and animation. To the film industry at large, animation was the vital craft that created elastic time and space, and the inside/outside of the sound stage. And in much the same spirit, full animation became standard throughout the animation industry after *Snow White* (sometimes more cheaply, sometimes more lavishly). This was big business in the era of bigger studios, a necessary overhead. Many cheaper animation techniques left over from the pre-sound era (again, graphic narrative; simpler merry-go-round stories) suddenly became unworkable, according to new systems of production. A very different set of priorities took over. Markets shifted; audience expectations changed. Much was, quite simply, wiped out, and by 1939 entirely replaced, almost as if it had never existed.

All this sounds like a vast improvement on the face of it. But certainly for cartoons, it was not simply a progression forward. It was also a form of corporate erasure, forced by circumstance. And these changes were not nearly as standardized as one might assume. Disney, Warners, MGM, and Lantz each applied full animation differently. And each look also changed a great deal from year to year.

Instead of an eternal, nominative case (a single grammar), we find a slang as changeable as the daily newspaper (or the movie set). The new graphics arrived in the mid-thirties, marked by the pressures of the Great Depression; and kept shifting its effects for another twenty years. There was not one "full animation": there were many. They varied according to studio and according to year.

That gave full animation extraordinary vitality. It was fractured, confabulated, and marvelously confused. And we honor its contradictions: gags moved at breakneck speed, generally faster than ever before or since. At the same time, gags moved very slowly, because full animation also invested a nostalgic epic style, which has cost the cartoon industry dearly. Walt gave, and Walt took away.

GRAPHICS: ADDING ATMOSPHERE

Full animation added so many elements foreign to the linear (or graphic narrative) tradition, the line itself was swollen and set afloat. Staging and layout lost what had been a rather simple formula. In cartoons before 1934, the drawing surface was fairly uniform. There were essentially only two contrasts: a soft background and a darkly outlined foreground, both as uniform in their way as flat latex walls. The background often resembled a vaudeville curtain or a scrim. The foreground moved like a comic strip. One surface fit conveniently behind the other, like cards shuffling.

In full animation, that simple program was broken apart into any number of "atmospheres." By atmosphere I mean a layout that suggests how the air, mist, and gravity should be seen. Previously, these had been omitted, as whimsical surprises. Now they had to be spelled out, in contrary mixtures, even in the same frame occasionally, as in *Mickey's Grand Opera*, a transitional example from 1936.

Donald is blundering his way through operatic recitative when, suddenly, Pluto runs on stage. The show is interrupted. Meanwhile, from the orchestra pit, Mickey as conductor watches, appalled. Pluto realizes his mistake gradually, then shivers, as the theater spotlight makes him obvious (also obviously painted, more like oil slicked on fur than light bathing a scene). Mickey (in flatter graphic, without shadow) tells Pluto to leave. Pluto is self-consciously round; Mickey is politely flat, as if no infrared light could ever reach him. Foreground and background seem to exist in very different atmospheres. The dramatic lighting on Pluto is so exaggerated, he looks trapped inside an isolated space lab, with outer space around him.

In some cartoons, the atmospheres were relatively consistent (Fleischer's Superman series, for example; though even there, the volumes of the faces can vary enormously from scene to scene; or when ray-guns blast). For the most part, however, the space and volume can be very contrary in full animation; and became even more so as the arsenal of techniques grew, year by year, from 1934 on.

Animators, layout and story men all found this variety very useful. It added new possibilities for gags: distances would collapse and telescope out quite suddenly; air quality might go from lunar to tropical — even in the same frame.

Atmospheric gags in full animation remind me of the early paragraphs in Italo Calvino's tale "The Distance of the Moon," a love story about conflicting atmospheres. Once upon a time, the moon existed only 100 feet off the earth. Then, quite suddenly, the tides pushed it up into its orbit. The tide and the moon conflict.

Round meets flat, with lunar lighting and plural gravities. Student animators particularly enjoy this story. It reads like an exercise. Two atmospheres meet at a single point. Consider how easily full animation might show these atmospheres lying on top of each other, as cels. The moon nearby dominates the background, like a floating island. It looks mysterious and yet, very ordinary — close enough to walk on or catch fish. Calvino writes:[4]

The spot where the Moon was lowest, as she went by, was off the Zinc Cliffs. We used to go out with those little rowboats they had in those days .... [Then at night] the water was very calm, so silvery it looked like mercury, and the fish in it, violet-colored. [Unable] to resist the Moon's attraction, [they] rose to the surface, all of them, and so did the octupuses and the saffron medusas. There was always a flight of tiny creatures — little crabs, squid, and even some weeds, light and filmy, and coral plants — that broke from the sea and ended up on the Moon, hanging down from that lime-white ceiling, or else they stayed in midair, a phosphorescent swarm we had to drive off, waving banana leaves at them.

How might someone animate these effects, primarily through the art department? A great deal of shading would be needed to capture the mist and conflicting atmospheres, the flashes of lightning across a body: by airbrushes, new tempera paints, Japanese greased crayon for rain; also with help from an effects department, at Disney; and new techniques in photography, various ranges of exposure. Otherwise, in a strictly linear style, the air would simply be made of paper, like the storyboard sketch, instead of teeming with primeval contraction. This shading would probably need full animation, where gravity has a specific weight, volume, speed, and can exert pressure on foreign objects. In full animation, the atmosphere can change or divide. One character breathes air; another breathes ink. A third never breathes at all, but simply exists in living watercolor. The foreground might be ink, the background naturalistic (or vice versa).

These contradictions made a new range of allusion possible, not simply comic strip versus vaudeville stage. Any number of media might be represented inside the same cartoon, even the same frame. An imaginary *movie* camera pans across an object that resembles an *oil painting*, or an *engraving*, or a *poster*, a *photograph*. The source does not seem to matter, as long it adds volume and atmosphere, makes the image look "full."

And a single atmosphere might be unstable for technical reasons as well. After all, how could dozens of artists, each in their own hand, keep all these variables entirely consistent for 24 frames per second (12 frames per 24 usually); and keep that going for 500–700 feet of film? Obviously, they never could.

Also, in the late thirties, there was still no way to print directly on the cel and thereby avoid some of the variation. According to Thomas and Johnston, the nitrate film "caused an unpredictable amount of shrinkage on each picture."[5]

With no consistency from one cel to the next, the quality of the whole process was in constant jeopardy. Walt continued to search for a way to make backgrounds three-dimensional, or having them animated in changing perspective on several pictures. While this gave startling effects for individual scenes, it further separated the flat characters on the cels from the rounded forms in the background by contrasting the two different techniques.

At first, full animation was slightly off-register. This helps explain why *Snow White* has a shimmering effect so different from Disney features of the fifties and after. We seem to sense a flicker, a pulse that adds even more charm.

As of the late thirties, full animation was "full" because it teemed with conflicting answers to a perceptual problem — how to give the hand-drawn surface a quilted density. It was collage redrawn to look like a single image. The more vividly its surface changed, the more it seemed to breathe life into the story.

Even *Pinocchio* was uneven (to its credit, in many ways). In a climactic sequence, we find Pinocchio and Gepetto inside Monstro the whale. The atmosphere (layout) is painted like a movie matte. To escape, Pinocchio and Gepetto set fire to their boat. They force Monstro to sneeze them out to sea, where the whale chases them furiously.

Once outside, however, drawing styles are shifted radically. The water looks more like a Japanese woodblock print. Even the thrashing by the whale looks different, like a Currier and Ives lithograph laid over a wood-engraved sea. Each medium is copied with stunning effect: the interior of the whale; the foaming sea. Frame by frame, they constrast very obviously. Even on the screen, if we pause to watch, the different atmospheres are unmistakable — and quite an astonishing achievement.

I also remind the reader that *Pinocchio* has the most sustained full animation of that era. And yet, very often, its layouts were so dissimilar from scene to scene, they seem to lift us from one movie simultaneously into another. Not until films of the late eighties, like *Blue Velvet*, have so many filmic atmospheres fought for our attention simultaneously on a single movie screen.

Nothing quite as eccentric appeared in live-action features of the late thirties. However much full animation strove to look cinematic, fortunately, it still wound up very much a cartoon. Scenes were still fitted together a bit crazily. The "acting" came on ridiculously broader than live film. Moods were enhanced like a quick injection by a nurse. Suddenly, the air went from heavy to lunar. Point of view seemed to vary according to species, like fly vision versus frog vision.

We find much the same in *Dumbo*, scenes that hop from bright circus poster to chiarascuro. The work day at the circus is over. The three-ring spectacle, in full makeup and bright colors, has been put aside. Now, at night, the proletarian clowns get drunk together. As we hear them yell in high Brooklynese, the chiarascuro of the night looks entirely different from the poster colors of the day, a jump to another movie.

Disjunctions like that are rare in live action. If we saw jumps as erratic as that in films other than cartoon, we might worry that some drunken editor had spliced together two films from the wrong tables (or perhaps made a music video).

AMAZING GRACE

Full animation is quintessentially an art of intrusion, held together by wonderful knockabout — leaps and pratfalls as graceful as Astaire/Rogers, Keaton, or Chaplin. That exaggerated grace, particularly in madly implausible situations, gives full animation the tensions of an acrobat walking the tightrope. The acrobat wobbles for an instant. He tests our fear of falling, hovers, seems about to fall. The fully animated world also looks too controlled to stay in balance. A stormy forest looks painfully pristine — landscaped to look life a golf course; we feel the storm ready to blow everything to pieces at any minute.

The dance sequences from *Dance of the Hours* in *Fantasia* are a stunning parody of thirties dance films, as well as formal ballet. A costumed crocodile sinks as he catches a hippo ballerina leaping with infinite grace into his arms. This hippo ballerina was drawn from footage made of Marjorie Belcher dancing, in a number she also choreographed. This is the same Marge Belcher who had posed for the character of Snow White, and later The Blue Fairy in *Pinocchio*, and would eventually develop the dance team of Marge and Gower Champion. That team, by the way, began their careers hoping to dance for the movies. In fact, for a time, Howard Hughes had wanted to remake all the old Astaire/Rogers films starring Marge and Gower Champion.

Full animation is implausibly graceful, with numerous cinematic bits burned upside down. We see the kind of easy landings only possible as hand-drawn fantasy. Like a Lubitsch touch, there was a Disney touch, or a cartoon Warners touch. Bob Clampett and Frank Tashlin at Warners particularly loved to exaggerate a graceful turn: the stupid hunting dog caught in mid-leap; the wild scream held through impossible turmoil. That small pause preceded the graceful move. As another way to go, Disney would throw his characters into implausible atmospheres, and make them dance so awkwardly, they became graceful, as Goofy does in a giant bowl of jello. Goofy was very much the master of awkward grace (i.e. *Clock Cleaners*, as a I have already mentioned), his limbs like an aquatic bird attached to an eggbeater.

Full animation has a conflict inherent in the "smooth" graphics, not unlike a conflict in character or plot. Will the attempts at self-control be sustained? We know that this natural look takes great effort, or at least cannot last forever. We wait for chaos to reconquer the scene. In the meantime, however, the graceful movement demands that we hold our breath. It keeps us suspended. It looks smoother than nature itself.

Frame by frame, however, it is not smooth at all; rather schizoid in fact. It is alive with a conflict built purely out of contradictions in drawing styles. Different atmospheres translate as changes in mood: love turns to anger, hope to jealousy. When characters feel different, they leave one atmosphere and enter another, like the siren lover in Calvino's story, who floats up to the moon, then is frozen into a dream once the orbit widens. Or like the anger literalized in the following scene from a Woody Wookpecker cartoon, *Smoked Hams* (1947).

Wally the Walrus has a night job, so he sleeps during the day, or tries to, because Woody is out in the yard pounding away, even burning leaves, until the smoke invades the house. Gradually, we see Wally struggling to contain his anger (his face, as usual, is about to burst with all he's had to swallow). For the moment, he is still in control. How do we know, graphically? He still exists in full volume, even as the smoke insinuates itself brilliantly through his brass bed. Then Wally explodes. We see a raging phosphorescence — hooting bed posts, blasts of fury. He funnels into another atmosphere, where the gags must be drawn in a somewhat flatter style, with deeper colors and elaborate metamorphoses. The flatter medium stands in for anger, the rounder for Wally's anxiety as he tries to maintain self-control.

Solid versus flat: this give-and-take becomes one of many crucial story elements in full animation (blam goes Tom into a wall; his face metamorphoses from soft to hard, into a squashed frying pan. We hear his head spin like a coin on a glass table).

At the heart of full animation is the conflict between self-control and explosion, usually in short bursts throughout. Faces were supposed to show more expression, but in extremes, rather like a cartoon manic depressive. A single expression could swing from cheerful to deeply crazy in perhaps five seconds (i.e. Pluto deciding to be devious). Animators also had to be masters of a *fast* burn; there was not always enough time for slow burn. Indeed, these wild mood swings did suggest personality, as the Disney tradition suggests, but consider how crazy the moods were. No wonder they worked equally well in chase cartoons or in dramatic features.

Fully animated stories are built out of the hopeless struggle to contain anxiety in a single style. In the end anxiety loses, and we jump into another style or dimension. Which will win out, the manic face or the acrobatic movement?

Again, what held the explosions together was ridiculously graceful movement, in practical terms: more poses for a single movement. The disjunctions might go from sadism to motherly love, but they were supposed to be handled on toe in some way.

Fluid movement made transitions in character possible. Bodies could be beamed off into atmospheric space, then retrieved into abstracted flatness in a single gesture. Characters could make ideogrammatic jumps from line to movie space and back again, but land on toe, or fall as nimbly as Keaton.

Time and space did not have to fit. A ridiculous contrast was, in itself, graceful. In *Pinocchio*, the wagon of the evil Stromboli is blanketed with rain and mist as it crosses the screen. Then, suddenly, the light changes, and the air gets more dense. We feel as if we have been transported thousands of miles away, but we are really only inside the very same wagon, watching Pinocchio in his cage.

Even the characters do not look very consistent when they stand next to each other. Mickey is still more of a comic-strip drawing than Donald. No matter how chubby Mickey got, his ears could never make a three-quarter turn, never show volume. Animators tried to add depth to Mickey's ears (1942), but that created even more problems; it tampered with Mickey as logo (remember those same flat ears worn by Mouseketeers only twelve years later).

THE DANGER OF BEING PREDICTABLE

Trying for absolute continuity could be risky. Marc Davis explains that the most delicate continuity was needed for closeups. These would be left to the top animators. The running scenes did not need quite as much matching. Better to design those to allow for little alterations. No animators could be quite certain how the shadow or light would be painted. Fully animated volume was harder to control frame after frame than straight linear gags. A little shift in the aureole made by a brush could make an object, quite suddenly, much slimmer, fatter, alter the imaginary light, and ruin the effect. After all, this light existed only inside the mind of the painter, not as continuous lighting inside a sound stage. *A cartoon should resemble a sound stage, but in an upside-down way.*

Allusions to movies themselves were hard to sustain, just as elusive as "atmosphere," and just as murderously expensive. Consider the labor hours involved for any of these effects, the tricks needed, the oversimplification of story (constantly whittling away gags), the struggle to keep craziness somewhere in the cartoon, or else nobody would remember to laugh when it played. It was very apparent early on that audiences were not all that excited by a dull exercise on how many ways a rabbit swells with love (particularly since the swelling had to avoid looking sexual). While the lovestruck rabbit is busy inhaling, what happens to the gags? While struggling to look like a movie, animators tried to remember that gags must move crazily, like a cartoon. This battle to be both movie and cartoon added tension. Ultimately, as I will show (particularly in Warners cartoons), that tension created even more ways for antics to take over.

But the full vocabulary took years to develop. Meanwhile, full animation had to struggle as a hybrid art. The uneven swings gave it subtlety and showed off its craftsmanship — as well as its unique possibilities. Without those crazy breaks in dimension and mood, full animation could easily feel as dull as Muzak played in a seven-minute elevator, or a computer-generated copy of a traditional Chinese landscape (the same composition, but no clever brushwork, only fields of colored dots).

Characters move in relation to each other like wrestlers. Full animation reminds me most of wrestling matches on the screen: first, between one atmosphere and another; then, between one medium and another (film versus drawing, etc.).

By 1939, virtually every cartoon studio still in business had developed its unique brand of fully animated wrestling match. They certainly told very different stories: this is apparent from Disney features, to Tex Avery's blackout spoofs of newsreels, or the very first Tom and Jerry cartoon (*Puss Gets the Boot*). But the anarchic element survived, even if the graphic narrative was taken out. In its way, like linear animation, full animation was still a war of all against all.

Clearly, this wrestling with atmospheres was brought on primarily by pressures from the movie industry (as I explained in earlier chapters). The client demanded it. From the mid-thirties until the early fifties, the film industry controlled more aspects of cartoon production than it had before, or has since, for that matter. This forced the cartoon into both satire and homage to movies as its primary role. It also forced massive restructuring of the cartoon, as the preceding chapters indicate.

The emergence of full animation follows the growing monopoly of the film industry. After 1934, cartoons shift rather quickly toward movie allusion and movie graphics. In chapter 12, I reviewed some of the problems in marketing that led to this situation. In this chapter, I have discussed the changing layout and staging. Next, I concentrate on how the graphics shifted after 1937, at Warners in particular, how the *contradictions* of full animation came to dominate in the chase cartoon.

CHAPTER FOURTEEN

Production: 1940

By 1940, even the doggedly cautious Paul Terry was producing cartoons by a system similar to Disney's, but without many of the frills. All the studios had done much the same, adding more story men, a larger art department, more assistants, and layout men double-checking along the way, more conferences, more division of labor on top of the systems for in-betweening and tempo set up in the twenties. There was simply a much larger paper trail: storyboards, more detailed bar sheets, more background layout. Animation went from a Model T to a fully loaded Plymouth Sedan — a fully animated mode of production:[1]

Storyboards (more time and money spent mapping out the plot beforehand)   After a story idea was first conceived, *sketch artists* and gag men worked with the director. Afterward, an interim synopsis might be written down and passed round. But more often, the layout man would block out the story (rough sketches of the characters and of the background).

Several hundred rough story sketches would be made, in continuity, often with dialogue underneath the drawings. On large storyboards, these were presented to a final conference of some sort, made up of the director, musical director, and animators.

After the conference (sometimes contentious, often involving many changes), a *rough timing sheet* was made for the director. From this the director wrote the script, on *"music detail sheets,"* which were

overgrown music sheets, with bars and musical format. Horizontally, they are divided into four parts — the top part for the music (which the director leaves blank), the next for sound effects, then dialogue and the largest space for detailed action.

For animators, and later photographers, there would also be columns listing the *consecutive numbers,* or *levels* of the cels to be placed over the background (generally no more than four). The background layout was finished.

In successive stages, the number of stages depending on the studio (Disney the most, Terry the least), what emerged was a *working "script,"* a visual scenario that resembled live-action production scripts far more than cartoons had earlier. Along the paper trail were *exposure sheets, bar sheets*, what Disney called *dope sheets*; and a much more cinematic layout for the larger and deeper *field of action*.

Next, the director timed each gag sequence. A lot of pantomime acting was involved (assistants or directors imping at each other) to check how the cycles and attitudes might look in the time allotted.

With the music director, the tempo of the action — and dialogue — was established, often on a bar sheet. Sound effects might be indicated as well.

All this was laid out on *exposure sheets*, "a blueprint of the entire production," with a space (horizontally ruled) for each frame; and every tenth, twelfth or sixteenth frame marked off — for tempo, including how many frames it will take for a piece of dialogue to be spoken.[2] There were also columns identifying each layer of cel.

Then the director made the working scenario, a final script of sorts, numbering each scene, frame by frame, and its field of action. This became a checklist once a scene was finished; also a guide sent to the camera department later on.

Background   The size of the *field of action* (backgrounds) had already been determined by the layout man (who was often considered as a kind of co-director). This defined how much of each character would be seen for a certain action, and for how many frames, scene by scene; also the angle for each scene, and how the camera might *truck*, as in live action. (At Disney, for larger productions, there would also be "inspiration" sketches and an effects [EFX] department.)

Head Animators, Assistants and In-Betweeners   Meanwhile, animators worked on individual scenes, while referring to *model sheets*, showing key poses and the comparative sizes of each character. Standard rules of personality animation were known, as in the requirement in the Fleischer Studios Handbook: "The character should *anticipate* their mood prior to saying or doing anything."

Also, as another tool for animators, there was often a *sculpture* department. Plasticine dolls were made of characters (sometimes even of objects in the story). These helped animators "get the feel" of characters, from all sides and angles. There are other implications, however, about cartoons and literalism, beyond the fact that these dolls, like fine Swiss figurines, remind me of the miniatures used in live-action special effects. They also remind me of Mickey and Donald dolls sold in stores at the time, and, finally, of Disneyland. Full animation made fantasy very literal — sculptural — in a way that Disneyland commodified later on.

The animators worked at their light tables (a desk with a large circular disk that is lit from below). This light allowed the image from multiple sheets to be seen (even to pre-scan the background).

Animators drew on five-holed paper (three round, two square) which goes on

MOTION PICTURE PHOTOGRAPHY

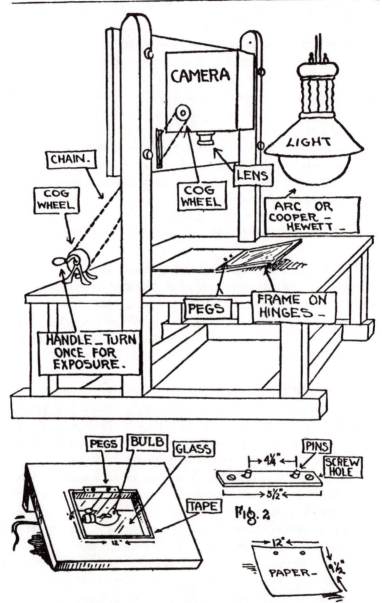

FIGURE SHOWING DETAILS OF THE CONSTRUCTION OF A CAMERA
STAND FOR MAKING ANIMATED CARTOONS AND DIAGRAMS

Animation equipment before the coming of sound (1927).

pegs to keep the registration uniform. Four or five head animators drew *roughs* (*originals*) of the high points (*extremes*) of each cycle, about every fifth drawing (not religiously every fifth, however; that varied). Then the assistant animator made the *breakdown* drawings, about every third; and the *in-betweener* drew the second and the fourth.

Next, the assistant animator *cleaned up* the drawings (erased extra lines, sharpened the images), and also added missing details. The action regularly was "flipped," the sheets thumbed like a flip-book.

Then the drawings were sent to a camera man who shot an *action test* (also called a *running reel*; if with sound, at Disney, a Leica reel), which was projected on the screen (or examined by Walt in a "sweatbox"). Not all studios were as judicious as Disney about this stage, who even approved reshooting or editing out, and throwing out unwanted footage. There was tremendous variation here. By whatever process, a final agreement was reached. Certain sequences were redone until those responsible were satisfied. Then, the technical department checked the sound, camera effects, uniformity of clothing — details that could be out of synch with all the steps involved — also because full animation demanded much more fluid movement.

Finishing the Backgrounds The colors were pre-selected and labeled according to number from color charts. Then the backgrounds were painted by the Art Department. The layout man drew rough pencil sketches, which were passed along. These were redrawn on heavy paper and painted usually in washes (with added touches — dry brush, airbrush, depending on the studio and the project).

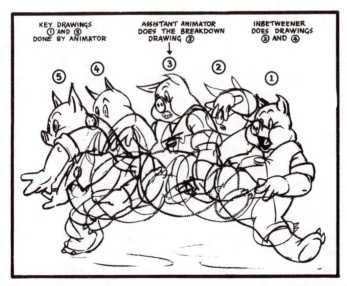

The division of labor between animator, assistant animator, and in-betweener (1940).

Some backgrounds were *still*, meaning that the characters did not move beyond the boundaries of a single frame. Others, much larger, usually three times larger, were *panoramas*, as in *pan*, for running action.

Backgrounds could be tested against the action once all the colors were assigned, and the *cels* could be inked and painted.

Cels First, the drawings of the action were *traced*, in black or colored ink, on to clear celluloid *cels* (or *cells*). These cels also had five register holes, to align with the drawings. Once traced, the shapes on the cels were *opaqued* (on the back) for solidity and smooth surface in paints specially designed for animation. (There were often references in articles about the new paints Disney was designing; these were apparently true. There were even more stories about new paints developed at Warners, though I suspect those were bogus.)

Once the *master color cels* were inked and painted — not even necessarily shaded yet — and only the key characters opaqued, these cels could be laid over the background, to make certain the contrast worked for the action. To make the action more readable, increasingly, more muted colors were used in backgrounds (though I like thirties cartoon color, what some called "picture-book colors"). They have a polyglot, intercepted look, as in my description of Disney "Nouveau." The background seems to be creeping up to attack the foreground.

Anyway, full animation demanded a great deal of shading, as well as many more shadows. It also required complex versions of solidity and surface — metallic and heavy, waved and slippery, sunken and mysterious, protruding and painful, wrinkled and feeble, bulging and stupid. This involved ink and paint work far beyond the multimorphic look of the early thirties. For example, a cartoon like Van Beuren's *Balloonland* has a special irony for 1935 that it could not have later on. First of all, *Balloonland* (also called *The Pincushion Man*) was made just before the Disney monopoly with Technicolor ended and all studios could use three-strip color. But most of all, the story summarizes the world of rubber-hose animation. It is the last cartoon where squeezable sausage bodies could be considered familiar. That style was rapidly going out.

Nasty pincushion men threaten balloon people and deflate them, until justice prevails. The entire universe is balloony, rubbery, and inflatable; but not for long.

Clampett's "rubber band" in *Tin Pan Alley Cats* (1943) may seem similar. They are certainly a rubbery band, even make rubbery music, or tinny, Mickey Mouse music. They are a ten-second throwback to the 1931 musical cartoons, to the paper/comb and kazoos of early sound. But the cartoon as a whole is not like that. It reminds me of the staging for *Porky in Wackyland* (1938), a far cry from the "innocent" and flatter rubber-hose style. Even as black and white (it was colorized later, in the forties), Wackyland is a deep-focus movie puzzle, only possible in fuller (if not "fullest") animation.

160

As the final step, the finished cels, after being checked for any unpainted or off-register spots, were photographed, frame by frame, in coordination with the background and story, about 10,000 times. A little over 500 feet emerged on the reel, which ran for between six and seven minutes.

CHAPTER FIFTEEN

The Chase Cartoon: Machina Versatilis

In chapters 16, 17, 18 and 20, I will study the dynamics of the well-made chase cartoon, beginning first with two chapters defining the form, then two more going over the history.

Elmer tiptoes on to the screen. We already know what comes next: Bugs, an insult, the chase. Undoubtedly, this is one of thousands of chase cartoons made between 1937 and the sixties — and represents a return to cartoon anarchy.

The chase returns to more antic gags: nuisance, over-reactor, and controller, very much upside down in the spirit of early sound cartoons. The return began as a late thirties "anti-story," a reaction against cartoon melodrama. It is a bridge, from the antics of 1930, past full animation in 1937, and into the forties.

Chases are not necessarily "faster." In the chase, when we stop to watch, the hand is slower than the eye, not the other way around. There is something in the subtlety of the form that allows for many pauses, a lot of contrast, not simply velocity.

At first, the chase cartoon was mostly about velocity. The early Daffys or *Porky's Railroad* are "jumpy." Early Avery and Tashlin chases, before 1940, clatter madly like runaway trains, like machines going haywire. But the timing fails in some essential way, compared to the later standard. Similarly, in Clampett's early chases, like *Porky in Wackyland* (a brilliant piece of nonsense) or *Daffy Doc* (less brilliant), one senses colossal acceleration, but something is missing. No matter how quickly that crazy Dodo bird moves through Wackyland, the scene does not register in that architectonic way that makes the train really speed along madly. For speed to make an impact, it needs to undermine time and space in ways that freeze the characters, as though they were clinging to an elevator running by upside-down gravity, as if they could feel the chill of a new atmosphere, as if the world held a grudge against them. Clampett already sensed this when he scribbled on a Wackyland thumbnail sketch: "Dodo appears from screwy places. Porky tries vainly to get a glimpse of him."[1]

I am counting on the reader to remember scenes where Porky or the dog

Willoughby stood around, stick still, while anti-gravity took control of their future. They were caught going against traffic in a wind tunnel. And watching them caught at the cross-wind makes the hazards of speed even more profound. That's "faster" in a chase. By 1939, some of these "cross-wind" effects are being added. In Avery's *A Feud There Was* (1938), Egghead is walking very slowly, ambling through a bomb-site of crazy hillbillies firing at each other. His aimless shuffle (as controller) adds a loopy bit of suspense. It makes the rifle fire in *A Feud There Was* even more upside down (faster). Why? Because the universe around Egghead is so unreliable. Only he seems to know where it's heading. The space he inhabits could accommodate many intrusions at once. Imagine a rubberized room filled with unlikely doorways, each to another universe. Like standing in a meteor shower, the more Egghead or Elmer stands still, the more quickly he is inundated. That is why Elmer has to tiptoe.

Chases were not necessarily faster because they ran faster. It soon became apparent that speed wasn't enough. Chases needed to look unpredictable and unreliable — even raw. Inside this rubberized room justice never prevailed, and revenge was always extremely sweet. A hapless war between incompatibles worked best: incompatible atmospheres, incompatible graphics, volumes, even ideologies. That's

The Schlesinger Studio (*c.* 1936), a Christmas mailer by the master caricaturist T. Hee (who also worked at Disney for decades).

why a chase looks so very, very fast. Simply put: *The chase is the collision of improbables meeting on a field where only greed and invasion operate.* The more levels of collision in a single gag, the funnier it is.

No wonder the form evolved more quickly after the war in Europe started and flourished during eras of military paranoia, during the Second World War and the early Cold War.

Nor is the chase disorderly. It is a very orderly state of anarchy, because it is completely ruthless. It cleans house, wipes the slate clean.

This is particularly true of chases in live-action films. Again, I rely on the reader's memory. A quick flash to the car chases in the final scenes of recent movies: the crunching of car bodies; or the wall-to-wall fist-fights during an atomic meltdown. These resolve the story conflict, but charred flesh does not resolve *neatly*, except when it is called "collateral damage" (as in the 1991 Gulf War). A devastated battle site is not a *neatly* made hospital bed. It is final agony. The bad guys get theirs. They are "totalized." When we cut to a chase, the moral ambiguities go away; poetic justice takes over, like a vengeful mountain god. Afterward, the audience applauds. They're refreshed, ready to face the traffic going home.

It is relaxing to see total annihilation in the form of a chase (don't ask me why). Buildings collapse. Limbs fly in all directions. Live-action chases, from westerns to *Terminator II*, are supposed to be extremely chaotic (and destructive). Revenge is great fun for the audience. Loud and heavy objects collide at once, cars spin through plate-glass windows and burst into flames. The camera pulls back for the full effect.

A chase, whether in cartoon or live action, is highly contrary. It blows things apart. It also glues things together. It runs by the clock, but the clock runs sideways.

In the language of critical theory, the chase cartoon is both diachronic and synchronic: hardly a simple task. To use Bakhtin's terminology, it is both dialogical and carnivalesque. In the lexicon of modern art, it qualifies as Brechtian defamiliarization. That would make it a postmodern, modernist, pre-modernism (pre-modernist in terms of its graphic pantomime). And finally, as a document about American history, it is even more contradictory: a satire of American violence, imperialism, and naivety, while at the same time, the classic form used for military propaganda during the Second World War. No wonder Elmer is always confused. Look at how many universes he has to fall through just to stay in the same room with Bugs.

In terms of animation history, however, the chase cartoon fits into a more settled category: it revived the anarchic cartoon (1928–34), but revived it as anti-melodrama (1937–45), a crash of metal and bodies when story is not enough. For example, an Avery chase takes the paradoxes that enriched *full animation* (crazy atmospheres and volumes), and invests them with *the anarchy of the early sound cartoon* (amoral, upside-down anti-gravity). It combines the anarchic elements found in both of these eras (1928–34; 1934–37), then adds even more, new gags that belong strictly to the era of the Second World War, 1937–46.

Avery took a very established gimmick, generations old — the chase as a gag, not a cartoon, more a cycle, twelve or fifteen frames running past. The chase cycle had unique properties which until 1937 were seen as essentially technical more than a form of narrative.

Fundamentally, the chase cycle operates like a magic trick, showing off the machinery of animation. Only later does it evolve into a form of cartoon story. But something in that magic trick makes the story easier to develop.

As film grammar, the chase was understood very early on as "pure" animation, a trick that, more than any other, separated the art of animation from live action. In 1915, an animator at Bray Studios named Wallace Carlson wrote:[2]

The comedy is easily injected by slap-stick actions, and they always produce a laugh. The audience will break into an uproar over a dog *chasing* a cat, whereas they would probably not even smile at this same action in a photoplay.

This is a very curious statement, particularly for 1915. We know that audiences certainly did smile at chases in live action, in Sennett comedies in 1915, and in slapstick films made throughout the silent era. Those were enormously popular. What the animator meant here was the way that chase gags operated as dramatic structure. In live action, even as early as 1915, with Chaplin two-reelers for example, the chase comedy was beginning to evolve into a *form of drama*, away from the vaudeville pratfall. For animation, the path was entirely different. The chase clearly did not evolve into drama. In cartoons, the chase was understood primarily as an artful flourish, and little more. Cats and mice ran one behind the other as the easiest way to hold the audience's interest — not to move the story, simply to move the drawings.

The chase was another form of machina versatilis. It displayed the machinery of animation. The characters were not expected to be thinking as they ran in cycle. When they were annoyed enough to run, their faces revealed little of envy or revenge, only a vague impatience, a scowl perhaps. Along with this indeterminate scowl came a charming, but relatively unmotivated scrambling of legs against a flat background.

The early chase was a magic act. One character followed another magically, but mindlessly, as if they were on a rotating drum, even in the Koko cartoons, or the Dinky Doodle cartoons (which Walter Lantz made for Bray Studios in the mid-twenties). The chase was part of the rhythm more than part of the story. The story was not as important in silent animation anyway; it was secondary to graphic narrative.

Cats chased mice in the way dogs chase their own tail. Like a windup illusion, these loops where one figure ran behind the other operated like a gimmick inside a trick film. Animators chased their own drawings, who escaped from sheets of paper or from inkwells. The movement of body behind body stood in for the machinery of reproduction, as in *Koko's Cartoon Factory* (1926). With Koko at the controls,

165

multiples of Max are stamped out and begin running madly, like the insensate army of toy soldiers in Laurel and Hardy's *March of the Wooden Soldiers* (1934, slapstick version of *Babes in Toyland*).

From 1928 to 1933, cartoon chases in sound were not much different. Mickey and Betty Boop ran mostly to show off the hardware. Pegleg growled until Mickey jumped. Fleischer goblins hooted until Betty scooted away. Warners' Bosko moved in chases the most mechanically of all, mostly to music, as in the car chase in *Bosko the Speed King* (1933).

There were crucial exceptions, however, which suggest the transition toward the chase cartoon, and the importance of Disney early on. In 1932, in *Playful Pluto*, Norm Ferguson (Fergy) animated Pluto at war with a sheet of flypaper, a sequence that veteran animators cite consistently as a turning point. Thomas and Johnston explain:[3]

It was the first time a character seemed to be thinking on the screen, and though it lasted only 64 seconds, it opened the way for animation of real characters and real problems.

Disney animators in the thirties were advised to study the sequence carefully, to see how "each *hold expression* after a surprise action was carefully planned, and expressed some definite attitude causing the audience to laugh. Each small climax builds up into a better surprise."

It seemed a way to take the chase beyond *machina versatilis*. It added a nervous intensity, very much a part of Fergy's own personality. (He was a jittery fellow apparently.) As the animator Wilfrid Jackson explained:[4] "You can take that same gag without running over the dog's thoughts or emotions, just mechanically do the thing, and it wouldn't be funny."

The range of expressions on Pluto's face became a benchmark for personality animation. Pluto went from curiosity to greed to sadism. This cycle also became essential for the chase cartoon. Without a range of moods, without a mobile face on at least one of the adversaries, the chase remained little more than a motorized ballet, as indeed Disney used it continuously, for *The Band Concert*, and others. I have already discussed a few examples.

In *The Clock Cleaners*, the giant mainspring attacks Donald, but not because these coils of steel have become a character. The mainspring is perfectly dumb, an annoying force of nature, which cannot think. It is an apparatus, like a sheet of flypaper sticking to Pluto or a hurricane attacking Mickey's band concert. It wreaks havoc because it cannot, and never will, think.

The Moose Hunters (1937) came much closer to character chase, and was an influence mentioned by Warners' animators. It starts with the usual Disney formula, Mickey leading his merry band into one entrepreneurial activity or another. Out camping, Mickey and friends tire of eating beans and decide to hunt for moose. Very quickly, they attract a huge bull moose, then give chase in a graceful mixture of confusion and acrobatics, very typical of the best personality animation from Disney in the thirties. Some of the gags, however, suggest a change toward what became the chase cartoon. A mating scent brings the gigantic beast into the open. But he is surprisingly peaceful, ready for love. His nostrils widen, or, should I say, swell and pulsate with romance. Suddenly weightless, he floats like a sail. Then, just as suddenly, like so many chase cartoon monsters later (bulls, beefy wrestlers, hairy ghouls), the dumb beast gets wise. He realizes he's been had and screeches to a halt. His eyes change first. He sees red, before he begins to pound his hooves angrily. Using various hold expressions, the chase reverses directions. The mood on each character's face is markedly different. Their chests slump or expand differently. Now the moose is the hunter. Matters get out of hand. Finally, Mickey gives up the struggle and settles for the can of beans instead.

A chase cartoon needs two thinking adversaries taking turns — scheming, dreaming, mixing greed, naivety, sadism, and revenge. For them to take turns, their moods have to switch from one extreme to another, in very vivid anatomical ways. Even if one character is as unexpressive as the Roadrunner (meep-meep), the other has to be Wile E. Coyote, an ever-hopeful manic-depressive, with wild emotional swings which make the roar of the chase more vivid. Without full animation or personality animation, these mood swings would not register enough to sustain the simple act of characters running after each other for seven minutes.

From 1937 on, Tex Avery and others (mostly at Warners, of course), continued what Disney essentially had started, but not developed further. Warners' animators dropped the other shoe, precisely the shoe that Disney tried hardest to hold on to. Walt disapproved of the raw quirkiness that a chase-oriented cartoon required. He thought that full animation was correcting that problem, not instigating it.

The key difference lies in the use of "anticipation." Thomas and Johnston define "the anticipatory gesture" at Disney: "Before Mickey reaches to grab an object, he first raises his arms as he stares at the article, broadcasting the fact that he is going to do something with that particular object."[5] Anticipation made movement more predictable. It was understood as the opposite of "the surprise gag." It telegraphed to add continuity. In the Avery cartoon, however, anticipation was used to create suspense, because the nastiness that came next was not predictable.

But rather than center my argument on Disney/anti-Disney, there is also another way to say much the same thing. In another sense, Avery simply went back to the pre-1932 cartoon and bypassed Disney altogether. The old-fashioned *machina versatilis* chase gag was isolated. Then elements were added in stages:

1. Characters were drawn differently, more fully animated, with emotional extremes in their expressions.
2. The anti-story of the pre-1934 cartoon was given a more ritualized structure: a more systematic version of the nuisance/over-reactor/controller story form.
3. The melodramatic overlay was removed, until the chase had more of the antic and amoral spirit of the pre-1934 cartoon.

There also were elements added that specifically referred to life in the late thirties:

4. Elaborate parodies of live-action movie formulas.
5. Adding gags about the insanity of consumer life, at home and in public spaces, from the radio to movie studios to the modern kitchen.

What resulted was a very complex package indeed. Cat-and-mouse went from narrow metonym to a multilayered story form.

Still, the heart of the chase cartoon remained — what I call *machina versatilis*, a simple effect practiced for decades, with roots going back centuries. However elaborate the form became, gags that revealed the clockwork of animation still regularly turned up in chase cartoons. Film historians often compare that clockwork effect to a Brechtian device. The motorized look of the chase gag distances the character from the drama. Abandoning what seems to be motivated action, the character will suddenly talk to the silhouette of someone in the audience, stop to show us a sign: "Silly isn't it?" Or get sucked from the projection booth onto the screen, like Keaton's Sherlock Junior.

As a result of these mechanistic gags, chases are very often labeled "modernist," and Avery as "the Manet of vulgar modernism."[6] Perhaps these critics sense a parallel between the emergence of modern art and the growing importance of *machina versatilis* in cartoons. But the term modernism requires some explanation.

DEFINING CARTOON MODERNISM

The Chase as Machina Versatilis

In animation theory, when the term *modernist* is used, it usually refers to what narrative poetics define as "self-reflexive." That can have an extremely broad meaning, essentially the entire tradition of anti-illusionism. For studying cartoons, anti-illusionism would include virtually every animated short ever made, almost every gag, and so is not a very useful tool.

In terms of my argument, therefore, a narrower term is needed. I equate the term self-reflexive with *machina versatilis*: how chases operate like theatrical machines to reveal the technology of animation to the audience, either through direct address or through machine-like gags, like the chase, or like the staging in Fleischer cartoons.

But this explanation still leaves the term modernism fluid. It is very frequently used in animation histories, and with varying meaning. Sometimes, it refers to abstraction, sometimes to reflexivity, sometimes to defamiliarization, sometimes to graphic design.

Briefly Defining Modernism in the Fine Arts: Truth to Materials

In art theory, the source of the term "modernism" remains one of those all-purpose generics, a *logos* more than a narrow process. Practically no two critics mean precisely the same thing when they label a problem as modernist.

Histories of modern art have changed considerably in the last decade or more. As a result, modernism has come to be seen as very pluralistic. Dozens of modernisms have replaced the singular version. Many of these literally contradict each other. Nevertheless, one strategy seems to be cited most often as common to virtually all the artists defined now as modernist, including Tex Avery. The strategy can be found in hundreds of texts, across the disciplines, particularly in those written during the first half of the twentieth century — in modern poetry, modern dance, the twelve-tone technique in music, and so on, including painting. It was given various names and nuances, terms like facture (FAKTURA) or "truth to materials." The texture or surface of an art-form was supposed to be displayed nakedly, as a way of maintaining honesty and avoiding camouflage: naked surface before illusion or decoration; show the seams.

Truth to materials also amounted to a simple act of isolation. Locate a device that is essential to your medium, like the texture of paint, then isolate it. Keep the device quarantined from the standard vocabulary in that art-form. Eventually, after a great deal of work, the device replaces the vocabulary altogether and becomes the entire piece.

Of course, many of the devices selected were well known, even centuries old. They were often techniques used to accent or apply counterpoint to paintings or plays. Only the extreme isolation of these techniques was really new. This is uniquely true of cartoon "modernism," defined as *machina versatilis*.

Coordinating Cartoon Modernism with Fine Arts Modernism

For animation, *machina versatilis* dates back earlier than the seventeenth century. This is also true of graphic narrative, discussed in chapter 1. That begins at least with Hogarth, if not earlier. For centuries, illustrators commonly used devices we might define as self-reflexive and label as "modernist." That distinction can be confusing, because the standard definitions of modernism begin with Manet or with Cubism, not with seventeenth-century theater, or with pre-industrial traditions of pantomime. And yet, cartoon "modernism" dates back almost to the late middle ages.

Still, we must remember that there are parallels in the fine arts and in literature as well. For hundreds of years, certain devices in novels and plays had served mostly to alienate the story, to provide a pause or lurch, a cliffhanger of sorts. They might also be called "self-reflexive," and labeled as "modernist." They certainly have been called "intertextual." The character in a story suddenly drifts into a reverie in the midst of the action (*Prince Frederick of Homburg*, 1806). The action stops just as the final blow is about to be delivered. The effect is not all that different from intercutting to add suspense. The suspense grows because the story has stopped while the fuse is still burning. The problem is then a matter of degree.

There are *"abstracted"* elements in Velázquez paintings from the seventeenth century. The hands in certain of Velázquez' portraits look very much like paints mixed directly on the canvas, without the opacity of veins beneath the skin — very unfinished compared to the varnished detail of the sleeves, or the sense of bones and flesh on the face. If these hands were abstracted, they might resemble the hands Picasso painted in the *Demoiselles d'Avignon*, for example; and in fact, there is extraordinary variety in how he rendered the hands in that painting. One might say that there are seventeenth-century references there.

That need not surprise us. A great painter in any era might decide, once in a while, to ignore the rules of resemblance, if only to play with the alternative, or merely to stop the audience in its tracks. The modernism in chase cartoons came more out of that undifferentiated process — testing possibilities — than the "experimental" studio of the modern artist.

It is similar to examples like the following. In the early nineteenth century, there were self-reflexive (or "modernist") elements even in popular Romantic literature, what was termed "Romantic irony," borrowing from the eighteenth-century novel (particularly Sterne). In music, dissonance was a necessary feature of "harmony." In eighteenth-century French painting, from Watteau to Chardin, the surface has scarification, erasure, or a velvety presence — not simply a varnished window; it is tactile in a way that suggests what we might call "modernist." But "modernism" remains a slippery category when taken too formally.

It is particularly slippery when the term is applied, as a crossover, to the mass-culture object. In small doses, many of the techniques we might classify as "modernist" were used regularly, over centuries, as narrative hooks, in mass culture, like vaudeville. They were tricks to arrest the viewer. They were engaging, not difficult to follow. Tex Avery essentially counted on how engaging spot gags and blackouts were. Even when "tricks" that we might label modernist are isolated ("abstracted"), the results might affect the audience more as suspense (anticipation) than as "distancing." They become pepper in the sauce. The audience senses that a piece is missing; the story, however naked and fractured, completes through absence.

Mass culture has been adding "absences" (elisions; debordements) even in our era (perhaps faster than ever). Popular storytelling is continually under erasure. Eventually, as MTV girdles the world, the appeal of jump-cut techniques will grow; and audience tolerance for more absences, more pluralist short subjects, will grow as well. That is very much how the cartoon has operated, by distilling the fractures in story to create parody. It is, in fact, a parody of transgression itself, of its innocence before the audience. And yet, these seven minutes will not be transgressional or modernist. In mass culture, there will always be a shadow of the missing picture on the wall, particularly as the modernity of mass culture absorbs the modernism of the fine arts.

According to cartoon modernism, there is no pure form, only erasures based on audience memory. Mass culture is alive with a sense of erasure similar to a Tex Avery chase. That this can be compared to the fine arts is a challenge to our sense of classification, whether modern art is a subset of mass culture. Cartoon modernism reminds us of the obvious. All white light is made up of memory, of other lights — nothing of itself, no pure form, only pale sparks of signification.

Cartoon Modernism: 1937

The chase gag, *machina versatilis*, was isolated, by Avery in particular, and others afterward. Before 1937, the chase had been used primarily as a showcase, to emphasize that the drawing is free to escape as it pleases. When used only as a part of the whole, the chase was a paradoxical stone in the road, the loopy suspense added when the plot became too slow or self-indulgent. But when the chase became the entire objective of the cartoon, these gags began to resemble what many writers today identify as modernism, a "Daffy" modernism.

The Advantages of Being Boneless and Incomplete: Daffy Duck (1937—42) and the Zip-Crash School

By the late thirties, at Warners, the chase became a coherent system, understood throughout the industry. The simplest way to show how the system started is through Daffy Duck, as created by Tex Avery in 1937 with help from his animator at that time, Bob Clampett. On the model sheet for *Porky's Duck Hunt*, the still unnamed character was called "the crazy darnfool duck."[1] He was essentially an early thirties rubber-hose design (not a full anatomical character) — mostly two circles attached by a cylindrical neck, inked entirely in black, not much volume, mostly skin without bones. In early cartoons, he would pull his skin back to show he was just skin and bone, but there would be no clear sense of an anatomy inside.

He was virtually dematerialized, able to hop across water as if he had no weight whatsoever, or the water were simply a drawing. On various cels, he was also inked with a blur along his back, one of many devices Avery used to accelerate sudden bursts of speed. Slowed down on moviola to one cel at a time, these blur drawings suggest a body disintegrating under its own momentum, or a body intentionally incomplete, as if part of the outline were missing.

There were advantages to being boneless and incomplete. Daffy was designed to move as improbably as possible, the first of many such characters that Avery developed — enigmas who lived outside the rules of plot, space, and time. Some were loud and nasty, like Screwy Squirrel. Others were very quiet, like Droopy and Egghead (and *Bad Luck Blackie*, 1949). They merely showed up wherever they pleased, as if they lived in a closet from another dimension.

Chuck Jones developed a similar enigma in the Minah Bird, and was told that Walt Disney found these cartoons (Inki and the Minah Bird) annoying to watch. Where was the story? Walt apparently would ask: What did the Minah Bird want? These were not characters who possessed "personality" in the sense that Disney preferred, even though Jones used Disney techniques more than any other Warners animator at the time. As Frank Thomas explained about the Disney approach, "spot laughs" do not build a character. Personality required "acting," "presence," "being there," "working with volume." Disney did not go for the "zip-crash, zip-crash school."[2]

Avery understood that he was contradicting the Disney dicta. But Avery was working on a very different model of story than Disney, one based predominantly on the shock of the improbable. In his stories, characters exceed the possible step by step, gag by gag. They literally jump off the edge, then suddenly off an even crazier edge. That meant, for example, that the slower a character was, the more likely that he would get there first. For Disney, slower movement allowed for more grace, more twisting of the anatomy, for details that showcased the animator's art.

Avery, a small-town Texan who knew the intricacies of bird dogs and duckshooting very well, was also very taken with the idea of the hunt. He liked to work on characters whose entire existence was dedicated to foiling the hunter. They made up their own rules about who shot whom and when. They were anti-prey (like anti-matter), absolutely in control of gravity, space, time, even the future of the story. They had infallible inside information. Egghead or Droopy would explain in various cartoons: "I'm [going to be] the hero of this picture."

The purpose of such characters was clearly to undermine the restrictions of cartoon melodrama. This is most evident in *Screwball Squirrel* (1944, at MGM), where the melodrama is so boring, the only recourse is to sadism. Screwy beats up a smaller squirrel simply for acting too cute.

But more than anti-melodrama, characters existed to speed up the gags, to pile them up faster. Screwy is relentless, a ruthless controller. He forces a dumb

Courtesy of the Bob Clampett Collection

Daffy Duck in 1937.

bloodhound to stay on his trail, but never in his tracks. The dog, worn out by defeat, finally asks to end the picture. Screwy offers a game of hide-and-go-seek instead, then promptly has the dog run over by a train.

Machina versatilis is built into *Screwball Squirrel* as well. In mid-chase, the music sticks, like a bad record. The sound goes out of synch. Later, Screwy pulls back a page to find out what he does next to "that guy." Animators called these "spot gags," throwaways that generally slowed down the rhythm. But in Avery's case, the spot gags accelerated the action. By not fitting, they made the chase feel even more unpredictable.

In 1969, Avery explained how he sped up the gags and why, in a passage frequently cited, from an interview with Joe Adamson:[3]

I think I started that faster trend. We started filling in more gags. Prior to that, they felt you had to have a story. Finally we got to where the "story" was just a string of gags with a "topper." I found out the eye can register an action in five frames of film. Five frames of film at twenty-four a second, so it's roughly a fifth of a second to register something, from the screen to your eye to the brain. I found out, if I wanted something just to barely be seen, five frames was all it needed. What would ruin it would be two or three seconds of film ... no, you'd have nothing. Say we had an anvil falling, we would bring it in perhaps four or five frames before the hit, that's all you need — Djuuuuuu ... Bam! it's there, and you don't know where in the hell it came from. It makes that gag much funnier. If you saw this thing coming down, and you panned down with it, and it hits — uh uh. But I kept speeding up my timing and I think I was followed, with the Roadrunner and all that stuff.

Daffy was the first continuing character that Avery designed like one of those anvils — purely for speed. Daffy moved fast enough to "string" together gags. He was free enough from story to show up anywhere. In the conclusion of *Porky's Duck Hunt*, we learn that Daffy is an escaped mental patient. Then we learn that he can escape even from his own body, and become two ducks at once — the duck driving the ambulance, and the crazy duck riding inside. Then, in the end-titles, Daffy returns for a final bow, running crazily inside the letters, and through the studio.

Clampett frequently mentioned how proud he was of working on that first Daffy, the absolute incoherence of Daffy's behavior, defying weight, space, and having Daffy appear in the credits. Apparently, while finishing the cartoon, it became clear that the duck was a very strong character, but there was no other place in the story to use him, so they slipped Daffy in for a few extra feet literally at "The End."

As more hunting cartoons came out of the Avery unit, and other Warners units, Avery saw that the contrast between slow and fast also made these gags seem even faster — and funnier. The slow moments left room for quizzical double-takes, extra blackout visuals, or even a sign held up by the character ("Silly isn't it?"). While speeding along, he could screech like a rubber tire, or go "sproing" like a spring bolt, and skid to a furious stop.

Crazy pauses became a feature in virtually all the Warners chase cartoons, to exaggerate the speed of characters who moved like bullets, both physically and mentally. A fast Daffy or fast Bugs went against characters who were incredibly slow and dim. Clampett also liked to punctuate the sudden breaks with a few stock phrases (directly to the audience, and always in a slow drawl), like "I'm only three and a half years old." Or the character, in a sudden fit of remorse, often with a bit of homoerotic pleasure thrown in, would say: "Agh-go-nee" (*An Itch in Time*, 1943, and others). This was an age of radio, so the audiences were very tuned in to the nuances of voice: when an arch tenor says "agony," it sounds like a bad reading from a high school play. Any number of radio soap operas come to mind. Or at the end of a cartoon (again, *An Itch in Time*), after the blur of insane gags, a passive observer, a fish or a cat, says: "Now I've seen everything." Then, the viewer puts a pistol to his head, blam, and zips backward, stone dead in five frames or less.

It is difficult to identify what I mean by "fast versus slow" without a small chart:

Fast	*Slow*
Bugs	Elmer
Yosemite Sam	Bugs
Daffy	Bugs
Wolfie	Droopy

When Bugs played against Elmer, he was the fast character. The slow Elmer was developed to match the speedy Bugs. However, against Yosemite Sam — always rushing, cursing ("blphmtzpstrkk!"), always impatient — Bugs became a very deliberate character, as he was also against Daffy. This was Bugs in the know, sly: "Ain't I a stinker?"

No one was much slower than Droopy. That was why Wolfie had to be manic. Similarly, in the last Wolfie/Showgirl cartoon, *Little Rural Riding Hood* (1949), the city wolf is suave and patient, with a velvet touch modeled on Ronald Colman. His rube of a cousin, the country wolf, however, is just a horny darn fool, can't sit still, melting, exploding, ejacu-bobbing his eyes and body parts. Meanwhile in his excitement, he is all but masticated into paste by his suave counterpart. At the end, however, the city wolf loses it over the buck-teethed, freckled country gal. "Sohrry," says the country wolf calmly, with a Goofy syrup in his voice. They switch roles, fast to slow. Country wolf wheels his frantic cousin away in a wheelbarrow, then back to the city into a limousine: "I guess you're just not ready for the country."

The elements of melodrama had no place here, no time. Faster gags left little room for moralizing. Melodrama also required a much more fixed universe, a poetic justice. The twists of the chase often made fun of poetic justice very directly, starting with homilies from Disney or from children's books, then having characters complain that they were fed up with the way the story ends. In *Red Hot Riding Hood*, first the wolf, then the girl, and finally the grandmother all start talking like actors interviewed in radio who are going on strike. They can't stand all this corny stuff. Pep it up! And pep it up he does, with Hollywood nightclub gags and hormones on tap.

There's no reward for a shy little girl in that kind of chase cartoon. The meek get run over. There's no room for a straight shooter either. The eager young champion gets blown up. If you're cute, you had better use that cuteness for a ruthless purpose. The cute little guy often hides a streak of sadism in chase cartoons, as in Clampett's early Tweety: "The poor little puddy tat. He fall down and go *boom*." And the hapless cat drops thirty feet below and slams into the pavement (*Birdie and the Beast*, 1944). Then little Tweety, literally designed as a hairless infant bird, even modeled on one of Clampett's own baby pictures, snickers cruelly in mock innocence to the audience.

Chase cartoons play directly against the moralizing of the mid-thirties. For contrast, let us go back to Disney's *The Tortoise and the Hare* (1934), often cited as an influence on Warners, because Bugs looks so much like Max Hare. There is a race, a chase. But Disney's chase is still a morality tale of sorts. Max Hare suffers from pride. He is too darned sure of himself and takes the race for granted. He has no gumption. He is cocksure, and that makes him lazy. He loses the race with the tortoise because he deserves to lose. The tortoise, a plugger, beats him through hard work.

In the early forties, Avery and Clampett made a few hare/tortoise cartoons also,

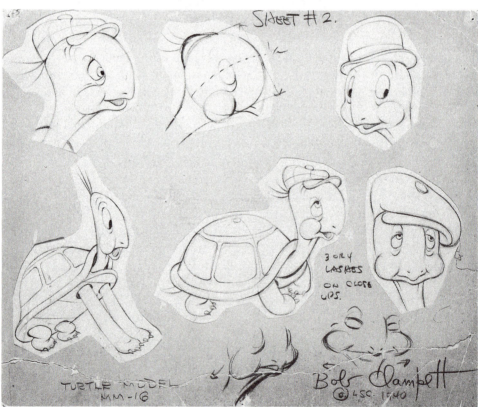

Model sheet of Cecil Turtle (1940), designed to look slow, to heighten the contrasts of the chase.

but with a very different twist. Cecil Turtle knows that hard work alone will not win the race. He needs to be sneaky too. He needs to cheat. Also, Bugs is not quite so cocksure. He senses his problem, and works hard, exercises, gets an early jump. Bugs is even repentant and clearly industrious enough to deserve to win. And yet, somehow, Bugs still loses. Even when he wins he loses. In *Tortoise Wins by a Hare* (1943) Cecil lets him win as a form of entrapment. At the finish line, traffic cops wait to arrest Bugs for speeding. In *Tortoise Beats Hare* (1940), Cecil cheats by using hundreds of identical relatives, who dress essentially like a criminal racing syndicate.

That is hardly a moral mesage compared to the Disney fable. But these cartoons were designed to subvert the moral messages that usually go with fables. Avery and Clampett were not alone in this. Many cartoon directors turned away from thirties melodrama. According to interviews, they discovered that sentimental cuteness hurt the rhythm of the chase. They grew uncomfortable with what Walter Lantz calls "birds and bees pictures," or the story man Leo Salkin remembers as "boy scout pictures."[4]

Chase cartoons also proved to be good business, popular with audiences and therefore distributors. And they were cheaper to make, at a time when costs were soaring. Distributors wanted full animation, but a fully animated cartoon cost $50,000 or more to make. Only Disney was prepared to spend that much. Other studios made theirs at $20,000–$35,000 apiece. (I've heard claims that some cartoons at Warners were made for even less, but I wonder if this was possible.) Therefore, animators who worked with smaller budgets had to find shortcuts. Faster gags and complex chases required less elaborate in-betweening, with less volumetric characters, less fussy work on atmosphere. Chase cartoons took far fewer work hours than a full-blown Silly Symphony.

Even Disney was under the gun, very seriously in fact, almost to the edge of bankruptcy for a time. By 1941, even before America entered the war, Disney began to economize. Not only were he (and Roy) skimping on salaries — and then finding themselves caught in a strike, sparked in part by salary restrictions — Walt also cut budgets for cartoons and features alike, even approved rather simplified sequences for some of *Fantasia*, presumably because it saved a few dollars. Specifically, animators felt that he shaved a few dollars in the mushroom dance, where silhouetted backgrounds, not at all Disney's fulsome style, were approved. (Ironically enough, the backgrounds for this sequence, by Jules Engel, were among the forerunners of the UPA style a decade later.)

At Warners, many of the early chase cartoons were made in black and white, at budgets low even for Leon Schlesinger, and long after the market for cartoons in Technicolor had been established. By the late thirties, the musical melodramas at Warners were made in color (usually directed by Friz Freleng, as a special "perk," he being the senior director at Schlesinger's studio). Chase cartoons, however, the Looney Tune series, were specifically *not* supposed to be color melodramas. And indeed they were not.

From 1937 to 1942, the format for chase cartoons continued to evolve, primarily around the work of Avery at first, then, secondarily, Bob Clampett and Frank Tashlin. By 1940, both the MGM and Lantz studios had shifted toward the chase cartoon as well. Then, when America entered the Second World War the agit-prop chase cartoon arrived — more pointed, more adult, for the boys overseas. These came at a time when a considerable portion of animation, particularly from Disney and Warners, was contracted out by the War Department.

The war altered the look of all cartoons. The Second World War chase is considerably more linear, more like three lines actually, toward what I will define later as the "pyramidal" style of cartoon, even in Avery's work. Certainly, the Tom and Jerry series (Hanna and Barbera for MGM) was more linear, as were the Woody Woodpecker shorts.

The war adds a third element. The earlier two were the antic cartoon of pre-1934, mixed after 1937 with Disney full animation. For almost four years, the chase cartoon dominates as it never would again, to capture the spirit of the war against the Axis Powers, to chase Hitler into hell and beyond. By 1945, the ferocious speed of these cartoons had been fine-tuned. For example:

- The Goofy series at Disney, and *Hockey Homicide* in particular (1945). Their director, Jack Kinney, wrote: "These shorts were just the way I liked 'em — loud and fast, with continuous dialogue. I threw everything in, everything but the kitchen sink."[5] The How-To Goofys resemble various training films Kinney and others made at Disney during the war.
- The gremlin cartoons at Warners (Clampett), based on an idea developed at first by Disney, for the War Department.
- The first Wolfie cartoons by Avery at MGM, after the anti-Nazi *Blitz Wolf*.
- Chuck Jones' first faster Bugs cartoon, *Hare-Raising Hare* (1946), done with gags similar to his army Snafu cartoons.
- The basic wartime format established for Tom and Jerry shorts, for Woody Woodpecker shorts, Heckyl and Jeckyl, Tweety. The dog-eat-dog world of the chase cartoon has been assembled.

By 1946, two cycles of chase cartoon had already come and gone: 1937–41 and 1942–45. The next cycle began more obviously in 1948, in response to the postwar anxieties and the expanding consumerist world. It is a more epic variant of the earlier chase, more simplified, even more stripped down, in some cases past the gears. Avery and Chuck Jones are the master innovators of the chase in the fifties, particularly Jones and Freleng. But the chase genre was dissolving in the fifties. In many ways, all the three I mentioned above (Avery, Jones, Freleng) are producing epitaphs of sorts to the theatrical cartoon. Their cartoons become odd parodies about the uncertainty of the form itself, not always intentionally, most as a response to diminishing prospects, as the studios are being continually cut back.

Then in the fifties, the UPA style has a considerable impact (see chapter 22). But that is not the immediate subject. Our subject here is the poetics of the chase, both a new and a worn area of study. So much has been written on Warners over the past decade or more, and on Avery, that there seems little point in retracing the same road. At the same time, however, the narrative structure of these chases, so crucial to live-action cinema in the eighties and nineties, has not been examined quite as carefully, except to praise it, as an alternative to Disney personality animation. Very little has been written on the use of background, plot, or dialogue in these cartoons. And beyond work on the wartime cartoons (1942–45), the social history and the audience reception have not been discussed in any detail. That is the central argument of this book, about the importance of antic narrative and graphics as defining a poetics for animation. The chase cartoon became the governing paradigm for the antic (anarchy) after 1940. As such, a few reminders are needed, to keep the cupboard organized, and up to date, into the forties.

DISNEY ANIMATION MADE THE CHASE POSSIBLE

In the late thirties, many of the Warners animators had the Disney training, even went to Don Graham's classes. But how they interpreted full animation a few years later reveals a great deal about the hidden anarchies within the Disney style — the loose ends that add charm and humanity, the mismatched volumes and atmospheres I discuss in chapter 12 on Snow White, for example.

Then, by the late forties, what these animators developed went in two divergent directions: the rhythm was made faster, or much, much slower. And again, by faster, I do not mean more velocity (as I explained in chapter 15 on the chase cartoon). In many way, what those working on chase cartoons discovered was similar to what UPA animators discovered in the late forties. So, in that sense, UPA was also "faster." Is that the way it was? The UPA style looks so deliberate; and yet, its flatter graphics also relied on contradictions spilling into each other at once, as in a Warners chase.

So, as a generic problem, cartoons of the forties and fifties tend to move much faster; or simply stand still and let crazy meteorites bump into them, as in UPA animation. Whether fast or slow, more was being trimmed away, removed from the frame, as in a cartoon like *Gerald McBoing-Boing*. Therefore, another boundary shifted.

UPA CARTOONS ARE "CHASES" THAT STAND STILL

In the fifties, "less becomes more" in animation. But this simplified style was used throughout the industry, not only at UPA, but also at Warners, MGM, and Lantz. Interviews with layout artists of the time (like Maurice Noble) indicate that the backgrounds were not simpler merely as a way to save money. They appear partly as a natural extension of earlier work. In fact, the chase cartoons of the forties help lead to breakthroughs in stylized animation, like *Gerald McBoing-Boing*. And these breakthroughs took place years before UPA became established. Again, I will be covering this material more thoroughly as we proceed, but for now, a summary statement might be useful: The rhythm of the chase allows the slower Disney poses, like "anticipation," to be simplifed into a kind of streamlining. This streamlining suggests more abstract background and space.

The obvious example is Chuck Jones' *The Dover Boys at Pimento University* (1942), a chase made up almost entirely of anticipation poses, as part of its parody of old "mellerdrammers." Beck and Friedwald, in their thorough survey of Warners animation, explain:[6]

The characters pop from pose to pose, with a few frames of "smear" action between each position — resulting in a new cartoon "logic" that would be used in Warner cartoons for the next fifteen years, making them faster and funnier.

This *pop-and-smear* style resembles the background and double-takes in the Roadrunner series, begun by Chuck Jones six years later (1948). However, it also resembles *Gerald McBoing-Boing*, made eight years later (1950), and directed by Bobe Cannon (the animator for *The Dover Boys* in 1942). By speeding up the chase, the cartoon moves in two contradictory directions: (1) toward cutting frames, and (2) cutting away some of the space.

Either way, the movement begins to flatten the volumes more and alter the backgrounds. The chase shows us that full animation is incomplete at its best. More volume and atmosphere does not make the graphics more orderly, no matter how cute the bunnies get. It adds more ways to be out of control, more ways to collide. The chase reconfirms the essential anarchy of the form.

CHAPTER SEVENTEEN

Citizen Kane, the Cartoon: Screwball Noir, 1941–46

The material in the last chapter — fast versus slow in the chase — suggests another obvious connection that needs consideration in its own right, about the mood of the audience and the film-maker, about links with live action.

The best way to suggest this is by recalling the first four minutes of *Citizen Kane*: the dying Kane remembers "Rosebud." Through special effects (animation effects), we journey into the object in his hand, an animated space. It is a journey that enters the improbable, and structurally, imagistically, shows the film dissolving (literally through lapse dissolves) into Kane's death. So also, the cartoon chase goes from pure velocity (in 1937) to stillness (in the late fifties), a journey imagistically about its own death, like a *grand guignol* with a touch of film noir.

THE NOIR GAG: ANXIETY IN THE CHASE

The chase cartoon seems to preview some of the attitudes that emerged later in film noir. I would not call these cartoons petits noirs; that would be ludicrous. But the chase cartoon after 1937 reacts against melodrama in a way that parallels the crime films of the mid-forties. Both forms were antic and amoral. In both, poetic justice can be an evil in itself. Sentiment becomes a sneaky trick to cheat the gullible. And very wry, sardonic jokes undercut the plot.

A closer point of comparison might be the screwball comedy, which is also rather sardonic and indeed very fast in its movement from scene to scene, with slapstick gags added. Of course, there is no compelling evidence that directors of the chase cartoon modeled their work on pre-noir or on screwball comedies any more than on other cinema genres in Hollywood. Clampett was apparently a fan of Capra films, and claimed that some of the carrot gags with Bugs had loose links to scenes from *It Happened One Night*; or that La Cava's *My Man Godfrey* (1937) set many at the cartoon studio thinking about new uses for slapstick. But the argument still sounds hesitant. Avery certainly studied the Marx Brothers carefully, but not Frank Capra,

Howard Hawkes, or Preston Sturges. As for "noir" gags, Warners cartoons frequently referred to Bogart and Robinson, *Thugs with Dirty Mugs* being the most cited; but this was done essentially as Warners company business, but not much more really.

The parallels with screwball and noir are useful only to identify a boundary in public taste which was gradually emerging — a boundary that the film industry was beginning to notice. A segment of the movie audience was beginning to shift away from the moralizing of thirties melodrama. There was a growing market for faster, more raucous anti-melodramas, first in screwball comedies of the thirties, then in chase cartoons, and finally in crime films. The war, of course, made all that inevitable, as I will explain in chapter 18. But in a peculiar way, cartoons show us that there was a certain continuity between screwball comedies and film noir (*Double Indemnity Meets Screwball Squirrel*). Or the cartoon moment where Bogart, on the screen in *To Have and to Have Not*, shoots Wolfie out in the audience trying to get in to howl at Lauren Bacall (*Bacall to Arms*, 1946, Warners: Clampett).

BACKGROUND

In the films by Sturges and Hawkes in particular, and in Capra by the late thirties,

Drawing for *Porky in Wackyland* (Warners, dir. Bob Clampett, 1938). Porky trapped again, now in Dodo-bird land, where freaks of nature entertain themselves at his expense.

the first enthusiasms of the New Deal appear exhausted, painful to sustain. The economic downturn of 1937 seems to leave very little to cheer about.

The crisis in Europe also had an effect, which is not evident in the films directly. Before 1940, references to Nazis and appeasement generally are left out of cartoons (and films). But the Spanish Civil War had an uneasy effect on the politics of the film industry. Political arguments in Hollywood grew between isolationists and interventionists, between leftists and union-busters, during the first wave of HUAC investigations in 1938.

These anxieties have a narrow but identifiable effect on the cartoon industry, where the range of political response was somewhat narrower. For animators very directly, the burning issues were miserable wages, unionization, and feeling utterly marginalized within the studio system (treated and paid like crafts workers who did not make movies, only provided a related service). At the lower levels, from assistant animators to inkers, there was a very strong impetus for unions, and this involved a number of animators as well. (Many animators also ignored union fights or tried to stay "neutral," and crossed picket lines.) Major strikes and threats of strike among animation studios began in 1937 at Fleischer in New York, and peaked

Drawing for *The Daff Doc* (Warners, dir. Bob Clampett, 1938). Porky undergoes malpractice as Daffy's unwilling patient.

with the Disney strike of 1941, with near-strikes at Schlesinger and even at MGM. These struggles were actually more in the thick of Hollywood politics than one might suppose. The Disney strike, for example, was pivotal in beginning the battle between rival craft unions (CSU and IATSE) which led ultimately to the Warners strikes of 1945—46, which set up much that became the Hollywood Ten and the blacklist in 1947. Virtually every extended interview with Warners and MGM animators mentions the neglect many felt while working there, the isolation from the rest of studio business, the affronteries from Schlesinger or Quimby. And of course, at Disney, some of the wounds from 1941 still remain. Some of the diaries that Disney animators kept at the time are still not made public. Animators like Art Babbitt, who went to the Supreme Court in a case against Disney, still rage over how they were treated. And rumors about Walt Disney assisting in setting up the blacklist began the saga of anti-Disney lore — about Disney as reactionary — and remains a sore point in animators' biographies and animation histories even today.

It is hardly surprising, then, to find many gags about the movie business in cartoons — darker gags. Chase cartoons from 1937 to 1941 have more about bad contracts than about the Great Depression, more about a callous film industry, about disputes with management. In *The Big Snooze* (1945), for example, Elmer tears up his contract, but is haunted in his sleep by Bugs until he pastes it back together and gets back to work. The strike is over. Elmer is forced off a cliff, because that's his job, to get pounded by Bugs as controller (a kind of foreman), who says: "I lo-ove that man." This cartoon was made during the massive Warners strike, months before Leon Schlesinger decided to sell his company to Warners, and a year before Clampett simply left, for Columbia, then Republic, and in 1949 to his own show on TV, *Time for Beany*.

There was a quirky sense of capitalist hierarchy built into the chase format, a hierarchy that suggests the place where cartoons "belong" — near the bottom.

In Freleng's *You Oughta Be in Pictures*, Porky leaves a flat drawing to enter human live action on the Warners lot. Then, after countless insults and collisions, he goes back to the two-dimensional safety of the cartoon.

Even in Tom and Jerry cartoons, the humans are seen only at ankle height towering above the animals. The humans seem to stand in for the world denied the animator.

Throughout the animation industry, except for Frank Tashlin, none of the cartoon directors found any way to get into live action, though many of them expressed a desire to try it. Avery, like Tashlin, Jones, Clampett, and the various gagmen, would take breaks watching the films being shot on various sound stages. Occasionally, they would meet actors or directors. Lantz had many friends in the industry, including Capra.

Avery, though very shy about promoting himself, would occasionally go to comedy directors on the Warners lot and give advice. One of Avery's gagmen of the forties, Heck Allen, remembers how coldly he was received:[1]

Five hundred dollars' worth of jokes in a minute. Unbelievable. The most unbelievable thing was that they didn't appreciate it, that they didn't snare him and elevate him to the papacy of humor on the front lot. Tex could have been a Frank Capra or whatever in this business, could have gone completely to the top. The cartoon business is full of brilliant people like that who never get heard of. Their tragic flaw is that they're hung up on these goddam little figures running around on that drawing board. See? They've been infected with that. Literally, the animation bug is in the blood.

A BRIEF ASIDE

There is another angle to this matter of cartoons/live-action. Heck Allen's reference to the "animation bug" was rather apt. Working on a frame-by-frame film art took the animator away from traditional Hollywood film-making. It was still essentially a graphic not a dramatic form of film narrative. Many left cartoon animation not to go into live action, but rather to go into more experimental forms of graphics and cinema (as with UPA expatriates John Hubley or Jules Engel in the sixties). Among the animators of the late thirties, only Tashlin regularly considered jobs in live-action, even as a gag man for Harpo Marx in *Night at Casablanca* (1945). I do not see why other animators could not have worked in much the same way when a job in cartoons fell through, except for the matter of temperament and preference. In tracing the job-hopping of most animators, they rarely headed toward live-action work at all, as we will see in studying the formation of UPA (1943). Animators then (and today as well) were essentially graphic artists rather than film/story men, at least for features. Tashlin was an exception, essentially a screen writer who also made cartoons — and very energetic, surprising cartoons, because they were "cut" like a film, with closeups, long shots, and camera angles, which added to the ironic effects.

There are indications, by the way, that more animators have been trying to enter live-action cinema since 1977, beginning with *Star Wars*, and on into the nineties, with the growing importance of special-effects animation in Hollywood. The animator-turned-movie director Tim Burton causes quite a stir when he visits animation programs. An increasing number of animators are training more in live action and taking on more classes in screenwriting and film history than earlier. Next time, perhaps Wolfie will shoot Bogart. Animation and live action are moving closer together. I will explain why in the final chapter of the book.

CHAPTER EIGHTEEN

The Anarchy of Wartime Chase Cartoons: Coal Black and de Sebben Dwarfs

From 1942 to the end of the war, about half of the cartoons produced were "war-related," and at some studios for a time the proportion ran as high as 70 percent.[1] In addition, many training films were animated, because soldiers often remembered military data shown in cartoon form more easily than in printed manuals. And finally, cartoon documentaries proved extremely effective, after the success of Disney's *The New Spirit* (1942), on the touchy subject of Donald Duck paying his income taxes ("Taxes to beat the Axis"). The critic Bosley Crowther called *The New Spirit* "the most effective of the morale films yet released by the government."[2]

By 1943, Disney, Schlesinger (Warners), MGM, and Lantz were all under contract to produce animated shorts for the armed forces. At Disney's Hyperion Studios, many areas were treated as top secret and off-limits; employees had to get government clearance. The term "aerology" is remembered by all the veteran animators. The range of projects was staggering: training films for sea captains; films on how to load and fire rifles; on cloud formations (like primitive flight simulators); 3D models of Lake Mead; 3D models for mariners.

In addition, many animators enlisted and went to work at the FMPU, the army film-making unit at the old Hal Roach Studio in Culver City, where more animation was produced than at any Hollywood Studio during the war. Between both the studios and FMPU the range was amazing, from cartoon documentaries on aerial warfare (Disney's famous *Victory through Air Power*) to shorts on venereal disease, or for bond drives. Animators became court engravers, like Callot in the seventeenth century, who produced patriotic engravings about sieges for the Duke of Lorraine. The cartoon industry recorded the sieges and the great campaigns.

Virtually every major animator spent some time on one project or another linked directly to the war effort, developing gags about bombs, spies, and the medical hazards of war, like the Snafu series. Made for the *Army and Navy Screen Magazine*, these were five-minute warnings about a dead-beat soldier who keeps making mistakes. In *Rumors* (directed by Chuck Jones), the rumor "nice day for a bombing" starts in an army latrine, and is spread by Snafu, until baloney-shaped monsters haunt him into the madhouse.

Animators were asked to find what was "funny" — or at least inviting — about bombing raids; or the workings of a rifle; or even a military map. Some of the darkest, most brutal images took on a blissful, amoral enthusiasm.

The anarchy I describe in earlier chapters, particularly the chase, was remodeled for the military. Apparently, GIs overseas particularly enjoyed fast and violent chase cartoons. Animators often remember being told that soldiers asked for certain chases to be shown over and over again. The Snafu cartoons reflect this dark mood very clearly. Snafu dies often for his foolishness.

The humor for GIs was racier and blunter as well, with pinup gags, ass and latrine jokes, and gags about whores. The mosquito, Malaria Mike, stares at Snafu's naked buttocks and says: "I knew I seen that face before." In another Snafu cartoon, *Anopheles Annie*, a mosquito as a fat, drunken, rundown madame has her whores attack and infect Snafu with malaria.

In southern California there were even racy USO shows by animators. Ward Kimball remembers a lively jazz review he and other Disney animators performed, a burlesque of the famous old melodrama *The Drunkard*. As the show stopper at the end, a character named Professor "Alberti" played a xylophone while an animator drew pictures of a woman stripping. A surveyor's plumb line was made into her v-crotch. Then panties were added. It was frolic to keep up morale — sex and magic — like Orsen Welles' USO magic act, with a scantily clad assistant.

The GI market influenced cartoons made for movie theaters at home as well. The soldier's eye-view became, more or less, a governing paradigm for a faster style of chase cartoon. Hundreds of these, from Warners, Columbia, Disney, and Lantz, were released with GIs clearly in mind. According to many veteran animators, the model audience was the soldier and his anxious family. Cartoon chases became a kind of USO in a can — anarchy to beat the Axis, Hitler as *Blitz Wolf*, confessions of a "Nutsy" spy, Superman retooled for *Japoteurs* (Famous Studios, after the Fleischers were removed), Snafu retooled as Snafuperman; Donald getting brainwashed in *Der Fuerher's Face*, Gremlins getting the best of Bugs, Pluto finding saboteurs, Jerry throwing "hen" grenades against the Nazi Tom. In Lantz's *Pass the Biscuits Mirandy* (1943, Culhane), hilbilly biscuits turn into artillery shells.

As a result, chases often referrred to the hysteria of battle. Even old gags were dressed over in battle fatigues. For example, standardly in cartoons, when the character would run very fast, he left a trail of scorched earth or a powerful wind behind him. The trail would flatten or spin everything in its path. This was an easy device, the hurricane in the eye: everything stood still so that the momentum could be exaggerated madly. Now this old gag took on a wartime, worrisome look. In *Draftee Daffy* (1945, Clampett), Daffy burns up the plaster and the rugs as he flees from Elmer, "the little man from the draft board."

Gags about bombing raids were very common. In *A Tale of Two Kitties* (1942, Clampett), Tweety, up a tree, is attacked by Catstello, who is dressed like a spitfire, cruising in the sky. Suddenly, Catstello is lit by spotlights. Air-raid sirens go off.

Anti-aircraft guns shoot him down. He falls and flattens Babbit below. In Tweety's words, "The poor little puddy tat. He fall down and go *boom*."

In numerous cartoons, birds of prey (hawks, buzzards) were transformed into bombers, turning metallic, more angular, starting to buzz like a bomber and swooping. Even Daffy became a bird of prey. In *Scrap Happy Daffy* (1943, Tashlin), he turns into A-Man and bombs the Axis in his sleep. He howls while he defends his Allied scrap pile against a Nazi goat.

The noise level also grew more warlike. While defending his scrap pile, Daffy's screaming is as loud as his bombing and just as relentless, rather typical of many Warners cartoons during the war. The Warners dialogue, particularly for Clampett cartoons, was often at a high shriek, building on crescendos, with cycles of shock, followed by even more hysterical shock — again, typical of Clampett, but even more evident in Avery's Wolfie, with his ejaculative triple-takes, eyes shooting out like springs, jaw thudding like an anvil.

As part of the frolicsome spirit, a number of swing cartoons about "negroes" were made, most notably *Coal Black and de Sebben Dwarfs* (1943, Warners). In all, wartime cartoons have more black caricature even than cartoons from the thirties, ripe as they were. Lazy "negroes" and cute piccaninnies mixed in with the patriotic barrage against buck-teethed Japs and bulldog-necked Nazis.

How these black stereotypes fit into the anarchy of the wartime chase cartoon is perplexing, and yet they do. They were made by the same studios, the same units. Somehow, a war about the "master race" also sparked more gags about the black race (what many saw as positive associations somehow, a polyglot America). It was also part of the id in id-eological, a kind of explosive cathexis, or a projection/release that is soothing: to see the old comic plantation again; or the grinning zootsuiters. Many of the same tensions that made anarchic chases a favorite of the GIs apparently also made black stereotypes more appealing. Such is the peculiar dynamic of race.

Perhaps it was a white response to the number of blacks who moved to the big cities during the war, becoming a more visible presence, or went to black units fighting in Europe. It certainly was *not* an acknowledgement of the racist treatment of blacks in the military, of the Oakland mutiny by blacks during the war after many died in a callously mismanaged explosion in Oakland Harbor. Instead, it was musical racism. These blacks were essentially whites on the loose, "in the groove." They were nervously antic black-faced whites (or black retelling of white problems); and secondarily a direct comment on the condition of blacks. I am convinced that black stereotyping often cloaks white anxiety about modernization. At least in these cartoons it does — the same stress that is caricatured so often in gags about women working the swingshift at Lockheed; or paranoia about staying alert to air raids, shortages, spies. Many of the gags exaggerate the quick study needed for new job skills, for meeting quick deadlines — the chase in the workplace, the family without men.

In LA, where most of the cartoon industry remained, the war altered the economy very quickly, bringing in heavy industry on a level previously unknown in southern California. Defense plants working all night resulted in massive smogs, first in the summer of 1943, when the daylight downtown seemed to vanish for hours. This was a symptom of the enveloping reality. Defense contracts took on a determinant economic role — the haunting reliance on continual war that became a part of the American psyche afterward. At the same time, massive black and Mexican immigration brought on a white backlash which led to violence, even riots. Like all American cities during the war, LA seemed on the edge of oblivion and salvation at the same time. The chase cartoon hovered around that very sense of the manic, and many "abductive" associations the manic had, including blacks jitterbugging. And in a circuitous way, that may be why we find more gags about blacks as the soul of the American libido.

Thus, the wartime chase, with all its multiple codings, operated as an "abduction," to use the phrase from Peirce as reinterpreted by Eco: an uncertainty in the coding of metaphor; meanings emergent in imagery, but not yet commonly agreed upon.[3] So they take on an emotional scattershot: multiple inferences, a kind of heteroglossia, or spot gags as language. The cacophony of gags starts to make a bizarre kind of sense: Nazis meet Rosie the Riveter, while blacks in zootsuits go into swingtime to help bombers hit Berlin. The chain of inferences evokes a mood of happy hysteria. This mood unifies as it breaks apart. As the chase proceeds, the story abducts the mood from one image to another — a gag about blackmarket whitewall tires reinforces the next gag, about covetous Nazi agents or a vengeful evil stepmother. The inferences run in a mad scramble, but they run. This scramble is a great teacher, about how inferences in a chase, however unlikely, can enhance each other. Throwaway gags can now be insane movement enhancers, like grease on a road. By making cartoons for the army, about battle fatigue, bombings, and morale, animators learned new techniques for putting hysteria into motion. The wartime cartoons may look uncontrolled, but they were lessons toward a simplified chase format afterward, toward new ways to make throwaways follow each other. They were a laboratory.

Using Bob Clampett's classic *Coal Black and de Sebben Dwarfs* (1943) as my centerpiece, I will discuss how anarchic gags developed during the war, how they addressed the moods of the audience — not simply the patriotism, but also the anxieties and prejudices.

To keep some order to the anarchy, since the matter of black caricature is central here, I will start with a brief survey of black stereotypes in cartoons, then of Clampett's approach, and of parallel examples, in cartoons from other animators.

There were indeed quite a few to choose from beside *Coal Black*. At least a dozen vividly "racist" cartoons were made during the Second World War, only a few of these from Clampett — some from Chuck Jones, and others at Warners and from the Lantz Studio from George Pal. Many of the best are well known to cartoon buffs, and are available on special video cassettes: *Tin Pan Alley Cats*, made soon after *Coal*

Black and de Sebben Dwarfs; Inki and the Mynah Bird, in 1940; color "swingtoons" from Lantz; the Jasper cartoons from George Pal. Clips from these appear regularly in documentaries about the history of American racism. At film rental houses, many are listed with a warning about content. And none of them makes it to kid-vid on TV. They are "specialty" pieces. Audiences still whistle at the rubber-lipped, bug-eyed faces, at the caricatures of negritude: cannibals with bones through their noses (in early thirties cartoons more than in the forties, when the look changed a bit); little nappy boys in jungle costumes; oily zootsuiters; brassy mammies in slippers. A certain bounce was added by the forties, more big band references and city blacks. Stepin Fetchit went through a cartoon rinse cycle during the war, but still came out just as fretful and dumb: "Feet, don't fail me now."

Other cartoons, not defined as racist, have occasional black caricatures, nothing very central to the story, an extension of business as usual from the thirties. The inference is still very clear: the shuffling mammy in Tom and Jerry cartoons; the piccaninny centaur-ettes working as maids in *Fantasia* (they were removed from the film when it was restored for re-release in 1991).

And yet, at the time all these cartoons were made, relatively few complaints

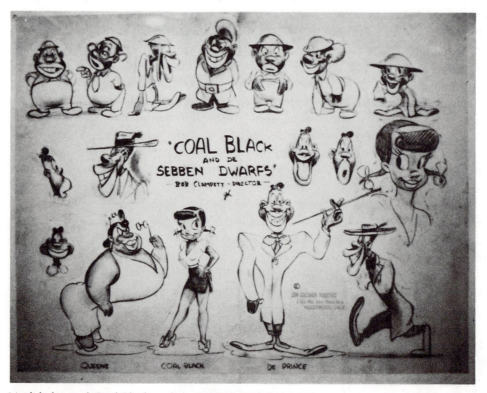

Model sheet of *Coal Black and de Sebben Dwarfs* (1943).

appeared about the racist content. In some cases, black musicians even helped script the gags. I do not imagine that this surprises the reader, when one considers how deep are the problems of race in America. Racist imagery will sometimes be acceptable to blacks too, even while it is given respectability by whites. To Clampett, *Coal Black* was a homage to black entertainers, and by extension, I suppose, to the growing black community in Los Angeles (on Central Avenue), a change he apparently sensed. He presented the war fever as a cartoon jitterbug, in what he believed to be a positive statement about race. Such are the peculiar inversions of white over black in America.

SOURCES OF THE GRAPHICS

Stereotypes of African-Americans have their own modernity, specifically within the twentieth century: blacks in entertainment; Broadway shows about blacks; blacks in cities; blacks "resisting" industrialization. They obviously resemble older racist imagery, the slapstick of blacks since the Renaissance, if not earlier — at least as old as colonization and the slave trade. But I would rather concentrate in this book on how the animators in 1943 specifically remembered and visualized — how they drew the African-American (then allowed broader implications in). This was wartime, in a city utterly consumed by the war in the Pacific, and by the movie marketing of patriotism. Strictly as a problem in figure drawing, the animators relied on sources from popular illustration after another war, after 1865:

1. The freed slave: E. W. Kemble, the widely copied illustrator for Mark Twain, used less broad caricature than other illustrators at the time, seemingly more about the look of recently freed slaves. However, in the way Kemble drew, one sees angles of the lean body and face that reappear in work by many other illustrators, suggesting the black tramp, the itinerant "darky".
2. Uncle Remus Tales (finding their way into Disney's *Song of the South*, 1945).
3. The Dogtown lithographs of Currier and Ives (blacks caricatured in silly re-enactments of white gentility).
4. Gags taken from minstrel shows, then transcribed to Broadway in the musical *Showboat*, or *Green Pastures*.
5. Or even from Kingfish in *Amos and Andy*, on radio, and in comic strips.
6. Finally, from the one-reelers of black swing bands made in the thirties and forties.

These were mostly images that originated in northern cities, about southern problems. Taking 1865 as the starting date, a new crop of racist illustrations came from the northern press looking whimsically at the defeated South. Apparently the abolition of slavery, and the crises after the Civil War, induced a new wave of mass caricature in northern newspapers, satires about blacks failing on their own.

Did these become a cartoon version of Jim Crow? That sounds exaggerated. However, they continued well past Reconstruction, very vividly into the 1880s and afterward, during the period of Jim Crow repression, when the worst of racist hostility started up yet again. These were illustrations about a shiftless, anarchic black, newly freed, never prepared, out of place.

Then, in the 1920s, there was an identifiable change. These "negro" gags were given a modified, much sweeter, look to match the appeal of ragtime and jazz: "This place is jumping," taking the shiftless theme directly into entertainment — blacks ever ready to party. Little black boys became much more musical. They plunked at banjos, did mad jigs, or banged on cat-house pianos. There is our immediate starting point. That is why Flip the Frog played his piano with body gestures very much like a black musician. Or why Bosko was clearly a little black man, often at the piano, then breaking into a fast dance.

Mickey himself started out with touches of black caricature in his first cartoon, wearing tattered pants, with bare, black legs and saucer eyes. But these signifiers were never labeled simply as black. They were part of the generic vaudeville costume, even though many veteran animators of the era (e.g. Freleng and Jones) identify them as obviously influenced by black slapstick.

That leads to yet another peculiar question about racism and cartoons. Had black stereotypes become so generic by the thirties and forties that they were not consciously seen as being about negroes? Blacks in musical comedy had so powerful a meaning in American entertainment, and they were so often played by whites themselves, they almost transcended the issue of race itself. *Almost*, but certainly never entirely. To say "almost" merely captures the sense of how essential "blackface" was to the cartoon form.

Blacks in vaudeville and film became virtually a cartoon in themselves, the *zanni* (zanies) and harlequins of American mass culture. "Negro" characters were instrinsically upside down. Responsible behavior was presumably "beyond" their brain power, and amoral behavior was simply "how they were." Blacks were shown as primitive and fancy free, dancing on the soft shoe, the soul of poor folk. At the same time, they were presumably very calm and trusting (translation: lazy and unimaginative). They were bucolics trapped on the farm, while the world passed them by (translation: unable to master machines and city life).

COAL BLACK AND DE SEBBEN DWARFS

As I mentioned earlier, Bob Clampett was apparently interested in black entertainment. His primary source for *Coal Black* was *Harlem as Seen by Hirschfeld* (1941), a book of caricatures well known to many animators (as were Hirschfeld's drawings in general, for the work of T. Hee, for example). But here again, Hirschfeld specialized in theater entertainment imagery; it was the mystique of the black entertainer that attracted Clampett. In preparation for this spoof on Disney's *Snow White*, he took his animators club-hopping one night to various black music spots in Los Angeles, particularly to Central Avenue, which was very much the Harlem West for black entertainment at the time.

The animator Virgil Ross, who had specialized in designing dancing figures for Tex Avery since his days at Lantz, modeled his Prince Chawmin' partly on a black man he had seen on the dance floor that night — a man so limber and tall, with a partner so short, that he swung his foot over her head as they danced.

Ross also gave Prince Chawmin' a broad manic smile (a very common device already at Warners, the gummy wild grin) and dice were added as front teeth. He was a very fluid and graceful character, with the stooped movements of the zootsuiter; or suit-o-r, since he is the "prince" who woos the heroine. She was named "So White," a spunky little pinup designed by Clampett and Rod Scribner, and a particular favorite of Clampett himself, who used to keep a drawing of her, winking back like a teenage Betty Grable, in his office forty years later.

As late as the seventies and afterward, Clampett regularly defended *Coal Black* against charges of racism, explaining that he had hired Eddie Beals (jazz piano, on Central Avenue, but also in Hollywood) and others to help with the gags. The voices were Vivian Dandridge as Coal Black, her mother Ruby as the Evil Stepmother, and Zoot Watson as the Prince: all black radio and film performers. He also had the trumpet in Beals' band add a few blasts for the scene when Prince Chawmin' tries to wake up the sleeping So White with his "dyn-o-mite" kiss. Apparently, Clampett had wanted Beals to do more of the music, but either Carl Stallings or Schlesinger stopped him.

Clampett was clearly a fan of Beals' work, and used him a few months later for the cartoon *Tin Pan Alley Cats*. He also admired Duke Ellington's *Jump for Joy* cavalcade of 1942, which had toured Los Angeles, and saw *Coal Black* a bit in that variety mode. He was not himself a musician, though some of the animators (like Virgil Ross) knew some honky-tonk piano or were part of a weekend band. In his unit, there was a generalized appreciation of the movements and vocabulary of black entertainment, but not necessarily much more.

Coal Black was not intended to be a statement about black life, only about big-band anarchy as a raunchier alternative to Disney. It opens with a Hattie McDonald style mammy talking to a little black girl on her lap, while the fire radiates in yellows very similar to Disney effects, spinning with atmospheric lighting.

The mammy agrees to tell the real version of Snow White, entirely with blacks. This opening resembles Avery cartoons at the same time, like *Red Hot Riding Hood* or even *Screwy Squirrel*: characters resist being in a sentimental fairy-tale cartoon; there is a break, and then the raunchier version takes over. In the case of *Coal Black*, Disney's *Snow White* is inverted, with dialogue re-cited in jitterbug singsong.

We open with "So White," pigtails and all, re-enacting in jitter-rap the Disney scene where Snow White wishes at the well, the piece about the prince who will come some day. Just then, lo and behold, Prince Chawmin' does zap in, like a spring-loaded projectile, and dressed to the teeth. They start a minuet, then break into a jitterbug.

Meanwhile, the evil queen, a brawny, growling fat momma with huge biceps and expensive tastes, hires Murder Incorporated to "black out So White." They, of course (like the huntsmen of yore), fall for her instead, in what appears to be a group petting party. Afterward, faces patched with lipstick kisses, they wave goodbye to her as they ride off, leaving her alone in the dark, deep forest.

There she finds the seven dwarfs (Dopey is a ringer for Disney's Dopey, and is labeled so in the storyboards). They are GIs in tents at camp. Very quickly, under a label USO, she becomes their bouncy fry cook. But not for long: the evil queen, in disguise with rubber nose and food cart, delivers the poisoned apple. So White takes one bite, falls down, "and that ain't good," say the dwarfs. Cut from grieving to battle: they take their revenge like soldiers, fire anti-tank artillery to dispose of the evil queen.

But So White is still lying there dead. On cue, Prince Chawmin' zaps in again, grinning with enthusiasm, ready to kiss her with his "Rosebud" lips. He gets to work kissing. Try as he might, though, none of his kisses wakes her. Finally, he gives up; he is old now, white-haired and shriveled. Next in line, little Dopey takes over, and with one slippy kiss pops her back to life. She bounces off the ground, as if by electricity. Her pigtails wave the American flag. She prefers the GI over the civilian — the little guy in uniform. Patriotism gets her going.

An exhibitor's flyer called it "blackface in swing." Soon after it was released, the Library of Congress complained about the dwarfs, not so much as racist stereotypes, but as an unheroic way to display the American soldier.

Most of all, *Coal Black* was intended as a declaration of personal independence. Black music was literally presented as an antidote to Disney sentimentality. The atmospheric Disney opening is dropped as soon as the story really begins. We leave the atmospheric plantation for a very contemporary castle, the queen with her stash of whitewall tires. An almost crude layout follows, in the violets and reds so common to Warner backgrounds during the war (though not as violet and red as the washed-out colors of old prints suggest — more blues in the original). Nevertheless, the background does have a very sketchy landscape, rather typical of the war years, to cut costs under multiple deadlines, to put all the labor investment into movement. The dances were very carefully choreographed, almost in the Disney manner.

POINTS OF COMPARISON

The space in Clampett-land is very identifiable, different than Tashlin — the long crane shots and cinematic cuts; different than Avery, who emphasized the edges

From the storyboards by Rod Schribner for *Coal Black and de Sebben Dwarfs*, the scene where Prince Chawmin' tries to revive So White with his "dyn-o-mite" kiss. But his "Rosebud" lips fail, and he withers into an old man. (The little private who resembles Dopey wakes her up instead.)

of the frame (flat versus deep). Clampett's "eye-view" is more like a staged set, perhaps even shallower, and hovers very much at the ground level, like a wacky set of roads made for stretching around corners. Clampett characters and objects have a peculiar elasticity: they stretch and snap quickly into position, like spring-loaded caterpillars. On the storyboards by Rod Scribner, which are astonishingly well done and very close to the final film (unusual for Clampett, who usually made many changes along the way), Clampett writes that the car must be stretched; and the road already stretches like a rubber band.

The background is not as cluttered or cinematic as those in Avery cartoons, where the blackout gags need a kind of cinematic overhead shot or optical illusions up high. However, Clampett's throwaway gags have the same obsessive sense of contemporary detail, pot shots at rationing and petty corruptions, a cheerful look at brutality. Murder Incorporated announces its rates:

> "We rub out anybody ... $1.00.
> Midgets ... half price.
> Japs ... for free."

(That last line always gets a sour groan from the audience. It might have drawn applause in 1943.)

On the storyboards the gangsters of Murder Incorporated are called "poisonalities."

While it is difficult to fit all the wartime product into a single arc, a few obvious changes passed throughout the cartoon industry, changes that are evident in *Coal Black* as well.

RESISTANCE TO THIRTIES SENTIMENTALITY

Clearly, the wartime chase cartoon "resembles" film noir, as I mentioned in chapter 17. Sentimental characters become the butt of the jokes, a kind of anti-melodrama, in Wolfie, Screwy Squirrel, and even Woody Woodpecker cartoons; also in the numerous updated fairy tales made during the war, like *Pigs in a Polka, Red Hot Riding Hood* (and the other showgirl cartoons); *Tortoise Beats Hare; Bugs Bunny and the Three Bears; Goldilocks and the Jivin' Bears*. Nostalgia is replaced by big-city cynicism. Characters become Brooklyn grifters of a sort, like Bugs. Los Angeles is treated as a city of scams, as in Clampett's early effort *Get Rich Quick, Porky* (1938), where a flim-flamming real-estate salesman sells Porky and Gabby an oil well salted with a few cans of gasoline. Hollywood has a bit of flim-flam also, in Avery's *Hollywood Steps Out* (1941: Dinners at Ciro's $50. "Six months to pay, small down-payment"). The Warners lot becomes a special hell for Porky in *You Oughta Be in Pictures* (1940), Freleng's first cartoon back at Warners after trying a year working for Quimby at MGM. Like the animator given a raw turn, Porky is hoodwinked by Daffy into tearing up his contract. Porky tries to get into features, then gets chased and generally brutalized by live-action movie people, even by a genial Leon (voice dubbed).

Along with the cynical thread of gags came further refinements in the element I call "nuisance/over-reactor/controller." This was particularly evident in the Tom and Jerry cartoons, a compendium in many ways of the chase formulas at that time — a more causal, more ontological path for the chase to follow; more complicated obstacles made for less waste.

Tom and Jerry

At the Oscars certainly, the period during the war was dominated by Hanna and Barbera, and their dual velocipede cartoons — state of the art chases. These contrast a great deal with the cartoons Hugh Harmon directed for MGM at the same time, like *Goldilocks and the Three Bears* (1939) or *Lonesome Stranger* (1940), which are stunningly animated, in a fullness that still has some of the older rubber-hose body types, but with highly deliberate movements, not quick turns and crushing chases. It was much, much closer to Disney, and quite remarkable. The Tom and Jerry series also used the best of Disney, but the best of Warners as well. The characters had Disneyfied faces and skeletal movements as elaborate as Disney might do, with a lot of "anticipation" and overlapping movement. However, they were chases, flat and simple (of the "baseboard" variety), with sudden breaks and skids similar to Warners' timing. The stories started around a single formula, and managed to repeat for seventeen years, with the variety based on a familiarity that is unique to the animated cartoon. The formula, with exceptions, can be summarized briefly as follows: Jerry and Tom take turns as controller, because the balance of power keeps shifting, whenever Butch or the maid accidentally joins the chase. The balance is ultimately held by a third party. In wartime cartoons, this was often a pretty lady cat, like the black kitten in *Zoot Suit Cat* (1944). Tom in *Zoot Suit Cat* might be considered a parallel to *Coal Black*, for lack of another. Tom fails to impress his girlfriend (as always). He literally pads his performance by putting a hanger in his coat to get that "V" across the shoulders. He's bound to fail. The point of *Zoot Suit Cat* is that Tom cannot pull off the streetwise look. He is simply a house kitty, like Sylvester, tough on his own turf, but not very good outside.

Tom and Jerry cartoons were like juggling acts, where nothing is allowed to fall. Often a bobbling object is left hanging treacherously, lingeringly. Tom tries desperately to hold it in his mouth, or by one toe, until it finally falls, and brings him down with it.

Usually Tom is not permitted to release his fury, to go against his own nature. Don't make a mess, he's warned. Don't make a noise. Don't touch the mouse. Most of the laughs come from Tom's struggle to overcome these controls. They were marvelously inventive cartoons within that very simple discipline — how to pit repression against Tom's anarchy and let the little guy take revenge. In that sense, they were as much about cathexis (attempting to escape from repression) as any chase cartoons ever made.

From the Lantz Studio we have black swing cartoons like Broadway musicals; or Woody doing a pilot-to-bombadier routine in *The Beach Nut*, or tormenting the sergeant at the base in *Ace in the Hole* (one of many "you're-in-the-army-now" cartoons) (1942).[4] The range from Lantz is still fairly limited, as also from Famous Studio, with Popeye dive-bombing in *Scrap the Japs* (1942). As far as prophets for the wartime chase, only Avery and Clampett cover the field widely. For Avery, the best parallel to *Coal Black* would be his showgirl in *Swingshift Cinderella* (released soon after the end of the war), a sequel of sorts to *Red Hot Riding Hood* (1943). We should look at both for a moment, to see how different 1943 was from 1945, and gain a sense of the range of the chase during the war and what was learned about making gags about the world upside down.

Avery's Red Hot Riding Hood vs. Swingshift Cinderalla

Many readers may have seen *Swingshift Cinderella*, on a Tex Avery tape. She does her act in a combination New York/LA nightclub world, at the Castle Mañana, where the sex-starved fairy godmother holds on to Wolfie (in scraggly debonair moustache), knocking him senseless each time he makes a move after Red, until she flees in overalls at midnight to the swing shift at Lockweed Aircraft, where more wolves on the bus howl after her.

Rushed as the action in this cartoon is, *Red Hot Riding Hood* was even madder, with even faster cuts. I suspect that Avery was already balancing the tempo of his cartoons (fast versus slow); as I discuss in chapter 20 on the postwar chase. Wolfie is less ejacula-ramic, perhaps to satisfy the censor. His eyeballs do not literally ejaculate, swell out and spurt. His ghost does not stiffen like an erection at the sight of Red in the spotlight.

In *Swingshift Cinderella*, Red is slimmer and slinkier than in *Red Hot Riding Hood*, less bouncy. It also opens with less fury: Wolfie escapes from a boring Little Red Riding Hood cartoon to a sexier one. *Red Hot Riding Hood* opened almost the same way, for ten seconds, but then broke into a threatened strike by the characters: "If you can't do this thing a new way, I quit!" *Swingshift Cinderella* has more gags about vehicles metamorphosing: a pumpkin into station wagon; a bath tub into a limousine; a junk pile into a clattering jeep. But overall the manic energy is more under control.

In many ways, *Red Hot Riding Hood* belongs more to the same year as *Coal Black*. It has more insane leaps in impossible space and time. Wolfie tries to escape the furious advances of the fairy godmother, and runs straight through any sense of perspective, a post-Euclidean game of line versus space. It has all the tumbling effect of the best Avery cartoons, like a room bouncing down a steep hill, never standing still. It is a world coming apart at the seams, and yet somehow operating by a four-dimensional guidance system. Avery certainly worked in the explosive spirit of the war, but without many gags directly about combat (except in his Hitler parody, *Blitz Wolf*, of course).

The sheer velocity of Avery cartoons was perfected during the war, particularly with *Dumb-Hounded* (1943), the first Droopy cartoon, where Droopy gets there first no matter how madly Wolfie tries to escape. From Swing-Swing Prison to the Arctic Circle, Wolfie keeps accelerating, and adding to his screeching hysteria, but Droopy shows up first anyway. Wolfie is daunted but determined. He turns an ocean liner into a speedboat (like the earlier "Pingo-Pongo" mock newsreels Avery made at Warners), and shoots across continents. But Droopy is always waiting, with a laconic, nasal: "Hi Joe." Shriek! When that doesn't work, he ties up Droopy and runs, or slams fifteen doors on him. Utter impossibility is defied again and again. That is the key for an era of extremes.

In less than 400 days of war, the United States put over twelve million Americans in uniform, from a startup of less than 300,000 soldiers, an escape trick if ever there was one — from the Great Depression into the integrated industrial economy of the postwar era. And during that transformation, the two cartoon masters of speed were Avery and Clampett.

1947: Roger Rabbit Then and Now

In 1988, the movie *Who Framed Roger Rabbit?* took Americans back to a mythic 1947 cartoon industry. Famous characters scrambled across the screen. Gags from classic cartoons and detective movies were brought back. Like a seance, it talked to us by the campfire, and made spirits dance in the smoke.

Some of these spirits were brewed out of the way we, in 1988, remembered cartoons, as well as our nostalgia for old Los Angeles as noir-town, and how it was replaced by the consumer fifties. According to *Roger Rabbit*, something vital was at stake in 1947 — a matter of life and death (or "death by dipping"). This serves very well as an introduction to chase cartoons after 1947; and to the unfocused, lingering disquiet beneath their silliness, to gags about erasure, about a city that specialized in leaving no traces.

The film opens in the midst of a chase cartoon, modeled on Baby Huey, Sylvester/ Tweety or, more likely, Tom and Jerry. It uses Avery-style fast breaks, one collision after another.

Suddenly, after a refrigerator falls on the hapless Roger Rabbit, a live action director bursts into the cartoon. The director is annoyed. Roger is forgetting his lines. He cannot keep his mind on his work.

We cut to live action, to find out what is bothering Roger. Does it have to do with his wife, the slinky torch singer Jessica? Mervyn Acme, owner of Maroon (cartoon) Studios hires a human detective named Eddie Valiant to find out. Eddie is a mess. He seems to be strangling in clichés lifted intentionally from old detective films.

His business has been going downhill for years. He's even shorter than Bogart and chunkier than Jack Nicholson. He dresses like a cheap gumshoe, in rumpled stripes. He can't buy anything but more bad luck. His hardboiled girlfriend needles him all the time. He lives in the slums of Los Angeles noir.

What's worse, now he has to go back to Toon Town, where his brother died. We gather very quickly that Toon is slang for cartoon, a "nigger" word for animated characters. Off camera, Toons are sleazy vaudevillians, anything for a laugh. They live in a parallel world called Toon Town, a film colony run by Maroon Studios. In Toon Town, cartoon logic governs; gravity and solidity go upside down. Anarchic gags are the rule. It is a rough neighborhood, like Chinatown or the Sonora — or better still, like the old Gower Gulch in Hollywood, where cheap B films used to be made. Humans don't go there much. Everyday logic has no chance.

Detective Valiant checks up on Roger. Immediately, he senses that Roger is in over his depth. His wife, Jessica, looks much too bosomy and sultry for Roger, too much of Avery's Showgirl, with a touch of Veronica Lake. The marriage can't possibly be working.

While looking for leads, Valiant manages to make matters infinitely worse for Roger Rabbit. Suddenly, Mervyn Acme, the owner of Toon Town, is murdered soon after Eddie speaks to him; and Roger is blamed. Roger was nervous enough before he was a murder suspect. Now, he is pure hysteria. Eddie has to hide Roger from the law for most of the movie.

They are chased by a dour comic-book villain named Judge Doom. Doom is the hanging judge in Toon Town, as well as its chief landbroker. He sends out "gun-sell" weasels to finish off Roger. The action pinballs from one narrow escape to the next, between the live-action world and Toon Town. At the last minute, Toon Town is saved, as well as Roger and Jessica. Judge Doom is "dipped."

The film is structured much like *Star Wars* or *Raiders of the Lost Ark*, a steady stream of roller-coaster effects, with whimsical asides, reminding us that this is a movie about movies, and about cartoons. Scenes are interrupted regularly by acrobatic cameos from famous cartoon characters (Donald, Daffy, Yosemite Sam, Bugs, Dumbo, and so on).

The story is also littered with "back to the future" gags, about what actually happened to Los Angeles after 1947. Someone wants to wipe out Toon Town, as part of a master plan to replace the old trolley system in Los Angeles with freeways. He almost succeeds, but history can be reversed in cartoons. What happens can be averted, in a fanciful last scene.

Meanwhile, as Judge Doom and his greasy weasels hunt for Roger, we root for the antic life of cartoon characters. Something essential in American life is in danger of being erased. We see how vulnerable the cartoon characters are. Like robots, they are programmed to finish jokes, or to entertain locals at a bar. They are comics addicted to slapstick. They are children in cartoons, but horny adults off stage. Inside their bodies, they contain something magically crucial — about what happened to cities in 1947, perhaps to movies, to American humor. Hand-drawn characters take on a life of their own, but that life is the social history of their industry and their moment. When they go, something vital goes too. We are told how serious it was to see them go. However, since this is a cartoon movie rather than a documentary, cartoons survive in the end. Also, the story is about memory more than characters. The more they are remembered, the more they survive.

The film obviously advocates the return of theatrical cartoons, as well as a sensible mass transit system. It seems to look "back to the future" of the fifties with some dismay. Judge Doom tells Valiant what the world of freeways will achieve: a ribbon of billboards and smooth traffic. The audience in the movie theater groans and laughs, having seen that ribbon turn into gridlock and the promise go sour.

In the roaring finale, the cartoon future and ours are mixed. We leave the movie through Toon Town and vanish into the credits. Porky turns to tell us: "That's all folks." The freeway invasion has been stopped, at least in cartoon 1947. A slow-growth coalition has saved Toon Town. Antic cartoon characters get to keep their unique ecosystem.

Now we enter the historical 1947, in order to place it alongside the audience memory version in *Roger Rabbit*. There are remarkable parallels and critical differences.

By 1947, the postwar recession was beginning to end, but fear for the future was very intense. A paranoia gripped both the film industry and the culture at large: the early Cold War; the Hollywood Ten, whose case marked the beginning of the anit-communist era. This also brought renewed problems for animation studios — this in spite of some good news.

The cartoon industry had adjusted to the end of the war with relative efficiency, even after losing financial suport from government contracts. There were a few shifts in management. Leon Schlesinger had sold his cartoon studio, and Warners had installed Eddie Seltzer in his place (a rather humorless, even inept man). Morale at Warners suffered, but survived. Clampett left, but the other directors stayed.

It was the future that looked risky. Rumors spread about the movie industry cutting back on cartoons, as this from the screenwriter Charles Palmer indicates: "In the past few months, Hollywood has periodically been reading the Requiem over the animation industry. Hat in breast, it waits reverently at the yawning grave."[1]

The year 1947 was a banner year in film attendance, but that could not last. The following year, the film monopolies would be broken up by anti-trust legislation. Television would begin to reach larger audiences. So there was already talk of cutting away frills. It seemed that the cartoon might be the loser. Disney continued to limit the number of cartoons it made, and even tried to shift toward live-action features.

Once again, cartoons were not profitable. Rental prices for cartoons were not increasing, despite inflation. Pressure for union wages continued. Cartoon studios saw the first signs of the movie industry pulling out of cartoon production (it became harder to get extended loans). Together, all these problems suggested what did indeed follow in the next eight years — a general decline for the animation industry.

Ways to cut costs were already developing, from UPA to Warners. These would require more limited animation, borrowing from certain shortcuts developed in educational films during the war. Even by 1947, before national television, a much leaner look seemed necessary. Palmer writes:[2]

Expensive character animation can be minimized in favor of diagrammatic portrayal, or symbolized by less expensive silhouettes and shadows; scenes can be planned so that they open on the high point of the action, omitting animated buildup, and then use animation only in the significant corner of the scene, against held backgrounds; animation can be "cycled" or replaced by sliding cells, and an illusion of animation can be inexpensively achieved by moving the camera over a still background.

This simplified look would suit American tastes as well, certainly in the fifties, from modern graphics to freeways. By 1947, early plans for the new America were well underway, in books on how to build shopping centers, in copies of paperbacks on modern architecture handed out as advertising at furniture conventions, in Harvard inviting Gropius, and Mies van de Rohe heading IIT, in Gabo becoming the anti-communist spokesman for Russian Constructivism, in new master plans quickly thrown into place in leading cities. A very different America was about to be built, out of profits gleaned by expanded European investment, out of the Cold War defense industries, and vast increases in consumer spending. The urban centers would be ignored and allowed to decay further. In architecture and design, the International Style would remove old markings. Old neighborhoods throughout America would be demolished in a heroic leap into the future.

In Los Angeles, the Red and Yellow trolley lines were endangered. They had been neglected since the twenties essentially, key lines abandoned. Private companies had built the system, and were now more involved in real-estate speculation than traffic patterns. By 1947, the city had owned the trolleys for a short time, even made a small profit, but considered them a liability nonetheless. City planners were far more committed to tearing down all forms of trolley, with avid support from corporate and real estate interests. Automobiles and buses, it was felt, could do the job better.

By 1947, plans to demolish much of downtown Los Angeles were being perfected, to make room for freeways and new office buildings. The old Chinatown had already been leveled. Soon, all the Victorian remnants downtown would go. Hills would be flattened and the area depopulated. All this was carefully planned, long before the growth coalition of the sixties put up bank high-rises in its place. Many Toon Town neighborhoods were about to vanish. Many were still run down from the Great Depression (and decline beginning as early as 1910). Los Angeles was preparing to push west and north once again, swallow up more vital farmland, and develop more suburban housing booms. (The first had begun in 1885 actually — a reminder to the reader that this was a pattern well established by 1947.)

Roger Rabbit reviews this memory: the clackety trolleys which look more like the Chicago or New York elevated than Red Cars; the cynical planners who blended utopian schemes with fast profit. These story points seem to advocate a whimsical political program based on what we remember today of all this. Since the consumer suburban expansion after 1947 erased many of the old neighborhoods, and no one likes to drive there much anymore, the film asks us to remember them cinematically

— as if they were movie sets or cartoon fantasies — gentrify them like movies, repair the worn façades, paint back the trim.

But like restored buildings in a gentrified downtown, based more on photos than original use, Toon Town cannot look the same as the original. The makers of *Roger Rabbit* clearly want it to look updated, different. Cartoon shadows do not look painted, as they did in full animation; instead, they are enhanced in ways that suggest television memory. They have the unfixed outlines of a glowing TV set. The volumes seem lit from the inside, a bit like the whiteness of Snow White, but with the eye-popping speed of Tex Avery editing. Cartoon substance seems multimorphic again, but not at all like early Mickey Mouse cartoons; it looks more like hologram made solid. It vibrates electronically. The spirit of special-effects films has been added to the hand-drawn image. Through gimmicks with levers (covered over by the cartoon itself) solid objects can be grasped and lifted by these electro-toons.

Cartoons always adjust their graphics to the audience perception of the time. *Roger Rabbit* is certainly no exception. Clearly, it honors the tradition of full animation and of vaudeville gags (Toons as old troupers). It remembers movie-centered cartoons (even Toon Town itself). It pays particular homage to the anarchic story in cartoons (nuisances and controllers everywhere).

But this cartoon is also a barometer of consumer memory in 1988. It "mis-remembers" full animation as though cartoons were electronic gimmickry. The characters look beamed down from a television or computer screen and given electronic flesh. They are TV memories of paint and ink — cartoons that we saw on TV first.

In other words, cartoons constantly adjust to media, perception, and marketing. They are constantly "redrawn" by the crises of modernity. And here indeed is a film where the crisis of modernity is identified as the story conflict itself. Toon Town is a memory chamber plugged into a wall: in 1947, cartoons, films, and old neighborhoods seemed to be teetering on the edge of extinction. Through cartoon myth, we see what was lost. Shifts in consumerism are registered, as audience memory, then and now. Even the graphics remind us where cartoons have gone since 1947 — on to the electronic screen, with its flickering, ghostly outline.

In *Roger Rabbit*, the energy of cartoons is equated with places where gangster/detective films lived in the forties — and died — like the old Los Angeles, as though urban decay were only a matter of high-key lighting and dirty alleys.

Fanciful exaggeration can reveal as much objective informative as historical events of a different sort, but very revealing nonetheless. In the next chapter, we will enter the world of 1948 and after — the consumer marketing that threatens Toon Town in *Roger Rabbit*. We observe cartoons adjusting to the many crises I described earlier. And finally, we see Toon Town fizzle after all, along with the old Los Angeles, to be revived as airbrushed fantasy generations later, like the City Walk going up at

Universal City, a movie mall version of urban spaces, directly adjoining the multiplex, right near the Universal lot.

Perhaps Toon Town (standing in also for full animation) always was a theme-park. In one scene, Betty Boop complains that she lost out when color came in, or when cartoons came to look more precisely like a movie sound stage. Perhaps cartoons show us the theme-park culture emerging, as I will show in the Conclusion. The cartoon is always heading toward its literal alternative.

Roger Rabbit opens a variety of questions of this sort, about the links between consumer memory and animation. No commercial film I know records as clearly the way cartoons died (and why they remain important as part of our collective cultural memory). It is a folk tale about the last two decades before cartoons essentially vanished from movie theaters; as well as a folk tale about how we misremember the past, nearly get it right, then settle for the movie. It seems to detail graphically and by gags how cartoons were structured before they died (and that the cartoon business was never healthy and safe). Finally, it shows us how theatrical cartoons have been updated as urban planning and fantasy architecture.

CHAPTER TWENTY

Chase Cartoons after 1947: Consumer Graphics

POSTWAR ANXIETY

Americans emerged from the war confident of a snowballing trend toward economic democratization and a classless future .... Instead [however], the postwar world brought bureaucratic complexity, cold war insecurity, and a shrunken sense of individual mastery. It produced a technology of atomic peril as well as material comfort. Inspired by the sweeping democratic promises of wartime ideology and a hunger for security and stability, Americans welcomed the notion of classless prosperity. Enticed by expectations of increased power and control, they reacted with dismay as they found themselves slipping into a condition of greater vulnerability and dependency. In response they embraced popular culture reveries that seemed to enhance their sense of personal dominion.[1]

The postwar euphoria did not last long, neither at the polls (red-baiting campaigns immediately afterward) nor at the movie theater. By 1948, even after the postwar recession improved, the mood of victory had been soured. An uneasy cynicism took its place, certainly in the animation industry, where new crises followed each other in lockstep.

After 1948, the number of screens reserved for cartoons began to slip after the movie studios were forced to divest themselves of their theater chains. Without block booking, cartoon distribution was handled by independent jobbers, who drove the rentals down, adding even more insecurity to an already uncertain industry.

Then came television, and the search by movie moguls for the bigger movie screen as a way to compete. The impact on cartoons was nearly catastrophic. In 1953, Jack Warner ordered the animation units to close down, to make way for 3D movies, the wave of the future that never happened, despite the box-office success of *House of Wax*. After the Warners animation units were brought back a year later, cartoons were seen increasingly as warehouse backlog, libraries for sale. Warners sold TV rights to cartoons at a fraction of what they actually earned. In 1955, hundreds of thousands of Warners cels were incinerated to make room for other storage.

The public access to movies was also diminishing. The number of movie screens declined throughout the fifties, as inner-city movie houses went out of business. Not until the multiplexes of the late seventies would the number of screens surpass what it once had been.

By the sixties, backlots would be sold as part of a broader strategy that began in the fifties. More American movies were being shot outside of the United States, just as many American industries were shifting toward global production. Increasingly, cartoons were animated abroad as well, where salaries were lower (compared with the improved union contracts in America of the forties).

Thus began the cartoon version of the stripped-down and yet paranoic fifties — the prosperity as well as the empire-building, from the Marshall Plan investments in Europe to the globalization of media and advertising — along with the Cold War, the strange priorities of the "military-industrial complex." Like a Roman Republic entering an Augustan Age, Americans naively planned for a world in their own image; but at the same time, were constantly obsessed with their dwindling window of opportunity. How many years of advantage were left? How vigilant should Americans be?

This same mixture of ebullience and paranoia can be seen very clearly in fifties cartoons, in the stories and the graphics. It is particularly evident in cartoons about consumer life, from the Goofy How-To series on tourism and new-fangled products, to Warners cartoons making fun of television and shopping. In Lantz's *Little Televillain* (1958, directed by Lovey), Smedley the Dog tells the story of how he was ruined by the television industry. We flash back, some time in the past.[2]

Smedley is about to be fired by the producer. To take his revenge, Smedley tries to wreck the TV camera. Instead, he crashes through the camera and winds up inside a TV set, in someone's living room. He has literally gone right through the glass, like a transmission.

Meanwhile, Chilly Willy is at the control panel in the studio. He is playing with the switcher (which moves the image on the screen), chopping Smedley up laterally and horizontally. Finally, to escape from the screen, Smedley hides in a refrigerator on the set. Then Betty Furness (famous as the TV hostess for Frigidaire) walks to the display. She opens the door of the Frigidaire and finds Smedley there. Disaster! This is live TV — a terrible mistake. But the audience loves it. Smedley is given his own TV show, which brings us to the present. Smedley is a love slave of daily television. He has to stand there, letting Chilly Willy brutalize him, while everyone laughs. A pie hits him the face.

This cartoon also helps explain business references hidden inside Chuck Jones' *Duck Amuck* (1953), made about the time of the "3D" crisis at Warners. *Duck Amuck*, very widely discussed in film journals,[3] is a classic about the machine that throws Daffy's world upside down. No matter what role Daffy begins to play, the background contradicts him, like the final gags in The Marx Brothers' *Night at the Opera*, where Harpo has background curtains dropping inappropriately during the opera. Daffy tries to do his job, but is constantly undercut by the layout and inking, then by the machinery of film-making itself, by the camera and sound equipment. In the last gag, the obnoxious controller, off screen, is finally revealed to be Bugs, who says: "Ain't I a stinker?" Daffy, like Smedley, falls victim to *machina versatilis*, but also to anarchic management. Both Daffy and Smedley resemble the animator caught in the anarchy of new marketing, while Chilly Willy and Bugs are cast as the mad "controllers" at the switch, like carnival kings turning management upside down.

That was 1953. Conditions worsened until, by 1963, Warners, UPA — even Disney — had stopped making animated shorts altogether. In 1958, Chuck Jones left Warners, the same year Hanna and Barbera left for television. Soon after, MGM bowed out altogether. Only Lantz, Terrytoons, and Famous (Paramount — Casper cartoons) remained, in what was called the "filler" business. In 1963, Lantz outlined the crisis for an interview in *Variety*.[4]

Annual cartoon production had dropped from 200 in 1953 to only 85 ten years later (and many of those were reissues). The number of cartoon play dates had declined from 24,000 to 14,000. Even worse, it cost an exhibitor from $3 to $5 to book a cartoon, while the average house yield was only $3.50. And worst of all, the animation house had to wait five years to recoup the cost of that cartoon (about $85,000 after prints).

The only solution, Lantz felt, was to diversify. He was following a path already laid out by Disney. Lantz had set up a licensing deal with Kellogg Foods, another with Western Publishing, along with TV residuals for old cartoons. This was quite modest; Disney had gone far beyond that, even in the thirties. By 1954, Disney had grown into the first communications or "entertainment" corporation to emerge directly out of the film industry. In generations to follow, Universal, Warners, Paramount, and Columbia would follow suit.

After the crisis of 1953, animators began to leave in increasing numbers to work for TV commercials, while animation studios shifted toward TV as well, and toward stories more appropriate to a shopping medium, stories about department stores and spending sprees. In this spirit, Friz Freleng made three cartoons glamorizing shopping — and the economics of consumerism — for the conservative Sloane Foundation. The first of these, *By Word of Mouse* (1954), lays out the ethic as clearly as any film of that period, and suggests related issues as well, very useful for studying how the cartoon adapted to the fifties markets.

In *By Word of Mouse*, Hans, a German mouse, visits his American cousin Willie. Hans is surprised by what he sees. Everybody is rich in America, he declares, eyes bulging. He sees new cars pouring through an underpass. No, Willie disagrees proudly, not everybody is rich. Some have cars that are more than one year old. Willie lives in Stacy's department store, a consumer cornucopia. They enter. From the elevator, we see the flood of merchandise: bikinis on one floor; machines that wash poker chips on another. Lines of sedate shoppers carry packages and slide across the screen in a lateral scroll.

Willie tries to teach Hans about the economics of shopping, about "mass consumption and mass production." But Hans can't quite follow. Finally, Willie takes Hans to a bespeckled mouse professor at Putnell University (PU). A few chase gags are thrown in as Sylvester appears. Between moments of narrow escape from Sylvester (described as the danger of "mouse" consumption), the professor lectures from charts, each presented like a balance sheet. One chart is designed like a telephone book: The white pages for consumers are laid beside the Yellow Pages, for producers. In another, stacks of TVs appear on the left column, while profits are shown on the right. Another resembles a pressure gauge. Costs rise up one side of the screen, toward a red danger signal, then are pushed down by volume (and lower wages I suppose), because slim profits can "only go so far."

Finally, as Hans and Willie run down the street, and out of view from Sylvester chasing them, the professor reminds the mice that "all this [profit through mass production] has given Americans the highest standard of living in the world."

Gag by gag, this is an unrelenting defense of consumer marketing, as the Sloane Foundation requested; but there is also a hidden message, a message inside the *graphics* itself. The layout of Stacy's department store will clarify what I mean. It is a very limited staging, a cheaply made cartoon, less than $30,000 apparently. But some of the reduction did not particularly cut costs. The background would have cost about the same, whether simplified or not. The backgrounds were an ideological decision of some sort. The slim, reductive surfaces look mathematically rationalized, like a blueprint for a panopticon, very utopian. This probably pleased the people at Sloane even more; and yet, the graphics reveal other issues as well. It borrows from the faded backgrounds of many Second World War industrial documentaries, about systematic movement of armies; and from early TV commercials, about easily readable product display. The anarchy of desire has been replaced by the efficient game plan of easy consumer gratification. Instead of anarchy, we see a pre-planned world dedicated to satisfying desire. It resembles dancing linoleum cutouts or plastic overlays out of a die cut. The flat overlays move smoothly through the rational channels of capitalism. We see the utopia of one-stop shopping in the fifties style, set inside an ahistorical, simplified consumer architecture. The department store is a controlled world for patterning the busy shopper. The elevator is crowded, the aisles packed with browsers, the traffic outside is bumper-to-bumper, but everything is enclosed by a very orderly set of grids. The activity is presented in clearly defined right angles, including the charts, the file drawers where the mice hide, the rude oblongs of the TV sets, even the simple quadrilaterals in the opening credits.

They all refer to simple architectonic spaces, which are easiest to express as flat surfaces. Clearly, the layout for animated space was refashioned after the war, even for chase cartoons. The anarchic elements were no longer drawn as movie-scapes; they were converted into themes about consumer desire. They became a highly *controlled* setting, not unlike the Disneyland park that opened in the same year this cartoon was made. The animated space adjusts from movie allusion to consumer allusion, a very noticeable difference — not simply about flat or deep focus. It was more about the changing role of cartoons, from film toward more obviously consumer-driven television.

These are still modest, early fifties versions of consumer efficiency. Many inner-city areas suffered far more. Flattened spaces became even more evident once civic projects started up, as many poor neighborhoods were leveled to make room for a world "without class differences."

CONSUMER CUBISM

Individualism and democracy were being redefined in terms of consumer desire. The homogeneous surface, open and "free," came to stand in for America's imperium. Remember Eisenhower's speeches equating democracy with refrigerators, or Nixon's kitchen debates against Khruschev? The door of a refrigerator (or any appliance) became the ultimate grid for consumer gratification, opening like a little diorama into the new highway or the new airport. By cartoon logic, the consumer object arrived (or was packaged) to the happy consumer at right angles.

After 1954, as television matured, as the highways, airports, shopping centers, and suburbs filled in, a consumer cubism took over, an obsession with the efficient, angular plan. Less became more, as the consumer aesthetic became associated with reductive strategies of all sorts, from shopping architecture to cartoons. The smoother the passageway from buyer impulse to the cash register the better.

Through the International Style, the design of buildings was adapted to this new consumer ideology, much as cartoons were. Consumer activity was supposed to be as rationalized as fifties architecture. Shopping was presumably just as sleek and functional as the glass-curtain wall or the simplifed room. And cartoons, ever the barometer of changes in entertainment, became consumer cubist as well (borrowing heavily from UPA, of course).

As a style of graphics or graphic design, the look of consumer cubism was obvious enough. The theme of consumer life in the early fifties was the grid, in the new suburbs and shopping centers. They were squares within squares, like the new TV-centered living room, with its great wooden cabinet which housed a small glass screen. That solid cubic shape became an object of cohesion — an oblong that kept a watchful eye, as it stood against the square outlines of the wall. This grid pattern was equally evident in the new massive road systems that began mostly in the fifties (even though many followed twisted, old trolley lines, or had to curve through valleys). Even if highways were built along old rutted rights of way, the immediate impact of the cement outer walls as you drove past was not rutted at all. The intersection of bridges with these massive, high channels of cement suggested a conquest of chaos. Very early on, one saw the consumer prairies emerging, outlined by geometric space.

210

In terms of entertainment architecture, one example was copied as much as any other — the new Las Vegas Strip, an auto/freeway world where sin and anarchy were promoted, yet domesticated, a well-lit and monitored city of services, where a family could have "lots of fun."

The appropriate term would be "controlled desire." All the examples above suggest a world obsessed with mechanical control, not unlike Bob McKimson's cartoon *Design for Leaving* (1954), where Daffy as salesman chases Elmer up and down his house, trying to sell robotic gadgets designed to make the world come to you, like hydraulically bringing the second floor downstairs instead of taking the steps (again, the grid that helps the consumer).

So also in Avery's *Car of Tomorrow* and *Farm of Tomorrow*, both postwar cousins of his "pingo-pongo" newsreel parodies of the late thirties. They contain one running gag (in Roadrunner and Goofy cartoons as well, and various cartoon parodies of TV commercials) — exaggerated convenience. It is so exaggerated that it looks insanely *uncomfortable*. The hapless consumer is *victimized* by the very machines that promise an easier, more extravagant life.

Convenience as brutish as this looks rather cynical compared to Grampy's cute devices in the Fleischer Boop cartoons of the late thirties. Such conveniences in thirties cartoons were pictured as beyond the reach of any technology, like Grampy's Christmas surprises for neighborhood children. But in fifties cartoons, such conveniences were a common vernacular, a new, upside-down language, as in Avery's *Symphony in Slang* (1954).

A young man, recently deceased, enters the gates of heaven, where he is asked to explain his life. However, he speaks in metaphors which Saint Peter, and even his chief angel wordsmith, Noah Webster, cannot understand at all. Every metaphor the man uses, when taken literally, conjures up insane mental images, of someone "chewing the rag," or "painting the town red." Speech is detached from language. Like Wile E. Coyote's literal use of his machines from Acme, the instructions detach from their meaning and float off the cliff. These are not simply Avery blackout gags, thrown in, as in Avery cartoons from 1939, to say hello to the audience. They are commentaries on speech modernizing too fast for language, as simple a definition of consumer overdrive as any film I can think of. Metaphors collapse into nonsense.

Even tourism in the fifties resembles consumer cubism. It is pleasure designed off a short, grid-like menu, a system based on coordinated pauses, where the tourist walks a simplified linear path. Tourist space was not as reductive as a freeway, of course; it tended to be much denser, like Disneyland — a kind of pre-packaged surprise.

However, it is very important to recognize how much the ethic of *control* includes tourism as well, why I am putting it into the category of consumer cubism. It too is "controlled anarchy," the oxymoron at the heart of fifties mass culture. Tourism, particularly fifties style, emphasized the simplified options, each scrupulously timed. With that in mind, the classic parody of the frustrated tourist/shopper is Jones' *Ali*

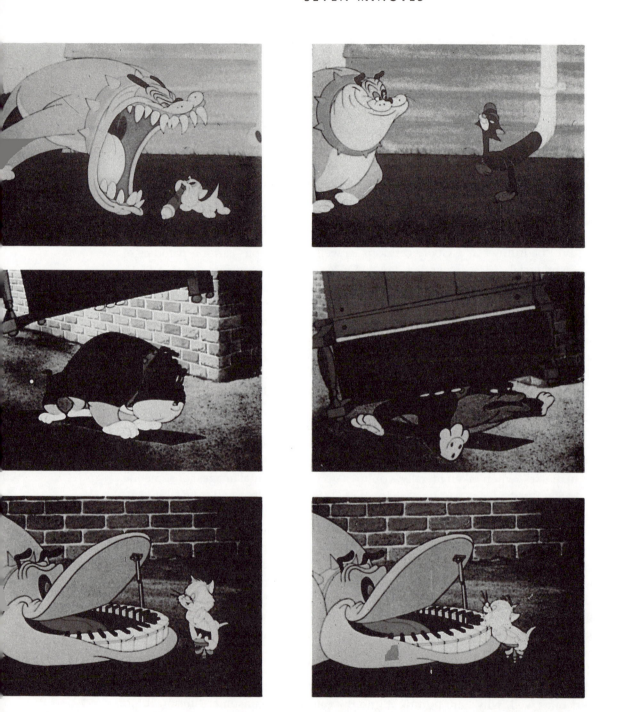

Tex Avery's *Bad Luck Blackie* (MGM, 1949). The nasty bulldog, with the hissing laugh (voice by Avery himself), runs into bad luck, and gets more than his just deserts, on an ever escalating scale.

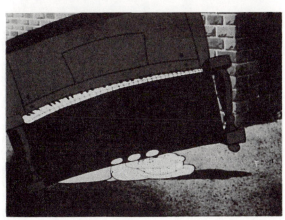
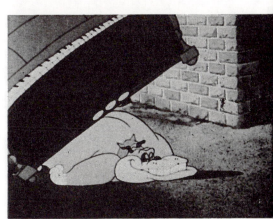

Baba Bunny, where Daffy's anarchic desire for the treasure in Ali Baba's cave is constantly thwarted, while he rants on like a frustrated shopper, craven with dreams of middle-class comforts.

Jones' cartoons in the fifties often refer to consumers on a hopeless quest, the loop from hunger to denial and back again. His ultimate shopper, by mail order no less, was Wile E. Coyote, addicted to fetishistic appliances from Acme.

Jones also left consumerist clues in the backgrounds as well, in the cartoon desert. With its reduced color fields, these flat planes reveal a shift from movie space to consumer/tourist space, about suburban belts of roads going into flat pastel desert-scapes (with treacherous, rubberized telephone lines and killer trucks).

Another obvious connection — before digging deeper — would be the Avery approach to consumerism. Like the consumer world he parodied, his cartoons are highly coordinated. So often is Avery praised as the mad alchemist of the gag that we forget how brilliantly structured his postwar cartoons were. They were not simply chases; they were competitions between seemingly well-matched foes, beginning

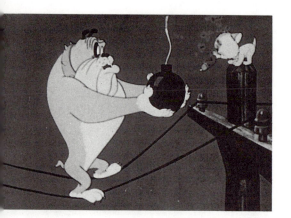

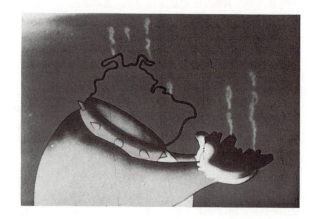

Bad Luck Blackie

with *King-Size Canary*, for Christmas of 1947, then *Lucky Ducky*, and *The Cat that Hated People*, both 1948, then *Bad Luck Blackie* (1949), *Ventriloquist Cat* (1950), *Magical Maestro* (1952), and finally *Dragalong Droopie* (1954).

The objects fly at quantum speed in *Magical Maestro*, or *Bad Luck Blackie* most of all, a blizzard of possibilities. In *Bad Luck Blackie*, the audience can barely fathom what bizarre — and very heavy — object will next fall on the hapless, sadistic bulldog. Since his path has been crossed by a black cat, he must now wait for bad luck to land on him. The bulldog looks up, to something out of view, beyond the frame. He pauses, then shrieks. We don't see it until it lands, thud. Finally, as his luck goes from bad to worst, bathtubs, horses, and ocean liners come crashing down and pursue Spike into the distance. The topper gags may be the funniest bits of *any* cartoon made, based on the gut-wrenching laughter I always hear from students whenever I show it.

Avery was doing another series at the same time, which was directly about consumer life. Starting with some titles I have already mentioned, *House of Tomorrow* (1949) was followed immediately by *Symphony in Slang* and *Car of Tomorrow*. Then he stopped making "spot-gag" cartoons for a while, and went back to the rivalry-chase cartoon, starting with one about sleep and noise: *Cockadoodle Dog*. He did not return to pseudo-newsreels again for two years, not until *TV of Tomorrow*, during the fateful 1953; and finally, the dullest of that series, *Farm of Tomorrow*, in 1954. In each of these, sight gags follow each other like a what-if from *Mad Magazine*, or a jokebook from *Science Digest*. Avery was clearly going after the inanity of fifties promotion, in the same way that he loved to poke fun at the newsreel of the thirties in his "Pingo-Pongo" series at Warners.

Of course, there is a general gag common to practically all of Avery's work from 1947 on — the pyramidal pursuit of objects, or the pyramiding of power, as in the cornerstone of his postwar style, *King-Size Canary*.

For those who do not remember this nearly perfect cartoon, *King-Size Canary* is an ever-spiraling competition/chase involving a hungry cat, a canary, a bulldog, and a gravel-voiced, good-natured mouse. The object that drives the story is a bottle of "Jumbo-Grow," passing from one to the other, the magic elixir for the consumer who needs to get bigger fast. Whoever drinks from the bottle last becomes the larger, and then chases his prey over bridges, or hops the Grand Canyon.

Some have compared this cartoon to an insane arms race; that is vaguely plausible, given the year it was made, but not quite as probable for Avery. More likely, it was simply a story about gluttony, a favorite theme of his: the ever-expanding, unquenchable need to eat your neighbor, in a food pyramid of ever-larger bodies. The three animals take turns growing larger, then getting dwarfed. They switch from hunter to hunted, and back again, until the cat and mouse dwarf mountains and cities. Finally, they get so big, they straddle the world together, like two superpowers. They are both thousands of miles tall, with no more room left on Earth. As the mouse narrator explains, "We just ran out of the stuff." The bottle of Jumbo-

Grow is empty, tossed away. Pals again, cat and mouse wave goodbye. The Earth is a tiny ball underneath them.

In 1954, Avery left MGM to work for Walter Lantz, who he may have felt was cheating him (a very debatable issue). Then, in 1955, he left Lantz as well. More clearly, by 1955, he had grown tired of making cartoons in that furious way he had, leaving no detail unworked, doing some of the voices himself, being what Heck Allen called "a one-man band." He went to work instead on TV commercials for Cascade. Amazingly enough, he found the advertising world less stressful (as ulcerous as advertising would seem to be) compared to the grind of meeting deadlines on cartoons. (The animator Phil Monroe said almost the same about leaving Warners to work for the Burnett Agency; nevertheless, it is so difficult for us as outsiders to comprehend how stressful animation can be — inching along hour by hour, flipping the sheets, back to the roughs.) Avery won some prizes in the late fifties for his TV commercials. He made what seem to be sensible adjustments to the 30-second format, a small slice of cartoon. He simplified his pyramid down to a single gag, relying more on the slambang, slingshot style of the early forties, on variations of blitzes, bombings, and sudden revenge. His spots for "Raid" roach

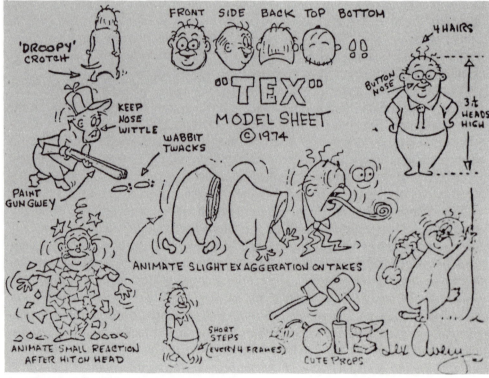

A self-portrait by the retired Avery (1974).

spray are probably the best remembered. They start off with a mob of gangster cockroaches, deep into mischief. Then, looking off-screen (not unlike the bulldog in *Bad Luck Blackie*), they go into paroxysms when they see a can of "Raid." It wears a spray nozzle like a helmet. The can is also bulky, squarely built, with a handsome, chiseled chin. It steps toward them, and, with one spritz, "kills them dead." The bugs get crushed, torpedoed, extirpated, always in a new way with every commercial. They are slammed between walls, swatted more than blown up. Generally, they collapse into a neat pile, often into tombstones, a common gag from wartime chases. For half-minute commercials, the bombastic lessons of wartime animation seemed very appropriate. At least they were easier to put across quickly (on deadline) than cynical seven-minute stories about consumer gluttony, like the cartoons he made before he went into TV work.

As I explained in the last chapter, the war was a great teacher for many animators. But so was the postwar. The chase format matured considerably after 1947, even while it recorded the steady decline of the cartoon industry, under the impact of television and consumer planning. These cartoons tried to outrace their own erasure, but finally vanished from the big screen anyway.

In the next chapter, I will examine what the animators at Warners and MGM had learned by 1948, after a decade of working on these chases — the refinements and shortcuts.

CHAPTER TWENTY-ONE

Villains and Victims: Timing the Chase

By 1948, for many animators, the erratic twists so common to the wartime chase had given way to a highly reductive story, with less direct address and much more dialogue between characters. There were more pauses between frantic action, rather than throwaway gags in mid-motion. Characters spent more frames simply *deliberating*. Chuck Jones explains very clearly how this postwar style worked, and he will serve as our point of entry. As he often says in his talks: "By 1948, I had learned my trade." He had become a master of *timing*, on when to hold back the action, when to go faster. Here is one famous example.

In *Rabbit Seasoning* (see p. 223), after a little verbal give-and-take, Bugs tricks Daffy into declaring that it is duck season, stupidly of course, but with absolute conviction. Daffy, thinking he's ahead of the game, demands that Elmer fire his gun right away. "Fire! Fire!" Daffy screams. The camera concentrates entirely on Daffy's expression as he waits. A few frames are added, setting up his gleeful expectation; then blammo! His beak is blown around his head. We see his eyes still staring, shocked and embarrassed.

A few frames add surprise just before the disaster. One sees similar gags in Tashlin and Clampett ten years earlier, but not with the same continuity.

Jones had learned when to pause on a close shot or a two-shot of the nuisance character (i.e. Daffy or Wile E. Coyote). He shows Daffy deliberating at close range — the facial expression or the body language of the nuisance.

Since disasters like Elmer shooting Daffy were crucial to the chase, there were essentially three places where these extra frames could be added for maximum effect: (1) before, (2) during, or (3) after the shotgun blast (or the dynamite blast, or the anvil falling). Each animator developed a special point to pause, a signature of sorts.

Jones was particularly fond of lingering on the character's expression immediately *before*. We watch Wile E. Coyote glowing with confidence just *before* he slams into the side of the mountain, or notices, at last, that the rock where he sits is plummeting 5,000 feet straight down.

I'll explain by contrast: For Avery, the trademark was often the insane double-take (eyes or jaw in explosive shock) *during* the disaster. *Recognition upon impact* is stretched out in Avery cartoons; whereas for Jones, that moment is often ignored altogether, simply identified by a ring of dust as the coyote hits the bottom.

As yet another contrast, Freleng's trademark was the slow burn — the character's expression *after* disaster had done its worst, when Yosemite Sam, in tatters, grumbles to Bugs that he "hates rabbits"; or when Sylvester, with Tweety discovered inside his mouth, has to face the wrath of Grandma.

CHARACTER

At the heart of the motivation that drives the chase is the "scheme," how one character plans, at some length, to outdo the other. For Jones, the character had to be shown scheming at ridiculous length immediately *before* the worst happened. A little hubris takes the chase a long way. Wile E. gathers his equipment, pulls hardware and parts furiously out of the Acme box, then patiently puts his scheme into operation. In *Gee Whizz-zz* (1956) he puts on a bat suit, seemingly with ease, then drops like a stone into the canyon, until he suddenly figures out how the wings work. He rises back into view, we see him gliding laterally, in peaceful silence, only a flapping sound, toward the unknown beyond the edge of the screen. He throws a satisfied glance at the audience — a pause. Then, immediately afterward, at the moment of deepest embarrassment, he slams into the side of the mountain (offscreen). After bouncing back on screen, his wings in shreds, he flaps furiously in the stillness. We only hear the sound of his arms in the cavernous desert, as he drops . . . down, down (up to twelve frames down) to that little puff of earth below.

Consider how little waste is involved here. All the character's expressions are built toward getting the plan in motion — no random crashes. Every pratfall is the result of bad planning, every expression designed to make his failure look even more embarrassing. This deliberate over-preparation allowed for more pauses, more subtleties in what characters thought was about to happen.

Scheming, Jones explains, was centered on the problem of greed — or rather, the "futility" of greed. "The fanatic is someone who redoubles his effort, when he has forgotten his aim" (a quote he likes to borrow from Santayana).

Comic characters portray "human frailty." That is why "nearly all great comedians are failures or villains," and above all "victims." How much more amoral (and foolishly unforgiving) can a universe get?

Greed for Jones is too fundamental simply to be labeled as good or bad. Greed takes no prisoners. Whether characters are good or evil, greed will dominate most of what they do.

That makes certain twists in their nature less predictable once the disaster strikes. They might get manic afterward, or then again, surprisingly, they might get very passive, try to retrace their steps. It's all part of scheming for what lies ahead. In

219

Rabbit Seasoning, Daffy says, with appropriate pauses: "Let's [pause] go through that [pause — a sizzling glare] o-once . . . a-gain." He is fuming but rigid. He goes jaw to jaw with Bugs. He knows he's been shafted. He senses that he has no chance of success.

Evil is hard work. Daffy wants very much to do bad, but his nasty schemes never work out. So he redoubles his efforts. He gets even nastier. He is "grasping" enough to be evil; he's greedy enough. But he cannot maintain his concentration. He gets too flustered in a crisis, and either through Murphy's Law, or mad egotism, he winds up empty-handed anyway, and exhausted. Then, to add insult to injury, Bugs can't be bothered; he just skates along, no fuss, no mess. The same with the coyote: it's always insult after injury: The Roadrunner "meeps" once and zips away, never anything but cheerful.

In 1986, I asked Jones what he thought of my distinction between nuisance, over-reactor, and controller. Elmer is a nuisance character, Jones agreed, but "he doesn't see himself that way." That is an important distinction for Jones, one he makes often. Nuisance characters have practically no self-knowledge, at least not when they need it most. Even Elmer cannot see his own greedy side. He is too busy scheming or being duped. As a result, there is no "pure evil." In that sense all characters are both villains and victims.

Along with ignorance, there is denial. Nuisances go to any length to rationalize what they do. That takes time, and it's hard work. Throughout Daffy's scheming, he explains (to anyone who might ask, or stops to look) precisely why he has to be greedy. You're all against me, he declares. I deserve more. I'm talented and extremely greedy ("a greedy slob"). You're jealous. I have to defend myself.

Daffy admitting he's greedy, as he sneaks away in *Rabbit Seasoning* (1952).

220

GRAPHICS

Finally, as if destiny were not foolish enough, nuisances are designed according to their problem (sometimes very ostentatiously, as in the classic *Duck Amuck*, but often in hidden ways as well). They are each given a twist in their body type, a useful malfunction according to their level and sense of greed. Bugs (long legs, big feet) slouches and struts, as if he had eyes in the back of his head, but also as a way to show off.

He remains the controller who knows he can afford simply to stand around. We rarely see Bugs scheming. He pauses mostly to ask his dumb adversary what's up (Doc). His battle plan is already in place.

By contrast, the coyote looks unprepared when he struts. He is drawn with one knee lower than the other; walks in a shuffle that almost resembles a limp. This fixes him as the victim who never gives up, but can never succeed either.

The purpose of these flaws is simple enough. Greed makes a character vulnerable, no matter how nasty the intentions. For example, in Jones' words, cartoon characters should be "scary" rather than "frightening." The forgetful Hassan in *Ali Baba Bunny* is "scary," but not frightening. He keeps saying "Hassan chop," in a very basso, menacing way, brandishing a huge scimitar. And this scares Bugs and Daffy, who are in the cave that Hassan is sworn to guard. But Hassan is too stupid to be frightening to the audience. He is not like a horror character who stalks his prey in a slasher movie. Hassan is too robotic to be a nightmare.

© 1993 Warner Bros., Inc., LJE, Inc.

Chuck Jones' drawing of Daffy trying some body English (1993).

This is intentional. Hassan is made vulnerable to give Daffy a false sense of security. Again, a few frames are added, as Hassan fails to move fast enough, or seems to lack hinges. In talking about *Ali Baba Bunny*, Jones explained how these details worked, by giving an example from an Avery cartoon. He asked: "Do you know what makes Avery's *"King-Size Canary* [1947] funny?"

He meant this in terms of how it was drawn. Jones, as acute animator, saw any number of crucial details I certainly missed, particularly in the design of a character. Did you notice, he explained, "that Avery didn't let the heads grow?" That is entirely true. Their heads do indeed look like buttons, while their bodies keep swelling. In fact, animators on the cartoon had been instructed by Avery to draw "hands and feet tiny," and to emphasize the "Bull Neck."[1]

In Don Graham's class, Jones had learned that if you want to make something look really big, leave one part of its anatomy small: the head or arms. Indeed, all the Jones wrestlers and bulky monsters are designed in that way, even the bull in *Bully for Bugs*. Some body part in these oversized torsos will be tiny; this contrast gives the characters an awkwardness, a foolishness, a vulnerability. They look like beefy oafs who can't button their shirts.

Of course, tricks like these could be learned without going to Don Graham's classes. Avery never went to them. He learned by experience, and also through his unique and sardonic gift for designing foolish characters with stumpy legs, or slimy, but lovable, long snouts.

Chuck Jones' drawing of Daffy (1993).

CONTINUITY

But, whatever the source of the tricks, by the late forties there was something of a system for animating the chase, what Jones calls "action as character." The clearest explanation of the system came from Preston Blair, who seemed to have integrated his time spent at the three leading studios: Disney, Warners, and MGM. Blair was arguably the most famous animator in Avery's unit at MGM. He specialized in female characters, particularly Red, the irresistible showgirl. He also designed and animated the dainty hippos for Disney's *The Dance of the Hours* in *Fantasia*. In 1949, he published a systematic analysis of how to animate, particularly for chases, since that was much of his experience. His forty-page how-to workbook contains useful insights into what animators had learned by 1949, and fits well, even in its contrasts, with what Jones has to say. There is very little of the story element here, more about how the Avery poses were translated by animators.[2]

In one section, the book lists a few basic character types, each built for the chase, like his version of the nuisance: the "screwball" type, which seems to include a generic Bugs, Donald/Daffy type, a Woody, and a screwball squirrel (but much cuter than Avery's version). These "cocky wise guys" need elongated heads, low foreheads, and little or skinny legs.

Blair was essentially adding another element to those I have already given. Instead of over-reactor, I would call it an *under-reactor* — the dumb one who deliberates, but never sorts the matter out fast enough. Blair calls it the "Goofy" character, clearly identifying a key source from Disney. We see a page of tired bloodhounds and dumb hicks, each with a "long skinny neck." They are "hump back, stoop shouldered," with "long droopy arms . . . big hands, overhanging fanny, pants low and loose and baggy." Most importantly, they have "enormous and clumsy feet." They cannot move easily, not with a "sunken chest, [a] big stomach [that] protrudes," and "low crotch in pants." They won't be going very far that

Chuck Jones' *Rabbit Seasoning*. During a verbal duel with Bugs, Daffy mistakenly asks Elmer to shoot the duck, and gets his beak blown off.

223

way, since they are designed to help the timing by adding pauses and slow burns.

They are important for "The Cartoon Take": "Almost anything can happen in a take. The figure may stagger or fly through the air. The eyes may pop out. Loose hair and coat tails, etc. All fly up and contribute to the surprise effect." There are "subdued" takes and "wild" takes.

These pauses provide essential balance for the chase, like "the Sneak: a walk . . . that gives the illusion of stealth." "The Strut" was a Blair trademark — the Blair Showgirl. Like so many of these movements, it is awkwardly graceful, a lingering before the harmony. When she sings, she throws her body back, almost as if she might fall. The in-betweens are intentionally made uneven, until she actually takes a step, plants her foot on the ground.

By 1949, much more emphasis had been put on movement between characters, primarily because of the chase cartoon. For Disney, the focus of energy went very much into "personality," into elaborate uses of body volumes (faces, moments of compassion, fear, etc.); and from there into motion. Blair's model is "line of action," clearly a different emphasis. Action is character very directly. The character is made either to hustle or to pause, and to reveal intention en route. Blair compares this to the way a ball bounces when it is filmed frame by frame — to what he calls "a path of action," literally a line cutting across circles, which squash and recoil. He recommends a "spacing chart" with "two lines charting the top and bottom of the character in its flight."

As in Jones' theories, this is also an indication of where cartoon anarchy had gone next, from bumpy, surprise movements to a kind of cartoon suspense. Earlier, from about 1937 to 1947, chases relied more on collisions and the ballet of near-misses. Now the chase was built far more around scheming — scheming more than brawling. Even the characters were built according to how well they schemed. Disney certainly understood this aspect of the cartoon, in character descriptions by Ted Sears in the thirties. But not much of this was put into practice, as it had to be at Warners or in Avery cartoons. Mickey and the Beanstalk is a superb chase cartoon, but more the exception than the rule.

From Disney full animation, Blair still emphasized three principles: overlapping action, squash and stretch, and follow-through. But even there, he was isolating what lay at the heart of cartoon movement. Overlapping means that not all of the body arrives at the same time when it moves. Squash and stretch is compared to a sandbag moving through the air. Follow-through shows parts of the body (or clothing) still moving even when the character stops.

The purpose of all of these is timing, particularly when characters go slower, or suddenly go into a skid. Under the category of "timing," he writes:[3]

Vary speeds of actions in a scene. A change of pace is usually highly desirable in animation.

Learn the value of a "hold," that is, just the right amount of time to linger on a "pose" so that it will register with the audience for all it is worth. Study the art of going in and out of "holds," of cushioning into "holds," of when to "freeze" and "hold" dead still, and when to keep up subtle animation during a "hold" to give it that breath of life. These points and others under "timing" are the essence of the art of animation as they are also of the art of acting, and an animator is the actor of the animated cartoon film.

As a third source, after Jones and Blair, here are a few comments gleaned from Friz Freleng, about Tweety and Yosemite Sam, his featured players after the war. Freleng's approach to timing was fixed more or less on two problems:

(1) *A near-equality between characters*, to sharpen the nuisance/controller format. Elmer was, in Freleng's words, "the hunter who was the victim," but much too stupid, too much of a victim ("brains like a chicken"). After the war, Freleng worked on Yosemite Sam instead, as a better adversary for Bugs. To enhance the timing between them, which required a seeming equality, Sam was always drawn slightly larger when he went face to face against Bugs, and had a voice much deeper than his tiny body would seem to hold.

(2) *A deceptively even rhythm*. Freleng set up his gags systematically on a musical bar sheet (standard for the animation industry, but rarely with as much precision as Freleng used). Movements always follow in sets of three or twelve, but Freleng made a habit of watching these very carefully, to give the gags a strange inevitability and elegance, perhaps a continuation of the many musical cartoons he made in the thirties. (Although he grew up hating his violin, after all those lessons he had as a child, he was still something of a musician.) This precision made the slow burns of a Yosemite Sam or the existential embarrassment of a Sylvester just a little more agonizing, a little funnier. Caught once again trying to eat Tweety, Sylvester looks up hopelessly. A shadow looms, really large. It's a broom. The lady of the house (seen only at ankle level) pounds him with it — rhythmically. The sound has to be piercing, like a rifle shot — thwack! It rises above her voice warning him to leave that little birdie alone. She is screaming, but in a rather gentle voice, gentle by comparison with her violence. She has to sound quite sweet to make that joke work, as if she didn't know her own rage, or her own strength. We watch the ominous broom descend on him again, as if it were blocking out the sun. Beneath the darkness, we see only the white ellipses of his eyes, which are all-suffering and lopsided. (Again — SLAM! rap! SLAM! rap! even louder this time.) The shadow chases his flattened body, while the smacking stays in rhythm, like a metronome from hell. Sylvester's agony is the payoff. And as gruesome as this might seem, given how harmless we all imagine ourselves to be, the crushing impact gets a huge laugh (from me too). If it is timed right. Freleng explains: "Tweety is just the instigator of all those problems. Sylvester is the fall guy. He defeated himself at all times."

ONE CARTOON EVERY FIVE WEEKS

"It's duck season."
"It's rabbit season."

Blam! As always, it's duck season. Daffy gets his face blown away yet again. Elmer looks on. He is intentionally drawn to look only mildly concerned, as if he were watching from a bus, rather than the person who actually fired the rifle. This perceptual blank adds a note of idiocy which makes the jokes funnier. As Hal Roach said of Laurel and Hardy, they got three laughs out of one gag just by looking at each other. Less is more when the timing is precise.

The chase was simplified through experience. At the same time, the work system at Warners remained very simplified as well. Necessity was literally the mother of invention. There was no money for previews. Every frame of film had to be planned before the cels were painted. This was standard everywhere but at Disney. At Warners, the entire process, from start to finish, took five weeks. Occasionally a few weeks might be tacked on — for quality shorts — but only if another cartoon were finished early. No exceptions. With block booking, a pattern had been set in the thirties, and it was followed right to the last days of the studio: five weeks for a unit of five plus a supervisor (code word for director); then inkers and painters afterward, and the voices done by Mel Blanc; and finally, the music. Jones began each cartoon by working for three weeks with the story man. (Michael Maltese was his favorite.) During that time, the story man would draw a fairly crude storyboard. Jones would redraw from there, keeping some of the schemes, rejecting others (between 300 and 400 drawings). The dialogue would be written directly onto the storyboard. Then, finally, when everything was more or less ready for the three animators, a secretary typed the dialogue. Over a period of two decades, the work system itself became something of a chase cartoon, where waste was steadily trimmed away (even the muscle in many cases as well; it took intense concentration to stay on schedule). Most of all, in production and product, pacing became razor sharp.

During the same first three weeks, the layout man (Maurice Noble was Jones' favorite) would bring in drawings and watercolors of the background. There was generally not much time to coordinate and rethink that element. As a result, story and background were often topsy-turvy in chase cartoons. Only the essential "discipline" held the pieces together, through a few story conferences. In Jones' case, the discipline of his stories tended toward simplified, almost UPA backgrounds, unless there were a direct spoof of a movie genre, as in *Duck Dodgers of the 23½ Century*. But even in *Duck Dodgers*, the black space, the icy, glass, bubble shapes, and the paradox of deep perspective look stripped down compared to Freleng backgrounds, for example, like the painterly pirate ship for *Buccaneer Bunny*. The

226

world of Duck Dodgers looks more like an empty store window out in the blankness of empty space, spare and monumentally vast.

Jones wanted his characters to appear almost naked, as in the Roadrunner cartoons: a coyote by the road, near a sheer cliff; or *In Duck Amuck*, Daffy's background is literally his enemy (almost a parody of how the system of production had to work).

For Jones, much of the impact had to be managed through the poses of the characters themselves. Their mad pursuit of utter folly had to be shown mostly through physical ambiguities, the everyday movements. He often reminds listeners that humans tend to walk slightly off balance, "a process of falling over, but catching yourself," until the front foot finally touches the floor again. Or he elaborates on how design is movement is character:

Our characters have a skeleton and obey the way they're built, with Bugs' big feet and long legs, there is only one way he could walk.

Each of these details seems modest. Many are still taught today, on the job, or at animation programs. Others are still being discovered. Not as much is being discovered about the anarchy of the chase, however. The new lexicon of tricks comes out of a very different tradition than that which motivated the fifties work. That tradition came out of vaudeville, pantomime, illustration, and the experiences on the job from 1928 onward. Today, character animation, as an industry, operates with tools developed through television and the occasional animated feature, less about the anarchic, and more about the consumer-driven narrative that started in the fifties, just as the chase cartoon reached its optimum efficiency.

There is also today a parallel world of animation tournées, or one-night programmers like Spike and Mike; or Liquid Television on MTV, or various animation festivals. In sum, for the future of the seven-minute cartoon only, this second range of markets offers an alternative way to work, though it is still very slim pickings for full-time employment. In Europe, there is an enduring love of the cartoon short, but also a weak market for them. As a final source, the impact of special-effects movies and what I call "animated" architecture will be discussed (p. 224). The animation industry is in transition, even temporarily growing. But whatever the next few decades accomplish, they cannot re-engender the timing in these chases; the momentum created by units of co-workers making hundreds of cartoons together, almost on an assembly-line, as the chase animators did for almost two generations. In practical terms, that seems impossible to recapture. Look instead to the computer anarchy of the future, the cyberchase, to debugged and corrupted files exploding like cartoon dynamite; and to Patriot missiles upside down, in a world as inverted and mad as any I have described thus far.

The next chapter completes my final analysis of the fifties cartoon, and where it fits in the scheme I have set up. We return to more or less where I began, graphic narrative, in this case a "cult of the line" from UPA, with implications quite different, however, than the silent cartoon of the twenties. UPA merged the lessons of the Second World War, of full animation, of the chase cartoon, of documentary film, and of "consumer cubism." It also turned the problem of simplification into an integrated narrative.

CHAPTER TWENTY-TWO

Back to the Animated Line: UPA and the Fifties

DURING THE WAR: WHEN PIGS AND BUNNIES COLLIDE WITH NUTS AND BOLTS

By 1946, the United Productions of America (UPA) had begun to find its way. It was moving toward a style based on simplified line, flat fields of color, and collage. The preparation for this style had come during the war, in animation produced for training films, particularly at Disney and Warners. For example, training films were more detail-oriented and less gag-centered. A docu-cartoon about a torpedo had to describe a thousand precision parts, clearly requiring more narrow detail than cartoons usually required. As a result, there was a greater need for images layered by multiple exposure. The result could look as if fifteen layers of cels were operating at once. Previously, six layers were the top limit, and this a luxury rarely possible outside of the Disney studio.

Military maps had to be animated in more detail as well. The background had to be as precise and as important as the characters. Also, live action was often mixed with animation and more object animation used, to display planes and tanks. The sum of these adjustments had their effect, particularly on those who finally left Disney or Warners and went to UPA. One of the UPA founders, the animator John Hubley, explained:[1]

The medium of animation has become a new language. It is no longer the vaudeville world of pigs and bunnies. Nor is it the mechanical diagram, the photographed charts of the "old training film." It has encompassed the whole field of visual images, including the photograph. We have found that line, shape, color, and symbols in movement can represent the essence of an idea, can express it humorously, with force and clarity. The method is only dependent upon the idea to be expressed.

In 1943, UPA began by producing animated documentaries (based on wartime systems) from *Hell Bent for Election* to *The Brotherhood of Man* — industrial films for large institutions, like the Navy or the American Federation of Labor. After the war this continued, until 1948, when UPA began producing cartoons for Columbia Pictures, cautiously at first, until this docu-modernist look replaced full animation entirely. With success by 1951, UPA launched something of an International Style for the industry, based on what was called then "stylized" animation. A highly reduced surface became standard practice for cartoons in the fifties. At its best, this flat graphics became story; the plot required characters who looked like color fields and moved mechanically inside a world that was practically empty, a sad, ironic, absurdist world; or a child's view of the adult madhouse; or simply the rhythm of an animated "Broadway Boogie-Woogie" (referring to Mondrian's vision of Manhattan in 1944 — and how abstract grids translated into film).

Obviously, much of this technique might have developed anyway (or had already developed) without UPA, emerging from German sources in the twenties, like the work of Hans Richter or Viking Eggeling; or the great Scotsman in Canada, Norman McLaren; or from Len Lye.[2] All of these film-makers were mentioned in established movie-industry publications, mostly in books published for the movie crafts (cinematographers, set designers, etc.) The word on modern animation had reached Disney as well. In 1940, Walt hired Oskar Fischinger to help design *Fantasia*, and even though Fischinger left unhappily only a few months later, the possibilities of abstraction and music had been groomed into the *Fantasia* project.

A broader trend was emerging, not as evident in the cartoon product yet, but already mentioned in articles by animators during the war, and well remembered in interviews generations later. During the Second World War, aspects of modern painting and design caught the interest of many in the animation industry, including Ward Kimball at Disney, and Clampett and Jones at Warners, but particularly layout painters and designers. Certainly, neither Disney nor Leon Schlesinger got the message, though. But animators sensed what was at stake, if more of these modernist issues were not brought into cartoons. In 1944, Chuck Jones wrote in detail about the possibilities of abstraction for cartoons, but concluded with a warning:[3]

We are dealing with a relatively new but horizonless medium . . . [but] only one serious danger confronts the animator: an underevaluation of his medium. If the motion picture producer, writer, or musician believes the end purpose of the animated cartoon to be the cartoon short of today, then it must follow that the end purpose of easel painting is the comic strip.

That last sentence is particularly revealing: suddenly, the term "comic strip" signifies boring animation, clearly a reversal of its meaning from only five years earlier.

In 1943, after a showing of a Disney docu-film on malaria, the animator Phil Eastman asked whether the use of dwarfs hindered the point of the picture.[4] He felt that bolder possibilities were at hand, "new ideas on presentation . . . new graphic symbols," particularly "the kind of pictures you are seeing in magazine advertisements today . . . an awful lot different from what you used to look at fifteen or twenty years ago." These ads take their ideas "from the whole field of art: from simple cave-man drawings, from Egyptian art, from Greek sculpture, from Botticelli, El Greco, Dufy, de Chirico, from Matisse, Picasso, and Miró." And you can find them not only in *Harper's Bazaar* and *Fortune*, but even in *Life, Collier's, Mademoiselle,* and *Saturday Evening Post*:

The magazine-reading public — and they're the ones who go to the movies too — accepts these new graphic media without even batting an eye. They not only accept them, but they demand them.

Why have animated pictures been so slow to make use of these media? Why are we so graphically out of date?

He also worries that producers who run the animation industry will junk its potential. He wants to convert them somehow. Knowing some on the management side could be listening, he lists possible techniques seen regularly in magazine advertisements, and starts with "college" techniques — a bizarre typo. Very likely, the proof-reader had corrected the spelling of *collage* to read *college*, an indication of the walls of antipathy the animators faced: this new graphics was the stuff "colleges" did. Eastman went on with his list: "combinations of line drawings and photographs, frank combinations of full forms and flat areas; . . . surrealistic handling of space and distance; [and] ignore perspective if it gets in [the] way."

The emphasis was clearly on design, not painting. And yet, modern painting was hardly an obscure subject either, not as it had been. By the late thirties, popular articles on Picasso were common, as were articles on Surrealism; and from 1946 on, about Abstract Expressionism, in *Life Magazine* and *Time*. In LA itself, many animators who had trained at Chouinard or Otis knew about a local group of abstract painters showing since the late twenties, notably John McLaughlin; and (after 1938) Rico LeBrun, who helped train animators working on *Bambi*; Lorser Feitelson, who also sponsored modernist shows in LA, through the WPA from 1937 to 1943; and Fischinger himself, whose work certainly was familiar to the animators, and fused animation techniques with painting.[5] There were also more exhibitions in LA during the war linking modern architecture with urban planning. And even more evidently, in the live-action movie crafts, art directors had been using aspects of modern design since the twenties.[6] There was indeed a strong essentialist or formalist interest in abstraction among many animators in Los Angeles as well.

On balance, however, with few exceptions, modern art was received by animators through mass culture, like the erector sets that were so popular at the time. It was approached essentially like a set-builder's fantasy; again, much the way it entered mainstream America — not as a painting really. It entered more as a new way to understand *space*, the belief that a modern space was hygienic and optimistic. In the new living room, modernism erased the cracked, varnished built-ins and dense intrusions, the so-called "dirt catchers." For millions of Americans, the modern building surgically removed memories of the Great Depression, as GI loans paid for homes out into the suburbs, or near jobs in new business districts. No blighted walls, no calcified water pipes. I suspect that was the definition of modern art that animators understood best — the hygienic fantasy. In cartoons, therefore, the most important shift could be seen in layout — in the animated *space*. In other areas — the way characters were drawn, for example — the changes were less consistent. The break was clearer in the way characters became part of the abstract space, like an Eisensteinian montage of attractions. Characters moved utterly differently in this suprematist non-space than they had in a rubbery universe, or a print universe. It was more clearly a universe based on ambiguity and absence, hardly suitable for the usual crash-bang chase cartoon or the famous slip on a banana peel.

Based on interviews, it appears that one turning-point occurred during the making of *Fantasia* in 1940. A strong case has been made for the mushroom dance (Tchaikovksy's *Nutcracker Suite*) as proto-UPA. The background layout was reduced to pure black (some say to save money), in a manner that suggests an abstract drawing, or more importantly an abstracted space. The man who did the preliminary drawings for this sequence, Jules Engel, was an abstract painter, but had been brought in as a specialist in dance choreography and design to synchronize movement to concert music. Engel later went to UPA as designer/coordinator, because color in the indefinable modern space was given a much higher priority than in full animation. Anyway, quite a few of the original UPA team also worked on *Fantasia*, with some leadership among equals from John Hubley.

After the strike at Disney in 1941, virtually none of these people returned. Some were later blacklisted. Meanwhile, during the war, at Camp Roach in Culver City, a group of them gathered around "Sergeant" John Hubley. While working on various shorts for the State Department, they began to draw flatter, simpler shapes, and restrict the layouts considerably. On first observation, this would seem to be a return to the older animated line, to the pre-1934 styles of animation. Hubley, for one, was well aware of the twenties and early thirties work. In a seminar from 1943, he said:[7]

[After Disney in the thirties] characters were imbued with a thinking process. The dotted line was out, the double take was in. In place of graphic symbols, you now saw physical and mental processes in terms of expressive drawing; the goat lowering its head in anticipation; Donald Duck's eyes literally popping out and neck stretching three times its length into an extreme take .... The question mark and the light bulb were replaced with expressive action drawings, color and design.

But he saw no way to go back simply to 1928. With the war, story material had to be far more complex. What he called "parody on human nature" demanded new animation techniques, particularly to remove any elements of racism and reactionary politics he saw in gag-oriented cartoons. A more politically complex story demanded a new style, with more variable graphics and layout, far beyond the earlier gags about line or volume.

So UPA was not simply a return to linear animation, much as they would give my argument an easy symmetry. In order to express political issues that grew more evident during the war (against racism, fascism, union-busting), the UPA artists were discovering a new way to describe space even more than character; and this evolved — after the war, during the political censorship of the McCarthy era — into a fascination with the public space, away from the movie space I identify with full animation. Actually, the term *"public"* is a bit misleading; I would do better calling it *"consumer space."* UPA helped establish a vocabulary for the emerging consumer world; this developed slowly, over a period of about seven years (by 1950), and then continued for a decade thereafter, and into TV.

The changes that took abstract animation into the consumer world do not fit into a neat summary. They seem, on the outside, highly contradictory, about displaced politics, changing public and private rituals. Eventually, modern art meets modern marketing. Similar transitions can be seen in abstract design, painting, and architecture as well, from 1940 to the late fifties. There too, so many unlikely factors figure. One is the political shift among New York painters away from thirties leftism; another is the impact of urban planning from 1939 on, as well as the use, after the war, of abstraction in advertising for TV, print, and in shopping centers generally. This may sound heretical, but the fine arts of 1946 were integrated into the consumer world years before Rauschenburg or Warhol announced it. Almost simultaneously, once the postwar era was in place, democratic individualism became consumer individualism, in the arts and in animation. I know that critics like Clement Greenberg defended modern abstraction precisely because it seemed free from consumer invasion.[8] But other critics point out how easily Jackson Pollock was mass-marketed, for example, in *Life* magazine (1949) and *Vogue* (1951).[9] Marketing often makes a mess out of one's best intentions. It has in the past, and it will do it again.

As of 1943–46, the UPA group felt patriotic toward animation as a new democratic individualism, as a way to open the entire cartoon to individual expression. Ten years later, the results were much more ambiguous. Aspects of that UPA style wound up as "limited" animation once the Hanna–Barbera shows started, and in TV commercials from 1953 on. Also, very early on, the crunch of studio financing (Columbia) was forcing UPA into compromises: racing deadlines; pressure to build continuing characters, all very distressing to Hubley in particular.

By then, Hubley had left the cartoon industry altogether and had entered the world of small film-maker (his own company by 1955; also TV commercials for Nabisco, Schott paper towels, and two "abstract" ads for AT&T). But, as of 1946, he had grand hopes for what theatrical animation might accomplish. He opened his lecture with a clever summary of where the cartoon had gone, and where he saw it going next:[10]

Select any two animals, grind together, and stir into a plot. Add pratfalls, head and body blows, and slide whistle effects to taste. Garnish with Brooklyn accents. Slice into 600-foot lengths and release.

This was the standard recipe for the animated cartoon. That is, it was standard until Hollywood's fantasy makers were presented the task of teaching people how to fight ...

Since that time, the lone educational short, dubbed by the industry a "nuts and bolts" film, has been augmented by hundreds of thousands of feet of animated educational film. Because of wartime necessity, pigs and bunnies have collided with nuts and bolts.

Thus, out of improvements in animated documentary film came a new approach to the theatrical cartoon. The animator Karl Van Leuwen describes a war-time instructional film on vaccination, and the sense of mission during the "good" war, an enthusiasm that gave these changes a moral imperative for many in the cartoon industry.[11] Abstract surface became linked with good political animation:

The body [is] a great walled city, which, when it is invaded, starts to build arms to fight the invader. But sometimes the invader strikes too swiftly and the defenses cannot be organized soon enough, and the city dies. It shows how the vaccine, which lets in weak invaders, gets the defensive machinery going full blast so when the real invader comes he is quickly put to rout.

Van Leuwen links this spirit directly with stylized animation:

The contribution of the war to the animation industry has been of tremendous importance. The nature of the work has demanded a return to symbolism, to stylization, and so to a graphic that is more universal .... The complexities and difficulties of the subject matter forced the industry to develop new methods and new tools, which have removed many of the old limitations which hampered expression.

GERALD McBOING-BOING

To reinforce my point about modernist space and cartoons, let us start by examining *where* animators worked the most obviously in this "modern" style — the space itself. The film-maker John Whitney remembered UPA best through the "novel architecture of the studio building ... put up in 1949 by John Lautner":[12]

The striking design had high roofs vaulted with corrugated metal, and the rooms were laid out along several corridors around a courtyard, so that every office, inside and outside, had a glass wall looking out on trees and flowers — some even had a country-club view. How pleasant those walkways were — and such a different ambience from Disney or the other animation studios I knew, which offered factory cubicles with artificial light and no view.

That studio building is often in the minds of animators and designers who think back to their time at UPA. It stood in for the critical difference there. It seems like a piece of hard evidence — the feeling within the building itself: the erasure of

Drawings by Jules Engel for *Gerald McBoing-Boing* (UPA, 1951, dir. Cannon). This features fifties stylized graphics: movement is simplified, the shading off-register, and the figure—ground ambiguity exaggerated.

inside—outside in LA modernist architecture that somehow fit the erasures animators made in their drawings. When animators stared away from their work, looking for ideas, what did they see: inside, a fluid space without bearing walls; outside, an unhindered, plate-glass view of the mountains north of Burbank — all this as part of the mood designed specifically for UPA. By the time everyone had moved in, the studio was about to start work on the cartoon *Gerald McBoing-Boing*, in many ways the quintessential UPA product.

Gerald opens with a blast of childlike music. In a sweet look at the ruthlessness of peer prejudice, we see the simplified, grid-story of the little boy who cannot talk, only makes special-effects noises. His mother and father are distraught. The doctor cannot help. The school sends him home for good. The other kids run away, as he toots, squeals, and roars. Finally, while he is in the process of running away from home (hopping a freight) a man from the radio station finds him at the stockyard and hires him as the special-effects wizard. Like Dumbo before him, his infirmity makes him a star.

Taken from a Dr Seuss story (many LA animators knew Ted Geisel during the war), this is a sly look at how greed and goodness make for good luck, and is very

Drawing by Jules Engel for *Madeleine* (1952), based on the classic children's book.

characteristic of the stories favored at UPA, from postwar children's books, like *Madeleine*, or from Thurber stories, like *The Unicorn in the Garden*. The linear/naive style of illustration that came into fashion in forties children's books clearly made an impact upon the designers, animators, and modern artists in the UPA group. Gerald, with his little hat, resembles the child in *The Carrot Seed*, a picture book in what was then called "the poster art style," in blocks of color that suggest a great stillness.

Gerald is made to stare and pause. When he actually opens his mouth, one almost expects silence. It is a system of illustration where poses are held in extra frames, to announce the design to the audience, where movement is more a form of mechanical locomotion, like a hydrofoil in space, a parody of walking.

Most of all, the colors are intentionally out of register, and the floor is generally left blank. Virtually the entire middle ground, so crucial to chase cartoons and full animation, is dissolved.

And instead of elaborate animated movement, the characters become a part of the layout, to suggest, at the very least, a deterministic omniverse, in the spirit of the wartime politics that had generated this style to begin with. The characters stop, then go — motorized — in a world that seems floating in a void. When Gerald is stopped by a stop sign, it drops by surprise, as if its solidity were startling him. He lives after all in a world without speech, a quilted world. Now he is out on his own for the first time.

The most stunning use of this omniversal void is the stairway that floats in the McBoing-Boing house, and then Gerald's escape to the stockyards, where night and abstract space are merged. The figures are like vehicles inside this void, driving all night to Reno in 1950, with only the geometry of lanes into a vanishing point and darkness everywhere else. Clearly, the spirit of the new world, isolated by automobile, into a detached distance, is captured here. It suits the moment when the first wave of shopping centers were being imagined, now (1950) just a few, but dozens, and then hundreds at once. It was to be a world of one-stop shopping, with a clear view from the parking lot to the cash register inside. It was also the world of the UPA studio building — inside–outside, with the isolation of sound by glass as the only major separation.

Gerald's world is tidy and reductive. He is something of a prisoner, rolling ahead like a mechanical toy with tiny wheels. How his space is defined makes it impossible for him to do otherwise, even if he were fully animated. Where could he run? Where could he crash? His world is inside a heavy American car of 1950, humming so quietly, there seems to be no sound at all.

And in the spirit of modern design, all his sounds are asynchronous, as they had been in cartoons generally, from Mickey to Bugs and Wile E. Coyote. Kisses are funnier when they snap like a balloon being pinched (Bugs giving Elmer the *coup de grâce*, the effortless kiss on the cheek, while Elmer is caught again). But the asynchronous sound is used as a form of awkwardness here, not anarchy. Here, the character is trying not to be anarchic, but he goes "boing" anyway (loudly!) and everyone is startled. In chase cartoons, no sound seems to startle any character, unless he is trying to sleep, in cartoons with Donald, with Elmer; or trying to keep a bulldog baby asleep, called Junior by big Spike, while Jerry forces Tom into noisy collisions. Otherwise, the clatter is fine in cartoons, because the story is built around different premises than *Gerald McBoing-Boing*.

Gerald is a reluctant cartoon character who simply wants to be a little boy. So often in UPA cartoons, the anarchic qualities (what is not erased) create the conflict, because the character is just trying to fit in, like the man in *The Unicorn in the Garden*. He keeps seeing that unicorn. His wife threatens to send him to the booby hatch. He sends her there instead. A sly grins finishes the cartoon, with the moral: "Don't count your boobies before they're hatched."

GAGS ABOUT INSANE NORMALCY

This style of animation is about quiet madness, about normalcy. Much the same is true of Bruno Bozzetto's cartoon shorts, like *Life in a Tin Can*. A tiny figure walks from one building across to another. The buildings change their purposes, from the hospital where he is born, to the office where he goes to work when he grows up. But he never ceases crossing the foreground, like a duck in a shoot, only rarely pausing for a bucolic break, until he dies. He is painfully driven by normalcy, not unlike the theater of the absurd characters Ionesco created.

The UPA style is of a piece with the "gray flannel" obsessions of the fifties world, about the marketing of experience into one-stop shopping, about the quiet withdrawal away from urban centers. At its heart, however, is the problem of the layouts, the backgrounds. They are particularly flat and void, brilliantly seasoned with poster colors, but expressed as an absence. The characters are trapped inside their self-reserve.

That becomes the quintessential world of UPA, where the outside is void and the inside (the character) is repressed. The conflict is displayed by watching how

> the inside (the self)
> colors outside — the void.

It uses distortion rather than metamorphosis and starkly elegant pauses. And between inside and outside, there is a clear viewing space, like a clear window — a cel, spare and linear against a field of color. Think of the effect from an architectural point of view. The space that frames the action is a field of color instead of a bearing wall. It resembles the feeling of looking out from the UPA building and seeing the hills around Burbank.

This is also a movie space. UPA used a great many camera angles and dissolves, even more than thirties full animation (almost in place of full animation). The movie syntax, from the mid-thirties on, was kept. The style was not really a return to the graphic narrative of the twenties. It was a redefinition of the movie space, in terms of the consumer modernism of the fifties — consumer cubism, very tidy.

Or was it tidy? The contrast of line against color field was often a central part of the story: linear Gerald escapes into the blank night, to hop a freight. In the language of the fifties, one might call Gerald's background a "buttoned-down anarchy."

A related matter: Critics generally summarize UPA's stories as follows, taking the lead from interviews with Hubley: "UPA preferred satire over slapstick." Or as Jules Engel remembers: "We preferred understatement." Most interviews with other veterans from UPA say much the same: we used more human characters, more adult fables. True enough, but how does cartoon understatement make its impact on the audience? The stillness deliberately runs (or stands still) against the grain of cartoon anarchy. All the leading UPA directors and the lead animators knew the chase format as well as they knew full animation. There was a choice involved here, of course, noted by one English critic, David Fisher:[13]

Gerald McBoing-Boing [is] a charming and ingenious fantasy about a child whose special predicament, like Magoo's, is a physical infirmity that turns to spectacular advantage

I believe that UPA instinctively selected stories about characters with bad eyesight, or with one of their senses reduced — or characters unable to act physically on the world — as a way to build more conflict into the erasures and refusals of those delicately cobbled poses. These were brilliantly colored stories about repression and sensory denial.

The antic impulse was intentionally repressed, but annoyingly present, as in the UPA adaptation of Poe's *The Tell-Tale Heart*: the murderer listening for signs of his victim's heartbeat beneath the floorboards. In the gray flannel world, the sound of unexpected breathing can take on the same drama as a character hit by a train in a chase cartoon.

After all, the fifties were hardly a peaceful era or a calm one. So the UPA characters are merely *pretending* that the world had normalcy. That is possibly why Magoo suited the studio as a continuing character. The more normal he pretended the world was, the more anarchic it became. Magoo is a classic example of the still character inside a rubberized, unpredictable world, very much a product of the chase cartoon I describe in earlier chapters. What was unique to UPA, however, was the animated space it presented, how its pauses seemed to collapse the background into the foreground. The simple line drawing — the character, Gerald or Magoo — was seemingly pressed against the enveloping color. The line, as the anarchic element, would attempt to hold out against the master plan.

Of course, this raises the question of whether modern design, as a graphic narrative, tried too hard to give a master plan to the world. At its most prescriptive, design could present a highly deodorized modernism; architects were encouraged to hyper-rationalize the public space, as in the frightful new business centers built from the fifties into the seventies, after the bulldozers cleared old neighborhoods. In that sense, UPA cleared old neighborhoods, took away the old vaudeville remnants, and replaced them with a buttoned-down whimsy — evacuated spaces — where the slightest asymmetry hit like a safe from ten storeys. Don't litter our cement vacuum.

UPA was a brilliant look at repression, consumer normalcy, and the new topology of the fifties — a world that promised freeways, housing projects, and a mechanistic normalcy, but was stricken by anxiety, like those little UPA characters. David Fisher added:[14]

Mr. Magoo represents for us the man who would be responsible and serious in a world that seems insane; he is a creation of the fifties, the age of anxiety; his situation reflects our own.

Magoo's situation also reflected the grim facts within the animation industry, as I explained earlier, in chapter 20 on the postwar chase. Cartoon production was thrown ever more dangerously toward the intersection, a nasty crossing of the axes, with less income and higher costs. Consumer marketing changed public habits considerably, particularly after the collapse of movie chains, and the arrival of the topsy-turvy world of television. As a result, the big studios were continually pinching dollars from marginal areas like the cartoon. The instability in the animation industry increased. Jobs in higher-paying TV commercials steadily took away many of the best animators. A shift toward the reductive surface of the TV screen made all sorts of subtleties rather gratuitous. When Hubley explained in 1946 that UPA was supposed to make animation an expressive, personal art, and keep away the invasions of marketing, there was a lot of wishful thinking there. (He left cartoon work earlier than any of the other founders of the UPA style.) By the time Bosustow sold UPA in 1960, most of its original team were gone. There was not much more than a shell left, mostly its film library, and characters to license or use in cheaper formats. So the anxious, reductive poses of those shy UPA figures bear witness to the crisis of a collapsing marketing: little boys who think they are chickens; men addicted to jaywalking; the frantic voice of James Mason in Poe's *The Tell-Tale Heart*.

CONSUMER LAYOUT

By the fifties, many at UPA would follow the journal *Graphis* regularly, to watch for new trends in design and practical links to abstract art. A sidelong alliance between "modern" advertising and the modern cartoon was being made, also with modern architecture, transportation, and urban planning.

But as I mentioned above, more than the characters, the key difference was in layout — the imaginary space, now an infinitely empty warehouse of lines and blank spaces. Even in chase cartoons of the fifties, or Disney melodramas, the background layout grew flatter. Flatter layout did not reduce costs. It was not necessarily cheaper that way. It was a decision, not a cheap answer; which brings us back to the central question about these layouts: what aspects of the world did these flat backgrounds turn upside down? I can make a few safe guesses by looking at the world around UPA. The backgrounds approximated the meaning of the fifties home, and how people traveled from home by car; and where they traveled — the horizontal consumer spaces of the expanding southern California. With its slices of color and crazy overhangs, one might call it googie space, like those luncheonettes of the period. With its see-through ambiguities — the missing floor, the lost walls — one might call it glass-curtain ballet, in honor of the Mies skyscraper. The googie metaphor seems closer to the horizontal spirit of fifties Los Angeles, when no building was permitted to be taller than seventeen stories, and the city was still empty enough to look like renovated farmland, in the San Fernando Valley where Disney had moved.

To repeat my central points here:

1. I see UPA cartoons of the fifties as primarily an adaptation to the fantasies associated with advertising, architecture, and open consumer spaces more than painting.
2. The most extreme adjustment came in layout, in the way animated space was erased, to suggest the ironies of reductive, linear movement — not so much about anarchy as restriction. This resembles the changes in architecture, home decors; and makes stories about whimsical alienation easier to tell, characters caught between consumer individualism and Cold War paranoia.

In the Conclusion, we enter these spaces through the eyes of the cartoon, into the virtual toon space, as nostalgia, as architecture. The animated space was built in Anaheim, with Disneyland. And while Disneyland seems to have a certain coquetry that UPA avoided, the implications of cartoon cubism became evident. Cartoon cubism in its American variation was certainly not a world of high formalism, not an Ad-Reinhardt erasure, not even a Norman McLaren cartoon, where the surface of each frame was hand-painted. It was a world where cartoons met their maker, where they made one more adjustment to consumer marketing. In that sense, the cartoon did not die after 1960; it metamorphosed yet again into a stucco butterfly. What began in the 1890s as a caricature of vaudeville space, on a surface borrowing from popular illustration, became, by the 1990s, a theme-park on a surface of electronic memory. The animated cartoon had been applied intimately to computer design, to TV narrative — and video games — to theme-parks, even to architecture. It was as if the viewer, not just the character, now lived in a world seven minutes long: the length of a world report on CNN; the length of the entertainment loop; the momentary stop of traffic around red, blinking ambulances after a drive-by shooting. That may be how our era will be remembered, as tourists who move like cartoon cels, in a layout gutted open like a fish — raunchy and confused. But who knows how historical memory will be recorded generations from now? In the context of this book, I can promise one certainty: There will be many cartoons about nervous tourists in a collapsing world — about the American white culture facing the new global uncertainty. And they'll be very funny.

CHAPTER TWENTY-THREE

From One Screen to the Other: Hanna—Barbera

The end of the cartoon as a staple for the movie theater was already hinted at as early as 1947. That year MGM, along with other studios, began re-releasing old cartoons. On reissue, an old cartoon could earn up to 90 percent of a new one.

By 1955, MGM planned to reissue more cartoons (14) than it produced (12).[1] Finally, early in 1957, it virtually closed down its animation units. (Some production dragged for a few more years, on very slim budgets.) I have already gone over many of the reasons for this decision, but another summary might still be helpful: between 1941 and 1956, cartoon production costs had increased by 225 percent, while rentals had risen only 15 percent.[2] Cartoons were not an industry for the big screen any longer Joseph Barbera remembered:[3]

It was a fateful day. Here we were thinking that we're at the top of the heap. Producing, writing, directing, and taking care of the full program. And our department on the MGM lot is successful. We didn't know what was going on. Without a hint, the phone rings — not to us but to an accountant, a bookkeeper. "Close the studio! Lay everybody off! Finish the few pictures we're doing. And then we're not doing any more cartoons." ...

[Afterward], Bill and I went to every agency, every studio. And they said: "We aren't doing any more cartoons. Too expensive." So we either had to find something in our field or leave the business entirely and sell insurance or open a chicken stand or wash cars.

They found a spot for a TV series in the fall schedule of 1957: *Ruff and Ready*, with a cat who looked sweeter than Tom, more like a Jerry-cat, and a bulldog a lot like Spike (white not brown, which would not register anyway), with a snout a bit like Droopy. Of course, after that show others came in astonishing succession, at least 138 series over a thirty-year period. Among the early ones were *Huckleberry Hound* (1958), *Pixie and Dixie* (1958), *Quick Draw McGraw* (1959), *Yogi Bear* (1960), *The Flintstones* (1960), *Snagglepuss* (1960), and *Top Cat* (1961). For decades, they added between four and seven new shows every year, until their film library grew so large that when Ted Turner bought it in 1991, he announced the beginning of a 24-hour cartoon channel, including Hanna—Barbera, as well as Warners and MGM cartoons.

The sheer volume prompted the comic Stan Freburg to call Hanna—Barbera the "Lockheed concept of commercial television."

In 1987, I visited Joe Barbera's office, then at Taft Entertainment in Burbank. Six-foot fuzzies of Fred Flintstone and Scoobie Doo rested like monuments as I passed. As mentioned earlier, I asked Barbera what adjustments he made in 1957 to speed up production. He said that he merely took away much of the second half of cartoon production, keeping the finished product more like pose reels, closer to the roughs that he used to produce with such velocity at MGM. But, of course, the changes go much deeper than that.

By removing the systems of full animation, and of antic early sound cartoons, Hanna—Barbera brought animation essentially back to the early twenties, to the cut-and-slash system used for Krazy Kat Cartoons, where only certain body parts might move, rather like Javanese stick puppets. Ironically, in 1957 he and Bill Hanna started working out of the old Chaplin studios on Highland Avenue, which had been built in the early twenties. Barbera often comments on the sensation that piece of history suggested to them, as if they were starting again. In the terms of this book at any rate, they were returning to the dusty remains of the character who had first inspired Otto Messmer in 1919.

There are other parallels with the twenties. And they make a useful lever to conclude this book, by returning to where it started (1928), to decide how far the animated space has come.

1957 versus 1921: In designing Felix the Cat, Otto Messmer specifically wanted to move away from the fuller animation of Winsor McCay. He was facing a problem in the technology. Animated film, for all the brilliance of McCay and Cohl, was still in its technological infancy in 1921. The motion picture camera was still a rather limited machine. The film stock was very slow and grainy, as I mentioned in chapter 1.

Similarly, television in 1957 was capable of remarkable innovation, but was still in its technological infancy. It was often little more than visual radio, or two-camera theater. When TV shifted away from live TV toward film, in 1955, it still borrowed principally from the movies. But broadcast machinery was still cumbersome. Ernie Kovacs' genius was to make fun of the crudeness of TV technology, to find a language based on its limitations, to find an essential facture to early TV.

TV was an intimate medium — that was in its favor, more or less, except for the ruthlessness of its salesmanship and censorship. But the picture could get muddy; it had all the stability of a song-and-dance act on a runaway bus, like a skit from *Your Show of Shows* perhaps. The cinematography often looked like a home movie. Even the image itself had the jitters. Like the animation of 1921, it did not resolve tonal gradations very well, and tended to flicker. It required simplification to be readable.[4] And all that took place on a smaller screen, in a highly synchronic, abrupt form, with frequent interruptions, which ultimately become their own grammar. I often remind students that the narrative structure of television is not the single story. The narrative structure is *three hours*. Whatever one sees in three hours makes up one story. And within those three hours, seven minutes is merely a punctuation. On the other hand, cartoons were always designed as media punctuation, to be sandwiched in while the projectionist changed reels. So instead of a newsreel, cartoons were followed by commericals about uranium-flavored barbecue chips or marshmallows as a breakfast cereal. Cartoons seemed to belong to this madly anarchic three hours on TV (with pretensions to domestic goodness), despite the extreme censorship, degenerated redundancies, and tiny budgets. Of course, one becomes what one does; and cartoons became TV.

Very quickly, these limitations evolved into a system of production, and then into a narrative form (as happened, in vaguely parallel conditions, in the cartoon of the twenties). The film historian Ted Sennett explains:[5]

As opposed to the intricate details of classical animation, a few moving parts of principal characters were animated and then photocopied on to the cels to simulate talking or simple action. The character walks and other standed movements were codified and reused in cycles, while a single background could serve for entire sequences.

Thus, cartoons took on the redundant movement and partial body animation characteristic of the period 1917—23, but, of course, with gags about the fifties. Instead of backgrounds similar to vaudeville, cartoons resembled the toy section of a shopping center — the consumer carnival rather than vaudeville.

To provide a setting for a barely moving character, Hanna—Barbera reversed the order to stylized animation (UPA, etc.). They made the background more in depth, while the foreground stayed flat. Thus, Huckleberry's Wild West or the Flintstones' town of Bedrock look more rounded than the characters do. As paper-thin as Fred and Barney look, the background resembles a walk through a deeper stage, a fuzzy theme-park setting; it is furnished in misshapen, rounded objects remade in synthetic materials (the kind of rocks that one might find in a toy playhouse). The objects suggest a cartoon Oldenburg effect, but in miniature scale, on a small screen. In its sense of depth, it reminds me of the Fleischer miniatures of the thirties, but much more airbrushed and intentionally synthetic (not industrial or cinematic at all).

With *The Jetsons* (1962) the background became more linear, perhaps to speed up production even more. I suspect budget was not the reason though. This linear look probably seemed suitable for *The Jetsons*. It allowed for gags about that degenerated late-modernist design which looks so lamentable to us today — a bald, plastic veneer poured over everything. In the early sixties, however, plastic modernism, beyond tupperware, suggested the space age, that last frontier promised by President Kennedy, where ever-lighter plastics and vacuum-packed food were needed to send men in aluminum and plastic suits to the moon. *The Jetsons* are indeed cartoons about "the (p)last(ic) frontier," where suburban bubble homes look out beyond the space station.

To enhance gags about a plastic future, the foreground and background were made to look identical. On first viewing, with a squint, one might equate this with the graphic narrative of the twenties, but that is utterly wrong. This look was more an accident of technology. *The Jetsons'* background is more like a plastic tablecloth in space than a Felix cartoon.

Rather than twenties graphic narrative, a clearer way to interpret the "Jetson" look would be the term *convenience*. I mean household conveniences, shopping for convenience, the myths of the four-day work week, labor-saving devices, a democracy by microwave, with wall-to-wall carpeting, dishwashers, and smooth surfaces, which can be wiped off easily with a damp rag. Too convenient consumer conveniences, when an animator has to draw them, look linear. How else should a smooth surface look? And the entire staging remains linear, front to back. In other words, the flat surfaces of *The Jetsons* allude to plastic comfort (like a kitchen galley, with washable walls). Compare this to the fuller background in the *Flintstones*; that looks more volumetric, like a rock garden near a shopping center, not quite Ralph Kramden's Brooklyn, despite the growling Fred and his bowling partner Barney. This looks more like cartoon suburb, a parody of the city as plastic, a caveman's theme-park as a kind of Disneyland.

In the Conclusion, I will enter the theme-park more directly, in discussing the neo-retro world of cartoon architecture.

Felix the Cathedral Meets the Swan Hotel

To conclude, I go from Bedrock to the Swan Hotel, into cartoon architecture, where the cartoon has found its new home.

Cartoon architecture started out as an imaginary problem in graphic narrative: In 1927, a British professor imagined what Felix the Cat would look like as a cathedral (as a teaching tool, not a building as we might find him today). We start with one Felix at the center:[1]

Suppose the teacher turned two other Felixes into pillars at his side and then constructed a Felix arch. It would be easy and amusing for him to show stresses and how they could be met. You would see the sagging at the knees or wherever it would sag.

Felix was an algebra of the fantastical, a bit Cézanniste: "when one thinks of Felix and mathematics — cones sliced in lovely sections, curves developing in a panoply of perpendiculars, and tangents to illustrate the secrets of growth and motion and form — why, on these lines we would have all the joys of Felix, Professor Einstein and the Zoo simultaneously."

By 1939, through Disney film staging, this architectural principle was already in practice. One wonders if Disney even in the thirties could have organized what he did for the 1964 World's Fair, those three exhibitions: General Motor's Carousel of Progress; the Ford show on dinosaurs and evolution; and Walt's fascination with the Walking/Talking President Lincoln, at least in their essential forms, as special-effects movie-sets where visitors stand in for characters in a story. All of these attractions had been transferred in part from Disney films, like *Fantasia*, or in amalgam through special-effects planners like John Hench at WED for Disneyland, or lighting technicians like J. S. Hamil (who had worked in Hollywood, and for the World's Fair of 1939).

In Disney's special effects department in the thirties, there were motorized models built for *Pinocchio*, not unlike rides (not unlike Pleasure Island, for that matter, as close a model for Disneyland as ever appeared in a Disney feature). As numerous documentaries show, Walt's love of trains was longstanding, existing long before he played conductor at the whistle on the opening day of Disneyland in 1955, in a copy of the full-scale locomotive he kept in his own backyard.

Of course, Disney's enthusiasms went far beyond trains in a park. At the time of his death, according to Marc Davis, Walt was already planning a "people mover" for downtown Los Angeles, and wanted to shift much more into urban development. There is considerable documentation at Cal-Arts about the city he planned to build for artists, with display windows where visitors could see artists at work. That's not what happened, of course, though we will never know what Cal-Arts might have looked like if Disney had lived another five years.

Ward Kimball, who may be the train enthusiast who started Walt collecting old engines, went with Disney to Chicago as part of a vacation they took to look at locomotives. (This was to help Walt relax after a modified nervous breakdown, brought on by extreme exhaustion.) As they sat in a Chicago subway, Walt went into excited detail about how the entire rail system worked in Chicago, talking about how he remembered each of the stops from the time he had been a mailman after the First World War. It was as if he were imagining Chicago as a blueprint.

Disney had a strong impulse to restructure old cities into small towns. In a radio interview, Ray Bradbury claimed that Disney's trip to Paris partly inspired his design for Disneyland, as unlikely as that may seem on first viewing. Perhaps it is Paris upside down, off the freeway, shrunken for convenience, with room for jungles and rides, stuccoed over, and twisted tight at both ends by Protestant fantasy. Imagineering (the name given by Disney for the architectural animation at Disneyland) has brought the whimsical innocence of the drawing art into real space on three continents, so who's to say what Paris or Disneyland may look like in the next century? Animation is the narrative art of simulation, for good or ill. And cartoons are the guidebook. When I asked Marc Davis how hard it was to switch from cartoons to designing the Pirates of the Caribbean at Disneyland he paused, and said not at all, with gentle modesty: he had simply applied the principles of space he had learned from the cartoon, in layout (as story man), and in movement. In an architectural sense, the tourist replaces the cel where the characters run and act; though, as a reminder that you are inside a cartoon at Disneyland, Mickey or Goofy in costume will wave or give you a fuzzy hug; or an animatronic body will talk to you.[2]

The rotating wraparound sets, the "*hyper*-cinematic simulations" of Futureworld and "Tomorrowland,"[3] remind us of the strong connections between movie-centered full animation of the late thirties and cartoon animatronic rides in theme-parks today, and how the miniatures and layouts for full animation resembled the Futurama conveyer ride at the New York World's Fair, how literally close to a movie set our world is becoming.

Animation, even by the late thirties, was already shifting toward a peculiar kind of architecture, when it tried to make cartoon layouts look like sound stages. In 1940, for an opening shot of *Mr. Bug Goes to Town*, Fleischer built a miniature of an imaginary Manhattan which very much resembled the New York World's Fair, except that, in its applications, it may have been even more elaborate. It could revolve up and down, on a large steel turntable, with a setback and "distorted perspective" for camera trucking to exaggerate the illusion of depth so crucial to movie-centered animation. "Each building has been painted, wired for electricity, and over 16,000 tiny panes of glass dot the windows of the various structures."[4] Then, two years later, the lights literally went out. Fleischer lost their studio partly due to expensive architectural gags like that.

REVIVAL OF THE GHOST

By the time that Max Fleischer died in 1962, a revival for the cartoon was underway, in numerous articles and festivals about Fleischer, about all the old studios; and always about Disney, particularly after the re-release of *Fantasia*, and a cult that surrounded it among the baby boomers. I don't know whether it was Disneyland or cartoons on TV, or even the reaction against Disney that actually sparked this revival. It had started long before Disney World opened in 1973. It was already well along by the late sixties, evident in what I call "anti-Mickeys".

In 1965, Disney purchased Chouinard Art Institute, to set up what became the California Institute of the Arts. Various disgruntled faculty at Chouinard, including John Van Hammersveld, produced "anti-Mickey" comic strips, about long-snouted, ratty Mickeys. Something of the anarchic edge of the animated cartoon seemed very appealing, even as a form of protest. From other sources came other anti-Disney printed paraphernalia: in New York, the magazine *The Realist*; in Chicago, anti-Mickey posters; in San Francisco, underground comics. Walt himself and his characters were criticized as Cold War imperialists in the United States and abroad, particularly in Latin America; in a controversial study entitled *How to Read Donald Duck*,[5] about the imperialist uses of Disney comics in Latin America. There was even an anti-war animated cartoon entitled *Uncle Walt* (1967), where an appropriated Mickey escapes from cannibals and winds up in a graveyard for the Viet Nam War.

By the late sixties, the anti-Mickeys in LA had been integrated into the visual style of the San Francisco underground comics movement (*Micky Rat* comics, for example, as late as 1980). Disney imagery also has become a staple in art installations about consumerism.

Disney filed at least one law suit to protect its interests, stopped the poster company in Chicago, and closed down a comic strip entitled *Air Pirates* (about Mickey as a recovered alcoholic, forced by studio politics to lie about his natural children, his so-called "nephews").

These were comic attacks on the growing influence of a global mass culture, as much as Walt's conservative politics. They cited a direct linkage between information industries and the war machine, a link no longer true about Disney, but true in a much broader sense of southern California: or of the way that, steadily, mass media have merged into the world economy. Obviously by the nineties, with computers, cable, video, and faxes, this is *much* more evident.

Also by the seventies, but from different sources, Betty Boop went through a sexy rediscovery. She got her Boop back, just as anti-Mickeys got their sharp bite back — the return of very anarchic cartoon imagery. Betty first reappeared in Grampy cartoons at Led Zeppelin concerts in the late sixties. Then she was featured as "feminist heroine" in various film festivals in the early seventies. Next campy marketers came up with buxom Boop candles, greeting cards (including a series designed by Leslie Cabarga), and Boop negligées at upscale emporiums by the late seventies. In 1980, during a Boop festival at Cal-Arts, honoring Grim Natwick on her fiftieth birthday, a young woman wearing only a slip and a garter intercepted me and gave me her card. She was in business renting herself out as Betty Boop, singing Boop-ograms at parties and birthdays. On stage, she booped a little number for us and pouted for Mr Natwick (then about ninety years old), while everyone cheered. There was even a rumor floating in 1980 that CBS was planning a muscial of Betty Boop (starring Linda Ronstadt?).

Any number of clues were evident: headline stories in Sunday supplements, as each character went through its fiftieth birthday, with a book, TV specials, a minute on the five o'clock news. Each by itself seemed trivial, but the mass of them together suggested a growing interest: articles about Disney's Epcot Center opening; new books on Warners cartoons; on Tex Avery; expanded showings for animation festivals, and always to huge crowds, even on weekdays. New journals on cartoons appeared, like *Funnyworld*, edited by Mike Barrier; crucial interviews by Joe Adamson and his book *Tex Avery: King of Cartoons* (1975); Leslie Cabarga's *The Fleischer Story* (1976); smaller journals like *Mindrot*; more attention to cartoons in film journals generally, particularly after events sponsored by ASIFA; documentary films and articles by John Canemaker; reviews by Charles Solomon; Leonard Maltin's *Of Mice and Magic* (1980); Donald Crafton's *Before Mickey* (1982).

The film industry also took notice, once Lucas and Spielberg started to promote animation. In cycles of media events after *Star Wars*, elements of the cartoon (more as staging than story) came into mainstream live-action films. The link may have started when large newspapers covered the story of George Lucas including *Duck Dodgers in the $23\frac{1}{2}$ Century* in special showings of *Star Wars*, up in San Francisco; then a Chuck Jones cartoon was added for *1941*; and a Fleischer-like *Cartoonland* segment in *The Twilight Zone: The Movie*.

Steadily, the architectonic meanings of cartoon nostalgia found their way. I say "architectonic" because so much of this revival was linked to special effects, miniatures, and to shopping malls. A kind of architectural significance was applied increasingly to cartoon imagery, as a sign for consumer desire (in shop windows, mall architecture). Even as consumer horror, starting with *Cartoonland*: an evil boy with animational powers forces strangers to serve his ten-year-old consumer fetishes or be sent to cartoon hell. If they annoy him, he throws them into a cruel cartoon, like a cautionary cartoon of the late thirties. They are shrunk, then dropped into an old fifties TV set. There, Boopish ghouls chase them forever, in a loop cycle that resembles the primitive chases of the twenties; or the nightmare we all dream occasionally, of endlessly running from something, but too slowly. Since then, with the *Gremlins* and *The Nightmare on Elm Street* series, characters empowered with cartoon imagination can look increasingly like the devil as interior decorator of their victim's unconscious.

It was only a matter of time before this storehouse of consumerist folklore would make its way into architecture directly — a broad-based application of Disneyland architecture, or what is generally called "Entertainment Architecture." By the late eighties, it had arrived. The theme-park had merged with the shopping mall across the United States, in glass, barrel-vaulted phantasmagorias, often with cartoon references (or at least special-effects staging). Then, after 1987, during the Eisner Disney era came Disney shops; and parallel to that, as part of the culture of collectables of the Reagan era, came the explosive growth of the cartoon cel as collectable. The first sale of an animation cel dates back to 1958, though it was not a serious business yet. In the mid-fifties, Warners thought so little of the old cels that they incinerated millions of them to clear warehouse space. By the late eighties, however, newly painted cels of old cartoons had become a sub-industry. A collection of original cels from *Snow White* was auctioned at Christie's for hundreds of thousands of dollars, and individual Disney cels have sold in the tens of thousands. Virgil Ross explained that many of his drawings from his years at Warners (featured in Steve Schneider's book *That's All Folks*) were valued altogether at over a million dollars. Cartoon cel galleries have opened throughout the country, like penny museums to the commodification of the cartoon image. Finally, there are museums in New York and London specializing in cartoon history.

More specifically, animation as a form of historical memory has entered real space. After all, any space or film that uses manipulated, interactive imagery must be called, by definition, a form of animation; and we are increasingly being submerged in life as a video game, even while our political crises deepen, and our class difference widens. I remember in 1978 following a teenager who had just seen *Star Wars* nineteen times, and frankly looked like it. He was inside the embrace of these images. He was part of an imaginary family. He kept talking about how intimate *Star Wars* made him feel. Then I watched him walk directly to a new video parlour nearby, as a finale to a perfect day. There, sitting beside Han Solo, so to speak, he entered *Star Wars* even more intimately — or more physically, at any rate. He could interact with the movie directly, as if he were a gunner in space; then shoot it out with Darth Vader. The age of hand-motor coordination had arrived, a rediscovery of the power of the prehensile thumb on the trigger. Video games, as we all know, may have arrived first in public video parlors, but they have since entered the living room, from Atari to Nintendo to Sega Genesis. Once in the privacy of the living room, along with cartoon shows like *The Simpsons*, cartoons had at last found a permanent home, more than a site on afternoon TV to dump reruns. Animated video is rapidly becoming the logon vocabulary for interactive media. Even Mickey, in his prime, never claimed that kind of authority. How these opportunities will be exploited in the future, and by whom, remains to be seen — or entered.

In line with the iconization of cartoons, Michael Graves was hired by Disney to design cartoon architecture. Three of his cartoon buildings are already built, with more to come: the Dwarfs' office building in Burbank (icons about work — heigh-ho); the massive Swan Hotel at Disney World ($120 million, 700,000 square feet, 758 guest rooms);[6] followed by the Dolphin Hotel, and more in the works. In both the Swan Hotel and Dwarfs' office building, the façades have cartoon columns, which stand guard over an interactive, animated space, like the massive elephants that held up Babylon in the 300-foot set for Griffith's *Intolerance* in 1916.

Coincidentally, these cartoon monuments were built at the same time that Disneyland became a central feature in critical theory, from Umberto Eco and Jean Baudrillard in particular, and any number of others.[7] A strange blend of innocence and malevolence has become associated with cartoons; they are tabula for the erasures and upside-down images of consumer memory. And they are merchandised as historic symbols of consumer desire, or, more accurately, anarchy as a menu for desire. You can order what you want, but the machine makes the meal. Cartoons are an electronic museum, about *machina versatilis*, the history of media, of vaudeville and live entertainment, and the rituals of consumption.

This revival then is also a return to the roots of animation, as the trick film in early cinema, as *machina versatilis* at Vitascope, or in the work of Cohl and Méliès. The power of animation was always understood — as with all early cinema — in the illusionary space, the staging unique to animation: the room upside down, within the darkness of the theater. First impressions of the movie machine often sounded like a script for a theme-park, like the following, published in 1895, about the presence of the projector itself:[8]

Its materials are paper, covered with pitch and profusely studded with tin nails. With its great flapping sail-like roof and ebon complexion, it has a weird and semi-nautical appearance, like the unwieldy hulk of a medieval pirate-craft or the air-ship of some swart Afrite, not lessened, when at an imperceptible signal, the great building swings slowly around upon a graphited center, presenting any given angle to the rays of the sun and rendering the apparatus independent of diurnal variations. The movable principle of this building is identical with that of our river bridges, the ends being suspended by iron rods from raised centerposts . . .

As we peer into the illusive depths we seem transported to one of those cheerful banqueting halls of old, where the feudal chief made merry with human terrors . . . a building for the better "taking" of kinetographic subjects . . .

No department of the wizard's domains is more fraught with perennial interest than this theater; none are more interwoven with the laughter, the pathos, the genius and the dexterities of life.

Now this presence of *machina versatilis* has taken yet another turn. Cartoons have transferred from the big screen into the boardroom of global culture for the emerging new world economy. They have become an architectural tradition, about the amoral as well as the repressive in consumer life. Through Disney, and then dozens of non-Disney theme-parks and malls, they have mutated into the fully animated city, into fully loaded, tourist family Babylons; and futuristic *machinae versatilae*, like at Epcot. In two decades, Orlando has grown from a town of 20,000 to the Rome of world tourism, with a population passing one million. With Universal installed there as well, Orlando is officially the cartoon Oz. It takes us seven minutes into the future, with hotel accommodations, Mickey dollars, and rides.

We act out stories inside cartoons now. The screen has been replaced by interactive video and tourism. The president of the Disney Development Company described "entertainment architecture," like the Swan Hotel, very succinctly: "In the end, it's all a bunch of stories, and you can pick the one you want." The critic Mark Alden Branch adds: "Michael Graves has proven himself one of Disney's best storytellers."[9]

Similarly, the TV commercials for Universal Studios in Orlando promise "everything that happens in the movies happens to you." Like the neo-Victorian world we live in, the classes may be distinguished between animatronic and real, two planets: the electronically engaged; and the lower depths. In the cyberpunk future of video, I can imagine games where, like an old Avery cartoon (*Thugs with Dirty Mugs*), cartoons on the screen shoot down someone in the audience. Human silhouettes crumple in the foreground. After the shooting, as in Robert Coover's short story "Cartoon" (1987), the real man can only find a cartoon policeman on call, who "hurries along about four inches above the ground . . . taking five or six airy steps for every one of his own . . . blowing his whistle ceaselessly" (like an old Keystone Comedy cop). "It's as though they were walking side by side down two different streets. The cartoon town, meanwhile, slides past silently, more or less on its own."[10]

Suddenly, the cartoon takes on the moonstruck erasures of a de Chirico painting, in the ruins of a century about to fold. The consumer world that animation chronicles is beginning to age in America. But the possibilities of an art form built on line, anarchic story and upside-down allegory remain. In Disney's *Aladdin* (1992), Robin Williams' Genie keeps morphing madly, like a TV remote control gone stir crazy. The result is an electronic interspace working like an Avery cartoon.

In real space, though, these seven minutes (not counting the wait on line at Disneyland) announce that someone else has pre-programmed your unconscious, rather like the man in *The Unicorn in the Garden* (1954) waking up to find a live unicorn eating flowers in his backyard. Between the computer and entertainment architecture, the world upside down, as a veil against the agonies of what is coming, has become a global civilization, a catholicity that explains wars and personal salvation. Cartoons are our version of a unicorn tapestry.

As an essential part of this global imagineering, many more animators may be needed to transfer into architecture — or back again, with video games, and video imaging, or Virtual Reality projects, where cartoons, interactive video, and theme-parks become simultaneous.

Perhaps this architectural side of animation will broaden the range expected of the animated film by those who run the industry. In the past, this has not generally been the case. And there is also a perverse implication here, where animators are asked to re-image events, to sweeten the vinegar. In 1915, a cartoonist for Pathé News wrote a rather vainglorious but charming summary of the ideal animator. This seems a solid place to end, at the birth of the corporate side of this business, leaving strong hopes for an art form that is too often stretched and squashed:[11]

An animated cartoonist must be able to talk English, Irish and Swedish, must know the Ten Commandments, the law of gravitation, locomotion and its uses, mind over matter, psychology and its action on cheese, the rules of the road, "cohesion," and its lifting capacity, navigation, [be] a strong believer in Darwin, [know] the art of tuning a bass violin, the internal combustion engine and its use in the home, how to fry an agg, many innumerable things touched upon so lightly by our famous men and, above all, the animated cartoonist must have a one-track mind.

Notes

CHAPTER 1 GRAPHIC NARRATIVE

1. As told to Hugh Kenner by Chaplin, January 1964.
2. Hieroglyph: how images and film editing resemble the principles of pictographic language. "Intellectual Cinema" (discussed at length in Eisenstein's *Film Form*): An allegorical use of montage, juxtaposing visual commentary within the narrative. (i.e. in *October*, "the king and country" sequence, with elaborate allusions). The contrasts between live-action use of this technique and its obvious virtues within animation remain a vital center to animation studies.
3. Sergei Eisenstein, *Immoral Memories, An Autobiography*, trans. H. Marshall (Boston: Houghton Mifflin, 1983), pp. 42–3.
4. See *Before Mickey* (Cambridge, Mass.: MIT, 1982), the chapters on Messmer, and references to Taylorism in the chapter on Bray (chs 5, 6, 8, and 9).
5. See John Canemaker, *Felix: The Twisted Tale of the World's Most Famous Cat* (New York: Pantheon Books, 1991). Useful quote, p. 103, from Bela Belazs (1945): "In Sullivan's drawn world there are no miracles, for in it there are only lines and these function according to the shape they take on."
6. Carolyn Lejeune, *Theater Arts*, February 1934. A similar quote, from movie historian Terry Ramsaye (1932): "Mickey Mouse is the crystalline, concentrated quintessence of that which is peculiarly the motion picture" (Michael Barrier, *Building a Better Mouse: Fifty Years of Disney Animation*, Washington: Library of Congress, 1979; for show in 1978).
7. *Eisenstein on Disney*, ed. Jay Leyda, trans. Alan Upchurch (London: Methuen, 1988). Third in Eisenstein series, edited by Leyda. Cover photo was taken in 1930, when Eisenstein visited the Hyperion Studios; however, the texts come from the forties, a markedly different Eisenstein than in 1930, on first arriving from the Soviet Union in the twenties. For example, from 1943: "*Bambi* is already a shift towards ecstasy — serious, eternal: the theme of Bambi is the circle of life — *the repeating circles of lives . . . Bambi*, of course, crowns the whole study of Disney" (p. 63). In the mid-forties, he compares *Snow White* to *Alexander Nevsky*, both examples of "sight-and-sound consonance"; Sergei Eisenstein, "The Embodiment of a Myth," *Film Essays and a Lecture* (Princeton: Princeton University Press, 1982; orig. 1968), p. 85.

   Eisenstein also used the term translated as "plasmicness" to describe animation (again the later essays). The term is discussed at length by Keith Clancy in his essay "The T(r)opology of Pyromania," in the anthology *The Illusion of Life: Essays on Animation*, ed.

Alan Cholodenko (Sydney: Power Publications, in association with the Australian Film Commission, 1991), pp. 248–9.

The way Eisenstein uses the term (as an "organic" variation, I suspect, on plasticity, so common in modernist criticism of the teens and twenties) links animation with "evolution," in other words, with biology, with morphic animus. Clancy links it to plasma as expanding gases (an application to cartoons I see one other time in a book by Huntly Carter, *The New Spirit in the Cinema* [London: Harold Shaylor, 1930], pp. 29–30, but only vaguely similar to what Eisenstein meant). I think the linkage is more to evolutionary biology, and thus to animation as folklore; or as an historically involuted — "plasmic" — journey (like *Alexander Nevsky*), and less to physics or chemistry.

8. Roman Jakobson, "Is Cinema in Decline? (1933)," *Semiotics of Art: Prague School Contributions*, ed. Ladislav Matejka and Irwin Titunik (Cambridge, Mass.: MIT, 1976), pp. 145–52.

Gilbert Seldes, *An Hour with the Movies and the Talkies* (Philadelphia: J.B. Lippercott, 1929), p. 103. On Seldes' film criticism at that time, see Myron Osborn Lounsbury, *The Origins of American Film Criticism, 1909–1939* (New York: Arno Press, 1973), pp. 214–19: the general interest among American film critics (Seldes in particular) in Soviet cinema, and how to apply its strategies to film theory. Seldes was also interested in the notion of "contrapuntal sound" or "sound as a montage instrument" (p. 218). Very much a popular journalist, he wrote often in support of animated cartoons, for example: Seldes, "Disney and Others," *New Republic*, June 8, 1932, pp. 101–2.

9. Max Horkheimer and Theodor Adorno, *Dialectic of Enlightenment*, trans. John Cumming (New York: Seabury, 1972; orig. 1944), p. 138: "Cartoons were once exponents of fantasy as opposed to rationalism ... [from] organized amusement to organized cruelty. All [cartoons] do today is confirm the victory of technological reason over truth ... the old lessons that continuous friction, the breaking down of all individual resistance is the condition of life in this society. Donald Duck in the cartoons and the unfortunate in real life get their thrashing so that the audience can learn to take their own punishment." Two issues are suggested by this quote: (1) How the "imaginary" machine, when it is still a dream about the rational — not in operation commercially — has a whimsical, fantastical meaning (as in Diderot's *Encyclopedia*, or even in Mary Shelley's *Frankenstein*, where her original manuscript was "scientifically" enhanced, given more accurate, but fantastical detail, as a Romantic flourish, by her husband Percy Shelley). Also, as in the history of science fiction, a subject in itself. Eventually, after 1820, once the wheels of the steam engine are grinding at the mills, this imaginary machine is understood very differently, not as whimsy, but as a metaphor for the cruel, mechanistic factory town. Much as I admire this essay by Adorno and Horkheimer, I cannot avoid the sense that they ignored the implications of *machina versatilis* (see chapter 7), that machinery in fantasy settings (or cartoons projected through machines) always force a double-reading by their audience — first, as the imaginary balloon ride into the upside-down world, but second (and simultaneously) as an ideological defense of how machines are beneficent, how machines domesticate our fantasies for us, as in the spirit of a theme-park. Through animation, industrial imagery takes on the code of the carefully controlled, even repressive, adventure (most recently in Virtual Reality and video games). But this has happened earlier, centuries before. There was no nostalgic moment when this split-reading did not exist. There never was a time when the audience could separate the ideology of animated machinery from its childlike escapism, if that indeed is part of what Adorno and Horkheimer mean by rational. It seems that they missed a beat here. Their argument

about the eighteenth-century Enlightenment as the birth of a kind of repressive mechanistic world-view does apply to the animated cartoon, but not as kindly technology gone bad in the thirties, but rather as "machinic" fantasy that was doubly coded from the start, even before the eighteenth century.

(2) However, the references to Donald Duck are accurate enough, given how Donald is used so often in Second World War cartoons (as the average GI), and (something Adorno and Horkheimer could not have known) in Latin American comic books from the forties on (as the obedient worker).

10. Fritz Moellenhoff, "The Remarkable Popularity of Mickey Mouse," *American Imago*, vol. 3, 1940, pp. 19ff (repr. in abridged form, Norman Cantor and Michael Werthman (eds), *The History of Popular Culture* [New York: Macmillan, 1968], pp. 610—13). To track down other articles of the period, see Thomas Hoffer, *Animation, A Reference Guide* (Westport, Conn.: Greenwood Press, 1981).

11. E. M. Forster, "Mickey and Minnie," *Abinger Harvest* (London, 1936), p. 53. First published, *Spectator* [London], January 19, 1934, pp. 81—2. Often excerpted (with the elaborate references to folklore left out); however these seemingly obscure references reveal a lot about how animation in the twenties and early thirties was understood as *culture populaire*, presumably an extension of old rural, peasant folk traditions, in other words, a nostalgic pre-industrial, people's culture.

12. Erwin Panofsky, "Style and Medium in the Motion Pictures," *Film: An Anthology*, ed. Daniel Talbot (New York: Simon & Schuster, 1959), p. 23. Originally a lecture published in *Bulletin of the Department of Art and Archaeology* (Princeton, 1934; then revised by 1947).

13. Huntly Carter, *The New Spirit in the Cinema*, pp. 29—30. Carter was primarily a theater critic.

14. Kenneth White, "Animated Cartoons," *The Hound and the Horn*, Oct./Dec. 1931 (White taught philosophy at Harvard). Also in *American Film Criticism from the Beginnings to Citizen Kane*, ed. S. Kauffman with Henstell (New York: Liveright, 1972), p. 258.

15. Harry Carr, "The Only Unpaid Movie Star," *American Magazine*, March 1931, pp. 55ff; also, references to article by Herman (Kay) Kamen in *Forbes*, 1934 (licensing executive for Disney); Arthur Mann, "Mickey Mouse's Financial Career," *Harpers*, May 1934, pp. 714—21; Alice Ames, "Animated Cartoon Pictures," *Motion Picture Monthly*, January 1931, pp. 7—8.

16. El Lissitzky, *Life, Letters, Texts*, ed. Sophie Lissitzky-Kuppers (London: Thames & Hudson, 1968). Lissitzky was very interested in what we might call the animated exhibition space, the active relationship between the machine, the image and the "proun" space. In that sense, he understood, it seems, the profound linkage between animation and architecture. See also his work on "the electromagnetic" puppet show; and particularly his *Tale of Two Squares*, with layered pages in a palimpsest that suggest animation. Also, *El Lissitzky: Architect, Painter, Philosopher, Typographer* (New York: Thames & Hudson, 1990), with material suggesting "animation" as an issue in Lissitzky's work.

17. El Lissitzky, *Life, Letters, Texts*, p. 359.

18. Maurice Horn (ed.), "From Cartoon to Comic Strip: A Pictorial Survey," *The World Encyclopedia of Cartoons* (New York: Chelsea House Publishers, 1980), pp. 46—64.

19. See Donald Crafton's comprehensive study on *Emile Cohl: Caricature and Film* (Princeton: Princeton University Press, 1990).

20. The most authoritative source is John Canemaker, *Winsor McCay: His Life and Art* (New York: Abbeville, 1987).

21. Hugh Kenner, "Miltonic Monkey," *Mazes* (San Francisco: Northpoint Press, 1989). Doré's

use of black-line wood engraving allowed for an atmospheric depth of field unique to his work. This atmospheric space, along with the theatrical lighting and monumentality of his settings, proved to be a valuable resource, generations later, for art direction in cinema.

22. These rolls of illustrated wallpaper were available to subscribers in 1853. They combined lithographic images from Philipon journals: *Le Caricature*, *Charivari*, and particularly *Journal pour rire*, by Daumier, Cham, Bertall, and Doré. Samples available at the Bibliothèque Nationale in Paris.

23. The term "cult of the line" refers to the transition toward a simplified surface, in illustration and design, during the Arts and Crafts Movement, where the expression originated; but also to similar transitions in the Jugendstil, the Werkbund, in designs by Mackintosh, Van der Velde, and, of course, Beardsley. Ornament was steadily transformed from elaborate scroll to simple diagram, particularly in Art Nouveau early in the twentieth century.

   Most important to remember: this transition was based, in great measure, on the power of mass publishing in the nineteenth century — on a visual vocabulary that was adjusting to popularity of print. One simplifies what the perceptual horizon of the viewer can follow. This is true also of the cartoon, where the graphics and story were simplified according to what the audience knew by heart, from daily experience.

24. King Features originally owned the rights to Betty Boop, though no licensing went on for decades, until the late seventies.

CHAPTER 2 THE GAG

1. Joe Adamson, "Recollections of Dave Fleischer," *Oral History Program of the Motion Picture in America* (UCLA, 1969). Also, apparently an interview with Dave Fleischer by Adamson, for the American Film Institute, entitled "Where Can I Get A Good Corned Beef Sandwich?"

2. The side shows, and the "Egyptian" dancers, the "Blowholes" (women's dresses blown upward), mechanical earthquakes, the crazy slapstick of the Insanitarium — all contributed to a bawdy vaudeville spirit throughout the eastern end of the boardwalk in Coney Island. As of 1910, there even were side-show dancers within the giant five-acre enclosed Steeplechase Park, as well as small skits performed along the boardwalk. On the Coney Island that Dave Fleischer knew: Oliver Pilat and Jo Ransom, *Sodom by the Sea: An Affectionate History of Coney Island* (New York: Doubleday, 1941).

3. John Dukic, who was a mine of information about old Edendale where he grew up, and returned, over a period of seventy-five years. The reference to "Gold" was probably from a Ben Turpin film.

4. Donald Crafton "Animation Iconography," *Quarterly Review of Film*, Fall, 1979, pp. 410ff. He expanded these sources thoroughly in *Before Mickey*, pp. 6ff; and in *Emile Cohl: Caricature and Film*.

5. While there were actually many magic lantern shows in France at the time and various toys that presaged the moving picture, the projection of *moving images on to a theater screen* was unknown, of course.

6. Viktor Shklovsky, "Art as Technique," *Russian Formalist Criticism: Four Essays*, ed. Lee Lemon and Marion Reis (Lincoln: University of Nebraska Press, 1965). How "art removes objects from the automatism of perception" (p. 13), how the appeal of narrative lies in the way it subverts expectations, and makes the daily routine suddenly unfamiliar, and

more intense (either as realism, or simulation; not as a way to make the story difficult, but as a way to hold the reader). This essay is a primary source, from the teens, on defamiliarization, at first applied to theories on the modern novel, then adjusted to the other arts (particularly when the term re-emerges in the sixties, in Western Europe and the United States).

7. Filippo Marinetti, "The Variety Theater," *Selected Writings*, ed. Flint and Copotelli (New York: Farrar, Strauss and Giroux, 1971; repr. Sun-Moon Press), pp. 116–22.

8. Erwin Panofsky, *The Life and Art of Albrecht Dürer* (Princeton: Princeton University Press, 1943), p. 38 (based on lectures from 1938).

9. Michael Kirby, *Futurist Performance* (New York: Dutton, 1971), p. 305 (*Improvised Balloon*, described as "cinemagraphic poem"). Also, the manifesto *Futurist Cinema* (1916), clearly identifies animation, and cartoon gags (p. 216).

10. Marinetti, *Selected Writings* (footnote 6).

11. Treg Brown was the sound-effects man at Warners for many years. Chuck Jones often mentions Brown, and how much he was part of the ensemble at Warners who learned, over some twenty years, how to make those fast gags funnier. (See also chapter 14, n. 2.)

12. Jakobson (chapter 1, n. 8).

13. Barnet G. Bravermann, "Mickey Mouse and His Playmates," *Theater Guild Magazine*, March 1931, p. 17.

14. The term "high industrial takeoff": Introduction in Richard Hertz and Norman Klein (eds), *Twentieth-Century Art Theory: Urbanism, Politics, and Mass Culture* (Englewood Cliffs, NJ: Prentice-Hall, 1990), p. 5.

15. Aristotle's *Poetics*, I.4.

16. Interview with Larry Garf, collector and specialist on early twentieth-century musical reproduction.

17. George Jean Nathan, *The Popular Theater* (New York: Alfred Knopf, 1918), p. 198. He complains about the "passing from vaudeville of its quondam irresistible slapstick tonic," replaced by the "tony society atmosphere" of 1918. Nathan was a theater critic and co-editor, with H. L. Menchen, of *The Smart Set* in New York.

18. Nathan, *The Popular Theater*, p. 199.

CHAPTER 3 STORY

1. The term "syntagm" refers here to *audience*-oriented signifiers, references to other films, to the act of watching, such as the way a character stares, is dressed, gestures, walks. Also applicable to video theory: Norman M. Klein, "Audience Culture and the Video Screen," in *Illuminating Video*, ed. Doug Hall and Sally Fifer (New York: Aperture/Bay Area Video Cooperative, 1990), pp. 375–403.

2. Creighton Peet, "The Cartoon Comedy," *The New Republic*, August 14, 1929, p. 342. See also, Creighton Peet, "The Movies; Miraculous Mickey," *Outlook*, July 23, 1930, pp. 472–3.

3. Jean Charlot, *Art from the Mayans to Disney* (New York: Freeport Press, 1939; repr. 1969), p. 279. The associations between animated cave drawings and animated film seem to have originated with this book, and certainly have reappeared often since.

4. E. M. Forster, "Mickey and Minnie,", p. 53. See chapter 1, n. 11.

5. E. M. Forster, "Story of a Panic," *Collected Tales* (New York, 1947; orig. 1928), pp. 8–9. His theories on how to apply fantasy to narrative (similar to animation) are stated very clearly in *Aspects of the Novel* (1927; repr. New York: Harcourt Brace, 1955).

6. From a plate in Leslie Cabarga's history: *The Fleischer Story* (New York: Da Capo, 1976).

7. Kenneth White, "Animated Cartoons." Reprinted: Kaufmann and Henstell, *American Film Criticism from the Beginnings to Citizen Kane*, p. 258.
8. Animism is a term in anthropology, for the most part (also the history of religion), about the worship of spirit forces — the animus — within all objects (theoretically a stage preceding organized religion, which suggests a "pagan" anarchy, unlike the more "civilized" monotheisms of the West. In other words, it has a built-in imperialist implication). As a broader term, it also came to include the animistic fantasies of children, or of the childlike in folklore. Clearly, animism (by this twenties, western imperialist definition) can apply to cartoons as well, in how drawings of objects take on life. In the late twenties and early thirties, cartoons often were described as "animistic."
9. Vladimir Propp, "Fairy Tale Transformations," in *Readings in Russian Poetics: Formalist and Structuralist Views*, ed. Matejikar and Promorsca (Ann Arbor: University of Michigan Press, 1978), p. 94: "We observe that the actors in the fairy tale perform essentially the same actions as the tale progresses, no matter how different from one another in shape, size and sex and occupation, in nomenclature and other static attributes. This determines the relationship of the constant factors to the variables. The functions of the actors are constant; everything else is a variable."
10. Bettelheim's approach to folklore has been widely debated (even while he was at the University of Chicago in the fifties, more than a decade before his *Uses of Enchantment* appeared). In addition to critiques of Bettelheim's methods and sources, a broader national debate centered on a reevaluation of Grimm's fairy tales, particularly in the writings of Jack Zipes, and in Maria Tatar's *The Hard Facts of the Grimm's Fairy Tales* (Princeton: Princeton Univ. Press, 1987).
11. Sigmund Freud, "The Occurrence in Dreams of Material from Fairy Tales (1913)," *Character and Culture*, intro. P. Rieff (New York: Collier, 1963). In this brief essay, Freud draws upon his earlier theories on "screen memory," to include popular illustration (i.e. Doré's illustrations of *Perrault's Tales*, the source I believe his patient was describing). The patient dreams of wood engravings of Little Red Riding Hood, from the Doré book in his childhood nursery, the images (particularly the girl and the wolf in bed together) as displacement for trauma.

    Freud himself did not bother checking on the source, understandably, as he was working clinically, not in a scholarly capacity here. However, there is a broader implication as well. Freud did not see mass culture as invading the interior psyche, in the sense that we do today (except perhaps in his work on jokes and on the "psychopathology of everyday life"). But those examples refer to involuntary speech acts, not mass media. Therefore, he did not make a point of searching out the printed sources for these dreams, because he considered the source images as incidental (as the objects where the gaps in memory, similar to displacement, took place). He describes the patient's memory of graphic imagery as interior information, logged inside the process Freud defines as cathexis, inside the topology of the preconscious. Freud looks at the objects of mass culture in a way typical of that era (i.e. Freud is interested in Andrew Lang's work, *Custom and Myth*, 1884; but not in Lang as the editor of children's literature). He sees popular illustration as the equivalent of folklore, an innocent collective memory translated for family audiences, which seems to make any further clinical study hardly necessary. Once classified, the problem is contained within the psyche. (I refrain from making comparisons with more critical attitudes toward mass culture by Ruskin, Morris, Gautier, Sainte-Beuve, Champfleury, Peirce, Saussure, etc., a galaxy of subjects in itself.)

Also this quote by Freud, from a letter (1910), about jokes, but not mentioning entertainment, except by inference: "Jokes, both erotic and of other sorts, which are in popular circulation provide an excellent auxiliary means of investigating the unconscious mind — in the same way as do dreams, myths and legends, with the exploitation of which psycho-analysis is already actively engaged" (*The . . . Complete . . . Freud*, trans. J. Strachey, Vol. 11, London: Hogarth Press, 1975, p. 234).

12. See also notes 8, 9, and 11. The parallels between illustration (or animation) and folklore studies often were discussed during the teens and twenties. Frequently, the illustrator's art was listed among the popular crafts still "hand-made." As a result, illustration was viewed as a symbol of a vanishing world, a vanishing folklore, because industrially made entertainment grew so quickly after 1910.

13. Histories of Hanna and Barbera: Ted Sennett, *The Art of Hanna–Barbera* (New York: Viking Studio Books, 1989); T. R. Adams, *Tom and Jerry: Fifty Years of Cat and Mouse* (New York: Crescent Books, 1991); Patrick Brion, *Tom and Jerry: The Definitive Guide to Their Animated Adventures*, trans. A. Michelson (New York: Harmony Books, 1990; orig. Paris 1987).

14. See chapter 7, n. 5. By the early seventeenth century, the masque referred clearly to two primary sources: (1) theater emerging from medieval carnival (reifying community, in this case, the court of the English king); (2) commerce, architecture, and military technology — the presence of machine-made spectacle.

Masque was, of course, a courtly theater. The popular variation of this same combination (carnival story with machines) evolved into vaudeville, and finally the cartoon.

15. Albert McClean, Jr, *American Vaudeville as Ritual* (Lexington: University of Kentucky Press, 1965). Other informational sources: Anthony Slide, *The Vaudevillians: A Dictionary of Vaudeville Performers* (Westport, Conn.: Arlington House, 1981); Charles Samuels and Louise Samuels, *Once Upon a Stage: The Merry World of Vaudeville*; Robert Sobel, *A Pictorial History of Vaudeville* (1961). For LA: Stanford Singer, *Vaudeville West: To Los Angeles and the Final Stages of Vaudeville* (UCLA dissertation, 1987), and the archives of the Variety Arts Theater in Los Angeles.

16. Interviews with Walter Lantz, 1987.

17. Disney Handbook, UCLA Theater Library; also, Disney Archives. Disney vastly expanded the role of the story department in animation, particularly after Ted Sears arrived from Fleischer, in the early thirties. According to Dick Huemer (*Funnyworld*, No. 18, p. 15; confirmed by others), Sears had already presented storyboards to the Fleischers, who remained uninterested. Then he went to Disney.

Most important, however, once Ted Sears was at Disney, the storyboard and the story department grew simultaneously. Since that time, cartoon-writing has been, and remains, a kind of drawing first, then script, with continuity storyboards instead of scripts, and the dialogue underneath the drawings. The final screenplay dialogue is not needed until the voice actors are brought in. Relying on the drawing-first approach provides a much more stable linkage for all the graphic artists who must work on these images.

Some of this drawing-first emphasis may change in the next generation, as Disney reaches out for more young writers who may not be used to storyboards primarily. *Little Mermaid* and *Beauty and the Beast* were certainly scripted initially much more like live-action features than earlier Disney animated features (though the storyboard still remains the central device, understandably). Live-action Disney may begin to coordinate more with animation, in general, as the cartoon industry grows (also following what seems to be happening at Amblin Studios, after *Who Framed Roger Rabbit?*).

Another symptom: Disney is offering more new writing internships than usual. Finally, there is the impact of video animation for adults, *The Simpsons*, etc. Still, most likely, not much will change for theatrical animated shorts in a major way. The canon for story is fairly fixed there. The nostalgic object is always difficult to modernize. Assumptions about cartoon melodrama and cartoon comedy remain essentially what they have been for generations, particularly after old cartoons on video tape became so marketable in the eighties. These attitudes are reinforced by market assumptions, of a cautious type — that cartoon story-telling has to look as it did in its golden ages, or audiences will not go to see it in large enough numbers. But consider: what if live-action features were limited *exclusively* to musicals and animal fables? Would that seem a bit narrow, a bit like a self-fulfilling prophesy? In balance, therefore, the thirties story department at Disney opened up a new range for what a cartoon or animated feature might contain, but also solidified ideological assumptions about the cartoon that seem impossible to expand very much.

18. Disney Handbook.
19. Ibid.
20. Ibid., "Tips to Remember."
21. John Blackburn, *Travels Through the Pyrenees* (London, 1874), reprinting the Doré illustrations from Hyppolyte Taine, *Voyages au Pyrenées* (Paris: Hachette, 1855).
22. Barthes, "The Blue Guide," in *Mythologies* (1957), trans. A. Lavers (New York: Hill and Wang, 1972). Once again, the venerable history of simulated spaces is discussed, here in terms of tourism, a vast narrative tradition in itself, with a vocabulary that is applied often to animation, particularly in cartoon features. The tourist vision of old Europe, from tourist albums of the nineteenth century, inspire some of the backgrounds for *Snow White* and *Pinocchio*. And then, these tourist visions were built literally in Disney theme-parks. Recently, the imaginary castle from Duc de Berry's *Book of Hours* was built in real space for EuroDisney. The illustration came from the lavish fourteenth-century de Berry edition of the most popular "tourist" album at that time, about pilgrimage and prayer, about animating imaginary spaces. Another standard source: Dean MacCannell, *The Tourist: A New Theory of the Leisure Class* (New York: Schocker Books, 1976).
23. Jack Kinney, *Sixteen Frames to the Foot, or Walt and Other Assorted Characters*, typescript biography, p. 1232 (1933, p. 18); printed in a much abridged form (with some new material) as *Walt Disney and Assorted Other Characters: An Unauthorized Account of the Early Years at Disney's* (New York: Harmony Books, 1988). The paragraph in this book where this footnote appears also includes material from interviews with Ward Kimball, Frank Thomas, and Ollie Johnston.
24. Frank Thomas and Ollie Johnston, *Disney Animation: The Illusion of Life* (New York: Abbeville Press, 1981), p. 147. Clearly the standard source for analysis of Disney technique.
25. Physiognomies resemble model sheets, and were common in illustrated albums and journals from the eighteenth century on. They were charts of facial attitudes that revealed the caricatural possibilities of a *physiognomic* type. A great deal has been written on the subject of illustrated physiognomy, debates about caricature, about the origins of Mannerism, Romanticism, and Expressionism. One useful summary: Rudolf Arnheim, "The Rationale of Deformation," *Art Journal*, Winter 1983, pp. 320–2.
26. Thomas and Johnston, *Disney Animation: The Illusion of Life*, p. 173.
27. The term Surrealism is applied regularly to animation, in articles, in lectures, rarely as a direct reference to work done by Surrealists themselves, more as a generic term. In the context of this book, the adjective "surrealist" refers to the disjunctive use of images

essential to what I call "anarchy." By "anarchy" I mean a specific narrative structure that relies on "upside-down" imagery. By contrast, in Poland during the sixties, Surrealist techniques (from cut-up montage to Surrealist detournement, as in the Situationist rereading of Surrealism) were used self-consciously by animators, like Jan Lenica.

CHAPTER 4 MARKETING

1. Norman M. Klein, "Mickey," *Journal*, No. 22, January 1979, pp. 29–35.
2. "Mickey Mouse, Financier," *Literary Digest*, November 21, 1933. Also, "Mickey Mouse is Eight Years Old," *Literary Digest*, October 3, 1936, pp. 18–19.
3. See chapter 1, n.14.
4. Cecil Munsey, *Disneyana: Walt Disney Collectables* (New York: Hawthorne, 1974), p. 17. Also, material on the early Mickey clubs can be found at the Disney Archives, in Burbank. And *Expo Disneyana*, at Annecy Festival (France) in 1981, reviewed *Positif*, October 1981, with quote, p. 53, from Pierre Tchernia: "Each country has its own Mickey Mouse. The German is less sexy, more severe, like a character from Brecht. The French is more lithe, with pointed teeth. My preference, however, is the American, who is rounder, more succulent. He looks like a tasty chicken that you want to fry up .... After 1935, look how vulgar he became. Since the forties, he has been dressing like a suburbanite."
5. "Father Goose," *Time*, December 27, 1954. The headline for the cover illustration of Walt is rather prophetic: "Walt Disney, to enchanted worlds on electronic wings."
6. Term, "Audience Culture": The voyeuristic aspects of mass culture become the paradigm for narrative structure, for political marketing. The audience becomes the central character hidden within the story, as in music videos, or even crime films like *Blue Velvet*.
7. The similarities between MTV and the cartoon have been noted very often, also applied directly, in numerous videos using cartoon sequences (for Paula Abdul, for the Rolling Stones, etc.). More recently, with Liquid Television (running on MTV), the merger between animation and music videos is a central feature. Liquid TV (Colossal Pictures in San Francisco), with its computer-enhanced imagery and effects, has become very interesting to various television executives as well, as a format for other shows. Computer animation seems to be bringing about a synthesis of live action and animation.
8. Abstraction in the late twentieth century may come to mean "genre" abstracted, genre as a signifier. Consider what this suggests: When European modernist painters *c*. 1913 elected to abstract (or reduce) the image to its "pure" form, the result came to be identified with non-objective painting, or the cubist facet, or the collage. Today, that same process suggests three frames of film, or a familiar haircut on a character's head — a signifier that carries within it a refracted half-memory of many films, as they operate (or vibrate) within the slimmest visual detail. Animated cartoons have played with this audience-oriented principle of abstraction since the medium started, at the end of the last century. Animation, therefore, is a collective digest (or at least a point of origin) for media narrative — video language as well as computerized storytelling.
9. Klein, "Mickey," p. 30. Also, Carolyn Lejeune, "Disney Cartoons," *Cinema* (London: Maclehouse, 1931), pp. 83–90.
10. Disney Handbook.

CHAPTER 5 FLEISCHER

1. Shamus Culhane, *Talking Animals and Other People* (New York: St Martin's Press, 1986), p. 3. Also, various printed interviews and columns by Dick Huemer (in *Funnyworld*, *Cartoonist Profiles*).

2. Felix Isman, *Weber and Fields: Their Tribulations, Triumphs and their Associates* (New York: Boni and Livright, 1924). In Anthony Slide, *The Vaudevillians*, p. 163. Among jokes they initiated: "In 1887 Weber asked Fields: 'Who is that lady I saw you with last night?' to which came the hoary answer, 'She ain't no lady; she's my wife.'"

3. Isman, *Weber and Fields*. Origins of famous pool-hall routine, in polyglot Germanic dialect, pp. 165–71.

4. Kazin, *A Walker in the City* (New York: Harcourt Brace, 1951), opening with: "Every time I go back to Brownsville, it is as if I had never been away."

5. Grandville (1808–47) was a profoundly important influence on "upside-down" fantasy illustration in the mid-nineteenth century, particularly on Sir John Tenniel's illustrations for *Alice in Wonderland*. Also, studies on popular illustration by David Kunzle.

6. Again, returning to the notion of "intellectual montage" (Eisenstein), many of the same visual problems were common in illustration, particularly political cartoons, or in the pseudo-journeys drawn by Grandville (wood engravings, mostly for books published in the 1840s). Like these illustrations, intellectual montage is very much a response to the narrative possibilities of a print-oriented visual memory. For that reason, intellectual montage probably operates much more clearly in animation than in live-action cinema.

7. See the TV documentary, available on film and video: *The Eye Hears, the Ear Sees* (1989, BBC).

8. Steve Schneider, *That's All Folks: The Art of Warner Brothers Animation* (New York: Henry Holt, 1988), p. 82.

CHAPTER 6 THE WORLD UPSIDE DOWN

1. Walter Benjamin, *The Origin of German Tragic Drama*, trans. J. Osborne (London: Verso 1977), p. 178. Benjamin's study, written in the twenties, had a profound influence on art criticism in the seventies and early eighties (Buchloh, Owens, Crimp), around the problem of collage-objects as ruins, and the allegorical "impulse" evident in conceptual art. Many of the same issues also apply to "anarchy" (as allegorical collage) in animation, as in the following by Benjamin, discussing a seventeenth-century German *Trauerspiel* play (p. 173): "With every idea the moment of expression coincides with a veritable eruption of images, which gives rise to a chaotic mass of metaphors." What animators call "spot gags" were a common practice in many areas of popular theater, not simply as farce (also in religious plays), in a tradition that later was overshadowed by the emergence of melodrama in the nineteenth century.

2. Margaret Blount, *Animal Land: The Creatures of Children's Fiction* (New York: Avon, 1977; orig. 1974), p. 70.

3. Lary May, *Screening Out the Past* (New York: Oxford University Press, 1980), p. 202.

4. Raymond Chandler, *The Big Sleep* (1939; repr. New York: Random House), p. 8.

CHAPTER 7 MACHINA VERSATILIS

1. Vitascope, begun by Edison, showcased the work of lightning artist/animator Stuart Blackton. Eventually, Blackton formed his own studio. This is a significant linkage for

early animation and early American cinema, often noted. Early cinema, with its painted backdrops and very shallow backgrounds, tended toward the animated space. Debate continues as to when the transition away from animated space occurred, when a definitive live-action staging (and editing) had finally replaced animation. Some argue as early as 1906; others earlier. The trend seems to point toward pushing the dates further back. One recent theoretical source: Noel Burch, *Life to Those Shadows*, trans. B. Brewster (1990). A standard source: John L. Fell, *Film and the Narrative Tradition* (Berkeley: University of California Press, 1986; orig. 1974). Key surveys: Donald Crafton, "J. Stuart Blackton's Animated Films," *The Art of the Animated Image*, ed. Charles Solomon (Los Angeles: The American Film Institute, 1987); Anthony Slide, *The Big V: A History of the Vitagraph Company* (1976); and essays by Russell Merritt.

2. An anthology on this subject: Norman M. Klein (ed.), *Lost Boundaries: A History of Media-Induced Experience* (Los Angeles: Center for Contemporary Arts Criticism, Cal-Arts, 1992).

3. See chapter 6, n. 1.

4. Ambrose Bierce, "Moxon's Monster," *Can This Be?*, Vol. III, *Collected Works* (New York: The Neale Publishing Company, 1910), pp. 102–3. Also, much has been written since Capek's play *URRS* (1919) about the term "robot" and various "Fordist" monsters; and the discourse on robots, cyborgs, in theories of mass culture during the 1980s.

5. Orgel, *The Jonsonian Masque* (Cambridge, Mass.: Harvard University Press, 1967), p. 196. Also, C. H. Herford et al., *Ben Jonson* (Oxford: Clarendon Press, 1950), Vol. X, p. 411: "[Here too] clouds play an important part in the scenery; they could be used, for example, to mask a change of scene" Appendix XXIV, pp. 689ff, on Jonson and Inigo Jones, as in the line (p. 691): "He is a mechanic, witness his cheap lighting-effects."

6. Jonathan Swift, *Gulliver's Travels*, Part III, Chapter 1.

7. There has been a longstanding debate between the "Lumière" and the "Méliès" theories on the sources of cinema. In a sentence, the debate suggests two reactions by audiences to the invention of film: (1) cinema was perceived, from the start, mostly as a "realist" medium (i.e. Lumière); or, (2) movies, from the start, were perceived primarily as an extension of the "trick" film, like those by Méliès. However, what if audiences, upon first seeing movies, made little distinction between Lumière or Méliès? Both were enjoyed as "magic acts." Aren't they still enjoyed as magic? What if all cinema in the late nineteenth century was received either as animation (Reynaud, Méliès, Cohl), or as part of the photographic paradox (which can be rather similar to animation, on the level of submission to the *machina versatilis*: photo/film is also hypnotic special effect, showing what industry can do to replace the physical world)? Another twist to the debate: Whether TV, the "personality" medium, removes that paradox (does the conversational style of TV "convince" the audience differently than cinema does?). In terms of this book, the issues can be narrowed in the following way: TV, cinema, video, even newsreels all have elements of animated narrative, and *machina versatilis*; and have used these elements for over a century. That is, more or less, what the final line of this chapter implies, much too cryptically, but I saw no point in pitching the argument in this direction, by adding pages more on the photographic paradox. From the internal experience of the audience, cinema and video operate a priestly function. They monumentalize as if by para-normal force: the audience remains forever awestruck (or confused — and that helps explain that hypnotic effect) by any manufactured simulation of real space, when it is regenerated on to a screen, in dim light, like an industrial seance. See also, Norman M. Klein, "Virtual Storytelling, 1400 to the Present," *Video Networks* (Summer 1992).

CHAPTER 8 WHAT MAKES BETTY BOOP?

1. Leonard Maltin, *Of Mice and Magic: A History of American Animated Cartoons* (New York: New American Library, 1987, rev.), pp. 96–7. This book is the most extensive history of the animated sound cartoon.

2. *Screenland Magazine*: plate in Leslie Cabarga's *The Fleischer Story*, early edition (see chapter 3, n. 6): a standard source. Also, the articles by Harvey Deneroff (and dissertation) on Fleischer; articles by Mark Langer; and by Michael Dobbs (i.e. a long review of "Betty Boop's Biographers," in *Funnyworld*).

3. A typical quote from Will Hays, from a speech before the LA Chamber of Commerce: "The industry must have toward that sacred thing, the mind of a child, toward that virgin thing, the unmarked slate, the same responsibility, the same care about the impressions made upon it that the best clergyman or the most inspired teacher of youths would have." Henry James Forman, *Our Movie Made Children* (New York: Macmillan, 1934), p. 121. The quote also appears in *Fortune*, December 1938, p. 71. That would hardly apply favorably to early Betty Boop cartoons.

   "Hollywood Censors its Animated Cartoons," *Look*, January 17, 1939, pp. 17–21: Schlesinger indicates how cartoons must be "proper for ... impressionable minds." Some of the rules of the censors were: no kissing on the lips (instead "hand holding"); avoid frightening monsters; no cruelty to animals; no blasphemies (halos of De Lawd, in *Cleaner Pastures*, Warners cartoon); no satires of Mussolini salute; no dogs at telephone poles; no spitting in public; put bad men in jail; no teats on cows; no thinly veiled hips.

   So many of these, by the way, were still subtly broken, but certainly during the Second World War were fractured.

4. Chuck Jones, *Chuck Amuck* (New York: Farrar, Strauss and Giroux, 1989), pp. 90–1.

5. Harvey Deneroff, " 'We Can't Get Much Spinach!' The Organization and Implementation of the Fleischer Animation Strike," *Film History* 1, 1987, pp. 1, 6, 7.

6. Donald Crafton (*Before Mickey*) discusses the impact of assembly-line or work efficiency systems at Bray Studios (where cel animation essentially began, where the chain of cartoon production was established, also where the Fleischers started out). Indeed, in the twenties, there was considerable interest in applying the "Fordist" model of office and factory organization to media. "Fordism" also influences popular fantasies of industrial evil (the classic example: the Mammon factory scene in *Metropolis*, 1925). It also apparently influenced literature on robots (of the pre-cyber-space variety); and has become a central plank of a general discourse on modernization (and modernism) in mass culture — a way to distinguish between a modernist and post-modernist stage in popular culture. "Fordist" cinema develops, in this argument, before the emergence of electronic, information industries (i.e. TV). After TV emerges — to follow the argument a bit further — mass culture becomes more polyglot in the way it organizes to make its product; it presumably takes on a different model of a very dispersed (even multinational) assembly-line, and, in turn, new systems for how adventure capital is used in media production.

7. Joe Adamson, "Working for the Fleischers: An Interview with Dick Huemer," *Funnyworld*, No. 16, 1975, p. 25. Huemer mentioned this anecote elsewhere as well.

CHAPTER 9 HOW MONEY TALKS IN CARTOONS

The information in this chapter came primarily from interviews with Grim Natwick, Friz Freleng, Walter Lantz, Chuck Jones, Jules Engel, Frank Thomas, Ollie Johnston, Joseph

Barbera, Bill Melendez, Maurice Noble, and Phil Monroe. There is also a body of published interviews (primarily about how the animators worked on specific cartoons), in *Funnyworld*, *Cartoonist Profiles, Animation Journal Animatrix, Graffiti, Millimeter, Animation*, (typescript) UCLA Oral History, *Velvet Light Trap, Mindrot* (Minneapolis), and in proceedings from ASIFA, from The Society for Animation Studies, and the AFI, among others. A thorough economic history of the Fleischer Studio is underway, by Harvey Deneroff and Mark Langer.

1. Shamus Culhane, *Talking Animals and Other People*, p. 113.
2. Jack Kinney, *Walt Disney and Assorted Other Characters* (see chapter 2, n. 23). Another unauthorized biography, very widely known: Richard Schickel, *The Disney Version* (New York: Simon & Schuster, 1968; rev. 1985).
3. *The Sho Card Cartoonist* (Minneapolis: Bart Publications, 1929), p. 24.
4. Charles J. Maland, *Chaplin and American Culture: The Evolution of a Star Image* (Princeton: Princeton University Press, 1989), pp. 16–17.
5. Charles Chaplin, *My Autobiography* (New York: Simon & Schuster, 1964), pp. 241ff.

CHAPTER 10 TRANSITION TOWARD FULL ANIMATION

1. Leonard Maltin, *Of Mice and Magic*, pp. 96–7. Also, Leslie Cabarga, *The Fleischer Story*, p. 110.

CHAPTER 11 DEPRESSION MELODRAMA

1. Robert E. Alexander, *An Index of Patents Concerning Theater Illusions and Stage Appliances* (dissertation submitted to UCLA, 1964), p. 57.
2. John L. Fell, *Film and the Narrative Tradition*, chapters 1–4, Appendix II.

   The discourse on melodrama is wideranging, from the classic study by David Grimsted, *Melodrama Unveiled* (1968), to essays from a feminist perspective (Laura Mulvey and others), to Robert Lang, *American Film Melodrama* (Princeton: Princeton University Press, 1989), whose first five chapters provide a very solid summary of much of the discourse on melodrama as fundamental to the narrative (and ideological) structure of American cinema. I admit to finding the theater summaries an objective balance for starting out, because I wanted a narrower model, a clear point of origin, since animation received the tradition from nineteenth-century theatrical sources as much as from twentieth-century cinema. Walt Disney, for example, used a turn of the century play of "Snow White" as the model for his film.

   Also, many of the critical essays presume that melodrama is a term generally agreed upon. I found that once I crossed disciplines, the term dissolved from one essay to the next. So I returned to older, practical explanations, even the Methuen short survey by James L. Smith (*Melodrama*, London: Methuen, 1973); also, the various collections of the old melodramas themselves (and histories of English theater in the first half of the nineteenth century); and studies on Ibsen, O'Neill, as melodrama — to avoid elitist assumptions. For a novelist's point of view, Robertson Davies, *The Mirror of Nature* (1982) was useful. It seemed clear that melodrama remained a coherent, even limited term well into the twentieth century, well into the teens, despite its vast range of applications. And even as late as the sixties, in *TV Guide*, the term "melodrama" appears as a category describing various TV shows and old movies (often film noir, ironically enough, since in many ways, noir was a reaction against the ideology of melodrama.

3. Alexander, *An Index of Patents Concerning Theater Illusions and Stage Appliances*, p. 132.
4. Maurice Disher, *Blood and Thunder, Mid-Victorian Melodrama and its Origins* (London: UCLA, 1949), p. 179.
5. Jack Kinney, *Walt Disney and Assorted Other Characters*, p. 38.
6. Forster, "Mickey and Minnie," *Animated Cartoon*, ed. Gerald and Danny Peary, *The American Animated Cartoon: A Critical Anthology* (New York: Dutton, 1980) p. 239. See chapter 1, n. 11.
7. Leland Price, *The City Slicker and Our Nell (A Rootin', Tootin', Shootin' "Meller Drammer")*, in anthology: Lawrence Brings, *Gay Nineties Meldrama* (Minneapolis, 1963), p. 5.
8. Lewis Jacobs, "The Mobility of Color," *The Movies As Medium* (New York: Farrar, Strauss and Giroux, 1970), p. 190.

CHAPTER 12 THE WHITENESS OF SNOW WHITE

1. Despite the many surveys and coffee table books on *Snow White*, like the "studio book" published in 1979 by Viking (strong background essay by Steve Hulett), the best primary source may still be Robert D. Feild, *The Art of Walt Disney* (New York: Macmillan, 1942). Feild centers his entire history of Disney on the making and longterm impact of *Snow White*. The Disney Archives have carefully maintained many of the key documents. Also, Christopher Finch, *The Art of Walt Disney: From Mickey Mouse to the Magic Kingdoms* (1973); Richard Hollis and Brian Sibley, *The Disney Studio Story* (1988).

   Beyond books on Disneyana (from the mid-fifties on), there are thirties sources on the Disney licensing of *Snow White*, for example: Margaret Thorpe, *America at the Movies* (New Haven: Yale University Press, 1939), pp. 118–19.
2. Karen Merritt, "The Little Girl/Mother Transformation: The American Evolution of *Snow White and the Seven Dwarfs*," *Storytelling in Animation*, ed. John Canemaker (Los Angeles: The American Film Institute, 1933), p. 106.
3. A central premise in Barthes's short essays from the fifties, collected into *Mythologies* (1957; English language edition, 1972) was the concept of the "natural" in a consumer culture, that when a product was marketed as "natural," this obviated any analysis of its inherent qualities. Natural, then, implied the absence of critical judgement. Clearly, this can be applied to the ideological use of the simulated natural in Disney, though that is hardly a secret to the Disney consumer. Animation proudly announces the lie within the natural; that lie is very much the charm of animation.

CHAPTER 13 FULL ANIMATION

1. George G. Clarke, "Putting Clouds into Exterior Scenes," *The Technique of Motion Picture Production*, for Meeting of Society of Motion Picture Engineers, Hollywood (New York: Interscience Publishers, 1944), p. 29.
2. Fred Sersen, "Special Photographic Effects," *The Technique of Motion Picture Production*, p. 40.
3. Allardyce Nicoll, *Film and Theater* (New York: Thomas Crowell, 1936), p. 92.
4. Italo Calvino, "The Distance of the Moon," *Cosmicomics*, trans. W. Weaver (New York: Harcourt, Brace, Jovanovich, 1976; orig. 1968), pp. 3–4.
5. Frank Thomas and Ollie Johnston, *Disney Animation: The Illusion of Life*, p. 245.

CHAPTER 14 PRODUCTION

1. This chapter is primarily a synthesis of the following sources: Nat Falk, *How to Make Animated Cartoons: The History and Technique* (New York: Foundation Books, 1941), virtually all the studios, mostly Terry — not much on Disney; Harold Turney, *Film Guide's Handbook: Cartoon Production* (Hollywood: A Film Guide Publication, 1940), Disney mostly; Robert D. Feild, *The Art of Walt Disney*; Earl Theisen, "Teaching Mickey Mouse to Walk," *International Photographer*, December 1935, used for publicity by Fox West Coast Theaters (Theisen was Honorary Curator of Motion Pictures for the LA Museum of Art); John Paddy Carstairs "Film Cartoons, As Told to The Author, by Walt Disney," *Movie Merry Go-Round* (London: Newnes, 1937), pp. 47–52.
2. Nat Falk, *How to Make Animated Cartoons*, p. 36.

CHAPTER 15 THE CHASE CARTOON

1. Bob Clampett archive.
2. David Callahan, "Cel Animation: Mass Production and Marginalization in the Film Industry," *Film History*, Vol. II, No. 3, p. 226. Article runs pp. 223–66, based on early Bray–Hurd animation patents, arguing that animation was "marginalized" by its definition as slapstick cartoon, not drama, a strange argument indeed for film of the silent era.
3. Thomas and Johnston, *Disney Animation: The Illusion of Life*, p. 100, two-page spread.
4. Ibid., p. 105.
5. Ibid., p. 52.
6. J. Hoberman, "Vulgar Modernism," *Artforum*, February 1982.

CHAPTER 16 THE ADVANTAGES OF BEING BONELESS AND INCOMPLETE

1. Joe Adamson, *Tex Avery: King of Cartoons* (New York: Popular Library, 1975), p. 49 (illustration). Clampett also mentioned that same phrase, in various interviews. Clampett was animator and gagman for Avery at the time.
2. Interview with Frank Thomas, 1987.
3. Adamson, *Tex Avery: King of Cartoons*, p. 188. Maltin also uses this quote. It probably is the most remembered quote within that interview.
4. Interviews with Walter Lantz, 1987; Leo Salkin, speaking at the AFI conference in 1987.
5. Jack Kinney, *Walt Disney and Assorted Other Characters*, p. 126. There were considerable variations in how Goofy was drawn: more like a human in Art Babbitt's *Moving Day* (1936), one classic formulation; to more extreme, stretchable "Goofs," like John Sibley's version.
6. Jerry Beck and Will Friedwald, *Looney Tunes and Merrie Melodies: A Complete Guide to the Warner Brothers Cartoons* (New York: Henry Holt, 1989), pp. 133–4. In their analysis, they also mention that this was a "mellerdrammer." The voice-over and the poses are indeed in that spirit (like the forties movie *The Strawberry Blond* upside down) more than the old theatrical mellderdrammers, I would guess; also like radio soap opera, in the voice of Dan Backslide. In the final scenes, where Dan is beaten to a pulp by Dora, I am reminded of the Showgirl (also tied) beating up Wolfie as he makes advances, in a very similar setting, in *Wild and Wolfie* (1945, Avery). What we have then is a spoof of

melodrama, and of the older style of live theater, along with clear elements of the chase cartoon. The sum of these indicates how easily the chase lends itself to stylized animation.

On the other side of the same issue — stylized animation as chase: UPA's *Magic Fluke* (1949) was remade by Avery as *Magical Maestro* (1925). Adamson, *Tex Avery: King of Cartoons*, p. 228: "The UPA stylization of the fifties comes off best here."

CHAPTER 17 CITIZEN KANE, THE CARTOON

1. Joe Adamson, *Tex Avery: King of Cartoons*, p. 149.

CHAPTER 18 THE ANARCHY OF WARTIME CHASE CARTOONS

1. Michael Shull and David E. Wilt, *Doing Their Bit: Wartime American Animated Short Films, 1939–1945* (Jefferson, North Carolina: McFarland and Company, 1987), p. 161.
2. Richard Shale, *Donald Duck Joins Up: The Walt Disney Studio During World War II* (Ann Arbor: UMI Research, 1982), p. 31.
3. Umberto Eco, *A Theory of Semiotics* (Bloomington: Indiana University Press, 1976), pp. 131–3.
4. Charles Solomon, *Enchanted Drawings: The History of Animation* (New York: Alfred Knopf, 1989), pp. 113–14.
5. Joe Adamson, *The Walter Lantz Story*, New York: St Martin's Press, 1989), p. 85.

CHAPTER 19 1947: *ROGER RABBIT* THEN AND NOW

Alan Cholodenko, "*Who Framed Roger Rabbit?*, or the Framing of Animation," *The Illusion of Life: Essays on Animation*, ed. Cholodenko (Sydney: Power Publications/Australian Film Commission, 1991). This essay applies critical theory to an analysis of *Roger Rabbit*, and to the principle of animation, as a mode within all cinema. The footnotes provide a useful general resource for articles on *Roger Rabbit*. The introduction to the book is particularly useful, as a survey of key texts in Animation Studies; and a plea for more theory in histories of the cartoon.

1. Charles Palmer, "Cartoon in the Classroom," *Hollywood Quarterly*, III.1, Fall 1947, p. 33.
2. Ibid.

CHAPTER 20 CHASE CARTOONS AFTER 1947

1. Roland Marchand, "Visions of Classlessness, Quests for Dominion: American Popular Culture, 1945–1960," *Reshaping America: Society and Institutions, 1945–1960*, ed. Robert Bremmer and Gary Reichard (Columbus: Ohio State University Press, 1982), p. 164.
2. Storyboards are in the Walter Lantz Archives, at UCLA.
3. A very influential article on *Duck Amuck* was written by Richard Thompson (*Film Comment*, January 1975), in a special issue on the Hollywood Cartoon, which sold out very quickly and became a collectors' item. The mid-seventies marks the beginning of a critical rediscovery of the chase. Also from Richard Thompson, "Meep Meep," *December*, Vol. XIII, or *Movies and Methods*, ed. Bill Nichols (Berkeley: University of California Press, 1976), where he compares Jones to Keaton in their "syllogistic" methods (p. 139) And: "Although Jones' work never quite reached the minimal stage, he came close" (p. 131).

4. "Inflation Squeeze and Long Films Make Animation Survival Chancy; Lantz on Slow, Slow Cost Recoup," *Variety*, November 27, 1963.

CHAPTER 21 VILLAINS AND VICTIMS

1. Joe Adamson, *Tex Avery: King of Cartoons*, p. 87.
2. Preston Blair, *Animation* (Laguna Beach, Calif.: Foster Art Service, 1949). This has remained a primary source for character animators, even today. Other basic "how-to" books that seem to be used by animators are those by Halas and Batchelder in England (since the sixties), a new workbook by Milt Grey, certainly Thomas and Johnston's *Disney Animation: The Illusion of Life*. Most of all, young animators rely on reprints in books of the old model sheets, the look of the roughs; and on the film itself, studying the cycles (almost frame by frame) of the old cartoons, whether by moviola or by video. It is still very difficult, however, for animators today to release the same contemporaneity into the gags that was evident in forties and fifties cartoons. A mix of nostalgia and caution often takes over. There are debates about how to avoid that quandary. On the subject of the cable TV series *Ren and Stimpy*, for example: animators argue about whether it has the timing of the older cartoons (at least one veteran animator has complained that it does not). And yet, its frantic look clearly is part of a rediscovery by young animators, since the mid-eighties, of the anarchic elements of the chase (working with their interpretations of Jones, Avery, and Clampett). Apparently, each generation has to discover a fresh way to time gags, by using the rhythms, movement, body types, and experience of its own time, as indeed is evident in Blair's book.
3. Preston Blair, *Animation*, p. 40.

CHAPTER 22 BACK TO THE ANIMATED LINE

1. John Hubley and Zachary Schwartz, "Animation Learns a New Language," *Hollywood Quarterly*, I.4, July 1946, p. 355.
   An interview with Hubley later on, about some of the same material: Lewis Archibald, "John Hubley," *Film Library Quarterly*, Spring 1970. Hubley said (p. 6): "We were able to experiment with everything in those days [early UPA] — forms and colors, collages and pastiches of famous paintings, everything."
2. "Rembrandt" effect, etc. Many art directors in live action and in animation were art school-trained.
3. Chuck Jones, "Music and the Animated Cartoon," *Hollywood Quarterly*, 1944.
4. Phil Eastman, "New Techniques and Uses," *Proceedings of Writers' Congress (1943), sponsored by Hollywood Writers' Mobilization and the University of California* (Berkeley: University of California, 1944), pp. 122–37. (This paper was read after showing of the Disney film on malaria, *The Winged Scourge*.)
5. Paul Karlstrom and Susan Ehrlich, *Turning the Tide: Early Los Angeles Modernists* (Santa Barbara Museum of Art, 1990). In conjunction with a show. Includes three abstract artists directly associated with animation in Los Angeles: Oskar Fischinger, Jules Engel, and Rico Lebrun.
6. See Donald Albrecht, *Designing Dreams: Modern Architecture in the Movies* (New York: Harper & Row, in collaboration with the Museum of Modern Art, 1986). Mostly about twenties and thirties. But even here, concentrating on an early period, he identifies an emerging source for modern cinematic design beyond graphic narrative, a certain utopian,

genteel fantasy, which suggests the cartoon cubism that finally arrives in cartoons and popular design by the fifties. He specifically indicates, from the Introduction on, that these movie sets were an "architectural" response, that went "deeper" than its "graphic value" (p. xi: the term graphic is compared, among other examples, to "comic-book illustrators," who also worked in "simple surfaces, lines and planes").

7. John Hubley, "The Writer and the Cartoon," *Writers' Congress* (1943), p. 108.

8. Clement Greenberg, "Avant-garde and Kitsch (1939)," widely reprinted, also (full text) in Richard Hertz and Norman M. Klein (eds), *Twentieth Century Art Theory*. The debate over this essay, in an anthology edited by Benjamin Buchloh, Serge Guilbaut, and David Solkin: *Modernity and Mass Culture* (Halifax: Press of the Nova Scotia College of Art and Design, 1983). The fundamental distinction that Greenberg made, about a rigid, canonical difference between kitsch (mass culture) and the fine arts, even entered criticism in the eighties as an adjective, "greenbergian," to identify the high formalist defense of abstract painting that Greenberg identified with the New York School. In terms of the animated cartoon, however, the greenbergian classification becomes impossible; however, the debates over cinematic formalism were common during the sixties and seventies, between graphic animation and character animation. Even these have diminished, as the widening impact of global mass culture has forced the arts to redefine its categories, or dispense with many categories altogether.

9. *Vogue, 1951*: Timothy J. Clark, "Jackson Pollock's Abstraction," *Reconstructing Modernism: Art in New York, Paris and Montreal, 1945–1964*, ed. Serge Guilbaut (Cambridge, Mass.: MIT Press, 1990) (1951 photo of *Vogue* fashions inspired by Pollock paintings are on the cover as well.)

   Life Magazine, 1949: "Jackson Pollock, Is He the Greatest Living Painter in the World?" (intro. Norman M. Klein), *Twentieth Century Art Theory*, ed. R. Hertz and N. Klein, pp. 351–6.

10. John Hubley and Zachary Schwartz, "Animation Learns a New Language,", p. 360.

11. Karl Van Leuwen, "The Animated Cartoon Goes to War," *Writers' Congress* (1943), p. 120.

12. William Moritz (ed.), "The United Productions of America: Reminiscing Thirty Years Later," *ASIFA* (Canada), XII.3, December 1984, p. 18.

13. David Fisher, "Two Premières: Disney and UPA," in Gerald and Danny Peary, *The American Animated Cartoon: A Critical Anthology*, p. 179.

14. Ibid. Here is more of the extended quote — on Magoo, pp. 181–2: "Because of his infirmity, the world around him remains a blur. Things are never as they seem: his idea of what is happening is always at variance with the reality. The comedy and situations arise from his refusal to recognize the fact . . . . He does not recognize the anarchy that surrounds him . . . . Mr. Magoo personifies a contemporary situation; the Disney heroes no longer do (they are too much creations from the 'madcap comedies' of the thirties . . .) Donald Duck, for instance was the arch anarchist . . . . Since [the thirties], however, we have experienced a hot war and are in the throes of a cold one . . . . We no longer admire (irresponsible action). Mr. Magoo represents for us the man who would be responsible and serious in a world that seems insane; he is a creation of the fifties, the age of anxiety; his situation reflects our own."

CHAPTER 23 FROM ONE SCREEN TO THE OTHER

1. Mark Mayerson, "The Lion Began with a Frog: Cartoons at MGM," *That's Not All Folks: A Primer on Cartoonal Knowledge* (London: BFI Distribution, 1984; orig. 1975), p. 37.

2. *Variety*, September 6, 1956.
3. Ted Sennett, *The Art of Hanna—Barbera: Fifty Years of Creativity*, p. 45.
4. Ibid., pp. 48—9.
5. See Norman M. Klein, "Audience Culture and the Video Screen," p. 376. Same reference in Dara Birnbaum, *Rough Edits: Popular Image Video*, ed. B. Buchloh (Halifax: Press of Nova Scotia College of Design, 1987), p. 99 ("Topology of the Screen").

CONCLUSION

1. W. O. Brigstocke, *The London Observer*, May 8, 1927; quote in Huntly Carter, *The New Spirit in Cinema*, p. 30.
2. By 1945, Walt was already experimenting with Audi-Animatronics, as indicated in a quote recorded by Richard Schickel, about tests with Buddy Ebsen dancing dolls electrically controlled, on a card that operated like a cross between IBM and a player piano. Richard Schickel, *The Disney Version: The Life, Times, Art and Commerce of Walt Disney* (New York: Simon & Schuster, 1968; rev. 1985), p. 332. Quote summarized in Anthony Haden-Guest, *The Paradise Program* (New York: William Morrow, 1973), p. 237.
3. Scott Bukatman, "There's Always Tomorrowland: Disney and the Hypercinematic Experience," *October* 57, Summer 1991, p. 76.
4. Leslie Cabarga, *The Fleischer Story*, p. 194 (insert from a Miami newspaper).
5. Ariel Dorfman and Armand Mattelart, *How to Read Donald Duck*, trans. D. Kunzle (New York: International General, 1975). Originally written not long after the Allende coup in Chile, then appeared in London, and (under some threats of infringement) into the United States, in an almost clandestine way. Also, to give a sense of the range: late-sixties psychedelic Mickey by Neon Park, *Chemical Wedding* (1971), in *Outlaw Visions*, ed. Tony Cohan and Gordon Beam (Los Angeles: Acrobat Books, 1977); and Max Apple's *Disneyad* (parody of Disney biography); and many more.
6. "Report: Disney in Florida," *Progressive Architecture*, March 1990, p. 80.
7. The two most cited sources: Jean Baudrillard, *Simulations*, trans. Foss, Patton, and Beichman (New York: Semiotext(e), 1983), p. 25: "The Disneyland Imaginary is neither true nor false; it is a deterrence machine set up in order to rejuvenate in reverse the fiction of the real." (Also in Baudrillard, *America*); and Umberto Eco, *Travels in Hyperreality* (New York: Harcourt, Brace, Jovanovich, 1985).
8. W. K. L. Dickson and Antonia Dickson, *History of the Kinetograph, Kinetoscope and Kinetophonograph* (New York, 1895; repr. New York: Arno Press and the New York Times, 1979), pp. 19—20.
9. Mark Alden Branch, "Report: Disney in Florida," p. 82 (closing comment).
10. Robert Coover, "Cartoon," *A Night at the Movies* (New York: Simon & Schuster, 1987; paperback, Collier), pp. 135—6.
11. Bert Green (cartoonist to Pathé News), "The Making of an Animated Cartoon," 1915, on file at Library of the Academy of Motion Picture Arts and Sciences.

Index